P. 261 — PITCH $= \dfrac{\text{RISE}}{\text{RUN}}$

RISE

$<$ $>$

Run

Career Mathematics

Industry and the Trades

MERWIN J. LYNG

L. J. MECONI

EARL J. ZWICK

Editorial Adviser
DANIEL H. MALIA

Technical Consultants
STEPHEN P. BALDWIN
BERNHOLDT R. NYSTROM
JACK SINEWITZ
LUCIANO S. VISCO

HOUGHTON MIFFLIN COMPANY · BOSTON
Atlanta
Dallas
Geneva, Illinois
Hopewell, New Jersey
Palo Alto
Toronto

THE AUTHORS | **Merwin J. Lyng,** Professor of Mathematics, Mayville State College, Mayville, North Dakota. Dr. Lyng has been a teacher of high school mathematics and has served as a mathematics consultant for the State of North Dakota. Articles by Dr. Lyng have appeared in professional journals.

L. J. Meconi, Associate Professor of Education, The University of Akron. Dr. Meconi has taught junior high and high school mathematics and has published articles in a number of professional journals.

Earl J. Zwick, Professor of Mathematics, Indiana State University. Dr. Zwick has taught high school mathematics, has published articles in professional journals, and serves on the Board of Directors of the Indiana Council of Teachers of Mathematics.

THE EDITORIAL ADVISER | **Daniel H. Malia,** Coordinator of Technical-Vocational Education, Newton Public Schools, Newton, Massachusetts. Mr. Malia has had experience teaching both industrial arts and mathematics in junior high and high school. He has working experience in industry, and has served as president of the Massachusetts Industrial Education Society.

THE TECHNICAL CONSULTANTS | **Stephen P. Baldwin,** Teacher of Career Education—Manufacturing, Warren Junior High School, Newton, Massachusetts. Mr. Baldwin is a registered professional mechanical engineer and worked in the field of manufacturing for many years.

Bernholdt R. Nystrom, Director of Manpower Development Training Act Programs, Nashoba Valley Technical High School, Littleton, Massachusetts. Mr. Nystrom has taught carpentry to high school students, bringing to them his valuable experience acquired during his years of working as a carpenter.

Jack Sinewitz, Graphics Instructor, Bigelow Junior High School, Newton Massachusetts. Mr. Sinewitz is an experienced writer and teacher in the field of graphic arts.

Luciano S. Visco, Automobile Instructor, Newton Technical High School, Newton, Massachusetts. Mr. Visco's many years of experience as an auto mechanic provide him with a rich background for teaching auto mechanics to technical-vocational students.

Printed in the United States of America

Student's Edition ISBN: 0-395-24552-4
Teacher's Edition ISBN: 0-395-24553-2

Contents

Start

Part II   Formulas from Industry

To relay messages from one place to another, the communications industry uses a wide variety of satellite and underground communication equipment.

CHAPTER 1 *Industrial Measurements*

After completing this chapter, you should be able to:

1. *Read several kinds of industrial meters.*
2. *Read and interpret bar and line graphs.*
3. *Make precise measurements with inch and centimeter rules.*
4. *Read technical drawings.*

Reading meters

1-1 Electric meters

Many industries depend on electricity as a source of power. The amount of electricity which they use is measured in kilowatt-hours (KWH). Figure 1-1 shows the dials on a common electric meter.

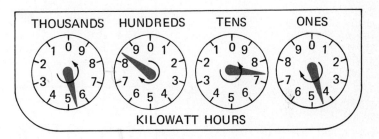

Figure 1-1

On this meter the last dial on the right records kilowatt-hours from 0 to 10. The other dials record the number of tens, hundreds, and thousands of kilowatt-hours used.

Here's how to read the meter: Note the position of the pointer on each dial. Starting at the far left, set the figures down in order. When the pointer is between two figures, use the smaller number. For example, the meter in Figure 1-1 reads 5874 KWH.

EXERCISES Read the electric meters.

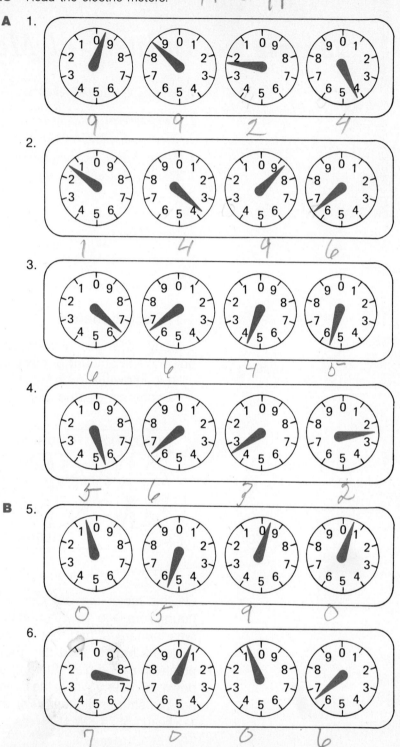

A 1.

   9   9   2   4

2.

   1   4   9   6

3.

   6   6   4   5

4.

   5   6   3   2

B 5.

   0   5   9   0

6.

   7   0   0   6

2

Gas meter

1-2 Gas meters

Natural gas is another energy source that is commonly used in industry. Gas use is measured in units of 100 cubic feet, which are symbolized CCF. Figure 1-2 shows the dials on a common type of gas meter.

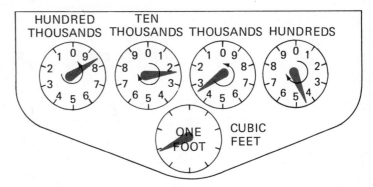

Figure 1-2

The upper four dials are used for reading the meter. The lower dial is used only to test the accuracy of the meter. Each mark on the dial at the far right represents 1 CCF, or 100 cubic feet. A complete revolution on this dial records 10 CCF, or 1000 cubic feet. The reading on the meter in Figure 1-2 is 8234 CCF, or 823,400 cubic feet.

EXERCISES   Read the gas meters. (The test dial has been omitted.)

A   1.

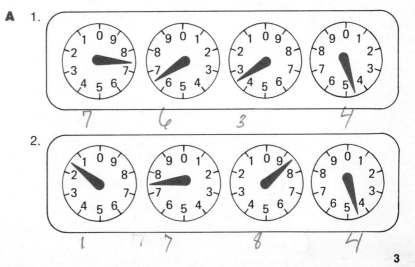

2.

3.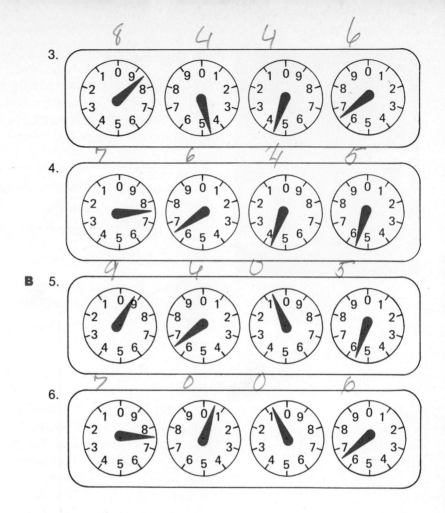

4.

B 5.

6.

1-3 Whole Numbers

Do you notice any similarity between the way we read electric and gas meters and the way we express numbers? Recall that the unit shown on a dial is 10 times greater than the unit on the dial to the right. Look at the electric meter in Figure 1-3. What is the reading?

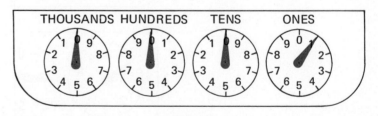

| THOUSANDS | HUNDREDS | TENS | ONES |

Figure 1-3

One kilowatt-hour is correct. When the pointer on the "ones" dial records 10 KWH and completes a revolution, the pointer on the "tens" dial moves 1 place, as shown in Figure 1-4.

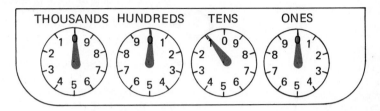

Figure 1-4

The same relationship holds true for the other adjacent dials. In this way, electric and gas meters are based on a system of tens.

Our number system is also based on tens. Look at the diagram below. The place value for each digit in the expression is 10 times the place value of the digit to its right.

billions	hundred-millions	ten-millions	millions	hundred-thousands	ten-thousands	thousands	hundreds	tens	ones
6,	3	2	7,	4	0	8,	2	5	6

We read this as "6 billion, 327 million, 408 thousand, 256." Note that we use a zero to show that there are no "ten-thousands" in this expression. Large numbers like this are common in industry—in measurements and sales reports, for example.

EXERCISES Read the following expressions aloud.

A
1. 2,324,617 automobiles

2. 379,340 pressure pumps

3. 627,229,367 rivets

4. 24,392 dado blades

5. 47,287,539 fasteners

Use numbers to write the following expressions.

6. 327 thousand, 216 ingots

7. 432 million, 627 thousand, 456 plastic bottles

8. 52 thousand, 293 brake shoes

9. three hundred twenty-nine thousand, six hundred fourteen employees

10. eighty-three thousand, twenty-nine cable reels

Frequently, in our work we will need to round numbers. The flow chart in Figure 1-5 can help us.

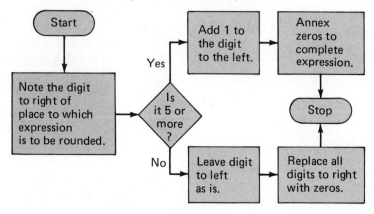

Figure 1-5

EXAMPLE 1   Round 3276 to the nearest hundred.

SOLUTION   The digit to the right of the hundreds' place is 7. Since 7 is greater than 5, we add 1 to the hundreds' place and complete the expression with zeros: 3276 → 3300.

EXAMPLE 2   Round 3276 to the nearest thousand.

SOLUTION   The digit to the right of the thousands' place is 2. Since 2 is less than 5, we leave the 3 in the thousands' place and complete the expression with zeros: 3276 → 3000

EXERCISES   Round to the nearest hundred.

A   1. 482   2. 927   3. 6284   4. 5728

Round to the nearest thousand.

5. 3298   6. 5899   7. 29,507   8. 68,426

6

Round to the nearest ten feet.

B **9.** 32 ft   **10.** 527 ft   **11.** 3291 ft

Round to the nearest 100 mi.

12. 428 mi   **13.** 3261 mi   **14.** 4556 mi

C **15.** Do you think rounding is used in reading electric and gas meters? Explain.

16. Name several examples to show how rounding is used in industry.

1-4 Tachometer

Automobile tachometer.
Figure 1-6

Tuning an automobile engine requires the use of precision instruments, like the tachometer shown in Figure 1-6. A tachometer measures the speed of a rotating object in revolutions per minute (rpm). To read a tachometer, take the reading on the dial shown by the pointer and multiply by 100. The reading on the tachometer in Figure 1-6 is 44 × 100, or 4400 rpm.

EXERCISES Read the tachometer to the nearest hundred rpm.

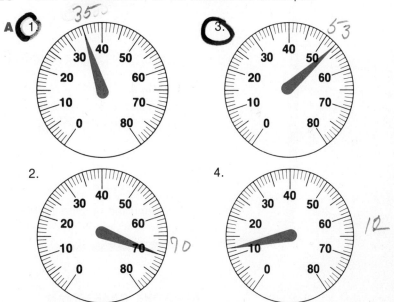

A **1.** 35⟋⟋

2. 70

3. 5 3

4. 12

B **5-8.** Round each of the above readings to the nearest thousand rpm.

7

Throughout this book you will find Self-Analysis Tests to help you check your understanding. After you finish the test, check your answers with those at the end of the book.

SELF-ANALYSIS TEST 1

Read the meters.

1.

KWH

2.

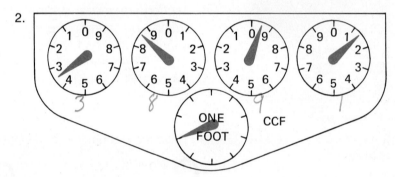

ONE FOOT   CCF

3.

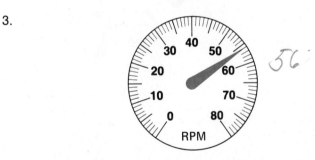

RPM

4–6. Round the reading on each meter to the nearest thousand.

CREATIVE CRAFTSMAN

Design and build a decorative object made from used soft-drink cans.

Reading graphs

1-5 Bar graphs

If you saw an industrial **bar graph** like Figure 1-7, would you know how to read it?

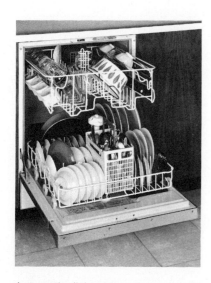

Automatic dishwasher—a household appliance.

Figure 1-7

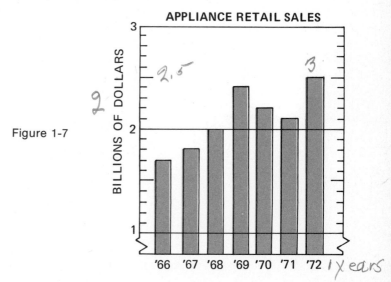

1. What information is given along the bottom of the graph?

2. What is the scale along the side of the graph?

3. In which year were appliance sales the greatest?

4. What is the amount of sales, in billions of dollars, for 1972?

We can get the answers to these questions directly from the graph. To learn even more from the graph, we need to use addition, subtraction, multiplication, and division.

EXAMPLE 1   What are the total appliance sales, in billions of dollars, for the last 3 years shown in the graph?

SOLUTION   *Addition*

Sales for these years are:

1970 →	$2,200,000,000
1971 →	2,100,000,000
1972 → +	2,500,000,000
	$6,800,000,000 (Total sales)

EXAMPLE 2   By how much did the 1972 sales exceed the sales in 1966?

SOLUTION   *Subtraction*

The sales figures for these years are:

1972 → $2,500,000,000
1966 → − 1,700,000,000
─────────────────
      $800,000,000 (Difference in sales)

EXAMPLE 3   The appliance industry expects to double its 1972 sales figure by 1975. What is the projected 1975 sales figure?

SOLUTION   *Multiplication*

1972 → $2,500,000,000
          × 2
─────────────────
1975 → $5,000,000,000 (Projected sales)

EXAMPLE 4   What is the average amount of sales for the years shown on the graph?

SOLUTION   *Addition and Division*

To find an average, we can follow the flow chart in Figure 1-8.

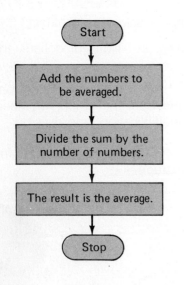

Figure 1-8

Step 1

$ 1,700,000,000
   1,800,000,000
   2,000,000,000
   2,400,000,000
   2,200,000,000
   2,100,000,000
+ 2,500,000,000
─────────────────
$14,700,000,000

Step 2

     $2,100,000,000 (Average sales)
     ─────────────
7)$14,700,000,000

Bar graphs may be drawn either vertically or horizontally. Sometimes two sets of facts are shown on the same graph, as in Figure 1-9.

Modern electric range.

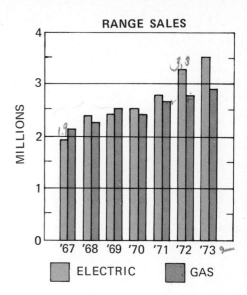

Figure 1-9

RANGE SALES

ELECTRIC GAS

EXERCISES Use Figure 1-9 to answer the questions.

A
1. How many electric ranges were sold in 1967? in 1972?

2. In which year were gas range sales the greatest? the least?

3. In which years did the sale of gas ranges exceed the sale of electric ranges? By how much in each case?

4. What are the total sales of electric and gas ranges in 1972?

5. If a gas range costs $250, about how much was spent for gas ranges in 1972?

6. Round the electric range sales for each of the years 1970 to 1973 to the nearest million dollars.

Exercises 7–12 refer to Figure 1-10 on the next page.

7. During which month did the housing starts reach their peak?

8. How many housing units were begun in May?

9. Between which two months did housing starts drop the most? By how much?

B 10. What is the average number of housing starts for the first six months?

11. Which month comes closest to matching the average?

C 12. Suppose the average asking price of a house is $28,990. What is the total value of the homes that were begun in June?

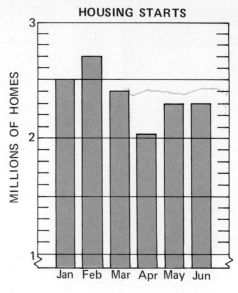

Figure 1-10

1-6 Broken-line graphs

Broken-line graphs are used in nearly every industry to show the changes in important trends. To make a broken-line graph, we join the tops of the bars of a vertical bar graph, as shown in Figures 1-11 and 1-12.

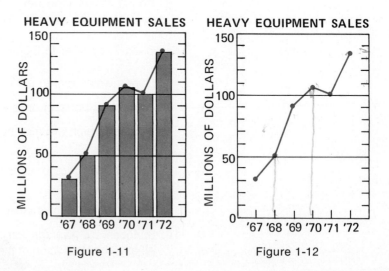

Figure 1-11   Figure 1-12

EXERCISES Use Figure 1-12 to answer the questions.

A   1. What were the sales for heavy equipment in 1972?

2. Between which two years did the sales increase the most? By how much?

3. How much of a decrease in sales took place between 1970 and 1971?

4. What will the sales be if the company doubles its 1972 figure?

5. What were the average sales in the period from 1970 to 1972?

Heavy equipment makes construction easier.

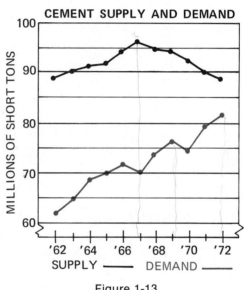

Figure 1-13

Exercises 6–10 refer to Figure 1-13.

6. In which year was the supply of cement the greatest? the least?

7. In which year was the demand for cement the greatest? the least?

8. What is the difference between supply and demand in 1972?

B   9. What does the graph show concerning the supply and demand? Explain.

10. Estimate when the demand will probably exceed the supply.

1-7 Curved-line graphs

Some graphs cannot be drawn exactly using only broken lines. For example, when an engineer tests the acceleration of an automobile, he records the results first in a table like Figure 1-14. Then the engineer transfers these results to a graph as a series of dots (Figure 1-15). Finally, he connects the graphs with a smooth curve to form a curved-line graph (Figure 1-16).

Acceleration Test

Time (Seconds)	Speed (Miles Per Hour)
0	0
5	12
10	23
15	30
20	35
25	39
30	42
35	45
40	47

Figure 1-14

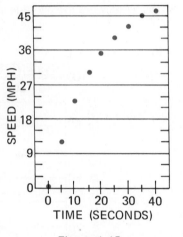

Figure 1-15

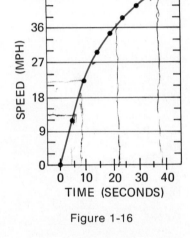

Figure 1-16

EXERCISES   Use Figure 1-16 to answer the questions.

A
1. By how much did the speed increase during each 5-second interval?

2. During which 5-second interval was the acceleration the greatest? the least?

3. What was the speed at 8 seconds? at 22 seconds? at 37 seconds?

4. How many seconds did it take the automobile to reach a speed of 14 mph? a speed of 26 mph? a speed of 35 mph?

5. Describe what you think the curved line will look like beyond the 45-second line.

Use Figure 1-17 to answer Exercises 6–9.

6. At what speed does the automobile get the highest mileage per gallon (mpg)?

7. What is the mileage per gallon at 25 mph? at 45 mph?

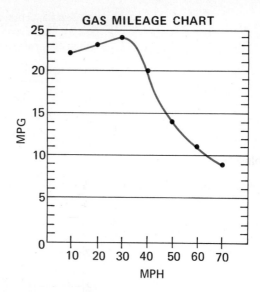

GAS MILEAGE CHART

Figure 1-17

8. What happens to the mileage per gallon as the speed increases beyond 30 mph?

9. Between which two speeds does the gas mileage per gallon drop the most?

B 10. Use the information in the table below to draw a curved-line graph.

Fuel Economy Test

Load (tons)	Miles per gallon (mpg)
2	18
4	17
6	15
8	12
10	8
12	7
14	6

RESEARCH PROJECT

To see how the speed of an engine affects its fuel consumption, try this experiment. Find out how long a power lawn mower will run at "LO", "MED", and "HI" speed, using the same amount of fuel at each speed. Show your findings in a bar graph. Can you think of ways for drivers to conserve gasoline in their automobiles?

SELF-ANALYSIS TEST 2

Exercises 1–4 refer to Figure 1-18.

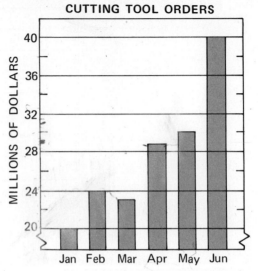

Figure 1-18

1. During which month were tool orders the highest? How much? 40

2. How much more was received from orders in May than in April? 90

3. What was the average amount received in orders for the first three months?

4. Using the information in Figure 1-18, draw a broken line graph.

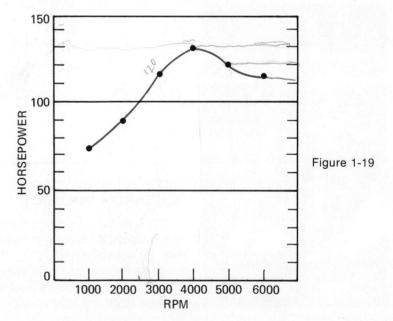

Figure 1-19

Exercises 5–8 refer to Figure 1-19.

5. What engine speed gives the maximum horsepower?

6. How much horsepower is developed at 2500 rpm?

7. Between which two rpm readings does the horsepower increase the most?

8. Estimate the horsepower rating at 7000 rpm.

SPOTLIGHT ON INDUSTRY

The discovery of the laser has changed many industries. A laser is a high energy beam which can be focused on points smaller than a millimeter which are miles away.

Clothing manufacturers are now cutting cloth with a computer-directed laser beam. The aircraft, engineering, plumbing, and oil industries are also benefiting from the use of lasers. In precision work with microscopic circuits and other electronic equipment, lasers are now a necessary tool. Holes can be drilled in a wire as small as a paper clip and wires as small as .08 mm can be welded.

Many uses for lasers have also been found in medicine, including eye surgery and improvements in contact lenses. A number of holes about .1 mm across are drilled in contact lenses to allow better circulation of the fluids around the eye and prevent itching.

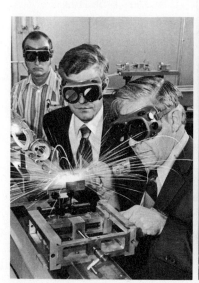 

Telephone and PBX Technician

As our population and economy grow, the demand for more and better communications systems increases. Efforts to meet these needs have created many career opportunities in the communications industry. One job that is becoming increasingly important is that of the telephone and private branch exchange (PBX) service technician. Perhaps this is the career for you.

Job Description

What do service technicians do?

1. They install and remove telephones in homes and places of business.
2. They fill customer's requests for new types of service and equipment. For example, they may change a party line to a private line in a home. Or they may install extension phones or replace older phones with newer ones.
3. They assist in locating faulty equipment, and help restore phone service to the customer.
4. They connect wires from terminals to switchboards and test to check installation.
5. They set up radio and television equipment for "on the scene" broadcasts.

Qualifications

Graduates from high schools or vocational schools are preferred.
Courses in mathematics and electricity are strongly recommended.
A pleasing appearance and the ability to deal effectively with people are desirable.
Good physical condition is needed for climbing telephone poles and ladders.

Training

Telephone companies hire inexperienced persons and train them for the job. New workers receive class instruction in

classrooms equipped with telephones, cables, and other equipment to <u>simulate</u> actual situations. After a few weeks of training, new workers accompany experienced servicepersons to learn while on the job. Service <u>technicians</u> receive training throughout their career to update them on the newest equipment.

Working Conditions

A 40-hour week, with possible overtime.
Availability for calls at all hours to restore service during breakdowns.
Indoor and outdoor work in all kinds of weather.
Common hazards include cuts, falls, and electrical shock.

Opportunities for Advancement

Due to the use of more <u>complex</u> equipment, telephone companies are <u>constantly</u> retraining their service technicians. Often a telephone service technician will be promoted to a PBX service technician, with an increase in pay. Those who prove themselves on the job and in the classroom are <u>frequently</u> promoted to supervisory positions.

1. Simulate
2. technicians
3. complex
4. constantly
5. frequently

Reading rules

1-8 Rules and lengths

To measure lengths precisely, we use a variety of rulers. Each ruler is made with different **scales**, depending on its intended use.

The ruler in Figure 1-20 has two scales. On the upper scale each inch is divided into 8 equal parts. Each part is $\frac{1}{8}$ inch long ($\frac{1}{8}''$). The distance AB is $\frac{5}{8}''$.

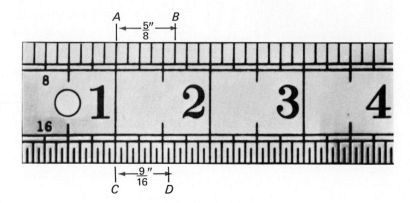

Figure 1-20

On the lower scale each inch is divided into 16 equal parts. Each part is $\frac{1}{16}''$ long. The distance CD is $\frac{9}{16}''$.

Do you remember the terms we use to describe fractions like those in Figure 1-20?

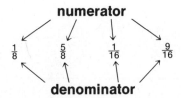

Many jobs require us to divide an inch into smaller fractions to make very precise measurements. In Figure 1-21 an inch is divided into 32 equal parts on the upper scale and into 64 equal parts on the lower scale. Each division on the upper scale is $\frac{1}{32}''$. Each division on the lower scale is $\frac{1}{64}''$.

Figure 1-21 (enlarged)

Some machinist's rules are divided into hundredths of an inch, as in Figure 1-22. The distance from the left edge of the scale to the number 10 is $\frac{10}{100}''$, or $\frac{1}{10}''$.

Figure 1-22 (enlarged)

Rules with scales divided into more than 100 equal parts are not used because of the difficulty in seeing the small sub-divisions. There are other instruments that can be used to make measurements that are accurate to $\frac{1}{1000}''$ or $\frac{1}{10000}''$. We will study these instruments later.

EXERCISES   Exercises 1–4 refer to Figure 1-23.

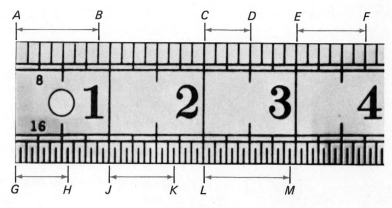

Figure 1-23

A   1. What is the smallest fraction of an inch

      a. on the upper scale?   b. on the lower scale?

  2. On the upper scale what distance is shown by

      a. 3 divisions?   b. 7 divisions?   c. 8 divisions?

  3. On the lower scale what distance is shown by

      a. 5 divisions?   b. 7 divisions?   c. 13 divisions?

  4. Give the length of each line.

      a. AB   c. EF   e. JK

      b. CD   d. GH   f. LM

Exercises 5–8 refer to Figure 1-24.

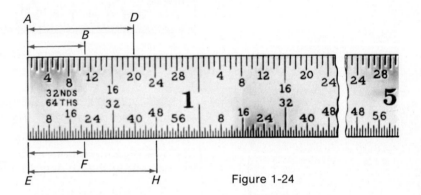

Figure 1-24

  5. What is the smallest division of an inch

      a. on the upper scale?   b. on the lower scale?

  6. On the upper scale what distance is shown by

      a. 5 divisions?   b. 15 divisions?   c. 23 divisions?

  7. On the lower scale what distance is shown by

      a. 27 divisions?   b. 43 divisions?

  8. Give the length of each line.

      a. AB   b. AD   c. EF   d. EH

Exercises 9–11 refer to Figure 1-25.

  9. What is the smallest division of an inch on the scale?

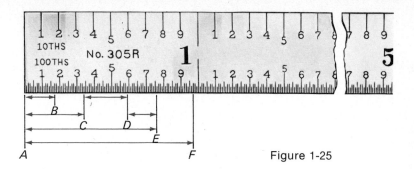

Figure 1-25

10. What distance is shown by

    a. 3 divisions?   **c.** 29 divisions?

    b. 17 divisions?   **d.** 57 divisions?

11. Give the length of each line.

    a. *AB*   **c.** *CD*   **e.** *AE*

    b. *AC*   **d.** *DE*   **f.** *AF*

B 12. Using a rule divided into sixteenths of an inch, draw each length.

    a. $\frac{3}{16}''$ **b.** $\frac{7}{16}''$ **c.** $\frac{11}{16}''$

13. Using a rule divided into thirty-seconds of an inch, draw each length.

    a. $\frac{7}{32}''$ **b.** $\frac{13}{32}''$ **c.** $\frac{25}{32}''$

1-9 Equivalent fractions

The ruler in Figure 1-26 is divided into eighths and sixteenths of an inch. Distance *AB* is $\frac{3}{8}''$. But *AB* is also $\frac{6}{16}''$. So $\frac{3}{8}'' = \frac{6}{16}''$.

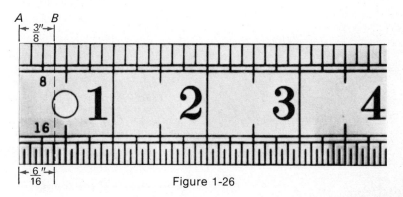

Figure 1-26

23

The fractions $\frac{3}{8}$ and $\frac{6}{16}$ are called **equivalent** because they have the same value. Do you think $\frac{5}{8}$ and $\frac{10}{16}$ are equivalent?

We can use an easy test to see if two fractions are equivalent. Cross-multiply the fractions. If the products are equal, the fractions are equivalent.

EXAMPLE 1   Is $\frac{5}{8}$ equivalent to $\frac{10}{16}$?

SOLUTION

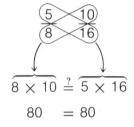

$$8 \times 10 \overset{?}{=} 5 \times 16$$

$$80 \quad = 80$$

Yes, $\frac{5}{8}$ is equivalent to $\frac{10}{16}$.

EXAMPLE 2   Is $\frac{9}{32}$ equivalent to $\frac{5}{16}$?

SOLUTION

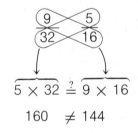

$$5 \times 32 \overset{?}{=} 9 \times 16$$

$$160 \quad \neq 144$$

No, $\frac{9}{32}$ and $\frac{5}{16}$ are *not* equivalent.

We can use the following rules for finding a fraction that is equivalent to another.

1. The numerator and denominator of any fraction may be multiplied by the same number (except zero) without changing the value of the fraction.

2. The numerator and denominator of any fraction may be divided by the same number (except zero) without changing the value of the fraction.

EXAMPLE 3   A metal strip $\frac{11}{32}''$ wide is needed to fasten two parts of a blower. Can a strip $\frac{3}{8}''$ wide be ground down to the required width?

SOLUTION   To change $\frac{3}{8}$ to thirty-seconds, multiply both the numerator and denominator by 4.

$$\frac{3 \times 4}{8 \times 4} = \frac{12}{32}$$

Since the $\frac{3}{8}''$ piece is $\frac{12}{32}''$, it can be ground down and used.

EXAMPLE 4   The hole in a lock washer measures $\frac{8}{32}''$. Can this washer be used on a $\frac{1}{4}''$ bolt?

SOLUTION   To change $\frac{8}{32}$ to an equivalent fraction, we may divide both the numerator and denominator by 8.

$$\frac{8 \div 8}{32 \div 8} = \frac{1}{4}$$

The washer diameter is $\frac{1}{4}''$. It will fit the $\frac{1}{4}''$ bolt.

When we can no longer change a fraction to an equivalent fraction by dividing its numerator and denominator by the same number, we say that the fraction is in *lowest terms*. Reducing fractions to lowest terms often saves time in calculating.

EXERCISES   Determine whether the following pairs of fractions are equivalent.

A
1. $\frac{4}{8}, \frac{1}{2}$ 3. $\frac{4}{16}, \frac{1}{4}$ 5. $\frac{1}{32}, \frac{2}{64}$

2. $\frac{9}{10}, \frac{90}{100}$ 4. $\frac{3}{7}, \frac{2}{14}$ 6. $\frac{2}{3}, \frac{8}{12}$

Change each measurement to sixteenths of an inch.

7. $\frac{1}{8}''$ 9. $\frac{1}{2}''$ 11. $\frac{3}{4}''$

8. $\frac{1}{4}''$ 10. $\frac{3}{8}''$ 12. $\frac{5}{8}''$

Change each measurement to thirty-seconds of an inch.

13. $\frac{3}{16}''$ 15. $\frac{7}{16}''$ 17. $\frac{1}{2}''$

14. $\frac{5}{8}''$ 16. $\frac{1}{4}''$ 18. $\frac{9}{16}''$

Reduce each fraction to lowest terms.

B 19. $\frac{6}{8}$ 22. $\frac{12}{16}$ 25. $\frac{4}{10}$

20. $\frac{4}{16}$ 23. $\frac{20}{32}$ 26. $\frac{20}{100}$

21. $\frac{8}{32}$ 24. $\frac{24}{64}$ 27. $\frac{25}{100}$

Reduce each measurement to the term indicated.

28. $\frac{8}{16}''$ to eighths   32. $\frac{48}{64}''$ to eighths

29. $\frac{24}{32}''$ to fourths   33. $\frac{40}{64}''$ to thirty-seconds

30. $\frac{16}{32}''$ to halves   34. $\frac{4}{20}''$ to tenths

31. $\frac{4}{64}''$ to sixteenths   35. $\frac{8}{64}''$ to eighths

C 36. The square head of a machine bolt measures $\frac{24}{32}''$ across. Will a $\frac{3}{4}''$ open-end wrench fit this bolt head?

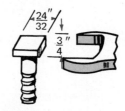

37. The owner's manual for a power lawn mower calls for an adjusting screw not less than $\frac{7}{8}''$ long. Will a screw $\frac{29}{32}''$ long fit?

1-10 Comparing lengths

Sometimes the end of the item you are measuring comes in between two marks on your rule. In such cases, you must estimate its actual length.

Look at the length *AB* in Figure 1-27. This length is a little more than $\frac{9}{16}''$, but less than $\frac{10}{16}''$. If you are measuring to the nearest sixteenth of an inch, you must decide which mark is nearer to *B*.

Now look at length *AC*. This length is more than $1\frac{1}{8}''$, but less than $1\frac{3}{16}''$. Point *C* falls between the $\frac{2}{16}''$ mark and the $\frac{3}{16}''$ mark. We estimate that it falls about halfway between, and give the length in thirty-seconds of an inch. We can find equivalent fractions for $\frac{2}{16}$ and $\frac{3}{16}$.

$$\frac{2}{16}'' = \frac{4}{32}''$$
$$\frac{3}{16}'' = \frac{6}{32}''$$

Halfway between $\frac{4}{32}''$ and $\frac{6}{32}''$ is $\frac{5}{32}''$. The length AC, then, is about $1\frac{5}{32}''$.

When we are using a scale with 16 divisions to the inch, we usually measure to the nearest sixteenth of an inch, or estimate to the nearest thirty-second. For more precise measurements, you may use a scale with 32 or 64 subdivisions to the inch.

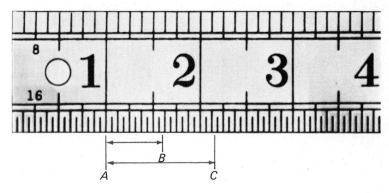

Figure 1-27

EXERCISES Using a rule, measure each line to the nearest sixteenth of an inch.

A 1. ├────────────────┤

2. ├──────────┤

3. ├────────────┤

4. ├──────────────────┤

5. ├────────────────────────┤

6–10. Estimate the length of each line in Exercises 1–5 to the nearest thirty-second of an inch.

Draw the following lengths. Use a rule with a scale of 16 divisions to the inch.

B 11. $1\frac{15}{16}''$ 13. $4\frac{1}{4}''$ 15. $3\frac{1}{2}''$

12. $5\frac{1}{2}''$ 14. $2\frac{3}{4}''$ 16. $4\frac{5}{16}''$

17–22. Check the accuracy of your drawings by using a scale having thirty-two divisions to the inch.

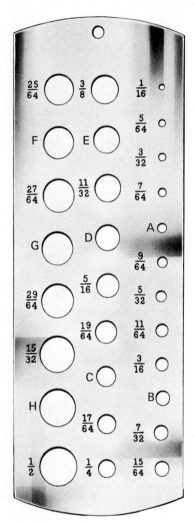

C 23. In working with sheet metal, you often need several pieces that are exactly alike. You make your pieces from a pattern, called a *template*. Measure each dimension in this template to the nearest thirty-second of an inch.

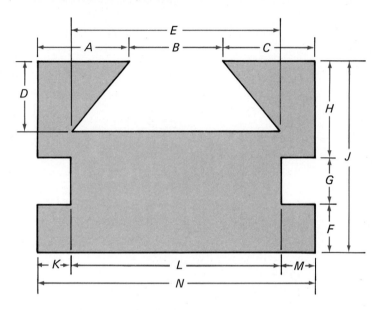

24. Machinists use a drill gauge like the one at the left to sort drill bits according to size. Each hole in the gauge is $\frac{1}{64}''$ larger than the next. Tell the size of the holes shown by letters.

1-11 Metric scales

The metric system is the standard system of measurement throughout most of the world. In the United States the metric system is being used more and more in the major industries. Tomorrow's skilled technicians will need to understand this important system of measurement.

Two of the most commonly used units of length in the metric system are the millimeter (mm) and the centimeter (cm). There are 10 millimeters in 1 centimeter, as shown on the upper scale in Figure 1-28.

The lower scale in Figure 1-28 shows an inch rule for comparison. Do you see that a centimeter is about $\frac{3}{8}''$? Would you say that a millimeter is about $\frac{1}{32}''$? You will use these metric scales frequently in this book.

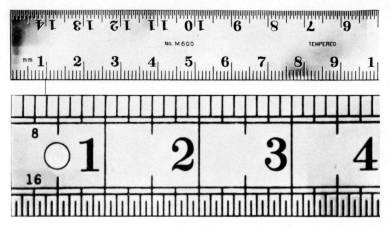

Figure 1-28

EXERCISES Exercises 1 and 2 refer to Figure 1-29.

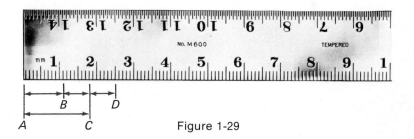

Figure 1-29

A   1. On the metric scale, give the distance between

   a. 3 divisions   c. 17 divisions
   b. 10 divisions   d. 29 divisions

   2. Name the distance for

   a. *AB*   b. *BC*   c. *CD*   d. *AC*

   3. Use a metric rule to measure the length of each line.

   a. ├────────────────┤

   b. ├────────────┤

   c. ├──────────────────────┤

   d. ├──────┤

   e. ├────────────────────┤

4. Use a metric rule to draw a line with a length of

    a. 18 mm   **b.** 29 mm   **c.** 4 cm   **d.** 9 cm

For Exercises 5–7 use a metric rule to find the lengths shown.

B 5.

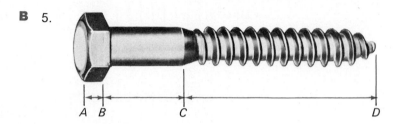

6.

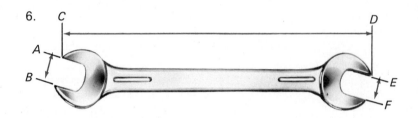

7.

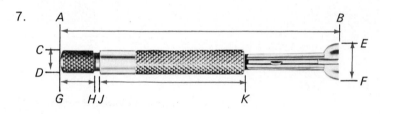

TRICKS OF THE TRADE

Here is a way to obtain two small square pieces of stock from a larger scrap. Just cut on the dashed lines and assemble the pieces, as shown.

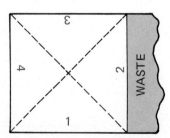
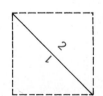

SELF-ANALYSIS TEST 3

1. Give the length of each line.

   a. *AB*   b. *AC*   c. *DE*   d. *DF*

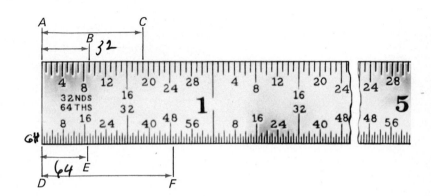

2. Use a machinist's scale to measure the line below to the nearest tenth of an inch.

3. Determine whether $\frac{3}{7}$ and $\frac{8}{21}$ are equivalent.

4. Change $\frac{21}{32}$ to sixty-fourths.

5. Reduce $\frac{24}{32}$ to lowest terms.

6. Give the length of each line in millimeters.

   a. *AB*   b. *BC*   c. *CD*   d. *AD*

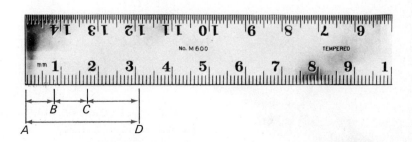

Reading technical drawings

1-12 Lines

Work in industry must be precise. Measurements are made with sensitive instruments. Parts are machined with precision tools. And technical diagrams are drawn with care. To help you read technical diagrams, you should know about the kinds of lines and dimensions used in drawings.

Look at Figure 1-30. If we rotate the object, its shape appears to change for each quarter-turn.

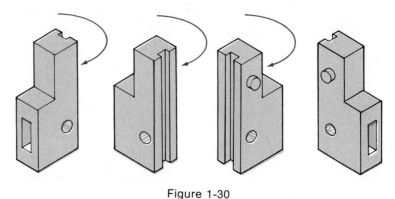

Figure 1-30

Figure 1-31 shows the same rotation in a technical drawing. Compare each drawing in Figure 1-31 with Figure 1-30.

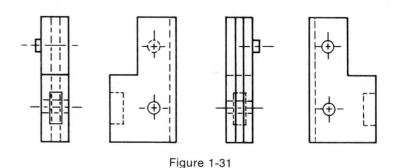

Figure 1-31

The most common lines used in technical drawings are shown in Figure 1-32.

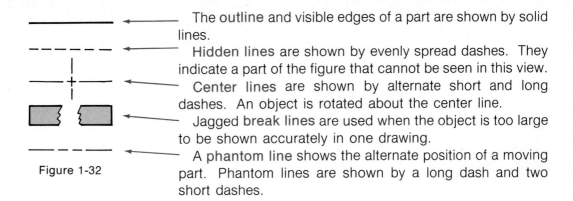

The outline and visible edges of a part are shown by solid lines.

Hidden lines are shown by evenly spread dashes. They indicate a part of the figure that cannot be seen in this view.

Center lines are shown by alternate short and long dashes. An object is rotated about the center line.

Jagged break lines are used when the object is too large to be shown accurately in one drawing.

A phantom line shows the alternate position of a moving part. Phantom lines are shown by a long dash and two short dashes.

Figure 1-32

EXERCISES

Match the technical drawing with the figure.

A 1.

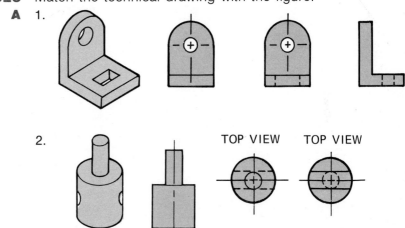

2.

TOP VIEW   TOP VIEW

Sketch 4 views of each object. Show hidden lines, center lines, and so on.

B 3.

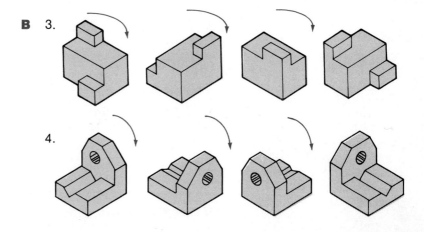

4.

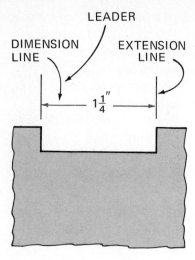

Figure 1-33

1-13 Dimensions

Special lines are used to show dimensions on a drawing like Figure 1-33.

Dimension lines with the arrowheads show the specified length of a part of the object.

Extension lines are used so that direction lines are not crowded into the space around the object. This adds to the overall clarity of the drawing.

A **leader** is used to direct information and symbols to a place in the drawing.

Sometimes it is more convenient to give a series of dimensions with respect to one fixed line, called a **datum line**. In this case the dimension lines have only one arrowhead. Figure 1-34 shows a datum line.

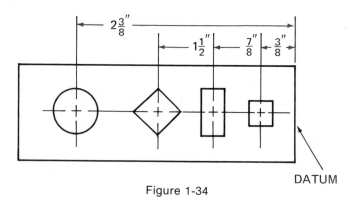

Figure 1-34

Dimensions are shown in one of two ways in technical drawings. With **unidirectional dimensioning** all dimensions can be read from the bottom of the page, as in Figure 1-35. Unidirectional dimensioning is commonly used in the aerospace and automotive industries.

With **aligned dimensioning** the dimensions are readable from either the bottom or the right side of the drawing, as in Figure 1-36. This type of dimensioning is used in blueprints and drafting work.

You may use either system, but you should not use them both in the same drawing. In this book you will find examples of both systems of dimensioning.

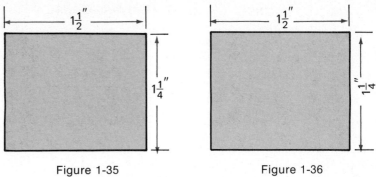

Figure 1-35   Figure 1-36

EXERCISES   Copy the figure. Then sketch in extension lines, dimension lines, and leaders to complete each drawing.

A 1.

2.

3.

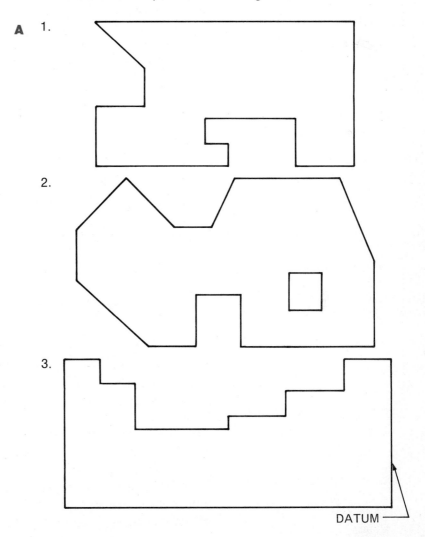

DATUM

35

B 4. Redraw the figure, using aligned dimensions.

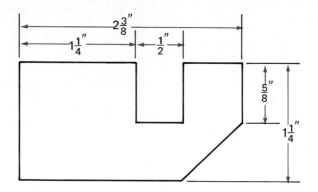

1-14 Curves and angles

Dimensions for circles are given in terms of the diameter, as in Figure 1-37. The center lines show the location of the center of the circle. The abbreviation DIA must always follow the diameter measurement.

In dimensioning arcs, we show the center of curvature and the radius of the curve. We indicate the radius with the abbreviation R, as shown in Figure 1-38.

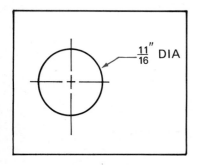

Figure 1-37

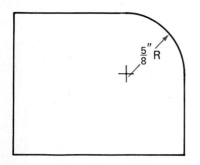

Figure 1-38

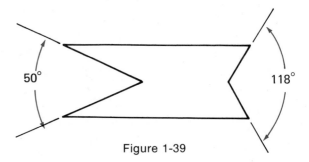

Figure 1-39

The size of an angle is given in degrees (°), minutes ('), and seconds (''), just as you would find them on a precision compass. Study the examples of angle dimensions in Figure 1-39.

EXERCISES Copy each diagram. Use a protractor and ruler to find the distances shown. Add these dimensions to your drawing.

A 1.

2.

3.

B 4.

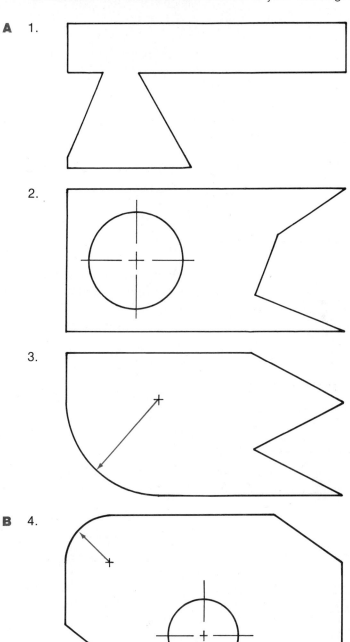

Match the sketch with the correct technical diagram.

1.

2.

TOP VIEW

Copy the drawing. Then measure the parts of the diagram. Show all the dimensions on your copy of this drawing.

3.

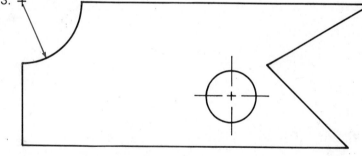

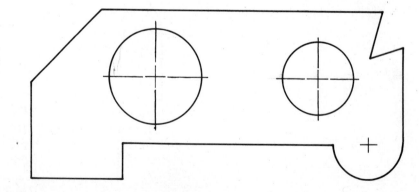

Accurate meter reading is part of a technician's job in a nuclear power plant.

TAKING INVENTORY

1. Industrial meters can be used to measure fuel use, speeds, and other quantities. (pp. 1–7)
2. Our number system is based on tens. (p. 5)
3. Information can be shown on bar graphs, broken-line graphs, and curved-line graphs. (pp. 9–15)
4. Rulers consist of scales divided into equal parts. (pp. 20–21)
5. The terms of a fraction are the **numerator** and **denominator.** (p. 20)
6. Fractions that are equal in value are called **equivalent** fractions. (pp. 23–25)
7. Two important systems of measurement are the United States system and the metric system. (p. 28)
8. Technical drawings show the dimensions and other information that is used in manufacturing an object. (pp. 32–37)

MEASURING YOUR SKILLS

Read the meters. (1-1, 1-2)

1.
KWH

2.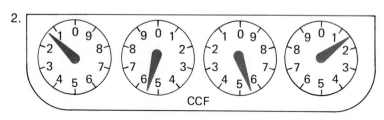
CCF

3. Use numbers to write the following expressions. (1-3)

    a. six hundred thousand, four hundred sixteen
    b. five million, five hundred thousand, five hundred

4. Round to the nearest thousand. (1-3)

    a. 5927　　b. 64,274　　c. 432,972

5. Read the tachometer at the left. (1-4)

Exercises 6–10 refer to Figure 1-40. (1-5, 1-6, 1-7)

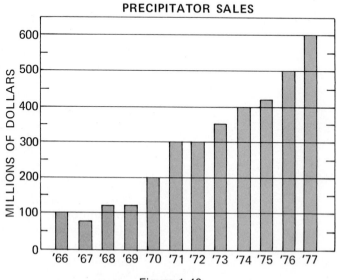

Figure 1-40

6. How many dollars were spent for industrial pollution control devices (precipitators) in 1972?

7. How much more was spent in 1972 than in 1970?

8. How many times greater is the 1972 figure than the 1967 figure?

9. Estimate the amount that will be spent in 1978.

10. Draw the bar graph in Figure 1-40 as a broken-line graph. Show the sales for 1972–1977 as a curved line.

11. Using a rule, measure each line to the nearest thirty-second of an inch. (1-8)

    a. _____

    b. _____

12. Write a fraction equivalent to $\frac{5}{8}$. (1-9)

13. Change $\frac{7}{8}''$ to thirty-seconds of an inch. (1-9)

14. Change $\frac{56}{64}''$ to eighths of an inch. (1-9)

15. Reduce to lowest terms. (1-9)

    a. $\frac{80}{100}$ b. $\frac{16}{64}$ c. $\frac{26}{32}$

16. In a set of combination wrenches which size is larger than $\frac{3}{8}''$ and less than $\frac{1}{2}''$? (1-10)

17. Give the length of each line in millimeters. (1-11)

    a. _____

    b. _____

18. Copy the drawing. Then measure the parts of the diagram. Show all the dimensions on your copy. (1-12, 1-13, 1-14)

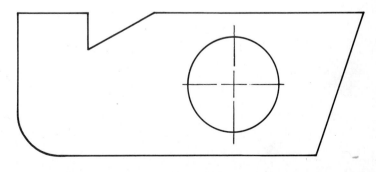

Wise forestry management by the paper industry is the first step in meeting the growing need for paper products.

CHAPTER **2** *Using Fractions*

After completing this chapter, you should be able to:

1. Add and subtract fractions.
2. Add and subtract mixed numbers.
3. Work with dimensions expressed in inches or feet and inches.
4. Plan projects carefully in order to minimize waste.

Adding and subtracting fractions

2-1 **Fractions with the same denominator**

Materials like aluminum and plastic can be shaped by forcing them through an open die, in a process called ex-trusion. To make the die, the machinist refers to a diagram which shows the required dimensions. By adding and sub-tracting fractions, he finds the dimensions that are not shown.

Figure 2-1—Stadium bench and automobile bumper of extruded aluminum.

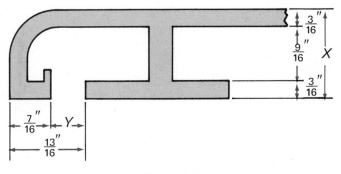

Figure 2-2

EXAMPLE 1 Find length X.

SOLUTION   Length $X = \dfrac{3}{16} + \dfrac{9}{16} + \dfrac{3}{16}$

$= \dfrac{3 + 9 + 3}{16}$

$= \dfrac{15}{16}$

Length X is $\dfrac{15''}{16}$.

EXAMPLE 2 Find length Y.

SOLUTION   Length $Y = \dfrac{13}{16} - \dfrac{7}{16}$

$= \dfrac{13 - 7}{16}$

$= \dfrac{6}{16}$

$= \dfrac{3}{8}$

Length Y is $\dfrac{3''}{8}$.

Examples 1 and 2 suggest the following rule.

> To add fractions with the same denominator, add the numerators and use that denominator.
> To subtract fractions with the same denominator, subtract the numerators and use that denominator.

EXERCISES   Add or subtract. Write the answer in the simplest form.

A   1. $\frac{2}{8} + \frac{3}{8}$

5. $\frac{3}{10} + \frac{1}{10}$

9. $\frac{19}{32} - \frac{11}{32}$

2. $\frac{7}{16} - \frac{5}{16}$

6. $\frac{21}{32} - \frac{17}{32}$

10. $\frac{27}{64} - \frac{23}{64}$

3. $\frac{3}{32} + \frac{5}{32}$

7. $\frac{29}{100} + \frac{47}{100}$

11. $\frac{9}{64} + \frac{15}{64} + \frac{33}{64}$

4. $\frac{15}{64} - \frac{7}{64}$

8. $\frac{29}{64} - \frac{13}{64}$

12. $\frac{27}{100} + \frac{37}{100} + \frac{17}{100}$

Find the lengths. (Do the work inside the parenthesis first.)

B 13. $\frac{29}{32}'' - (\frac{3}{32}'' + \frac{7}{32}'')$ 15. $\frac{33}{64}'' - (\frac{5}{64}'' + \frac{9}{64}'' + \frac{5}{64}'')$

14. $\frac{87}{100}'' - (\frac{33}{100}'' + \frac{23}{100}'')$ 16. $(\frac{49}{100}'' + \frac{17}{100}'') - (\frac{27}{100}'' + \frac{13}{100}'')$

Find the lengths shown by letters on the diagrams.

C 17.

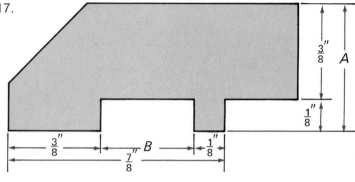

18.

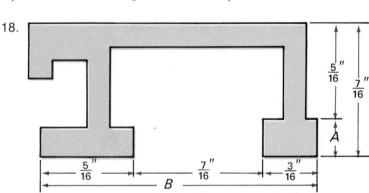

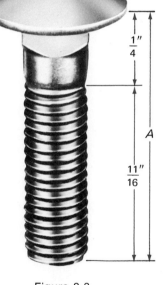

Figure 2-3

2-2 Fractions with different denominators

Figure 2-3 shows a carriage bolt, which is used widely in industry. In order to find the missing dimensions A and B, we have to add and subtract fractions with different denominators. The following rule can help us.

To add or subtract fractions with different denominators:
1. Change the fractions to equivalent fractions having the same denominator; then
2. Add or subtract the fractions, using the common denominator.

EXAMPLE 1   Find length *A* in Figure 2-3 on the previous page.

SOLUTION   Length $A = \dfrac{1}{4} + \dfrac{11}{16}$

$$= \frac{4}{16} + \frac{11}{16}$$

$$= \frac{4 + 11}{16} = \frac{15}{16}$$

Length *A* is $\dfrac{15''}{16}$.

EXAMPLE 2   Find length *B* in Figure 2-3 on the previous page.

SOLUTION   To find *B*, we must subtract the length of the flanges from the diameter of the bolt head. Thus,

Length $B = \dfrac{9}{16} - \left(\dfrac{5}{32} + \dfrac{5}{32} \right)$

$$= \frac{18}{32} - \frac{10}{32}$$

$$= \frac{8}{32} = \frac{1}{4}$$

Length *B* is $\dfrac{1''}{4}$.

Sometimes it is difficult to find a common denominator quickly. In such cases we may use a short cut. Study this example.

EXAMPLE 3 $\frac{7}{10} + \frac{1}{8} = ?$

SOLUTION $\dfrac{7}{10} \diagdown\!\!\!\!\diagup \dfrac{1}{8} = \dfrac{(7 \times 8) + (1 \times 10)}{10 \times 8}$

$$= \frac{56 + 10}{80}$$

$$= \frac{66}{80}$$

$$= \frac{33}{40}$$

The arrows show how we multiply to obtain the numbers in the numerator and in the denominator.

EXERCISES Use the short cut to find a common denominator, then add or subtract. Write the answer in lowest terms.

A
1. $\frac{1}{4} + \frac{5}{8}$

2. $\frac{3}{4} - \frac{3}{8}$

3. $\frac{1}{16} + \frac{7}{8}$

4. $\frac{5}{8} - \frac{5}{16}$

5. $\frac{7}{16} + \frac{1}{4}$

6. $\frac{9}{16} - \frac{3}{8}$

7. $\frac{1}{2} + \frac{1}{8}$

8. $\frac{1}{2} - \frac{3}{16}$

9. $\frac{7}{10} + \frac{1}{4}$

10. $\frac{5}{8} - \frac{3}{10}$

11. $\frac{35}{100} + \frac{3}{10}$

12. $\frac{9}{32} - \frac{1}{4}$

Find the lengths. (Do the work in the parentheses first.)

B
13. $\frac{5}{8}'' + \frac{1}{16}'' + \frac{1}{8}''$

14. $\frac{3}{4}'' - (\frac{1}{16}'' + \frac{1}{4}'')$

15. $\frac{3}{16}'' + \frac{5}{8}'' + \frac{1}{16}''$

16. $(\frac{5}{32}'' + \frac{3}{16}'') - \frac{1}{8}''$

17. $(\frac{7}{16}'' - \frac{3}{8}'') + \frac{1}{4}''$

18. $\frac{9}{32}'' - (\frac{1}{16}'' + \frac{1}{8}'')$

Find the missing dimensions in the following figures.

C 19.

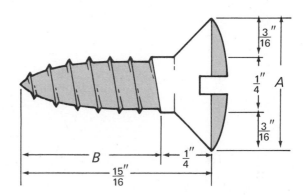

20.

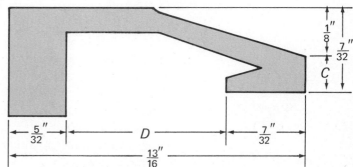

47

21.

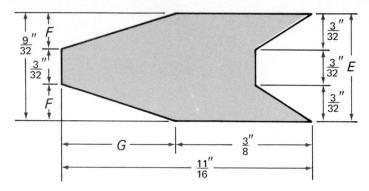

2-3 The least common denominator

To find the total length of the hydraulic valve lifter in Figure 2-4, we have to add 3 fractions that have different denominators.

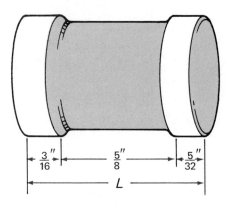

Figure 2-4

Usually it is easier to calculate if we use the smallest number that can be divided evenly by the denominators of the fractions. This number is called the **least common denominator (LCD)**. For the hydraulic lifter in Figure 2-4 the least common denominator is 32. Do you agree that 32 is the smallest number that can be divided by 16, 8, and 32 evenly?

EXAMPLE 1 Find the length of the hydraulic valve lifter in Figure 2-4.

SOLUTION
$$L = \frac{3}{16} + \frac{5}{8} + \frac{5}{32}$$

$$= \frac{6}{32} + \frac{20}{32} + \frac{5}{32} \text{ (32 is L.C.D.)}$$

$$= \frac{6 + 20 + 5}{32}$$

$$= \frac{31}{32}$$

Length L is $\frac{31''}{32}$.

We also use the LCD when we want to subtract fractions having different denominators.

To help us further in adding and subtracting fractions, we can use the flow chart in Figure 2-5. Follow the steps.

EXAMPLE 2

Find length T on the template.

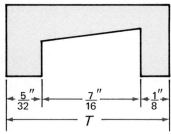

EXAMPLE 3

Find length R on the template.

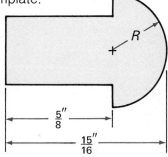

A
Write fractions to be added (subtracted).

B Same denominators? — No → **C** Find common denominator.

Yes

D Change to equivalent fractions with common denominators.

E Add (subtract) numerators.

F Place sum (difference) over common denominator.

G Lowest terms? — No → **H** Reduce.

Yes

J Write answer.

Figure 2-5

SOLUTION

A. $\frac{5}{32}, \frac{7}{16}, \frac{1}{8}$

B. No

C. 32

D. $\frac{5}{32}, \frac{14}{32}, \frac{4}{32}$

E. $5 + 14 + 4 = 23$

F. $\frac{23}{32}$

G. Yes

H. —

I. $\frac{23}{32}''$

SOLUTION

A. $\frac{15}{16}, \frac{5}{8}$

B. No

C. 16

D. $\frac{15}{16}, \frac{10}{16}$

E. $15 - 10 = 5$

F. $\frac{5}{16}$

G. Yes

H. —

I. $\frac{5}{16}''$

EXERCISES Find the least common denominator for the fractions, then add or subtract. Write the answers in lowest terms.

A

1. $\frac{3}{4} + \frac{1}{8}$

2. $\frac{9}{16} - \frac{3}{8}$

3. $\frac{23}{32} + \frac{1}{16}$

4. $\frac{45}{64} - \frac{5}{16}$

5. $\frac{1}{2} + \frac{3}{16}$

6. $\frac{13}{16} - \frac{3}{8}$

7. $\frac{43}{64} + \frac{1}{8}$

8. $\frac{9}{32} - \frac{3}{16}$

9. $\frac{3}{10} + \frac{1}{10} + \frac{53}{100}$

10. $\frac{1}{32} + \frac{1}{4}$

11. $\frac{29}{32} - (\frac{5}{64} + \frac{3}{16})$

12. $(\frac{3}{8} + \frac{3}{16}) - \frac{3}{64}$

B Use the least common denominator to find the lengths.

13. $\frac{83}{100}'' + \frac{1}{10}'' = $ __?__

14. $\frac{5}{8}'' + \frac{11}{32}'' = $ __?__

15. $\frac{17}{100}'' + \frac{1}{10}'' = $ __?__

16. $\frac{9}{16}'' - \frac{7}{32}'' = $ __?__

17. $\frac{43}{64}'' - \frac{15}{32}'' = $ __?__

18. $\frac{11}{16}'' - \frac{37}{64}'' = $ __?__

19. What is the total length of the rivet?

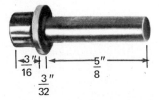

20. Find the lengths R and Q on the gasket.

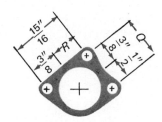

21. Find the lengths, X, Y, and Z on the latch plate.

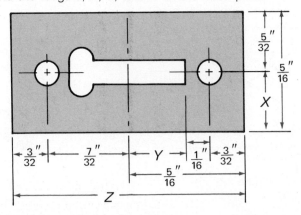

50

C 22. Draw a flow chart for finding the least common denominator of two fractions.

SELF-ANALYSIS TEST 5

Add or subtract. Write the answer in lowest terms.

1. $\frac{3}{16} + \frac{9}{16}$ 3. $\frac{7}{16} - \frac{5}{16}$

2. $\frac{1}{10} + \frac{7}{10}$ 4. $\frac{9}{32} - \frac{3}{32}$

Find the least common denominator for the fractions. Then add or subtract. Write the answer in lowest terms.

5. $\frac{11}{32} - \frac{3}{16}$ 7. $\frac{17}{64} + \frac{3}{8}$

6. $\frac{5}{8} + \frac{3}{32}$ 8. $\frac{7}{8} - \frac{23}{32}$

9. Find the lengths G and H on the door hinge.

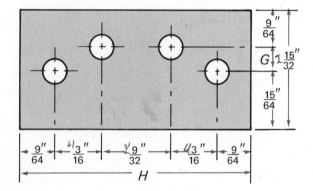

TRICKS OF THE TRADE

Here is an easy way to find the center of a piece of round stock. Hold a carpenter's square against the stock. Mark the points 1 and 2, where it touches. Now rotate the stock so that only one mark touches the square. Mark the point 3, as shown. Rotate again, and mark the point 4. Connect points 1 and 3 and points 2 and 4. The center is where the two lines intersect.

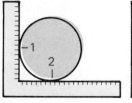 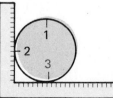 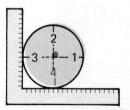

Adding and subtracting
mixed numbers

2-4 Whole numbers and mixed numbers

Most industrial measurements involve not only fractions but also whole numbers and mixed numbers. For example, to manufacture the radio case in Figure 2-6, we must be able to work with numbers like $5\frac{7}{8}''$, $3\frac{3}{16}''$, $2''$, $\frac{3}{4}''$, and so on.

Figure 2-6

EXAMPLE 1   Change 2 to a fraction.

SOLUTION   We can write any whole number as a fraction by placing it over 1 as the denominator. Thus, $2 = \frac{2}{1}$.

EXAMPLE 2   Change $5\frac{7}{8}$ to a fraction.

SOLUTION   *Method 1.* Write the whole number as a fraction, find the common denominator, then add.

$$5\frac{7}{8} = 5 + \frac{7}{8}$$

$$= \frac{5}{1} + \frac{7}{8}$$

$$= \frac{40}{8} + \frac{7}{8}$$

$$= \frac{40 + 7}{8}$$

$$= \frac{47}{8}$$

Method 2. Multiply the whole number by the denominator, then add the numerator.

$$5\frac{7}{8} = \frac{(5 \times 8) + 7}{8}$$

$$= \frac{40 + 7}{8}$$

$$= \frac{47}{8}$$

To simplify our work we often need to change fractions to whole numbers or mixed numbers.

EXAMPLE 3   Simplify $\frac{32}{8}$.

SOLUTION   *Method 1.* Write equivalent fractions using the same denominator.

$$\frac{32}{8} = \frac{8 + 8 + 8 + 8}{8}$$

$$= \frac{8}{8} + \frac{8}{8} + \frac{8}{8} + \frac{8}{8}$$

$$= 1 + 1 + 1 + 1$$

$$= 4$$

Method 2. Divide the numerator by the denominator. If there is a remainder, use it as the numerator.

$$\frac{32}{8} = 8\overline{)32} = 4$$
$$\quad\quad \underline{-32}$$
$$\quad\quad\quad\; 0$$

EXAMPLE 4 Simplify $\frac{43}{16}$.

SOLUTION *Method 1.* Write equivalent fractions using the same denominator.

$$\frac{43}{16} = \frac{16 + 16 + 11}{16}$$

$$= \frac{16}{16} + \frac{16}{16} + \frac{11}{16}$$

$$= 1 + 1 + \frac{11}{16}$$

$$= 2\frac{11}{16}$$

Method 2. Divide the numerator by the denominator. If there is a remainder, use it as the numerator.

$$\frac{43}{16} = 16\overline{)\,43\,}^{\,2} = 2\frac{11}{16}$$
$$\underline{-32}$$
$$11$$

EXERCISES Change to fractions.

A 1. 6

3. $3\frac{3}{4}$

5. $4\frac{7}{8}''$

7. $2\frac{3}{32}''$

2. 8

4. $2\frac{3}{16}$

6. $7\frac{1}{16}''$

8. $4\frac{11}{32}''$

Simplify.

9. $\frac{24}{8}$

11. $\frac{29}{16}$

13. $\frac{15}{4}''$

15. $\frac{65}{32}''$

10. $\frac{64}{16}$

12. $\frac{55}{32}$

14. $\frac{39}{8}''$

16. $\frac{29}{11}''$

2-5 Adding mixed numbers

A wire tunnel is to be constructed from sheet metal with the dimensions shown in Figure 2-7. In order to cut the strip of sheet metal to the correct width, we need to find the **perimeter,** or distance around the outer face.

$$\text{Perimeter} = 2\frac{1}{4}'' + 1\frac{3}{16}'' + 1\frac{5}{8}'' + 1\frac{3}{16}''.$$

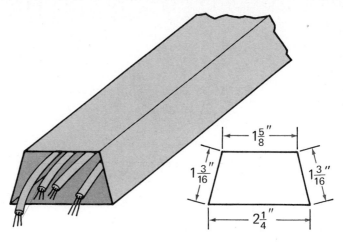

Figure 2-7

There are two ways of adding mixed numbers.

Method 1. Change the mixed numbers to fractions, then add. Simplify the answer.

EXAMPLE 1 Find the perimeter of the wire tunnel in Figure 2-7.

SOLUTION

$$P = 2\tfrac{1}{4} + 1\tfrac{3}{16} + 1\tfrac{5}{8} + 1\tfrac{3}{16}$$
$$= \tfrac{9}{4} + \tfrac{19}{16} + \tfrac{13}{8} + \tfrac{19}{16}$$
$$= \tfrac{36}{16} + \tfrac{19}{16} + \tfrac{26}{16} + \tfrac{19}{16}$$
$$= \tfrac{36+19+26+19}{16}$$
$$= \tfrac{100}{16}$$
$$= 6\tfrac{1}{4}$$

The perimeter is $6\tfrac{1}{4}''$.

Method 2. Add the whole numbers and the fractions separately, then combine to find the answer.

EXAMPLE 2 Find the perimeter of the wire tunnel in Figure 2-7.

SOLUTION

$$\text{Perimeter} \begin{cases} 2\tfrac{1}{4} = 2 + \tfrac{1}{4} = 2 + \tfrac{4}{16} \\ 1\tfrac{3}{16} = 1 + \tfrac{3}{16} = 1 + \tfrac{3}{16} \\ 1\tfrac{5}{8} = 1 + \tfrac{5}{8} = 1 + \tfrac{10}{16} \\ + 1\tfrac{3}{16} = 1 + \tfrac{3}{16} = 1 + \tfrac{3}{16} \\ \hline \qquad\qquad 5 + \tfrac{20}{16} = 5 + 1 + \tfrac{4}{16} = 6\tfrac{1}{4} \end{cases}$$

The perimeter is $6\tfrac{1}{4}''$.

Both methods are useful. The method you use will usually depend on the object you are measuring.

EXERCISES Find the sums.

A 1. $5\frac{1}{2} + 4\frac{3}{8}$

2. $2\frac{5}{8} + 7\frac{3}{32}$

3. $6\frac{7}{10} + 12\frac{47}{100}$

4. $9\frac{27}{32} + 3\frac{53}{64}$

5. $\frac{7}{8} + 10\frac{9}{10}$

6. $2\frac{1}{4}'' + 4\frac{1}{8}'' + 5\frac{3}{16}''$

7. $8\frac{7}{64}'' + 1\frac{9}{32}'' + 5\frac{5}{8}''$

8. $3\frac{3}{10}'' + \frac{3}{4}'' + 4\frac{1}{2}''$

9. $8\frac{15}{16}'' + 2\frac{7}{8}'' + 5\frac{3}{4}''$

10. $5\frac{5}{16}'' + 4\frac{7}{8}'' + 7\frac{3}{4}'' + 9\frac{1}{2}''$

B 11. Find the total length of the transmission gears.

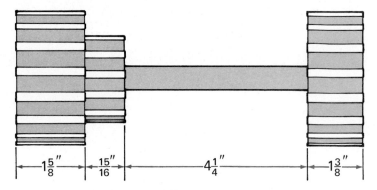

$1\frac{5}{8}''$ $\frac{15}{16}''$ $4\frac{1}{4}''$ $1\frac{3}{8}''$

12. Find the height of the I-beam.

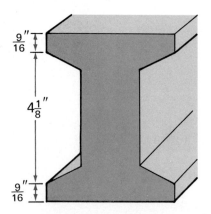

$\frac{9}{16}''$

$4\frac{1}{8}''$

$\frac{9}{16}''$

56

13. How wide is the kitchen chopping block?

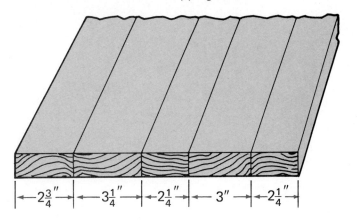

$2\frac{3}{4}''$ $3\frac{1}{4}''$ $2\frac{1}{4}''$ $3''$ $2\frac{1}{4}''$

14. How long is the hammer head?

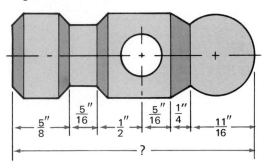

$\frac{5}{8}''$ $\frac{5}{16}''$ $\frac{1}{2}''$ $\frac{5}{16}''$ $\frac{1''}{4}$ $\frac{11}{16}''$

?

15. Find lengths A and B on the light switch plate.

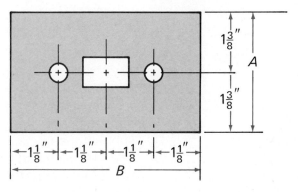

$1\frac{3}{8}''$

A

$1\frac{3}{8}''$

$1\frac{1}{8}''$ $1\frac{1}{8}''$ $1\frac{1}{8}''$ $1\frac{1}{8}''$

B

c 16. Draftsmen use a template when drawing common shapes in various sizes. Part of a drafting template is shown here. If the distance between each shape is $\frac{3}{32}''$, what is the distance between:

a. the first and last square?　　b. the first and last circle?

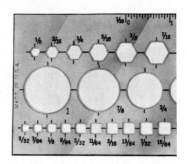

2-6 Subtracting mixed numbers

Subtracting mixed numbers is another skill which is used frequently in industrial work.

EXAMPLE 1　　An electrician needs $12\frac{1}{2}''$ of insulated wire to connect two terminals. He has a piece that measures $27\frac{3}{4}''$, but does not want to cut it unless there will be at least $15\frac{1}{8}''$ left to do another job. Should he cut the wire?

SOLUTION　　To answer this question, we need to subtract $12\frac{1}{2}$ from $27\frac{3}{4}$, as shown here.

$$
\begin{array}{rcr}
27\dfrac{3}{4} = & & 27\dfrac{3}{4} \\[2mm]
-12\dfrac{1}{2} = & & -12\dfrac{2}{4} \\[2mm]
\hline
& & 15\dfrac{1}{4}
\end{array}
$$

Since there will be $15\frac{1}{4}''$ left, he can make the cut.

To subtract mixed numbers, we change the fractions to equivalent fractions with the same denominator. Then we subtract the fractions and the whole numbers. Finally, we add the difference of the fractions to the difference of the whole numbers. (Remember: $15 + \frac{1}{4} = 15\frac{1}{4}$)

Electricians make many measurements in their work.

EXAMPLE 2 In modifying an automobile engine the mechanic bores the cylinder to $4\frac{1}{16}''$ (see Figure 2-8). The original bore was $3\frac{7}{8}''$. By how much has the bore been enlarged?

SOLUTION To find the difference between the bore before and after the machining, we must subtract $3\frac{7}{8}$ from $4\frac{1}{16}$, as shown here.

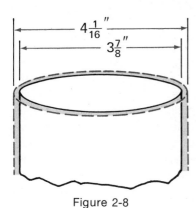

Figure 2-8

$$4\frac{1}{16} = 4\frac{1}{16} = 3\frac{17}{16}$$
$$-3\frac{7}{8} = -3\frac{14}{16} = -3\frac{14}{16}$$
$$\overline{\phantom{-3\frac{7}{8}}} \quad \overline{\phantom{-3\frac{14}{16}}} \quad \overline{\quad 3\frac{}{16}}$$
$$\frac{3}{16}$$

The bore was enlarged by $\frac{3}{16}''$.

Notice in Example 2 that in order to complete the subtraction, we must change $4\frac{1}{16}$ to $3\frac{17}{16}$. We can do this because

$$4\frac{1}{16} = 4 + \frac{1}{16} = 3 + 1 + \frac{1}{16} = 3 + \frac{16}{16} + \frac{1}{16} = 3 + \frac{17}{16}.$$

EXERCISES Subtract.

A 1. $5\frac{7}{8} - \frac{3}{4}$ 4. $9\frac{11}{16} - 8\frac{5}{8}$ 7. $3\frac{5}{16}'' - 1\frac{1}{8}''$

2. $3\frac{7}{16} - \frac{3}{8}$ 5. $1\frac{5}{32} - \frac{1}{16}$ 8. $4\frac{3}{8}'' - 3\frac{1}{4}''$

3. $6\frac{15}{16} - \frac{5}{8}$ 6. $2\frac{9}{16} - 1\frac{1}{4}$ 9. $6\frac{7}{16}'' - 3\frac{3}{8}''$

B 10. $4 - 2\frac{3}{8}$ 13. $2\frac{1}{4}'' - 1\frac{7}{8}''$

11. $3 - 1\frac{5}{16}$ 14. $16\frac{5}{8}'' - 12\frac{13}{16}''$

12. $9\frac{1}{8} - 3\frac{3}{4}$ 15. $17\frac{3}{8}'' - 15\frac{9}{16}''$

16. A plumber has a piece of plastic tubing $18\frac{1}{2}''$ long. He plans to use a piece $12\frac{3}{4}''$ long. How many inches of unused tubing will be left?

17. To check the layout of the bracket shown below, a machinist measured distances A and B. Find A and B.

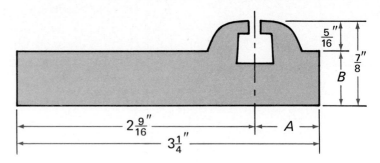

18. A sheet worker has to drill a hole in a metal plate, according to the diagram below. He centerpunched $22\frac{7}{8}''$ from the left edge and $1\frac{3}{8}''$ from the upper edge of the plate. To check the accuracy of the punch, he measured distance C and distance D. What should these measurements be?

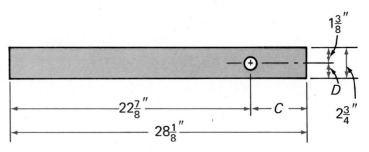

SELF-ANALYSIS TEST 6

Add or subtract.

1. $3\frac{1}{4} + 2\frac{1}{2}$ $5\frac{3}{4}$

2. $4\frac{3}{4} - 2\frac{1}{8}$

3. $15\frac{1}{16} + 2\frac{7}{8}$

4. $3\frac{5}{32} - 2\frac{9}{16}$

5. $4\frac{1}{16} + 3\frac{7}{8}$

6. $9\frac{1}{2} - 5\frac{15}{16}$

7. $4\frac{1}{10}'' - 3\frac{7}{10}''$

8. $5\frac{7}{16}'' + 9\frac{5}{8}''$

9. $14\frac{5}{16}'' - 12\frac{1}{8}''$

10. A machinist uses a grinder to remove $\frac{5}{16}''$ from a steel plate which is $3\frac{7}{8}''$ thick. How thick will the plate be after the grinding?

60

11. Find lengths *A*, *B*, *C*, and *D*.

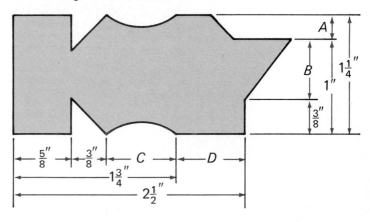

Dimensions in feet and inches

2-7 Changing inches to feet and inches

So far the dimensions which you have studied have been given in inches only. In industry most lengths up to 72″ are stated in inches only. Lengths greater than 72″ are usually expressed in feet and inches. For example, a strip of plastic may measure 21″ wide (*not* $1\frac{3}{4}'$) but a door frame may be 7′2″ high (*not* 86″). However, those who plan to work in industry should be able to make calculations with dimensions in either form.

EXAMPLE 1 A welder must butt-weld three sheets of sheet metal. The dimensions of the sheets are 22″, 18″, and 41″. What will be the total length of the welded sheet?

SOLUTION 22″ + 18″ + 41″ = 81″

Since 81″ is greater than 72″, we normally express this length as 6′9″. Therefore, the welded sheet will measure 6′9″ in length.

EXAMPLE 2 A section of extruded plastic tubing $17\frac{1}{2}''$ long is cut from a piece $6'4\frac{3}{4}''$ long. What is the length of the remaining piece of tubing?

SOLUTION In order to subtract $17\frac{1}{2}''$ from $6'4\frac{3}{4}''$, we change $6'4\frac{3}{4}''$ to $76\frac{3}{4}''$.

$$76\frac{3}{4}''$$
$$-17\frac{1}{2}''$$
$$\overline{59\frac{1}{4}''}$$

Thus, a piece of tubing $59\frac{1}{4}''$ long is left.

When most of the dimensions are given in both feet and inches, it is usually easier to express all of them in feet and inches. In this case we work with both units at once.

EXAMPLE 3 In installing an automatic car wash, a plumber joins three sections of pipe. The pipes are $6'8''$, $11'6''$ and $8'4''$ in length. What is the total length of the pipes?

SOLUTION To make the work easier, we keep the numbers in columns.

$$
\begin{aligned}
6'\ 8'' & \\
11'\ 6'' & \\
+\ 8'\ 4'' & \\
\hline
25'\ 18'' & = 25' + 1' + 6'' \\
& = 26'\ 6''
\end{aligned}
$$

The total length is $26'6''$.

Do you see why we change $18''$ to $1'6''$ and add it to $25'$?

EXAMPLE 4 A book binding machine used $237'3''$ of thread from a new spool to finish a job. If a spool holds $1000'$ of thread, how much thread is left on the spool?

SOLUTION In order to subtract $237'3''$ from $1000'$, we change $1000'$ to $999'12''$.

$$
\begin{aligned}
\text{Thus,} \quad 1000' \quad &= \quad 999'\ 12'' \\
-\ 237'\ 3'' \quad &= \quad -237'\ 3'' \\
\hline
&762'\ 9''
\end{aligned}
$$

There are $762'9''$ of thread left.

EXERCISES Add or subtract. Express answers in inches or feet and inches.

A

1. $14'' + 3\frac{3}{4}'' + 6''$
2. $19'' + 27\frac{1}{2}''$
3. $38\frac{3}{8}'' + 46\frac{3}{4}''$
4. $6'4'' - 26''$
5. $9'8\frac{3}{8}'' - 24\frac{1}{4}''$

6. $7'2'' - 10\frac{1}{2}''$
7. $13' + 6'3\frac{3}{4}'' + 5\frac{1}{4}''$
8. $9' + 2'4\frac{1}{2}'' + 5\frac{1}{2}''$
9. $8'4'' - (32'' + 6\frac{1}{2}'')$
10. $13'\frac{1}{2}'' - (36'' + 12\frac{1}{4}'')$

B

11. A plumber needs pieces of copper tubing in the following lengths: 8'6'', 12'4'', 9'8'', and 7'3''. How much pipe does he need in all?

12. The inventory sheet shows that the hospital stockroom has only three pieces of clear plastic tubing. The lengths are $16'4\frac{1}{2}''$, $24'5\frac{3}{4}''$, and 8'. What is the combined length of the three pieces?

13. Three hundred fifty feet of pipe must be laid in a new industrial center. So far 195'8'' of pipe has been laid. How much more pipe must be put in place?

14. The following lengths of rudder cable were required in an airplane: 10'3'', 13'9'', 7'9'', and 11'5''. Find the total length needed.

15. A piece 13'6'' long is cut from a 50' plastic hose. How much of the hose is left?

Laying pipe

63

C 16. From a sheet of fiberglass twelve feet long, three pieces are to be cut. The pieces are to be 11″, 6′3¾″ and 17″ long. What will be the length of the remaining piece?

17. A spool of copper wire contains 25′ of wire. Four pieces are cut off. Their lengths are $12\frac{1}{2}$″, $14\frac{3}{4}$″, $20\frac{5}{8}$″, and $36\frac{9}{16}$″. How much wire remains?

2-8 Conserving materials

Because raw materials are expensive, industries try to minimize the amount of waste. Sometimes the waste material is converted into another product which can be sold.

Figure 2-9 Vat of scrap paper pulp in a recycling plant.

For example, cardboard is made from tree bark at a paper mill. In other branches of industry waste material is recycled. Old newspapers, for example, are broken down and converted into other paper products.

Planning how best to use waste material is an important part of industry. It is also a habit that you should try to develop now.

EXAMPLE Two wedge-shaped metal brackets are to be made according to the specifications in Figure 2-10.

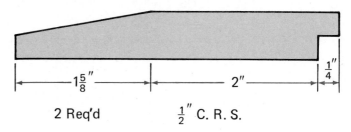

2 Req'd $\frac{1}{2}''$ C. R. S.

Figure 2-10

SOLUTION The machinist would find three important facts about the braces in Figure 2-10:
1. The length: $1\frac{5}{8}'' + 2'' + \frac{1}{4}''$
2. The number to be made: 2(2 Req'd)
3. The material: $\frac{1}{2}''$ cold rolled steel (C.R.S.)

Next the machinist would make a sketch showing all dimensions and allowances. He will allow $\frac{1}{8}''$ for finishing each end. He will also allow $\frac{1}{16}''$ for separating the pieces. His final drawing would look like Figure 2-11.

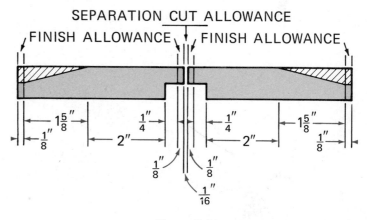

Figure 2-11

From the drawing the machinist can determine the length of the materials. Can you?

$$\tfrac{1}{8} + 1\tfrac{5}{8} + 2 + \tfrac{1}{4} + \tfrac{1}{8} + \tfrac{1}{16} + \tfrac{1}{8} + \tfrac{1}{4} + 2 + 1\tfrac{5}{8} + \tfrac{1}{8} = ?$$

waste allowance   separation   waste allowance
for finishing ends   cut   for finishing ends

Do you see how careful planning can reduce the amount of waste?

EXERCISES Answer the questions. Discuss how planning reduces the amount of waste in each case.

A 1. In planning to cut some stock, a printer found that he would have only the two waste strips shown.
   a. Find the width of the waste strip along the bottom.
   b. Find the width of the waste strip along the side.

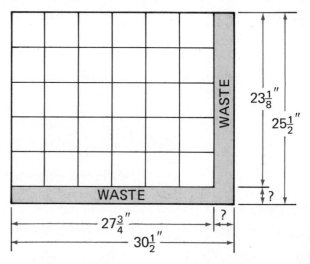

2. What length of steel stock is needed to make the U-bracket? Allow $\tfrac{3}{16}''$ for each bend and $\tfrac{1}{4}''$ on each end for finishing.

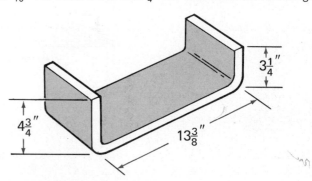

3. An electronics kit contains a spool of insulated wire 18′ long. The following lengths are to be cut: $12\frac{5}{8}''$, $33\frac{3}{16}''$, $4\frac{7}{8}''$, $25\frac{1}{2}''$. The instruction manual suggests allowing $\frac{1}{16}''$ for each cut.
   a. Draw a diagram to show how to cut the wire.
   b. What length will be cut from the spool?
   c. How much wire will remain on the spool after cutting?

SELF-ANALYSIS TEST 7

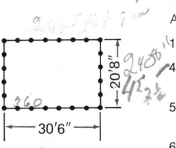

Add or subtract. Express answers in inches or feet and inches.

1. $38'' + 17\frac{3}{4}''$ 2. $9'3\frac{1}{8}'' - 22\frac{3}{4}''$ 3. $6'4\frac{3}{4}'' - (3\frac{1}{2}'' + 5\frac{1}{8}'')$

4. Find the length of woven wire needed to enclose a rectangular plot of ground with the dimensions shown at the left.

5. A piece of plywood 6′8″ long must be trimmed by $10\frac{3}{4}''$ to fit between shelf supports. What will be the finished length?

6. A photographer has a sheet of print paper measuring 17″ by 22″. He wants to cut the sheet into pieces $3\frac{1}{2}''$ by $5\frac{1}{2}''$.
   a. How should he plan the cuts to get the greatest number of pieces?
   b. How much waste paper will be left?

SPOTLIGHT ON INDUSTRY

The railroads have turned to the computer to solve the problem of sorting cars in switching yards. This process has always been time-consuming and very often inaccurate. Here's how the computer has solved the problem: A central computer keeps a record of every car's cargo, destination, location, and position on a train. This information, in coded labels on each car is "read" by electronic scanners as the car enters the yard. The scanners send the data to the central computer. The computer then decides on the proper destination for that car. It relays this information to a computer in each yard, which automatically switches the car to the proper track. To safely guide the car, track sensors pick up the weight and speed of the car, wind velocity, and other data needed for correct braking. The car is then controlled by the computer until it is stopped and coupled to its new train. This new computerized car sorting has resulted in fewer errors and faster, safer service.

RESEARCH WITH A COMPUTER

In Section 2-7 you learned how to deal with measurements given in feet and inches. If you have access to an electronic computer that uses the BASIC "language," you can use the program below to change a measurement given in feet and inches to inches only.

```
10 PRINT "NUMBER OF FEET";
20 INPUT A
30 PRINT "NUMBER OF INCHES";
40 INPUT B
50 LET I = 12*A + B
60 PRINT A; "  FT,"; B; "  IN. ="; I; "  IN."
70 END
```

EXERCISES

1. RUN the program, using the following measurements.

   a. 7′ 4″   d. 10′ 8″   g. 14′ 3″

   b. 6′ 3″   e. 55′ 10″   h. 104′ 5″

   c. 2′ 11″   f. 17′ 7″   i. 21′ 6″

2. RUN the program, using the values given in Exercise 11 on page 63. Give the answer in inches.

Use the program above to change the dimensions in the following problems to inches only. Then solve the problems.

3. An electrician needs 3 pieces of wire in the following lengths: 14′ 3″, 8′ 11″, and 10′ 1″. How many inches of wire does he need in all?

4. A plumber has a piece of copper tubing 12′ 6″ long. A piece 7′ 8″ must be cut off to make a repair. How much is left after the tubing is cut?

5. Pieces 12′ 5″, 15′ 4″, and 11′ 3″ are cut from a 50′ roll of carpeting. Is there enough carpeting left on the roll to carpet a room 10′ 6″ long?

6. Chain-link fencing is needed to enclose a rectangular storage area 3′ 5″ by 5′ 3″. Will a partial roll of fencing containing 17′ 10″ of fencing be enough for the job?

Sometimes you may see measurements given in yards, feet, and inches. The following program can change such a measurement into inches only. Working in inches only can often make your calculations easier.

```
10 PRINT "NUMBER OF YARDS";
20 INPUT C
30 PRINT "NUMBER OF FEET";
40 INPUT A
50 PRINT "NUMBER OF INCHES";
60 INPUT B
70 LET I=36*C+12*A+B
80 PRINT C; " YD"; A;" FT"; B;" IN. ="; I; " In."
90 END
```

EXERCISES   7. RUN the program, using the following measurements.

    a. 5 yd 2 ft 8 in.   **d.** 11 yd 1 ft 7 in.

    b. 4 yd 1 ft 2 in.   **e.** 22 yd 2 ft 5 in.

    c. 8 yd 1 ft 11 in.   **f.** 13 yd 1 ft 1 in.

Use the program above to change the dimensions in the following problems to inches only. Then solve the problems.

8. When a property line is surveyed, it is found to measure 50 yd 2 ft 3 in. What is this length in inches?

9. The fence along the edge of a football field extends 16′ 3″ beyond each end zone. The field measures 120 yards overall. What is the length of the fence?

TAKING INVENTORY

1. To add (subtract) fractions with the same denominator, add (subtract) the numerators and use the same denominator. (pp. 43–44)

2. To add (subtract) fractions with different denominators, change the fractions to equivalent fractions having a common denominator, then add (subtract). (pp. 45–46)

3. The **least common denominator (LCD)** is the smallest number that can be divided evenly by the denominators of the fractions which are to be added or subtracted. (p. 48)

4. A **mixed number** is made up of a whole number and a fraction. (p. 52)

5. Whole numbers and mixed numbers can be written as fractions. (pp. 52–54)

6. Dimensions not shown on technical drawings can be found by adding and subtracting fractions. (pp. 54–59)

7. Dimensions up to 72″ are usually given in inches only. Dimensions greater than 72″ are usually given in feet and inches. (pp. 61–62)

8. Careful planning and accurate measurements help conserve materials. (pp. 64–66)

MEASURING YOUR SKILLS

Add or subtract. Give the answer in lowest terms. (2-1–2-2)

1. $\frac{17}{64} + \frac{13}{64}$

2. $\frac{2}{32} + \frac{11}{32} + \frac{9}{32}$

3. $\frac{13}{16}'' - \frac{5}{16}''$

4. $\frac{5}{8}'' - \frac{3}{8}''$

5. $\frac{3}{8} + \frac{1}{4}$

6. $\frac{1}{8} + \frac{3}{16} + \frac{5}{32}$

7. $\frac{3}{4}'' - \frac{1}{8}''$

8. $\frac{7}{32}'' - \frac{3}{64}''$

Find the lowest common denominator for the fractions. (2-3)

9. $\frac{1}{3}, \frac{1}{4}, \frac{1}{5}$

10. $\frac{3}{4}, \frac{7}{8}, \frac{3}{10}$

11. Change $17\frac{5}{8}$ to a fraction. (2-4)

12. Simplify $\frac{106}{4}$. (2-4)

13. Simplify $\frac{56}{8}$. (2-4)

Wire being woven.

Add or subtract. Give each answer in lowest terms. (2-5–2-6)

14. $4\frac{1}{8} + 5\frac{1}{4} + 4\frac{3}{8}$ 18. $1\frac{9}{16}'' + 5\frac{5}{8}''$

15. $8\frac{5}{8} - 2\frac{1}{4}$ 19. $4\frac{5}{16}'' - 2\frac{3}{4}''$

16. $3\frac{31}{32} - 2\frac{11}{16}$ 20. $5'' - 2\frac{1}{8}''$

17. $7\frac{3}{4} + 1\frac{1}{8} + 9\frac{1}{16}$ 21. $12\frac{1}{2}'' + 5\frac{1}{4}'' + 6\frac{1}{16}''$

22. A contractor wants to add a 42″ section of stockade fence to his present fence. If the fence now measures 72′4″, how long will it be with the addition? (2-7)

23. In a warehouse cartons move along a conveyor belt that is 423′ 6″ long. Only 117′ of the conveyor belt is at ground level; the rest is overhead. How much of the belt is overhead? (2-7)

24. Three sections of insulated telephone cable are cut from a 1000′ reel. The pieces measure 37′ 4″, 68′ 2″, and 92′ 8″. How much cable is left on the reel? (2-7)

25. A 36′ roll of wall covering must be cut into strips to cover a wall 7′ 2″. Four inches are allowed at the end of each piece for matching the pattern.
    a. Draw a diagram to show how the wall covering will be cut.
    b. How many strips can be cut from the roll?
    c. How much material will be wasted? (2-8)

Hundreds of reels of cables are needed to keep up with the demand for telephones.

Extracting metal ore provides industry with the materials for a wide range of manufactured products.

More on Fractions

After completing this chapter, you should be able to:

1. Multiply fractions and mixed numbers.
2. Use cancellation when multiplying fractions.
3. Divide fractions and mixed numbers.
4. Make industrial calculations involving fractions and estimation.

Multiplying fractions

3-1 Multiplying a fraction and a whole number

Figure 3-1 shows a part of metal grille which covers the fan in an air conditioner. A grille like this is made in an automatic perforating machine, according to specified dimensions.

To find the distance from A to B, we could add $\frac{5}{16}''$ five times. For example,

length $AB = \frac{5}{16} + \frac{5}{16} + \frac{5}{16} + \frac{5}{16} + \frac{5}{16} = \frac{25}{16} = 1\frac{9}{16}''$.

However, we usually find it easier and faster to multiply. For example,

length $AB = 5 \times \frac{5}{16} = \frac{5 \times 5}{16} = \frac{25}{16} = 1\frac{9}{16}''$.

$\frac{5''}{32}$

A　$\frac{5}{16}''$ on center　B

Figure 3-1

EXAMPLE   Suppose there were 47 slots between A and B in Figure 3-1. Find length AB.

SOLUTION   Length $AB = 47 \times \frac{5}{16} = \frac{47 \times 5}{16} = \frac{235}{16} = 14\frac{11}{16}$

Length AB would measure $14\frac{11}{16}''$.

Do you see how multiplication helps us find the answer quickly? Study the following rule.

> To multiply a fraction by a whole number, multiply the numerator of the fraction by the whole number and place the product over the denominator.

EXERCISES   Multiply. Write the answers in lowest terms.

A 1. $7 \times \frac{1}{8}$ 5. $\frac{9}{64} \times 2$ 9. $100 \times \frac{5}{8}''$

2. $5 \times \frac{3}{4}$ 6. $\frac{3}{100} \times 25$ 10. $17 \times \frac{7}{10}''$

3. $\frac{3}{10} \times 6$ 7. $36 \times \frac{3}{64}$ 11. $\frac{7}{8}'' \times 8$

4. $\frac{5}{16} \times 8$ 8. $2 \times \frac{3}{32}$ 12. $\frac{7}{16}'' \times 16$

B 13. What is the total weight of 7 cast-iron pulleys, if each weighs $\frac{3}{4}$ lb?

14. A surveyor marks off 12 adjacent lots. The frontage of each lot measures $\frac{1}{10}$ mi. What is the total frontage in miles?

15. A printer sets the type for an advertising brochure in $\frac{3}{4}$ of an hour. How long would it take him to set 5 similar brochures?

16. The distance between the threads of the screw in Figure 3-2 is $\frac{3}{32}''$. How far does the screw travel if it is turned 8 complete revolutions?

Figure 3-2

C 17. A tile mason uses $\frac{7}{8}''$ square tiles to form a wall mosaic. How wide is the wall if he uses 184 tiles?

CREATIVE CRAFTSMAN

Design and build a device entirely of wood that
    a. is fun to watch;
    b. does something unexpected; and
    c. is powered by a stream of water.

3-2 Multiplying a mixed number and a whole number

Airplanes like those in Figure 3-3 undergo great stress when in flight. To provide strength in parts like the wing or body, aerospace manufacturers use rivets during assembly.

Figure 3-3   Inside an airplane assembly plant.

Figure 3-4 shows a portion of a wing panel with holes for the rivets. A "Caution" stripe is to be painted as shown. How long will the stripe be?

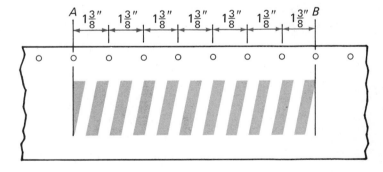

Figure 3-4

To find *AB*, we multiply $1\frac{3}{8}''$ by 7, or $7 \times 1\frac{3}{8}$. There are two methods we can use.

Method 1. The mixed number $1\frac{3}{8}$ can be changed into a fraction, $1\frac{3}{8} = \frac{11}{8}$. Now we multiply:

$$7 \times 1\frac{3}{8} = 7 \times \frac{11}{8} = \frac{77}{8} = 9\frac{5}{8}$$

The stripe between A and B will be $9\frac{5}{8}''$.

Method 2. Since $1\frac{3}{8} = 1 + \frac{3}{8}$, we can multiply 1 by 7 and $\frac{3}{8}$ by 7, then add the two results. Thus,

$$7 \times 1\frac{3}{8} = (7 \times 1) + (7 \times \frac{3}{8})$$
$$= \quad 7 \quad + \quad \frac{21}{8}$$
$$= \quad 7 \quad + \quad 2\frac{5}{8}$$
$$= 9\frac{5}{8}$$

Again, the stripe will be $9\frac{5}{8}''$.

Would you agree with the following rule?

> To multiply a mixed number by a whole number, we can work in two ways:
> 1. a. Change the mixed number to a fraction;
>   b. Multiply by the whole number; or
> 2. a. Write the mixed number as the sum of a whole number and fraction;
>   b. Multiply each part by the whole number;
>   c. Add the products.

EXERCISES Multiply. Reduce the answers to lowest terms.

A
1. $1\frac{7}{8} \times 4$
2. $2\frac{7}{8} \times 5$
3. $3\frac{5}{16} \times 10$

4. $8 \times 2\frac{7}{8}$
5. $22\frac{1}{2} \times 11$
6. $17 \times 12\frac{1}{8}$

7. $35\frac{2}{4}'' \times 8$
8. $20 \times 11\frac{7}{8}''$
9. $5 \times 7\frac{15}{16}''$

B
10. A furniture refinisher is calculating the amount of material he needs to repair the 4 legs of a stool. He finds that, allowing $\frac{1}{4}''$ at each end for waste, he needs a piece of lumber $13\frac{3}{8}''$ long for each leg.

a. How many inches of lumber does he need for 4 legs?

b. Give the answer in feet and inches.

11. The height, or riser, of a single step of a flight of stairs is $7\frac{1}{2}''$. There are 14 steps in the flight.

   a. What is the height of the stairs in inches?

   b. What is the height of the stairs in feet and inches?

12. Find the height and width of the storage area of the small-parts chest.

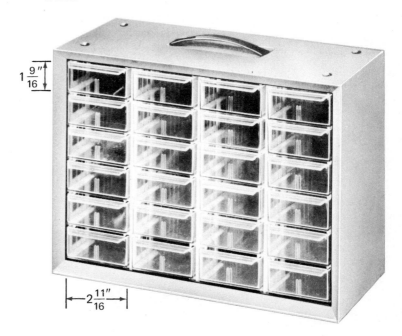

C   13. L is the length of the side of a dovetailed drawer.

   a. Find L.

   b. Can a matching piece be made from stock that is $9\frac{3}{8}''$ wide?

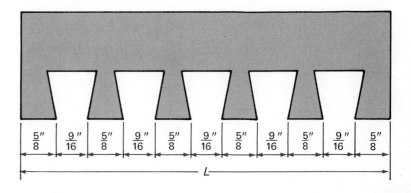

3-3 Multiplying two fractions

Many situations in industry involve multiplying two fractions. Study the following examples.

EXAMPLE 1   One turn of the handle of a bench vise in Figure 3-5 closes the jaws by $\frac{3}{16}''$. How much do the jaws close if we give the handle only a half-turn?

Figure 3-5

SOLUTION   Since we are making $\frac{1}{2}$ of a complete turn, the distance decreases $\frac{1}{2}$ as much as when we make a complete turn. Therefore, the distance decreases $\frac{1}{2}$ of $\frac{3}{16}''$. Note that $\frac{1}{2}$ of $\frac{3}{16}$ has the same meaning as $\frac{1}{2}$ "times" $\frac{3}{16}$, or $\frac{1}{2}$ "multiplied by" $\frac{3}{16}$. Therefore,

$$\tfrac{1}{2} \text{ of } \tfrac{3}{16} = \tfrac{1}{2} \times \tfrac{3}{16} = \tfrac{1\times3}{2\times16} = \tfrac{3}{32}''.$$

A half-turn of the vise handle closes the jaws by $\frac{3}{32}''$.

EXAMPLE 2   If a printing press uses $4\frac{3}{4}$ ounces of ink in 1 hour, how much will it use during a $3\frac{1}{2}$-hour run?

SOLUTION   Since the press would use $3\frac{1}{2}$ times more ink than in one hour, we can find the amount of ink used by multiplying $3\frac{1}{2} \times 4\frac{3}{4}$. Thus,

$$3\tfrac{1}{2} \times 4\tfrac{3}{4} = \tfrac{7}{2} \times \tfrac{19}{4} = \tfrac{7\times19}{2\times4} = \tfrac{133}{8} = 16\tfrac{5}{8}.$$

The printing press will use $16\frac{5}{8}$ oz of ink.

From these examples we can state the following rules.

> 1. To multiply two fractions, multiply the numerators together and the denominators together. Reduce the resulting fraction to lowest terms.
> 2. To multiply mixed numbers, change the mixed numbers to fractions, then proceed as above.

EXERCISES   Multiply. Write the answers in lowest terms.

A

1. $\frac{1}{2} \times \frac{1}{4}$ 4. $\frac{9}{10} \times \frac{4}{5}$ 7. $3\frac{1}{2} \times 2\frac{5}{8}''$

2. $\frac{5}{16} \times \frac{14}{16}$ 5. $\frac{22}{7} \times \frac{3}{8}$ 8. $3\frac{1}{2}'' \times 3\frac{1}{5}$

3. $\frac{1}{3} \times \frac{7}{8}$ 6. $\frac{7}{2} \times \frac{5}{3}$ 9. $3\frac{1}{10} \times 2\frac{1}{10}$

10. $\frac{7}{9} \times \frac{2}{3}$ 12. $\frac{15}{18} \times \frac{5}{3}$ 14. $6\frac{7}{8}'' \times 3\frac{4}{5}$

11. $\frac{3}{5} \times \frac{3}{4}$ 13. $\frac{7}{3} \times \frac{21}{5}$ 15. $7\frac{1}{5} \times 2\frac{1}{2}''$

Find each of the following:

B 16. $2\frac{1}{2}$ times 4.   18. $1\frac{1}{4}$ times $\frac{7}{8}''$.

17. Half of $4\frac{7}{8}$.   19. A third of $\frac{11}{64}''$.

20. One gallon of water weighs about $8\frac{1}{4}$ lb. What is the weight of the water in an automobile cooling system with a capacity of $4\frac{1}{2}$ gal?

21. An automobile gasoline tank can hold $15\frac{1}{2}$ gal. How many gallons are in the tank when it is $\frac{3}{4}$ full?

22. An automatic bottler has a capacity of $23\frac{1}{2}$ gal per minute. How much soda can it bottle in $3\frac{1}{2}$ min?

23. If it costs $1\frac{3}{4}$¢ per kilowatt-hour of electricity, what is the cost for $8\frac{1}{2}$ kilowatt-hours?

24. The weight of a sheet of aluminum is $16\frac{3}{4}$ lb. If $\frac{2}{3}$ of this sheet is cut and put back in stock, what is the weight of the piece that is used?

C 25. Using a machinist's rule, an engineer found the dimensions for a sheet metal patch. The patch must be $9\frac{3}{10}''$ by $7\frac{7}{10}''$.
a. What is the area of the patch in square inches? (Area = length × width)
b. If it costs $3\frac{1}{2}$¢ per square inch to rust-proof the material, what will it cost to treat this patch?

Automated bottling machine

TRICKS OF THE TRADE

Here is a method you can use to help you subtract lengths quickly. Suppose you want to cut a piece $2\frac{7}{8}''$ wide from a board $5\frac{3}{8}''$ wide. You may think like this:

$$5\frac{3}{8} - 2\frac{7}{8} = \underline{\quad?\quad}$$

$$\left(5\frac{3}{8} + \frac{1}{8}\right) - \left(2\frac{7}{8} + \frac{1}{8}\right) = \underline{\quad?\quad}$$

$$5\frac{1}{2} - 3 = 2\frac{1}{2}$$

The piece left is $2\frac{1}{2}''$ wide.

Can you see why this method works?

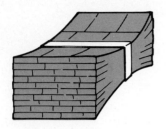

It takes 4 bundles of shingles to make a square.

3-4 Cancellation

If one bundle of shingles weighs $23\frac{3}{4}$ lb, what do $6\frac{1}{5}$ bundles weigh? To find the answer, we multiply $23\frac{3}{4}$ by $6\frac{1}{5}$.

$$6\frac{1}{5} \times 23\frac{3}{4} = \frac{31}{5} \times \frac{95}{4} = \frac{31 \times 95}{5 \times 4} = \frac{2945}{20} = 147\frac{1}{4}$$

Thus, $6\frac{1}{5}$ bundles will weigh $147\frac{1}{4}$ lb.

Sometimes we can save time in multiplying fractions by using a short cut. In the example above, notice that

$$\frac{31}{5} \times \frac{95}{4} = \frac{31 \times 95}{5 \times 4}$$

We can reduce $\frac{31 \times 95}{5 \times 4}$ before we multiply by dividing both the numerator and denominator by 5 because

$$\frac{31 \times (19 \times 5)}{5 \times 4} = \frac{31 \times 19 \times 5}{5 \times 4}$$

$$= \frac{31 \times 19}{4} \times \frac{5}{5}$$

$$= \frac{31 \times 19}{4} \times 1$$

$$= \frac{589}{4} = 147\frac{1}{4}$$

Here is a short way to show our work.

$$6\frac{1}{5} \times 23\frac{3}{4} = \frac{31}{\overset{}{\underset{1}{5}}} \times \frac{\overset{19}{\cancel{95}}}{4} = \frac{31 \times 19}{4} = \frac{589}{4} = 147\frac{1}{4}$$

This short cut is called **cancellation**. Here is a helpful rule to follow when you cancel.

> To cancel when multiplying fractions, divide the numerator and denominator of a fraction by the same number.
>
> **Caution:** Cancellation may be used *only* when multiplying fractions. It must *not* be used when adding or subtracting fractions.

EXAMPLE   The water in a public swimming pool rises at a rate of $3\frac{1}{8}''$ an hour during filling. What will be the height after $9\frac{3}{5}$ hours?

SOLUTION   To find the answer, we multiply $3\frac{1}{8}$ by $9\frac{3}{5}$.

$$3\frac{1}{8} \times 9\frac{3}{5} = \frac{\overset{5}{\cancel{25}}}{8} \times \frac{48}{\cancel{5}}\ \text{Divide by 5}$$

$$= \frac{5}{\cancel{8}} \times \frac{\overset{6}{\cancel{48}}}{1}\ \text{Divide by 8}$$

$$= 30$$

The water will be 30″ deep.

Notice that we can cancel twice. In actual practice we usually show all the cancellations in one step, as below.

$$3\frac{1}{8} \times 9\frac{3}{5} = \frac{\overset{5}{\cancel{25}}}{\underset{1}{\cancel{8}}} \times \frac{\overset{6}{\cancel{48}}}{\underset{1}{\cancel{5}}} = 30$$

Do you see how cancelling can shorten your work?

EXERCISES   Multiply, using cancellation wherever possible. Write the answers in lowest terms.

A
1. $\frac{5}{6} \times \frac{9}{20}$
2. $\frac{3}{8} \times \frac{8}{9}$
3. $\frac{2}{5} \times \frac{7}{10}$
4. $\frac{24}{10} \times \frac{5}{8}$
5. $\frac{15}{36} \times \frac{9}{10}$

6. $\frac{27}{64} \times \frac{4}{9}$
7. $\frac{20}{1} \times \frac{5}{6}$
8. $4 \times \frac{5}{16}$
9. $24 \times \frac{3}{4}$
10. $2\frac{1}{16} \times 1\frac{1}{3}$

11. $10\frac{1}{8} \times 7\frac{1}{9}$
12. $5\frac{5}{8}'' \times \frac{4}{9}$
13. $3\frac{5}{8}'' \times 8$
14. $3\frac{3}{4}'' \times 16$
15. $1\frac{1}{3} \times \frac{3}{4}''$

SELF-ANALYSIS TEST 8

Multiply. Write the answers in lowest terms.

1. $\frac{2}{3} \times 4$
2. $\frac{3}{5} \times 15$
3. $\frac{5}{16}'' \times 8$

4. $3\frac{1}{2}'' \times 4$
5. $6\frac{3}{8}'' \times 7$
6. $18\frac{4}{5} \times 3$

7. $\frac{3}{7} \times \frac{4}{9}$
8. $\frac{8}{11} \times \frac{3}{4}''$
9. $\frac{2}{5} \times \frac{15}{16}''$

10. A computer teletype terminal can print out $12\frac{1}{2}$ lines in one minute. At this rate how many lines can be printed out in $3\frac{1}{2}$ minutes?

Dividing fractions

3-5 Reciprocals

For every fraction there is another fraction such that when we multiply the two fractions, the result is 1. For example, if we multiply $\frac{2}{3}$ by $\frac{3}{2}$, we get $\frac{2}{3} \times \frac{3}{2} = \frac{6}{6} = 1$. The fractions $\frac{2}{3}$ and $\frac{3}{2}$ are called **reciprocals**.

Whole numbers have reciprocals too. Recall that 5 can be written as the fraction $\frac{5}{1}$. Since $\frac{5}{1} \times \frac{1}{5} = \frac{5}{5} = 1$, we see that $\frac{1}{5}$ and 5 are reciprocals.

We use reciprocals to solve common industrial problems that involve dividing fractions.

EXERCISES Give the reciprocal of each number. Then show that the product of the number and its reciprocal is 1.

A
1. $\frac{3}{4}$
    3. $\frac{7}{2}$
    5. $\frac{22}{7}$
    7. $\frac{31}{32}$

2. $\frac{2}{9}$
    4. $\frac{8}{5}$
    6. $\frac{15}{16}$
    8. $\frac{10}{3}$

B
9. 53
    10. 117
    11. $8\frac{2}{3}$
    12. $3\frac{7}{8}$

3-6 Dividing a fraction by a whole number

When a machinist has to make several identical small parts, he begins with a large piece of stock. First he does the detail work like drilling holes and knurling. After this, he cuts the stock into the required number of pieces. Dividing fractions occurs frequently in this kind of operation.

EXAMPLE Three rectangular insulators must be made from a nylon strip $8\frac{1}{4}''$ long (see Figure 3-6). How long will each be?

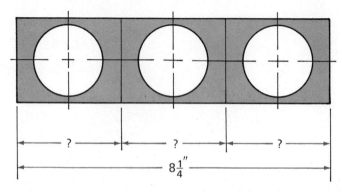

Figure 3-6

82

SOLUTION Since $8\frac{1}{4} = \frac{33}{4}$, we wish to divide $\frac{33}{4}$ by 3. But notice that

$$\frac{33}{4} = \frac{11 + 11 + 11}{4} = \frac{11}{4} + \frac{11}{4} + \frac{11}{4}.$$

Do you see that when $\frac{33}{4}$ is divided 3 times, the result is $\frac{11}{4}$? The width of each insulator must be $\frac{11}{4}$, or $2\frac{3}{4}''$.

An easier way to show the division is to multiply $\frac{33}{4}$ by $\frac{1}{3}$, the reciprocal of 3. In this case we get

$$\frac{33}{4} \times \frac{1}{3} = \frac{\overset{11}{\cancel{33}}}{4} \times \frac{1}{\cancel{3}} = \frac{11 \times 1}{4 \times 1} = \frac{11}{4} = 2\frac{3}{4}.$$

Thus, $\frac{33}{4} \div 3 = \frac{33}{4} \times \frac{1}{3} = \frac{11}{4} = 2\frac{3}{4}.$

Notice that dividing a quantity by 3 is the same as *multiplying* by $\frac{1}{3}$. Since we treat division as multiplication by the reciprocal, we can cancel.

Here's a helpful rule to remember.

> To divide a fraction by a whole number, multiply the fraction by the reciprocal of the whole number.

EXERCISES Divide. Cancel where possible. Give the answers in lowest terms.

A 1. $\frac{9}{10} \div 3$ 5. $\frac{15}{16}'' \div 3$ 9. $3\frac{1}{3} \div 5$

  2. $\frac{4}{5} \div 2$ 6. $\frac{27}{64}'' \div 9$ 10. $1\frac{23}{25} \div 4$

  3. $\frac{16}{35} \div 4$ 7. $\frac{63}{100}'' \div 7$ 11. $5\frac{1}{16}'' \div 27$

  4. $\frac{3}{7} \div 8$ 8. $\frac{5}{16}'' \div 7$ 12. $9\frac{3}{8}'' \div 25$

B 13. To make a six-sided stereo speaker cabinet, a piece of mahogony must be sawed so that A, B, C, D, E, and F are equal. What are these dimensions?

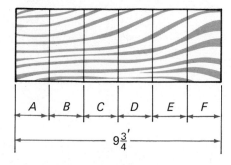

83

14. An earthmover removed $64\frac{1}{2}$ cu yd of gravel in 4 hours. What is its rate per hour?

15. A strip of aluminum $26\frac{1}{4}''$ long is to be sheared into 5 pieces of equal length. What is the length of each piece?

C 16. Three $8\frac{1}{2}''$ by $11''$ photographs are to be mounted on background stock. The photos will be equally spaced "east-west" and centered "north-south."

    a. Find dimensions A, B, C, and D.
    b. Find dimensions E and F.

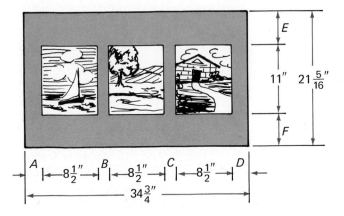

17. The cinder block in Figure 3-7 was formed with the dimensions given below. The three mortar holes are the same size.

    a. Find the width of the holes.
    b. Find the length of the holes.

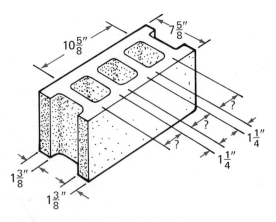

Figure 3-7

3-7 Dividing by a fraction

Frequently, industrial calculations involve dividing by fractions. Study the following examples.

EXAMPLE 1   The coffee table in Figure 3-8 is to be built with the top 30″ wide. The plans call for finished pine boards $1\frac{7}{8}$″ wide. How many boards will be needed to construct the top?

SOLUTION   To find the number of boards needed, we have to divide 30″ by $1\frac{7}{8}$″. We can show the work like this:

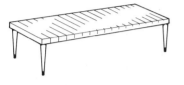

Figure 3-8

$$30 \div 1\frac{7}{8} = \frac{30}{1} \div \frac{15}{8}$$

$$= \frac{\overset{2}{\cancel{30}}}{1} \times \frac{8}{\underset{1}{\cancel{15}}}$$

$$= \frac{2 \times 8}{1 \times 1}$$

$$= 16$$

Thus, 16 boards are needed.

EXAMPLE 2   A numerical-control lathe automatically advances the cutting tool $1\frac{3}{8}$″ every minute. At this rate, how long would it take to turn an iron rod $24\frac{3}{4}$″ long?

SOLUTION   To find the time, we must divide $24\frac{3}{4}$ by $1\frac{3}{8}$.

$$24\frac{3}{4} \div 1\frac{3}{8} = \frac{99}{4} \div \frac{11}{8}$$

$$= \frac{\overset{9}{\cancel{99}}}{\underset{1}{\cancel{4}}} \times \frac{\overset{2}{\cancel{8}}}{\underset{1}{\cancel{11}}}$$

$$= \frac{9 \times 2}{1 \times 1}$$

$$= 18$$

It would take 18 minutes to turn the rod.

These examples suggest the following rule.

> To divide a fraction by a fraction, multiply the first fraction by the reciprocal of the other.
> In division involving mixed numbers, change the mixed numbers to fractions, then proceed as above.

Divide. Follow the flow chart in Figure 3-9 if you need help.

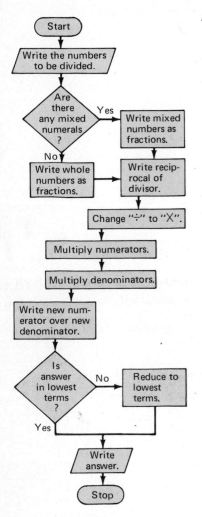

Figure 3-9

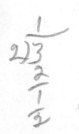

A

1. $12 \div \frac{6}{7}$

2. $18 \div \frac{3}{16}$

3. $7 \div \frac{4}{9}$

4. $4 \div \frac{8}{9}$

5. $\frac{4}{9} \div \frac{8}{9}$

6. $\frac{5}{16} \div \frac{5}{8}$

7. $\frac{22}{7} \div \frac{4}{3}$

8. $\frac{32}{5} \div \frac{1}{5}$

9. $8 \div 4\frac{4}{5}$

10. $46'' \div 1\frac{7}{16}$

11. $\frac{3}{4}'' \div 2\frac{1}{2}$

12. $8\frac{3}{4}'' \div 2\frac{1}{2}$

B

13. A sheet of vinyl plastic is $25\frac{1}{2}''$ wide. How many strips, each $2\frac{5}{8}''$ wide, can be cut from the sheet?

14. A piece of rubber weather stripping $26\frac{1}{4}''$ long is required along the bottom of a storm window. How many strips can be cut from a roll $43'\ 3''$ long?

15. One turn of the handle moves the tail stock of a lathe $\frac{3}{32}''$. How many turns must be made to move the tailstock $1\frac{1}{2}''$?

16. The adjusting nut on a plane lowers the blade $\frac{5}{64}''$ for each turn. How many times must the nut be turned to lower the blade $\frac{5}{32}''$?

17. How many roofing boards $\frac{13}{16}''$ thick are there in a stack $2'2''$ high?

18. How many pieces of solid copper wire $2\frac{1}{2}''$ long can be cut from a piece $15'\ 6''$ long?

C

19. Draw a flow chart to show how to find a reciprocal. Use it to find the reciprocals of:

a. $\frac{1}{3}$ b. 3 c. $\frac{7}{8}$ d. $2\frac{1}{4}$ e. $\frac{19}{8}$.

SELF-ANALYSIS TEST 9

Give the reciprocal of each number.

1. $\frac{5}{8}$

2. $\frac{7}{16}$

3. $\frac{5}{2}$

4. 32

5. $3\frac{1}{6}$

6. $4\frac{7}{8}$

Divide.

7. $\frac{14}{15} \div 7$

8. $\frac{3}{8} \div 9$

9. $6 \div \frac{3}{4}$

10. $16 \div \frac{8}{9}$

11. $\frac{6}{7} \div \frac{12}{21}$

12. $3\frac{3}{4} \div 1\frac{3}{5}$

13. How many $\frac{9}{16}''$ strips can be sawed from a board $5\frac{5}{8}''$ wide?

Combining operations with fractions

3-8 Estimating

The daily operation of some industries is so large that exact figures for important information cannot be given. For example, it would be almost impossible to know how many cartons are in a storage warehouse at a certain time. Instead, industries often rely on estimates to help them plan their operations.

Estimating is a way of making a "reasonable guess." Estimates can tell the amount of material that is available or how much is needed. Estimates can also help us see whether our calculations are accurate.

EXAMPLE 1   What is the total width of 5 pieces of $\frac{7}{8}''$ strapping?

SOLUTION   *Step 1.* Since $\frac{7}{8}''$ is slightly less than $1''$, we expect the answer to be less than $5 \times 1''$, or $5''$. Since $\frac{7}{8}''$ is slightly more than $\frac{3}{4}''$, we expect the answer to be more than $5 \times \frac{3}{4}''$ or $3\frac{3}{4}''$. We, therefore, estimate the answer to be between $3\frac{3}{4}''$ and $5''$.

Step 2. $5 \times \frac{7}{8} = \frac{5}{1} \times \frac{7}{8}$

$$= \frac{5 \times 7}{1 \times 8}$$

$$= \frac{35}{8}$$

$$= 4\frac{3}{8}$$

The total width is $4\frac{3}{8}''$. This answer is reasonable, since $4\frac{3}{8}$ is between $3\frac{3}{4}$ and 5.

EXAMPLE 2   An iron plate $65''$ long must be cut to form 6 pieces of equal width. Allowing $\frac{1}{8}''$ for each of 5 saw cuts, about how long will each piece be?

SOLUTION   *Step 1.* Since $65''$ is slightly less than $66''$, a reasonable guess for the upper limit would be about $11''$ ($66'' \div 6$). Considering the 5 saw cuts, each of which is less than an inch, we can allow at the most $5''$ for the saw cuts. Then the plate, less the saw cuts, would be about $60''$. The lower limit for each piece would be about $10''$ ($60'' \div 6$).

Therefore, a reasonable guess for the length of each piece would be between $10''$ and $11''$.   (cont. on next page)

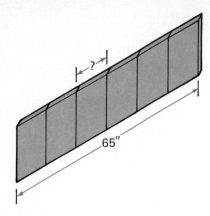

Step 2. Amount of material after cut allowance:

$$65 - (5 \times \tfrac{1}{8}) = 65 - \tfrac{5}{8} = 64\tfrac{3}{8}$$

Width of each piece:

$$64\tfrac{3}{8} \div 6 = \tfrac{515}{8} \times \tfrac{1}{6}$$
$$= \tfrac{515 \times 1}{8 \times 6}$$
$$= \tfrac{515}{48}$$
$$= 10\tfrac{35}{48}, \text{ or } 10\tfrac{3}{4} \text{ (approx.)}$$

Each plate will be about $10\tfrac{3}{4}''$ wide. This answer is reasonable, since $10\tfrac{3}{4}$ is between 10 and 11.

EXERCISES   Estimate the answers. Then use your estimates to check the answers.

A   1. In making a binding post $\tfrac{3}{4}''$ long, $\tfrac{1}{8}''$ of stock is wasted. How many binding posts can be made from a rod $25''$ long?

2. How many thumb screws $\tfrac{7}{8}''$ long can be cut from a bar of cold rolled steel $36''$ long, if $\tfrac{3}{16}''$ is wasted in each cut?

3. A plank $11\tfrac{3}{4}''$ wide is to be cut lengthwise into strips $2\tfrac{3}{4}''$ wide. Allowing $\tfrac{1}{8}''$ for each saw cut, find the number of $2\tfrac{3}{4}''$ strips that can be cut.

4. A garment worker cut 7 pieces of equal length from a strip of cloth $50''$ long. Allowing $\tfrac{1}{8}''$ scrap border for each of the 6 cuts, find the length of each piece.

5. Weight bars are used to press tablet sheets together before the glue is applied. How many bars $\tfrac{9}{16}''$ wide can be placed side by side in a space of $8\tfrac{1}{2}''$ wide?

6. A board $11'$ long is to be cut into partitions for displaying stereo tapes. How many partitions $6\tfrac{3}{4}''$ long can be cut, if $\tfrac{1}{8}''$ is allowed for each saw cut?

7. A street $340'$ long is to be curbed with blocks of granite, each $30''$ long. If $\tfrac{1}{4}''$ between the blocks is allowed for expansion, how many blocks are needed for the curb?

8. A $145'$ conveyor belt moves cartons from the storage area to the loading platform. Each carton is $18''$ wide. If a $\tfrac{3}{4}''$ space is left between cartons, what is the maximum capacity of the conveyor belt?

Laying out clothing patterns involves working with fractions.

3-9 Solving problems

Besides being able to estimate, tomorrow's skilled industrial worker must be able to solve problems involving several operations with fractions.

EXAMPLE 1 A printer is going to ship 44 used plates in a wooden crate. Each plate weighs $1\frac{3}{4}$ lb. If the crate can safely hold 75 lb, can the printer ship the plates in the crate?

SOLUTION *Step 1.* Estimate the total weight of the plates.

44×1 lb $= 44$ lb
44×2 lb $= 88$ lb

The total weight is between 44 and 88 lb.

Step 2. Find the total weight of the plates.

$$44 \times 1\frac{3}{4} = \frac{44}{1} \times \frac{7}{4}$$
$$= \frac{44 \times 7}{1 \times 4}$$
$$= \frac{11 \times 7}{1}$$
$$= 77$$

The plates weigh 77 lb.

Step 3. Compare with the safety weight.

77 is greater than 75.

Therefore, the crate cannot be used to ship the plates.

EXAMPLE 2 A tie rack is to be manufactured from a piece of clear plastic according to the plan in Figure 3-10. Equally-spaced holes must be drilled so that plastic pegs can be inserted. How many holes can be drilled?

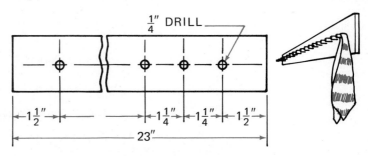

Figure 3-10

SOLUTION   *Step 1.* Estimate the number of holes.

$23'' \div 1'' = 23$
$23'' \div 2'' = 11\frac{1}{2}$, rounded to 12

There will be between 12 and 23 holes.

Step 2. Find the length of the space where the holes will be drilled.

$$23 - (1\frac{1}{2} + 1\frac{1}{2}) = 23 - 3 = 20$$

The space measures 20''.

Step 3. Find the number of holes.

$$20 \div 1\frac{1}{4} = \frac{20}{1} \div \frac{5}{4}$$

$$= \frac{\overset{4}{\cancel{20}}}{1} \times \frac{4}{\underset{1}{\cancel{5}}}$$

$$= 16$$

There will be 16 spaces. Therefore, there will be 17 holes.

EXERCISES   Solve the problems. Use estimates to check your work.

A   1. A printer's assistant must cut cards $4\frac{1}{4}''$ by $8\frac{1}{8}''$ from a 17'' by 22'' sheet of stock. The preferred method of cutting the stock is shown in the diagram.
   a. What is the width of waste strip A?
   b. What is the width of waste strip B?

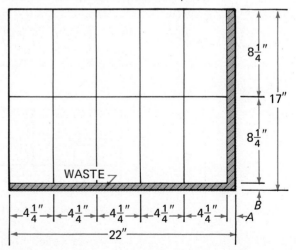

90

2. Twenty-five brackets with the dimensions shown must be stamped from a strip of No. 20 gauge sheet metal.
   a. How long is the bracket?
   b. How wide is the bracket?

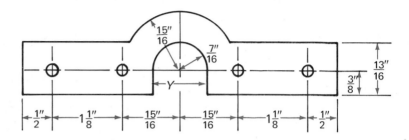

3. In making a bolt $2\frac{5}{8}''$ long, the allowance for waste is $\frac{1}{8}''$. How many feet of stock are used in making 36 bolts?

4. How many display shelves $2' \, 3''$ long can be cut from a board $14'$ long, if $\frac{1}{8}''$ is allowed for each saw cut?

5. A pattern for the cork sleeve on a woodburning pen is shown in Figure 3-11. The allowance for waste and cutting each piece is $\frac{1}{4}''$. How many cork sleeves can be made from a cork rod $24''$ long?

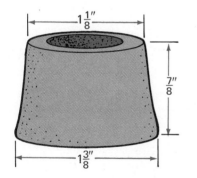

Figure 3-11

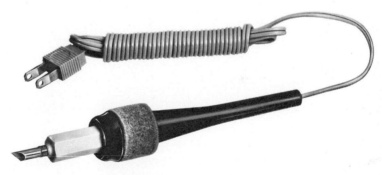

Electric woodburning pen.

6. A service technician finds that he needs pieces of copper tubing $8\frac{1}{4}''$, $9\frac{7}{8}''$, and $14\frac{1}{2}''$ long to install the cooling unit in an air conditioner. Allowing $\frac{1}{16}''$ for each cut, how much tubing does he need to assemble 16 such units? Give the answer in feet and inches.

7. A technical drawing $6\frac{3}{4}''$ wide by $8\frac{1}{8}''$ high is to be centered on a sheet of $12''$ by $18''$ paper. How much of a margin should be left on each side of the drawing?

B 8. A tenon $\frac{3}{4}''$ by $2\frac{3}{8}''$ is cut in the center of a piece $1\frac{1}{2}''$ by $3\frac{1}{4}''$.
   a. How wide are the shoulders on the sides?
   b. How wide are the shoulders on the top and bottom?

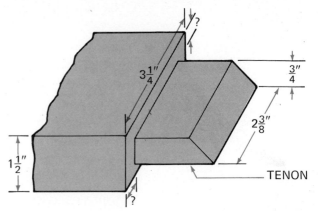

9. In building a brick wall 12′ long and 6′5″ high, bricks 8″ long and $2\frac{1}{4}''$ high are used. The mortar between the bricks is $\frac{1}{2}''$ thick.
   a. How many bricks are needed for one layer? (Count a fraction of a brick as a whole brick.)
   b. How many layers of brick are in the completed wall?

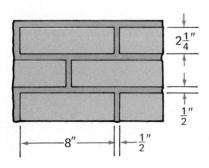

10. Eight T-rails are to be cut from a piece of stock 20′ long. In cutting each piece, $\frac{8}{16}''$ of stock is wasted.
   a. How much stock is used in cutting the 8 pieces?
   b. What is the length of the piece of unused stock?
   c. If the price of the stock is 62¢ a foot, what is the cost of the 20′ piece of stock?

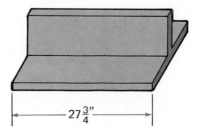

$27\frac{3}{4}''$

CREATIVE CRAFTSMAN

Design and build a device that is
   a. made from discarded materials;
   b. fun to watch; and
   c. powered by a falling weight.

SELF-ANALYSIS TEST 10

Estimate first, then solve the problems.

1. A service technician cut 10 pieces, each $3\frac{5}{8}''$ long from a piece of copper tubing $40\frac{1}{2}''$ long. Allowing $\frac{1}{8}''$ for each cut, how much tubing was left?

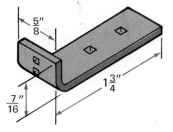

2. A duplicating machine requires 4 small brackets like the one shown at the left. The allowance for finishing each end of the bracket is $\frac{1}{16}''$. The allowance for the 90° bend is $\frac{1}{4}''$. How much stock is needed to make the brackets?

3. Two pieces of inlaid asphalt flooring $10'\ 4\frac{3}{4}''$ long must be cut from a 24' roll. A cutting allowance of $2''$ is made for each piece. How much flooring will remain after cutting?

SPOTLIGHT ON INDUSTRY

Urethane foam is creating a revolution in the building industry. It is replacing wood and producing a longer lasting product which insulates better against heat, cold, and sound. The possibilities for its use are unlimited. Some possibilities are in decorative beams, columns, and moldings which are lightweight and cost much less than wood. Urethane foam can also be used in the basic structure of buildings, such as for doors, door frames, windows, shingles, and even beams and walls. Spray-in-place urethane foam offers great possibilities in insulation. The photo at the left shows urethane foam being placed between concrete to make an insulated wall. Still another use for urethane foam is reducing the noise of appliances by spraying it on their inner surfaces.

EXERCISES

1. Wood beams on a living room ceiling cost $124.99. Urethane beams cost $45.98. How much can be saved by using urethane beams?
2. It takes 7 minutes to put a urethane door frame in place. A wood frame takes 45 minutes to assemble. If 18 door frames are needed in a house, how much time can be saved by using urethane foam?

Air-Conditioning, Refrigeration, and Heating Service Engineer

Each year the number of career opportunities in the air-conditioning, refrigeration, and heating trades increases. As more offices, factories, and homes are built with year-round climate controls, the need for skilled service engineers in these trades becomes greater. Perhaps you are interested in a career in this rapidly expanding field.

Job Description

What do service engineers do?
1. They install new equipment in homes and offices. The equipment may range in size from room air conditioners and space heaters to centralized air comfort systems.
2. They repair or replace faulty parts of equipment. Some repairs may be made at the site. If major repairs are needed, the equipment is taken to the repair shop.
3. They service the equipment during the off season. Service duties include lubricating motors, replacing filters, and checking coolant levels.
4. They test the equipment with meters and make the necessary adjustments to get the best performance.

Qualifications

Preference is given to high school graduates who have taken courses in mathematics, physics, electricity, and blueprint reading.
Good physical condition is needed for lifting heavy equipment.

Training

Service engineers usually begin as apprentices, combining technical training with on-the-job experience. In technical institutes apprentices study the design, operation, and repair of air-control equipment. In the field, apprentices work under the supervision of a trained engineer. They do simple jobs at first, like insulating coolant lines and cleaning furnaces. As they gain experience, they are given more complex jobs like installing pumps and checking electrical relays.

Working Conditions

A 40-hour week, with possible overtime.
Irregular hours are common during peak seasons.
Work at great heights, in cramped positions, is not unusual.
Common hazards include torch burns, metal cuts, electrical
   shock, and muscle strain.

Opportunities for Advancement

Many service engineers work for dealers and contractors who
specialize in installing, servicing, and repairing air-control
equipment. Some seek jobs as full-time maintenance engineers
for department stores, hotels, supermarket chains, and
industrial plants. Many service engineers prefer to operate their
own businesses. And, quite a few become "field service
engineers" for manufacturers of heating and air-conditioning
equipment.

TAKING INVENTORY

1. To multiply fractions, multiply the numerators together and the denominators together. Reduce the resulting fraction to lowest terms. (p. 78)

2. To multiply mixed numbers, first change the mixed numbers to fractions, then multiply. (p. 78)

3. **Cancellation** is the process of reducing to lowest terms before multiplying instead of after multiplying. (p. 80)

4. The **reciprocal** of a number is another number which, when multiplied by the first number, gives 1 as the product. (p. 82)

5. To divide fractions, multiply the first fraction by the reciprocal of the second fraction. (p. 85)

6. An **estimate** is a "reasonable guess" as to the amount of a certain quantity. (p. 87)

MEASURING YOUR SKILLS

Multiply. Give the answer in lowest terms.

1. $13 \times \frac{1}{4}$ 2. $4 \times \frac{4}{9}$ 3. $\frac{7}{8} \times 5$ (3-1)

4. $\frac{1}{7} \times 3\frac{3}{4}$ 5. $\frac{2}{5} \times 2\frac{1}{3}$ 6. $\frac{3}{8} \times 2\frac{1}{8}$ (3-2)

7. $\frac{3}{4} \times \frac{3}{10}$ 8. $\frac{7}{3} \times \frac{5}{4}$ 9. $\frac{5}{8} \times \frac{4}{9}$ (3-3)

Multiply, using cancellation.

10. $\frac{4}{5} \times \frac{3}{16}$ 11. $\frac{1}{8}'' \times \frac{4}{7}$ 12. $\frac{5}{8} \times \frac{2}{3} \times \frac{12}{25}$ (3-4)

Give the reciprocals.

13. 3 14. $\frac{1}{5}$ 15. $\frac{4}{7}$ (3-5)

Divide. Give the answers in lowest terms.

16. $\frac{15}{32} \div 3$ 17. $\frac{3}{4} \div 15$ 18. $\frac{18}{25} \div 9$ (3-6)

19. $\frac{2}{9} \div \frac{1}{5}$ 20. $\frac{4}{7}'' \div \frac{3}{8}$ 21. $3\frac{5}{8}'' \div 2\frac{1}{3}$ (3-7)

22. To make one engine head bolt $4\frac{3}{4}''$ of stock is required, including all allowances. How much stock is needed to make 48 head bolts? Give the answer in feet and inches.

23. An airplane uses gasoline at the rate of $15\frac{3}{4}$ gal per hr. How much fuel does it use in a flight of $5\frac{1}{2}$ hr?

24. Radio speaker grilles $3\frac{3}{4}''$ by $5\frac{3}{4}''$ are stamped from a strip of lightweight material $4''$ wide. A $\frac{3}{8}''$ waste piece is allowed between grilles. How long a strip is needed to manufacture 36 grilles?

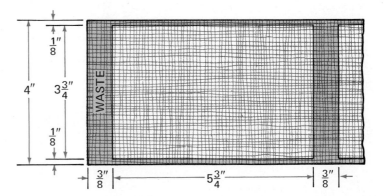

25. A panel of an airplane wing measures $9'\ 3\frac{1}{2}''$ by $54\frac{1}{2}''$. The rivet holes are drilled $1\frac{3}{16}''$ apart, and the end holes were located $1\frac{1}{8}''$ from the ends of the section. How many holes are needed
    a. along the length of the panel?
    b. along the width of the panel?
    c. around the perimeter of the panel?

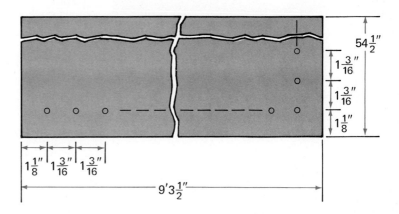

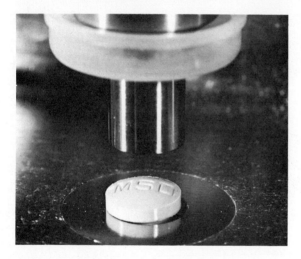

Reading patient-monitoring instruments and manufacturing pharmaceuticals require a knowledge of decimals and percents.

CHAPTER **4** *Decimals, Percents*

After completing this chapter, you should be able to:
1. *Write equivalent fractions, decimals, and percents.*
2. *Add, subtract, multiply, and divide decimals.*
3. *Use a micrometer to take precise measurements.*
4. *Use percents to determine discounts, tolerances, and efficiencies.*

Decimals and fractions

4-1 Reading and writing decimals

In Chapter 1 you learned about the machinist's scale (see Figure 4-1). Recall that this scale is divided into hundredths of an inch.

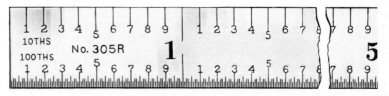

Figure 4-1

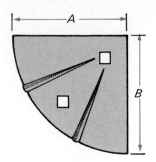

Figure 4-2

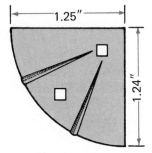

Figure 4-3

If a machinist's scale is available, measure the lengths A and B on the bicycle kick-stand mounting shown in Figure 4-2. Do you see that A is $1\frac{24}{100}''$ and B is $1\frac{25}{100}''$? The pattern for manufacturing this kick-stand mounting might look like Figure 4-3. Notice how the dimensions $1\frac{24}{100}''$ and $1\frac{25}{100}''$ are shown in Figure 4-3 as 1.24'' and 1.25''. Such numbers are called decimals.

Decimals are special fractions whose denominators are 10, or 100, or 1000, and so on. Instead of writing the denominator of decimal fractions, we write only the numerator, preceded by a decimal point. Below are several more examples of decimals.

Fraction	Words	Decimal
$\frac{3}{10}$	three tenths	.3
$\frac{37}{100}$	thirty-seven hundredths	.37
$\frac{217}{1000}$	two hundred seventeen thousandths	.217
$\frac{45}{10,000}$	forty-five ten-thousandths	.0045

The pattern in the decimals above suggests the following idea.

> In a decimal the number of digits after the decimal point indicates the number of zeros in the denominator of the fraction. For example,
>
>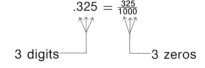
>
> 3 digits———— ————3 zeros

Write each as a common fraction and as a decimal.

A

1. four tenths
2. seven tenths
3. seven hundredths
4. thirty-six hundredths
5. ninety-three hundredths
6. nine thousandths
7. one hundred fifty-five thousandths
8. three hundred five thousandths

Write as decimals.

9. $\frac{2}{10}$ 12. $\frac{125}{1000}$ 15. $\frac{18}{1000}$

10. $\frac{9}{100}$ 13. $\frac{900}{1000}$ 16. $\frac{83}{100}$

11. $\frac{6}{1000}$ 14. $\frac{95}{10000}$ 17. $\frac{5}{10}$

Write as fractions.

18. .1   21. .27   24. .015

19. .12   22. .125   25. .0725

20. .322   23. .2737   26. .0069

B Using a machinist's scale, measure the lengths indicated in the diagrams. Write the dimensions as decimals.

27.

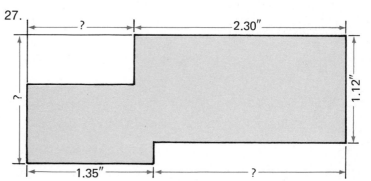

28.

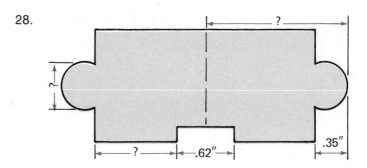

CREATIVE CRAFTSMAN

Design a device which uses a lever or a combination of levers and various geometric shapes to create a "balanced system."

4-2 Equivalent decimals and fractions

Decimal Equivalents

Number of 64ths	Decimal Equivalent	Number of 64ths	Decimal Equivalent
1	.0156	33	.5156
2	.0313	34	.5313
3	.0469	35	.5469
4	.0625	36	.5625
5	.0781	37	.5781
6	.0938	38	.5938
7	.1094	39	.6094
8	.125	40	.625
9	.1406	41	.6406
10	.1563	42	.6563
11	.1719	43	.6719
12	.1875	44	.6875
13	.2031	45	.7031
14	.2188	46	.7188
15	.2344	47	.7344
16	.25	48	.75
17	.2656	49	.7656
18	.2813	50	.7813
19	.2969	51	.7969
20	.3125	52	.8125
21	.3281	53	.8281
22	.3438	54	.8438
23	.3594	55	.8594
24	.375	56	.875
25	.3906	57	.8906
26	.4063	58	.9063
27	.4219	59	.9219
28	.4375	60	.9375
29	.4531	61	.9531
30	.4688	62	.9688
31	.4844	63	.9844
32	.5	64	1.

Figure 4-4

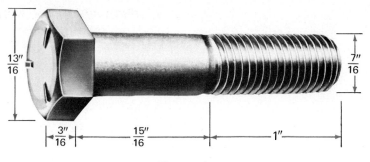

Figure 4-5

The dimensions of the bolt in Figure 4-5 are given in fractions. To machine a bolt like this on a metal lathe that is calibrated in hundredths of an inch, we need to know the dimensions as decimals. Usually we can find the most common equivalents in a table, as in Figure 4-4.

EXAMPLE 1   Change $\frac{5}{8}''$ to a decimal.

SOLUTION   First, change $\frac{5}{8}$ to an equivalent fraction with 64 as denominator.

$$\frac{5}{8} \times \frac{8}{8} = \frac{40}{64}$$

Now find the numerator 40 in the column headed "Number of 64ths". Next to it is the decimal equivalent, .625".

EXAMPLE 2   Change $\frac{5}{16}''$ to a decimal.

SOLUTION $\frac{5}{16} = \frac{20}{64}$. Next to 20 in the column headed "Number of 64ths" is the decimal .3125. Thus $\frac{5}{16}'' = .3125''$.

From time to time we may also need to find an equivalent fraction for a decimal. We can also use the table in Figure 4-4 to do this.

EXAMPLE 3   An optical lens must be precision-ground to a thickness of .0469". What is this dimension as a fraction?

SOLUTION   Find .0469 in the column headed "Decimal Equivalent." In the column to the left, read the numerator 3. Thus, .0469" = $\frac{3}{64}''$.

Sometimes in your work a table may not be close at hand. At other times the dimensions you are dealing with may not appear in the table. In these instances, you will need to find equivalent decimals and fractions. The following rules can be helpful.

---

1. To change a fraction to its decimal equivalent, divide the numerator by the denominator.
2. To change a decimal to a fraction:
   a. Count the number of decimal places;
   b. Write the fraction using that number of zeros in the denominator;
   c. Reduce the fraction to lowest terms.

EXAMPLE 4   Change $\frac{5}{8}$ to a decimal.

SOLUTION $\frac{5}{8} = 5 \div 8 =$

$$
\begin{array}{r}
.625 \\
8\overline{)5.000} \\
-4\,8 \\
\hline
20 \\
-16 \\
\hline
40 \\
-40 \\
\hline
0
\end{array}
$$

Therefore, $\frac{5}{8} = .625$.

EXAMPLE 5   Change 4.375 to a fraction.

SOLUTION $4.375 = 4\dfrac{375}{1000}$ Divide by 125

$= 4\dfrac{3}{8}$

Thus, $4.375 = 4\frac{3}{8}$.

EXERCISES   Use the table in Figure 4-4 to find the decimal equivalent of each fraction.

A   1. $\frac{3}{4}$ 3. $\frac{7}{8}$ 5. $\frac{9}{16}$ 7. $\frac{29}{32}$

2. $\frac{9}{32}$ 4. $\frac{41}{64}$ 6. $\frac{3}{16}$ 8. $\frac{1}{4}$

Use the table to find the fraction whose value is nearest each of the following decimals.

9. .62	11. .925	13. .280	15. .775
10. .525	12. .435	14. .385	16. .651

Give the decimal equivalent of each.

17. $\frac{1}{5}$	20. $\frac{3}{16}$	23. $\frac{3}{32}$	26. $1\frac{1}{4}''$
18. $\frac{2}{5}$	21. $\frac{5}{16}$	24. $\frac{5}{32}$	27. $2\frac{3}{8}''$
19. $\frac{7}{8}$	22. $\frac{15}{16}$	25. $\frac{9}{32}$	28. $1\frac{5}{16}''$

Write each decimal as a mixed number or fraction in lowest terms.

29. .25	32. .35	35. .875	38. 1.625″
30. .4	33. .75	36. .3125	39. 3.15″
31. .6	34. .125	37. .4375	40. 5.75″

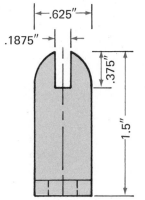

Piston, connecting rod, and rings.

B 41. An automotive-parts supplier lists the dimensions of all parts in decimals. What size piston rings must a mechanic buy to replace rings that are $3\frac{7}{8}''$ in diameter?

42. The thickness of a hexagon-shaped nut is $\frac{7}{8}$ the diameter of the bolt, reduced to the nearest sixty-fourth of an inch. Find the thickness of hex nuts for bolts with the following diameters:

    a. 1.125″   b. .625″   c. .6875″   d. 1.1875″

43. Write the dimensions of the bicycle shift lever in Figure 4-6 as fractions.

C 44. Find the fractional equivalent of each decimal to the nearest sixteenth.

    a. .4   b. .15   c. .125   d. 1.625

Figure 4-6

SELF-ANALYSIS TEST 11

Write the equivalent decimal for each.

1. $\frac{3}{16}$	3. $\frac{9}{64}$	5. $3\frac{1}{4}''$
2. $\frac{7}{8}$	4. $\frac{7}{16}$	6. $2\frac{3}{8}''$

Write the equivalent fraction for each decimal.

7. 4	9. .5	11. .64″
8. .875	10. .15	12. .125″

Using decimals

4-3 Adding and subtracting decimals

To find the length of the carpenter's brace shown in Figure 4-7, we must add several dimensions.

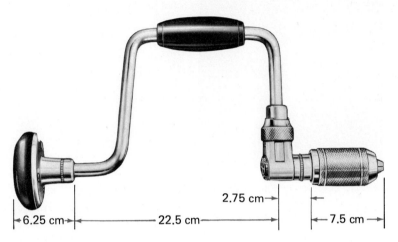

Figure 4-7

When adding decimals, we write them in a column, with the decimal points in a line.

Do this!		*Not this!*	
	6.25 cm		6.25 cm
	22.5 cm		22.5 cm
	2.75 cm		2.75 cm
+	7.5 cm	+	7.5 cm
	39.00 cm		?? cm

If we wish to find the length of the brace, excluding the handle, we need to subtract. Again we line up the decimal points. A helpful idea is to add as many zeros after the decimal point so that each decimal has the same number of places. Thus, to subtract 6.25 from 39, we write:

$$
\begin{array}{r}
39.00 \text{ cm} \\
-\ 6.25 \text{ cm} \\
\hline
32.75 \text{ cm}
\end{array}
$$

Placing zeros after the digit to the right of the decimal point does not change the value of the decimal. The numbers 39, 39.0 and 39.00 are the same.

We can summarize our work in this way.

To add or subtract decimals, write them in a column, making sure the decimal points are in a line. Then proceed as with whole numbers.

Did you notice that the dimensions of the brace in Figure 4-8 are given in centimeters? Because the metric system is based on tens, metric dimensions are usually written as decimals. For example, the shank of the brace measures 22 cm + 5 mm. Since 10 mm = 1 cm, 5 mm = $\frac{1}{2}$ cm, or as a decimal, .5 cm. Therefore, we write the length as 22.5 cm.

EXERCISES Add.

A

1. 4.03
    +2.91

2. 43.6
    +29.5

3. 16.82
    + 4.73

4. 53.39 cm
    +14.52 cm

5. 14.54 cm
    + 2.98 cm

6. 18.304
    + 7.683

7. 8.46 + 5.2 + .845 + .234

8. 10.76 + .18 + 4.2654 + 88.005

9. 68 + .056 + .0072 + 3.4

10. 1.65 + 2.0735 + .484

Subtract.

11. 3.9
    −2.7

12. 4.6 mm
    −3.2 mm

13. 5.93 cm
    −2.61 cm

14. 17.8 cm
    − 8.2 cm

15. 5.932
    −2.811

16. 16.38
    −11.97

17. 6.
    −3.71

18. 4.3
    − .582

19. 125.83
    − 14.7

U.S. System

B 20. The smaller end of a tapered pin is 1.125″ in diameter. The diameter of the other end is .385″ larger. Find the diameter of the larger end.

21. Find dimension A in the routed wood panel.

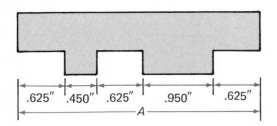

22. Find dimensions A and B in the step bracket.

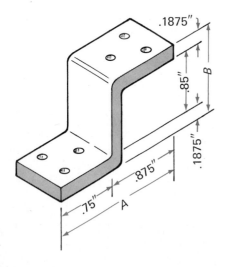

Metric System

23. Find the inside diameter, CD, of the extended plastic tubing. The outside diameter and the thickness are shown in the cross-section.

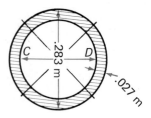

24. Find the distance between the centers of the holes in the drill jig.

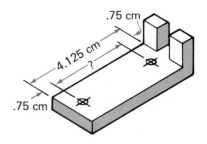

25. Two holes must be drilled in a lock template. Find dimensions A and B.

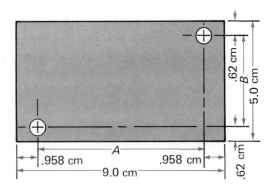

Figure 4-8

4-4 Multiplying decimals

The wood jointer in Figure 4-8 is set to cut at .125″. If a board is passed through the jointer 3 times, by how much is the board planed down?

To answer this question, we must multiply the amount planed each time, .125″, by the number of cuts, 3. We show our work as follows:

$$.125'' \leftarrow \text{3 decimal places}$$
$$\underline{\times\ 3}$$
$$.375'' \leftarrow \text{3 decimal places}$$

Notice that there are as many decimal places in the answer as there are in the decimal fraction. This fact suggests the following rule.

> The number of decimal places in a product is the sum of the number of decimal places in the factors.

EXAMPLE 1   Multiply .27 by .6.

SOLUTION $.27 \leftarrow$ 2 decimal places
$\underline{\times .6} \leftarrow$ 1 decimal place
$.162 \leftarrow$ 3 decimal places

EXAMPLE 2   Multiply 4.3 by .005.

SOLUTION $4.3 \leftarrow$ 1 decimal place
$\underline{\times .005} \leftarrow$ 3 decimal places
$215 \leftarrow$??

We should have 4 decimal places in the answer, but we only have 3 digits in the answer. In this case, it is necessary to insert a zero to the left of the digit 2. Then we locate the decimal point. Thus, the product is .0215.

It is a good practice to make an estimate before beginning your work. See how the estimate helps you locate the decimal point in Example 3 on the next page.

EXAMPLE 3   A strip of heat-treated steel 21.4 cm by 3.21 cm is needed to replace a defective piece. What is the area of this piece?

SOLUTION   *Step 1*. Estimate.

21.4 is about 21.

3.21 is about 3.

21 × 3 = 63

The strip has an area of about 63 sq cm.

Step 2. Solve.
$$\begin{array}{r} 21.4 \\ \times 3.21 \\ \hline 214 \\ 428 \\ 642 \\ \hline 68.694 \end{array}$$

Therefore, the area is 68.694 sq cm.

EXERCISES   Locate the decimal point in the answer.

A   1. .6 × .7 = 42   4. 2.5 × 25 = 625   7. .007 × 1.8 = 126

2. .4 × 7 = 28   5. .7 × .866 = 6062   8. .08 × .003 = 24

3. .7 × .21 = 147   6. .3 × 1.414 = 4242 9. .003 × .004 = 12

Multiply. Check the answer by estimating.

10. 1.732 × 5   14. 1.155 × 8.05   18. 68.8 × 1.43

11. .007 × 130   15. .063 × .0047   19. 4.276 × 24

12. .6 × .6   16. 57.3 × 35.2   20. 4.39 × 3.4

13. .15 × .15   17. 46.25 × 8.4   21. 130.2 × 5.006

U.S. System

B 22. Each pound of a brass alloy used for stampings contains .58 lb of copper, .405 lb of zinc, and .015 lb of lead. A bar of this alloy weighs 8.5 lb. Find the amounts of copper, zinc and lead in the bar.

Metric System

26. One meter of a steel rod 2 cm in diameter weighs 1.61 kilograms (kg). What is the weight of a rod of this steel that is 8.25 m long?

23. In a square the side, S, is always about .707 times the length of the diagonal, D. Find S when D is 1.75″ long.

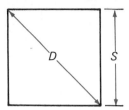

24. The countersunk-head rivet below has a diameter D of .5″. Dimension A is .425 times D. Dimension B is 1.85 times D. Find dimensions A and B.

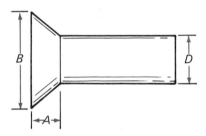

25. The thickness of a sheet of No. 1 gauge sheet metal is .28125″. How high is a stack containing 48 sheets?

27. The distance, F, across the flats of a hexbolt is .866 times D. Find F when D is 4.4 cm.

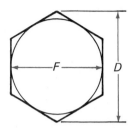

28. A mechanic must bore a hole large enough to seat the head of a bolt. The diameter of the hole must be 1.414 times the side of the bolt head. If the bolt is 3.2 cm on each side, what must be the diameter of the hole?

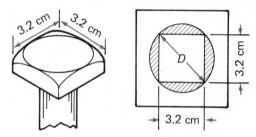

29. Using the diagram in Exercise 23, find S when D is 3.6 cm.

SPOTLIGHT ON INDUSTRY

Time spent in line at a checkout counter can be cut 60% by an automated checkout. Here's how it works: A coded label is attached to each product. An optical scanner at the checkout counter reads the label. It then sends a message to a minicomputer. The computer looks up the price and prints it out on a cash register. When the order is complete, the computer adds the prices and prints the amount. With this system the prices would not be marked on each item. Rather, they would be on the shelf and in the storage area of the computer. The prices would also appear on the customer's receipt.

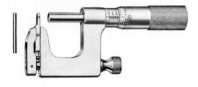

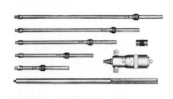

Figure 4-9

4-5 Micrometers

The micrometer is an instrument used in making precise measurements. Some micrometers can measure accurately to .001″. Others are calibrated to give accurate measurements in metric units. Figure 4-9 shows some of the different types of micrometers.

The important parts of a micrometer are shown in a cutaway view in Figure 4-10.

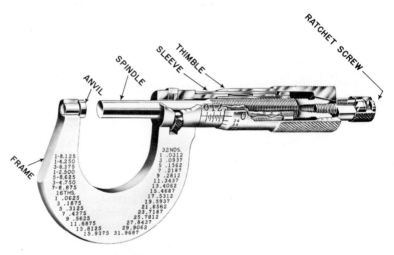

Figure 4-10

A micrometer is calibrated according to two scales—one on the sleeve, the other on the thimble. On a micrometer for measuring in the U.S. system each numeral on the sleeve indicates .100″. Each of the sub-divisions on the sleeve is .025″. There are 25 divisions on the thimble. Each division equals .001″. These relationships are shown in Figure 4-11.

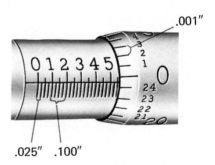

Figure 4-11

The flow chart in Figure 4-12 will help you read the setting on a micrometer.

EXAMPLE 1   Read the micrometer.

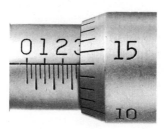

SOLUTION   A. $2 \times .100'' = .200''$
            B. $3 \times .025'' = .075''$
            C. $14 \times .001'' = .014''$
                         Sum $= \overline{.289''}$

EXAMPLE 2   What is the reading?

SOLUTION   A. $3 \times .100'' = .300''$
            B. $0 \times .025'' = .000''$
            C. $9 \times .001'' = .009''$
                         Sum $= \overline{.309''}$

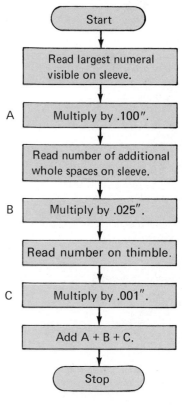

Figure 4-12

Metric micrometers also consist of a scale on the sleeve and a scale on the thimble. Figure 4-13 shows the basic units on these scales.

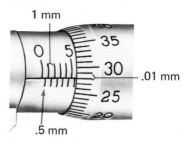

Figure 4-13

The flow chart in Figure 4-14 can be used to read the settings on a metric micrometer.

EXAMPLE 3   Read the micrometer.

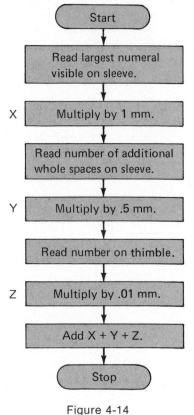

SOLUTION   X. $5 \times 1 \text{ mm} = 5$ mm
Y. $4 \times 0.5 \text{ mm} = 2.0$ mm
Z. $17 \times .01 \text{ mm} = .17$ mm
Sum $= \overline{7.17 \text{ mm}}$

EXAMPLE 4   What is the reading?

SOLUTION   X. $5 \times 1 \text{ mm} = 5$ mm
Y. $7 \times .5 \text{ mm} = 3.5$ mm
Z. $29 \times .01 \text{ mm} = .29$ mm
Sum $= \overline{8.79 \text{ mm}}$

Figure 4-14

Flow chart (Figure 4-14):

Start → Read largest numeral visible on sleeve. → X: Multiply by 1 mm. → Read number of additional whole spaces on sleeve. → Y: Multiply by .5 mm. → Read number on thimble. → Z: Multiply by .01 mm. → Add X + Y + Z. → Stop

EXERCISES

U.S. System   *Metric System*

Read the micrometers.

A 1.

7.

2.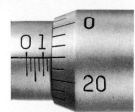

8.

3.

9.

4.

10.

5.

11.

6.

12.

TRICKS OF THE TRADE

To divide a number by 10, move the decimal point 1 place to the *left*. To divide by 100, move the decimal point 2 places to the *left*, and so on.

$$758 \div 10 = 75.8$$
$$758 \div 100 = 7.58$$

4-6 Dividing decimals

Frequently it is necessary to divide decimals in making calculations. Do you recall how to divide decimals? If not, look at the examples below.

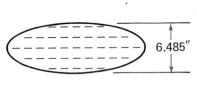

6.485"

Figure 4-15

EXAMPLE 1   Figure 4-15 shows the cross-section of a laminated helicopter rotor blade. Find the thickness of each sheet of laminating material if the 5 layers in the blade measure 6.485".

SOLUTION   To find the answer, we need to divide 6.485 by 5. We can show the work in this way:

$$
\begin{array}{r}
1.297 \\
5\overline{)\ 6.485} \\
-5 \\
\hline
1\,4 \\
-1\,0 \\
\hline
48 \\
-45 \\
\hline
35 \\
-35 \\
\hline
0
\end{array}
$$

Each sheet of laminating material is 1.297" thick.

Notice that the decimal points are lined up when we divide decimals.

EXAMPLE 2   It takes 13.5 volts to activate an electric relay. How many 1.5 volt batteries, connected in series, are needed to activate the relay?

SOLUTION   To find the number of batteries, we must divide 13.5 by 1.5. The flow chart in Figure 4-16 can help us.

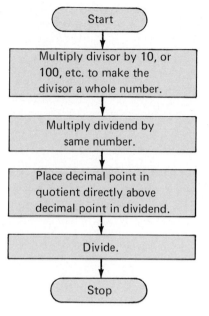

$$1.5\overline{)13.5}$$

Multiply   Multiply
by 10   by 10

$$\begin{array}{r} 9. \\ 15\overline{)135.} \\ -135 \\ \hline 0 \end{array}$$

Figure 4-16

It will take 9 batteries.

Once we become familiar with this process we can learn a short cut to divide decimals.

EXAMPLE 3   A rectangular drip pan is placed under a printing press to keep ink and solvent off the floor. The pan covers 1.725 sq m in area. If it is .75 m wide, how long is it?

SOLUTION   We must divide 1.725 by .75.

$$\begin{array}{r} 2.3 \\ .75\overline{)1.725} \\ -1\,50 \\ \hline 225 \\ -225 \\ \hline 0 \end{array}$$

The pan measures 2.3 m long.
   We multiply both the divisor and dividend by 100. We show this by moving the decimal point 2 places to the right. How many places to the right would you move the decimal point if you were multiplying the divisor and dividend by 1000?

These examples suggest the following rule.

> To divide decimals, follow these steps:
>
> a. If the divisor is a decimal, multiply both the divisor and dividend by 10, or 100, or 1000, and so on, to make the divisor a whole number. (This is the same as moving the decimal point to the right);
> b. Place the decimal point directly above the decimal point in the dividend;
> c. Divide as with whole numbers.

EXERCISES   Divide.

A
1. 4.2 ÷ 2
2. .248 ÷ 8
3. 78.84 ÷ 9
4. .4632 ÷ 4

5. 184.25 ÷ 5
6. 12.465 ÷ 3
7. 28.8 ÷ 12
8. .064 ÷ 16

9. 1.275 ÷ 75
10. 11.25 ÷ 25
11. .665 ÷ 19
12. 69.16 ÷ 28

B
13. 4.5 ÷ .5
14. .48 ÷ .6
15. 19.8 ÷ 6

16. 4.96 ÷ 4
17. 10.71 ÷ .07
18. .225 ÷ .15

19. .125 ÷ .25
20. .9 ÷ .003
21. .805 ÷ .0035

U.S. System

22. To find the outside diameter of a pipe, we divide the circumference of the pipe by 3.14. What is the outside diameter of a pipe whose circumference is 15.7″?

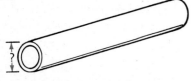

23. An airplane propeller 4.25″ thick is ⟩ of 5 layers of uniformly thick lami-⟩ material. Find the thickness of ⟩yer of this material.

Metric System

27. The inside diameter of a pipe is equal to the inside circumference divided by 3.14. Find the inside diameter of a pipe with an inside circumference of 23.608 cm.

28. Rust-proofing is applied to automobile frames by dipping them in vats. After 4 treatments, the coating on the metal surface measured 3.69 mm. About how much coating was applied each time?

24. A stack of 55 sheets of watch-spring brass is 3.520″ high. What is the thickness of each sheet?

25. Eight complete turns of a nut advance it 1.00″. How far does it advance on each full turn?

26. A 250′ roll of TV antenna lead costs $8.75. What is the cost per foot?

29. One square meter of No. 18 gauge sheet steel weighs .97 kg. What is the area in square meters of a piece of this steel weighing 7.954 kg?

30. A metric wood screw advances 1.8 mm for each complete turn. How many turns will advance it 12.6 mm?

31. It costs $3770 to fuel an atomic reactor with 4.4 g of radioactive material. What is the cost per gram?

SELF-ANALYSIS TEST 12

U.S. System

1. 3.97″
   +2.84″

2. 6.729″
   −4.167″

3. Find the cost of 44.5 gal of asphalt sealer at $.23 a gallon. 10,230

4. Give the micrometer reading in inches.

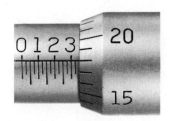

5. The weight of 7.5″ of aluminum wire is 1.575 oz. What is the weight of 1″ of the wire?

Metric System

6. 81.42 cm
   −16.85 cm

7. 199.7 mm
   +326.4 mm

8. Surgical tubing costs $3.27 per meter. What is the cost of 6.6 m of tubing?

9. Give the micrometer reading in millimeters.

10. The area of a rectangular iron plate is 3.08 sq m. If one side is 1.4 m long, how wide is the other side? 4.48

TRICKS OF THE TRADE

To multiply a number by 10, move the decimal point 1 place to the *right*. To multiply by 100, move the decimal point 2 places to the *right,* and so on.

$$.234 \times 10 = 2.34$$
$$.234 \times 100 = 23.4$$

Percents

4-7 Meaning of percent

In Chapter 1 you studied industrial graphs like Figure 4-17. Study this graph carefully.

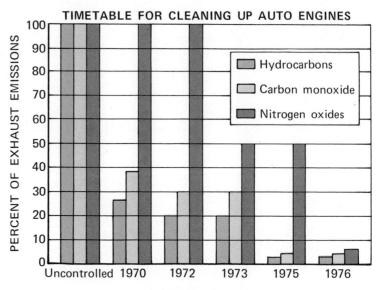

Figure 4-17

Notice the scale along the side of the graph. The air-pollution levels are given as percents. Percents are special fractions. They have 100 as denominator. Thus, 35 percent, written 35%, means $\frac{35}{100}$ or .35.

In your work you may have to change a percent to a decimal or a fraction. Here's how to do it.

To change a percent to a decimal:

a. Move the decimal point two places to the *left;*
b. Drop the percent sign.

EXAMPLE 1 Write 35% as a decimal.

SOLUTION 35.% → .35

EXAMPLE 2 Write 6% as a decimal.

SOLUTION 06.% → .06

> To change a fraction to a percent:
>
> a. Change the fraction to a decimal;
> b. Move the decimal point two places to the *right;*
> c. Add a percent sign.

EXAMPLE 3   Write $\frac{3}{4}$ as a percent.

SOLUTION $\frac{3}{4} = 4\overline{)\,3.00} = .75 = 75\%$

$$
\begin{array}{r}
.75 \\
4\overline{)\;3.00} \\
-2\,8 \\ \hline
20 \\
-20 \\ \hline
0
\end{array}
$$

EXAMPLE 4   Write $\dfrac{7}{8}$ as a percent.

SOLUTION $\dfrac{7}{8} = 8\overline{)\,7.000} = .875 = 87.5\%$, or $87\frac{1}{2}\%$

$$
\begin{array}{r}
.875 \\
8\overline{)\;7.000} \\
-6\,4 \\ \hline
60 \\
-\,56 \\ \hline
40 \\
-\,40 \\ \hline
0
\end{array}
$$

EXERCISES   Write the percents as decimals.

A
1. 3%	3. 78%	5. 25.3%	7. .2%
2. 4%	4. 93%	6. 16.5%	8. 108.2%

Write the percents as fractions in lowest terms.

9. 25%	12. 40%	15. $12\frac{1}{2}\%$	18. 100%
10. 50%	13. 60%	16. $37\frac{1}{2}\%$	19. .5%
11. 75%	14. 90%	17. $62\frac{1}{2}\%$	20. 1.5%

Write the decimals as percents.

21. .14	23. 1.45	25. .032	27. .4
22. .63	24. .062	26. .017	28. 1.25

Write the fractions as percents.

29. $\frac{1}{2}$ 32. $\frac{3}{5}$ 35. $\frac{7}{8}$ 38. $\frac{4}{25}$

30. $\frac{3}{4}$ 33. $\frac{3}{8}$ 36. $\frac{7}{20}$ 39. $\frac{7}{50}$

31. $\frac{2}{5}$ 34. $\frac{5}{8}$ 37. $\frac{13}{20}$ 40. $\frac{43}{80}$

For Exercises 41–44 refer to the graph in Figure 4-17 on page 120.

B 41. From 1972 to 1973 nitrogen oxides should drop to 50%. Write 50% as a fraction.

42. In 1976 exhaust should contain no more than 4% hydrocarbons. Write 4% as a fraction.

43. With no pollution controls, emissions would be 100%. Write 100% as a decimal.

44. By 1976 hydrocarbons should drop to $\frac{1}{4}$ the amount present in 1972. What is $\frac{1}{4}$ as a decimal? as a percent?

4-8 Discounts

When a dealer buys an item from a manufacturer, he usually pays a discount price, called the net price. Discount rates are often stated as percents. Since you may have to work with discounts on your job, you will need to study them now.

EXAMPLE   A $13.00 set of calipers is put on sale at 15% off the regular price. What is the sale price?

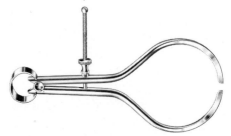

SOLUTION   Percent means "hundredths." Therefore, 15% = .15.

$$\text{Discount} = .15 \text{ of } \$13.00 = .15 \times \$13.00$$
$$= \$1.95$$
$$\text{Sale price} = \$13.00 - \$1.95$$
$$= \$11.05$$

The set of calipers will sell for $11.05.

EXERCISES Find the following amounts.

A
1. 20% of $840
2. 30% of $560
3. 25% of $84
4. 12½% of $80
5. 6% of $402
6. 15% of $90

Find the missing items in this purchase order.

7.

Quan.	Item	Unit Cost	Cost	% Discount	Net Cost
5	hinges	.35	1.75	20%	1.40
7	locks	.40	?	25%	?
2	sockets	1.15	?	30%	?
4	switches	2.35	?	15%	?
				Total net cost	?

Copy and complete this purchase order.

B 8.

Purchase Order No. 4279

ACME PLUMBING SUPPLY CO.

Date: 4/5

For: Ortega's Plumbing   Phone: 443-2921

Address: 1434 Ridge Blvd.   City: Waco, Texas

QUANTITY	ITEM	UNIT COST	COST	DISCOUNT	NET COST
5	$\frac{3}{4}''$ unions	.85	4.25	20%	3.40
8	$\frac{3}{4}''$ 45° ells	.65	5.20	30%	3.64
4	$\frac{3}{4}''$ valves	2.50		25%	
18	$\frac{3}{4}''$ X 6'' nozzles	.95		15%	
5	$\frac{3}{4}''$ faucets	2.00		20%	
12	$\frac{3}{4}''$ 90° ells	.75		30%	
18	$\frac{3}{4}''$ fittings	.35		35%	
8	$\frac{3}{4}''$ T-joints	.55		20%	

Total _____

Less 2% Cash Discount _____

Net Total _____

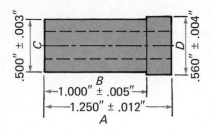

Figure 4-18

4-9 Machine tolerance

The bushing in Figure 4-18 must be machined to certain limits of precision. Notice that dimension A must be 1.250″ ± .012″. (The symbol ± is read "plus or minus.") These figures show that the basic size of A is 1.250″. However, to allow for errors in manufacturing, the length of A can vary from 1.238″ to 1.262″ and still be acceptable. The measurements 1.238″ and 1.262″ are called the dimension limits. The difference between the dimension limits is called the tolerance. The tolerance of dimension A is 1.262″ − 1.238″ = .024″.

EXAMPLE 1 Find the dimension limits and tolerance for dimension B in Figure 4-18.

SOLUTION

Basic size	1.000″	Basic size	1.000″
Oversize allowance	+ .005″	Undersize allowance	− .005″
Oversize dim. limit	1.005″	Undersize dim. limit	.995″

$$1.005''$$
$$- \ .995''$$
$$\text{Tolerance} \quad .010''$$

The specifications for some machined parts require very high levels of precision. This means that the percent of relative error must be very small, 1% or less. To determine the percent of relative error, we can use this formula:

$$\text{Relative error} = \frac{1}{2} \times \frac{\text{Tolerance}}{\text{Basic size}}$$

EXAMPLE 2 What is the percent of relative error for dimension A in Figure 4-18?

SOLUTION $\text{Relative error} = \frac{1}{2} \times \frac{.024}{1.250} = \frac{1}{2} \times .0192 = .0096$

Percent of relative error = .0096 × 100 = .96%, or 1% (approx.)

EXERCISES Copy and complete the table.

U.S. System

		Basic Size	Tolerance	Dimension Limits	% of Relative Error
A	1.	2.500″	±.125″	?	?
	2.	4.375″	±.005″	?	?
	3.	2.445″	±.002″	?	?
	4.	.828″	±.005″	?	?
	5.	1.875″	±.004″	?	?

Metric System

	Basic Size	Tolerance	Dimension Limits	% of Relative Error
6.	322 mm	±.5 mm	?	?
7.	45 mm	±.5 mm	?	?
8.	625 mm	±.3 mm	?	?
9.	83 mm	±.2 mm	?	?
10.	39 mm	±.25 mm	?	?

B 11. Draw two tables like those shown above. Complete the tables for dimensions *A*, *B*, *C*, *D*, and *E* in Figures 4-19 and 4-20.

U.S. System

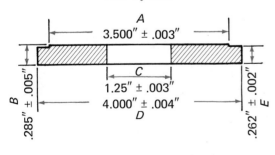

Figure 4-19

Metric System

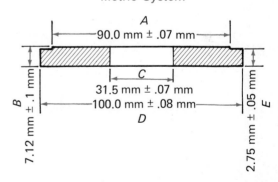

Figure 4-20

12. The cylinder bore on a certain engine is 4.062 ± .005″. Find the dimension limits, the tolerance, and the percent of relative error.

13. The specifications for an economy automobile engine show the bore as 856 mm ± .5 mm. Find the dimension limits, the tolerance, and the percent of relative error.

4-10 Electrical tolerance

Electronic resistors like the one in Figure 4-21 are used in radios and television sets to control the flow of electric current. Resistors are rated in **ohms**, the standard unit of electrical resistance.

Resistors have colored bands to indicate their ohms rating and their tolerance. Study the sample resistor and code shown below.

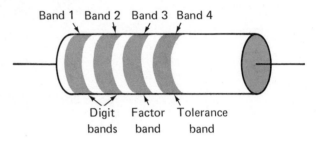

Figure 4-21

Resistor Color Code

Color	Band 1	Band 2	Band 3	Band 4
Brown(BR)	1	1	× 10	None ± 20%
Red(R)	2	2	× 100	Silver(S) ± 10%
Orange(O)	3	3	× 1000	Gold(GD) ± 5%
Yellow(Y)	4	4	× 10,000	Red(R) ± 2%
Green(GN)	5	5	× 100,000	
Blue(BL)	6	6	× 1,000,000	
Violet(V)	7	7	Grey(GR) ÷ 100	
Grey(GY)	8	8	Gold(GD) ÷ 10	
White(W)	9	9	Black(BK) ÷ 1	
Black(BK)	0	0		

EXAMPLE 1 Read the basic ohms rating of the resistor in Figure 4-22.

SOLUTION The color code is:

Figure 4-22

Band 1	Band 2	Band 3	Band 4
blue	orange	yellow	gold
6	3	× 10,000	±5%

630,000 ± 5%

The resistance is 630,000 ohms, ± 5%.

EXAMPLE 2   What is the ohms rating of the resistor in Figure 4-23?

SOLUTION   The color code is:

Figure 4-23

	Band 1 grey	Band 2 green	Band 3 gold	Band 4 silver
	8	5	÷10	±10%

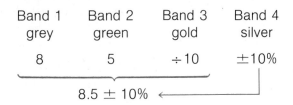

$8.5 \pm 10\%$

The resistance is 8.5 ohms, $\pm$ 10%.

EXAMPLE 3   What are the tolerance limits of the resistor in Figure 4-23?

SOLUTION   Band 4 is silver. The tolerance is $\pm$ 10% of the basic ohms rating, or .85 ohm. Thus,

$$\begin{array}{r} 8.50 \\ +\ .85 \\ \hline 9.35 \end{array} \qquad\qquad \begin{array}{r} 8.50 \\ -\ .85 \\ \hline 7.65 \end{array}$$

tolerance limits

EXERCISES   Find the basic ohms rating of the resistors. Use the color code on page 126.

A   1.   5.

2.   6.

3.   7.

4.   8.

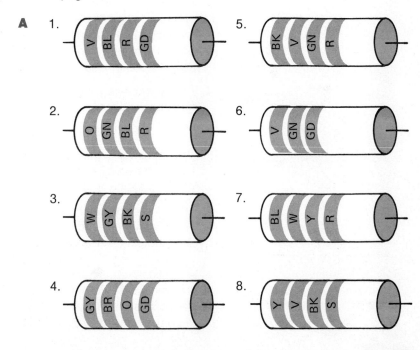

4-11 Efficiency

When power is converted from one form to another, some of the power is wasted. The efficiency of a conversion is the ratio of power produced to the power used. Efficiency is usually expressed as a percent.

EXAMPLE 1   A turbine in a hydro-electric plant converts power with efficiency rate of 60%. If the power of the water which drives the turbine is rated at 750,000 horsepower, how much electrical power is generated by the turbine?

SOLUTION   60% of 750,000 = .60 × 750,000
$$= 450,000$$

The electrical output is about 450,000 horsepower.

EXERCISES A   1. An automobile engine rated at 150 horsepower delivers only 120 horsepower to the transmission. What is the efficiency of the engine?

2. An improved, computerized welding machine which used to complete 75 pieces per day now completes 90 pieces each day. By what percent did its efficiency increase?

3. A metal machine company replaced an old lathe with a numerically controlled machine. With the old lathe, a machinist could produce 124 finished items in one day. With the new machine, production has increased to 284 items a day. What is the percent of increase in production?

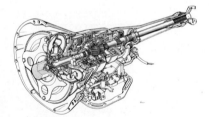

4. A torque converter behind a 222 horsepower engine loses 36 horsepower because of fluid transmission. What percent of the power is lost?

5. The input to a generator powered by a nuclear reactor is 15,000 horsepower. The efficiency of the generator is 63%. What horsepower is delivered?

6. An automobile engine develops 316 horsepower. The transmission and rear-end drive have a combined efficiency of 68%. What horsepower is delivered to the rear wheels?

B   7. A duplicating machine can make 9 copies every 15 seconds. It is replaced by a newer model which can make 48 copies per minute. How much more efficient is the newer machine in copies per minute? in efficiency percentage?

SELF-ANALYSIS TEST 13

Write the decimals as percents.

1. .35   2. .06   3. .935

Write the fractions as percents.

4. $\frac{4}{5}$ 5. $\frac{3}{8}$ 6. $\frac{11}{20}$

7. If a 15% cash discount is allowed on a $29.00 power drill, what is the net price?

8. Find the tolerance and the dimension limits of the aligning pin.

9. What is the ohms rating of the resistor?

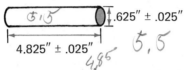

$.625'' \pm .025''$

$4.825'' \pm .025''$

10. A 200-horsepower engine loses 35% of its power due to worn rings. How much power does the engine actually produce?

TAKING INVENTORY

1. **Decimals** are fractions whose denominators are 10, or 100, or 1000, and so on. (p. 100)
2. To add or subtract decimals, write the numbers in a column with the decimal points in line. Then proceed as with whole numbers. (p. 107)
3. The number of decimal places in the product of two decimals equals the sum of the number of decimal places in the factors. (p. 109)
4. **Micrometers** are instruments used for making precise measurements. (p. 112)
5. When decimal fractions are divided, the divisor should first be changed to a whole number. (p. 118)
6. A **percent** is a decimal fraction whose denominator is understood to be 100. (p. 120)
7. A **discount** is a reduction in the marked price of an item. The discount price is called the **net price.** (p. 122)
8. **Tolerance** is the difference between the greatest and smallest acceptable dimensions or specifications. (p. 124)
9. A tolerance is usually given in specifying the size of a machined item or in specifying the ohms rating of electrical resistors. (p. 126)
10. The **efficiency** of a machine is the ratio of the power produced (output) to the power used (input). (p. 128)

MEASURING YOUR SKILLS

Write as decimals. (4-1-4-2)

1. $\frac{9}{10}$
2. $\frac{67}{100}$
3. $\frac{3}{8}$

Write as fractions. (4-1-4-2)

4. .25
5. .4
6. .65

U.S. System

Add or subtract. (4-3)

7. $\begin{array}{r} \cdot 3.72'' \\ +5.69'' \\ \hline \end{array}$

8. $\begin{array}{r} 19.637'' \\ -\ 8.298'' \\ \hline \end{array}$

9. Find the missing dimensions.

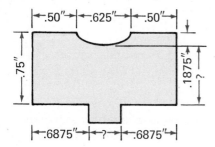

Multiply. (4-4)

10. $\begin{array}{r} 3.778'' \\ \times\ .4 \\ \hline \end{array}$

11. $\begin{array}{r} 29.73'' \\ \times\ 13.4 \\ \hline \end{array}$

12. Gold leaf has a thickness of .03''. What is the thickness of 7 sheets of gold leaf?

Read the micrometer. (4-5)

13.

Divide. Give your answers to the nearest thousandth. (4-6)

14. $3.7'' \div .58$
15. $9.12'' \div 3.9$

Metric System

Add or subtract. (4-3)

17. $\begin{array}{r} 3.217 \text{ cm} \\ +4.693 \text{ cm} \\ \hline \end{array}$

18. $\begin{array}{r} 14.09 \text{ mm} \\ -\ 6.97 \text{ mm} \\ \hline \end{array}$

19. Find the missing dimensions.

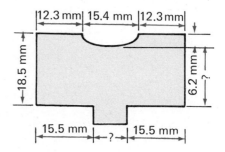

Multiply. (4-4)

20. $\begin{array}{r} 8.11 \text{ cm} \\ \times\ 1.5 \\ \hline \end{array}$

21. $\begin{array}{r} 13.45 \text{ cm} \\ \times\ 17.3 \\ \hline \end{array}$

22. A strip of copper used in making printed circuits is .4 mm thick. Find the thickness of 9 layers of this material.

Read the micrometer. (4-5)

23.

Divide. (4-6)

24. $2.1 \text{ mm} \div 5.1$
25. $13.07 \text{ mm} \div .08$

16. A punch press stamps lantern reflectors from a sheet of aluminum, as shown below. Dimension *A* shows how much is used for each piece. How many pieces can be stamped from the length indicated? (4-6)

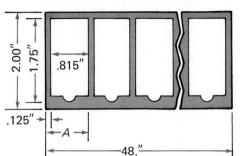

26. Solve Exercise 16, using the figure below. (4-6)

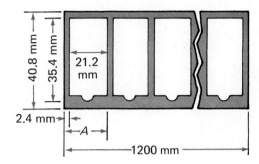

Write the percents as fractions. (4-7)

27. 16%   28. 65%   29. 113%

Write the percents as decimals. (4-7)

30. 40%   31. 25%   32. 120%

Write as percents. (4-7)

33. .6   34. 3.5   35. $\frac{4}{5}$ 36. $\frac{5}{12}$

37. An offset printing press retails for $7395. Find the net price if a 5% discount is allowed for full payment within 90 days. (4-8)

38. Find the dimension limits, tolerance, and percent of relative error. (4-9)

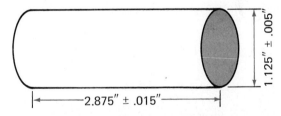

Give the ohms readings and the tolerance of the resistors. (4-10)

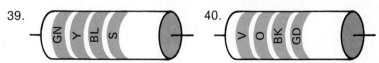

39.   40.

41. The input for an electric motor is 8000 watts. The output is 7200 watts. What is the percent of efficiency? (4-11)

RESEARCH WITH A COMPUTER

In Section 4-9 you learned about the precision of measurements. If you have access to an electronic computer that uses the BASIC "language," you can use the program below to find the precision specifications for an object. If you know the basic size and the degree of precision required, the program below will give the tolerance, the dimension limits, and the percent of relative error.

```
10 PRINT "BASIC SIZE IS";
20 INPUT D
30 PRINT "PLUS OR MINUS";
40 INPUT A, B
50 LET L=A/B
60 PRINT "TOLERANCE IS";2*L
70 PRINT "DIMENSION LIMITS ARE";D-L;" AND";D+L
80 PRINT "% OF RELATIVE ERROR IS";L/D*100;"%"
90 END
```

Compare the formulas in lines 60, 70, and 80 with the descriptions of these ideas in the text.

Note: The computer will print out "PLUS OR MINUS?" If the limit of precision is a fraction, type in the numerator, a comma, then the denominator. For example, if an object must be $5'' \pm \frac{1}{2}''$, the printout should look like:

$$\text{BASIC SIZE IS? 5}$$
$$\text{PLUS OR MINUS? 1, 2}$$

When the limit of precision is a decimal, type in the decimal, a comma, then 1. For example, for an object whose dimensions must be $3'' \pm .065''$, the printout would look like:

$$\text{BASIC SIZE IS? 3}$$
$$\text{PLUS OR MINUS? .065, 1}$$

EXERCISES   1. RUN the program above for the following measurements.

a. $3.25'' \pm \frac{1}{8}''$ d. .02 cm $\pm$ .001 cm

b. $1.5'' \pm .01''$ e. $25.5'' \pm \frac{3}{16}''$

c. 6.7 mm $\pm$ 0.2 mm   f. $2.85'' \pm .02''$

2. RUN the program, using the measurements given in Exercises 1-10 on page 125. Compare the results.

3. Which measurements has the smaller percent of error:

$60'' \pm \frac{1}{2}''$ or $1 \text{ cm} \pm 0.025 \text{ cm}$?

Frequently, specifications are given in terms of the percent of relative error. For example, the dimensions of an object may be $5.54'' \pm 10\%$. The following program, when given the basic size and the percent of relative error, will print out the tolerance, the dimension limits, and the relative error.

```
10  PRINT "BASIC SIZE IS";
20  INPUT D
30  PRINT " % OF RELATIVE ERROR IS";
40  INPUT P
50  LET L=P*D/100
60  PRINT "BASIC SIZE IS"; D;" PLUS OR MINUS"; L
70  PRINT "TOLERANCE IS";2*L
80  PRINT "DIMENSION LIMITS ARE";D−L; " AND";D+L
90  PRINT "RELATIVE ERROR IS";P/100
100 END
```

EXERCISES

4. RUN the program for each of the following basic sizes, with the percent of error as 10.

a. 5''   c. 2.15 mm   e. 10 feet

b. 7.2 m   d. 3.8 cm   f. 55.87 in.

5. Repeat Exercise 4, with the percent of error as 5.

MEASURING YOUR PROGRESS

Read the meters. (1-1-1-4)

1.

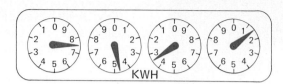

2.

Freight Shipments

Month	Tons
Jan.	34
Feb.	39
Mar.	36
Apr.	46
May	51
June	50

3. Show the information in the table at the left in a bar graph and a broken-line graph. (1-5-1-7)

4. Give the length of each line in sixteenths of an inch and in millimeters. (1-8-1-11)

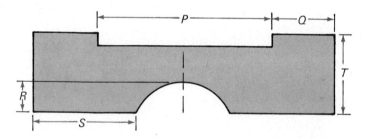

5. Copy the drawing. Measure the parts of the diagram that are not dimensioned. Show all the dimensions on your copy. (1-12-1-14)

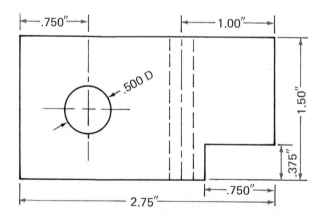

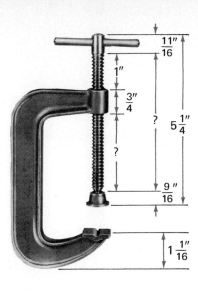

Add or subtract. (2-1–2-3)

6. $\frac{15}{32}'' - \frac{12}{32}''$ 7. $\frac{3}{8}'' + \frac{3}{16}'' + \frac{3}{32}''$ 8. $\frac{7}{16}'' - \frac{3}{8}''$

9. Find the missing dimensions on the C-clamp at the left. (2-4–2-6)

10. To fit between two fence posts, a split rail 8′ long must be shortened by $15\frac{3}{4}''$. What will be the length of the rail after sawing? (2-7–2-8)

Multiply. Cancel wherever possible. (3-1–3-4)

11. $8 \times \frac{5}{16}$ 12. $3\frac{1}{8} \times 4$ 13. $1\frac{5}{8} \times 2\frac{1}{4}$

Divide. (3-5–3-7)

14. $\frac{3}{4} \div 9$ 15. $\frac{5}{8} \div \frac{7}{16}$ 16. $\frac{1}{4} \div 1\frac{3}{16}$

Write the fractions as decimals. (4-1–4-2)

17. $\frac{3}{8}$ 18. $\frac{7}{20}$ 19. $\frac{5}{16}$

Write the decimals as fractions. (4-1–4-2)

20. .3   21. .75   22. .375

Perform the indicated operation. (4-3–4-6)

23.   3.172″
  +2.973″

24.   7.03 mm
  −1.73 mm

25.   4.273
  × .27

26. $.87\overline{)27.84}$

27. During a sale a set of high speed drills are marked down 20%. If the regular price is $9.95, how much is the sale price? (4-7–4-11)

28. What are the dimension limits and tolerance of *A* and *B*? (4-7–4-11)

A
2.437″ ± .003″

.687″ ± .005″ *B*

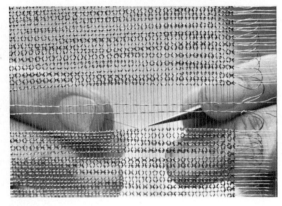

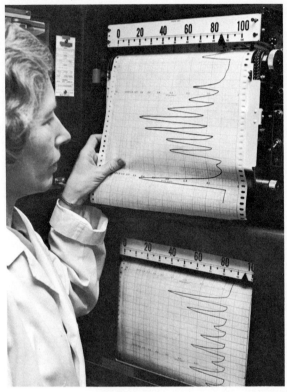

The formulas and equations stored in the memory cell of a computer allow industrial information to be analyzed quickly and accurately.

5 Equations, Formulas

After completing this chapter, you should be able to:

1. Simplify number expressions.

2. Solve equations by using addition, subtraction, multiplication, and division.

3. Use formulas to solve typical industrial problems.

Components of equations

5-1 Terms, expressions, and equations

A strip of stainless-steel molding must go around the edge of the table in Figure 5-1. To cut the strip to the correct length, we need to find the perimeter of the table top. We can show the calculation, as follows:

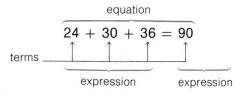

As you can see, an equation is a statement showing that two expressions are equal. An expression may consist of several terms, like 24 + 30 + 36. Or it may have just a single term, like 90.

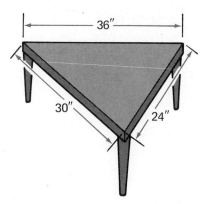

Figure 5-1

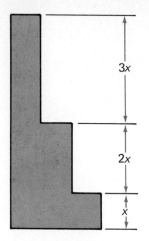

Figure 5-2

Sometimes in our work we deal with expressions that contain "unknown" terms. For example, Figure 5-2 shows the pattern for a step-block. Because step-blocks can be made in any size, we use the dimensions x, $2x$, and $3x$ to show the relative size of the steps. Thus, the steps could be 1 ft, 2 ft, and 3 ft, or 1 cm, 2 cm, and 3 cm.

The overall length of the step-block is $3x + 2x + x$. To make calculations easier, we can combine **similar terms**.

Thus,
$$\text{length} = 3x + 2x + x$$
$$= (3 + 2 + 1)\,x$$
$$= 6x$$

The overall length of the step-block would be 6 ft or 6 cm, depending on the unit of measure represented by x.

Study the following examples of combining terms.

EXAMPLE 1 Combine $6m + 3m - 2m$.

SOLUTION $6m + 3m - 2m = (6 + 3 - 2)m$
$$= 7m$$

EXAMPLE 2 Combine $l + w + l + w$.

SOLUTION $l + w + l + w = (l + l) + (w + w)$
$$= (1 + 1)l + (1 + 1)w$$
$$= 2l + 2w$$

Notice that we combine the l-terms with l-terms and the w-terms with w-terms. We cannot combine the l- and w-terms because they are not similar terms.

EXAMPLE 3 Write an expression for the length of the template.

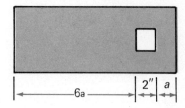

SOLUTION Length $= 6a + 2 + a$
$$= (6a + a) + 2$$
$$= (6 + 1)a + 2$$
$$= 7a + 2$$

Notice again, we can combine only the similar terms.

EXERCISES Combine the similar terms to simplify the expressions.

A
1. $4a + a$
2. $7c - 2c$
3. $3x + x$
4. $5t - 2t$
5. $x + x$
6. $3y + 2y$

7. $5m + 3m + 2m$
8. $2t - t$
9. $6s - 3s$
10. $5y + 2y + 9y$
11. $10r - 3r$
12. $2x + 2x + 2x$

B
13. $3x + 4x + 1$
14. $9y - 2y + 6$
15. $4t + 8 + 3t$
16. $2s + 2s + 5$

17. $3x + 2y + 4x + 2y$
18. $9a + 8b + 2b + 4a$
19. $5a - (3a + a)$
20. $12p - (7p + 2p)$

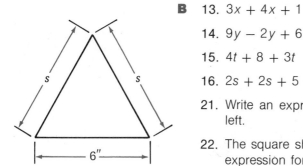

21. Write an expression for the perimeter of the triangle at the left.

22. The square shaft is milled from a round steel bar. Write an expression for the diameter of the bar.

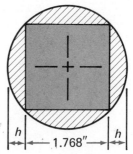

23. Write an expression for the length of the inside calipers.

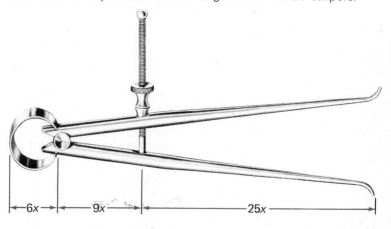

139

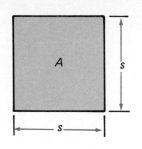

Figure 5-3

5-2 Exponents

The formula for the area of a square, as in Figure 5-3, can be written as

$$A = s \times s,$$

where s is the length of the side.

The formula for the volume of a cube, as in Figure 5-4, can be written as

$$V = e \times e \times e,$$

where e is the length of the edge.

Sometimes formulas can be written with special symbols to help simplify them. One such symbol is the *exponent*. An exponent is a small number written above and to the right of another number. It indicates how many times the number is used as a factor.

For example, $\quad 2^3 = 2 \times 2 \times 2 = 8$
or $\qquad\qquad 3^4 = 3 \times 3 \times 3 \times 3 = 81$

We can use an exponent to simplify the area and the volume formulas from above.

Thus, $\qquad\qquad A = s \times s = s^2$

and $\qquad\qquad V = e \times e \times e = e^3$

Many of the formulas which you will use in industry and the trades will contain exponents. Study these examples.

EXAMPLE 1   What is the area of a square microscope slide having a side 2.7 cm long?

SOLUTION   Area $= s^2 = (2.7)^2 = 2.7 \times 2.7 = 7.29$

The area is 7.29 sq cm.

EXAMPLE 2   Find the volume of a cube-shaped laboratory container which measures 6.3 cm along an edge.

SOLUTION   Volume $= e^3 = (6.3)^3 = 6.3 \times 6.3 \times 6.3 = 250.047$

The volume is 250 cu cm (approx.)

EXERCISES Calculate.

A
1. 3^2
2. 5^2
3. 7^2
4. 10^3
5. 8^3
6. 4^2
7. 5^3
8. 6^3
9. 4^4

B
10. $(1.2)^2$
11. $(2.3)^2$
12. $(5.6)^2$
13. $(3.9)^3$
14. $(7.9)^2$
15. $(5.4)^3$
16. $(21.7)^2$
17. $(3.04)^2$
18. $(12.6)^3$

U.S. System

19. Find the area of a square bench plate having sides $8\frac{1}{4}''$ long. Use the formula $A = s^2$.

20. Find the volume of a cube-shaped storage bin having an edge $2\frac{1}{8}'$ in length. Use the formula $V = e^3$.

21. The formula for the area of a circle is $A = 3.14\, r^2$, where r represents the radius of the circle. Find the area of a circular flower bed having a radius of $7'$.

Metric System

22. What is the area of a square pane of glass which is 22.5 cm on each side? Use the formula $A = s^2$.

23. A clear plastic cube is used to display photos. Find the volume of the cube if the edge is 12.2 cm long. Use the formula $V = e^3$.

24. The radius of a circle on a bicycle-safety test course is 14 m. Find the area of the circular region. Use the formula $A = 3.14\, r^2$.

5-3 The order of operations

During your work you may come across an expression like $(2 \times 7) + (6 \div (3 - 1))$. How would you simplify this?

To help us simplify expressions like this, we can use the steps in the flow chart in Figure 5-5.

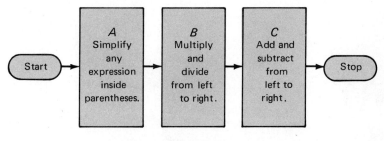

Figure 5-5

141

EXAMPLE 1 Simplify $2 \times 7 + 6 \div (3 - 1)$.

SOLUTION *Step A.* $2 \times 7 + 6 \div (\underbrace{3 - 1})$

         Step B. $\underbrace{2 \times 7} + \underbrace{6 \div 2}$

         Step C. $\underbrace{14 + 3}$

                17

EXAMPLE 2 Simplify $4 \times (9 + 2) \div 2 + 2$.

SOLUTION *Step A.* $4 \times (\underbrace{9 + 2}) \div 2 + 2$

         Step B. $\underbrace{4 \times 11} \div 2 + 2$

         Step B. $\underbrace{44 \div 2} + 2$

         Step C. $\underbrace{22 + 2}$

                24

EXERCISES Simplify each expression.

A   1. $4 \times 5 + 7$ 7. $(3 \times 15) \div 5$

       2. $18 \div 3 + 36$ 8. $(20 \div 4) \times 3$

       3. $3 + 4 \times 6$ 9. $5 \times 6 + 8$

       4. $(15 \div 3) \div 5$ 10. $25 - 3 \times 6$

       5. $21 - 6 \div 3$ 11. $8 \times 4 \div 2$

       6. $60 - 8 \div 2$ 12. $27 \div 9 + 3$

B   13. $8 \times (7 - 4) + 11$ 17. $(6 \div 2) + 1 \times 4$

     14. $(11 \times (3 + 2)) \div 5$ 18. $18 \div 9 + (3 \times 3)$

     15. $23 + (18 \div (5 + 1))$ 19. $(12 \times 2) \div 1$

     16. $12 \times 8 + (12 \times 2)$ 20. $(7 + 4 + 3) \div (2 + 1)$

C   21. $2 \times 3^2 - 5$ 22. $4^2 \div 8 + (3 \times 2)$

SELF-ANALYSIS TEST 14

Combine the terms to simplify the expression.

1. $5x + 7x - 2x$

2. $(8y - 4y) - y$

3. Write an expression for the length of the pipe wrench.

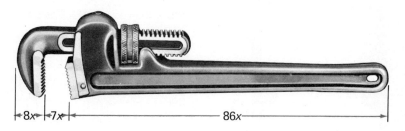

Simplify.

4. 3^4

5. $(2.5)^3$

6. $2 \times 4 + 8 \div 2$

7. $(8 \times 7) \times (3 + 2) \times \frac{1}{2}$

SPOTLIGHT ON INDUSTRY

Today there is a demand for large ships and tankers to carry raw materials and products. These ships are hard to maneuver, however. It takes two hours for a 250,000-ton tanker to reach cruising speed. Stopping a ship this size takes two to ten miles, and large spaces of open water are needed for turning. Research has produced a new rudder to solve these problems. Previously, rudders could not be turned more than 35°. Resulting choppy water conditions made it impossible to steer the ship. A new design for rudders uses rotating cylinders which control the flow of water to the back of the rudder. This has solved the choppy water problem. When the new rudder was tested on a 200-ton freighter, the ship was able to turn in place and stop in seconds. From this, engineers have figured that a 250,000-ton tanker should be able to turn in 180 yards and stop in $\frac{1}{3}$ of a mile.

EXERCISES

1. Assume it takes a 100,000-ton tanker half the distance to stop as it does a 250,000-ton tanker. How many feet would it take a 100,000-ton tanker to stop?

2. A tanker can travel 18 nautical miles per hour at cruising speed. How many hours will it take it to travel 400 nautical miles?

Solving equations

5-4 Solving equations by subtraction

Figure 5-6 shows a gasket used in sealing the rocker-arm cover to the head of an automobile engine. The length of the gasket can be stated in two ways:

A. $2 + x + 2$, or $x + 4$, represents the length.
B. The length is 17″.

The equation $x + 4 = 17$ indicates that the two quantities $x + 4$ and 17 are equal.

To solve the equation, we must find the number which x represents. We can solve this equation by using the following rule.

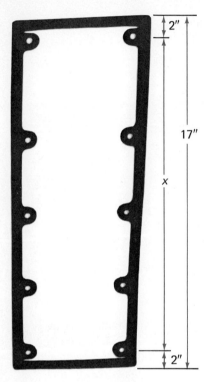

Figure 5-6

| Subtracting the same number from both sides of an equation does not change the equality of the equation. |

Thus,

$$\begin{array}{rcl} x + 4 &=& 17 \\ -4 &=& -4 \quad \text{(Subtracting 4)} \\ \hline x &=& 13 \end{array}$$

Therefore, the center portion of the gasket is 13″ long.

Study these other examples of solving equations by using subtraction.

EXAMPLE 1   Solve $a + \dfrac{4}{9} = \dfrac{2}{3}$.

SOLUTION

$$a + \frac{4}{9} = \frac{2}{3}$$

$$a + \frac{4}{9} - \frac{4}{9} = \frac{2}{3} - \frac{4}{9} \quad \left(\text{Subtracting } \frac{4}{9}\right)$$

$$a + 0 = \frac{2}{9}$$

$$a = \frac{2}{9}$$

EXAMPLE 2   A 2.7 cm hole must be enlarged to allow a cable connector to pass through. The cable is 3.6 cm in diameter. By how much must the hole be enlarged?

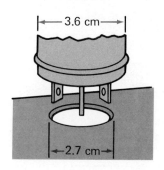

— 3.6 cm —

← 2.7 cm →

SOLUTION   Let y represent the amount that the hole must be enlarged. Then,

$$y + 2.7 = 3.6$$
$$y + 2.7 - 2.7 = 3.6 - 2.7$$
$$y - 0 = .9$$
$$y = .9$$

Therefore, the hole must be widened by .9 cm, or 9 mm.

EXERCISES   Use the subtraction rule to solve the equations.

A   1. $x + 7 = 11$ 6. $a + 37 = 198$

2. $y + 9 = 14$ 7. $b + 15 = 71$

3. $a + 11 = 20$ 8. $c + 31 = 103$

4. $b + 7 = 15$ 9. $69 + y = 311$

5. $c + 9 = 26$ 10. $84 + z = 99$

B   11. $a + \frac{1}{2} = 4\frac{3}{4}$ $A = 4\frac{3}{4}$ 16. $x + \frac{5}{6} = 3\frac{1}{6}$

12. $b + \frac{3}{8} = 2\frac{7}{8}$ $B = 2\frac{4}{8}$ 17. $y + \frac{4}{5} = 9\frac{1}{5}$

13. $c + \frac{5}{16} = 7\frac{9}{16}$ $C = 7\frac{4}{16}$ 18. $z + 1\frac{1}{4} = 8$

14. $d + .35 = 2.89$ 2.54 19. $89.01 + y = 205.44$

15. $y + 1.2 = 47.9$ 46.7 20. $z + 3.4 = 21.4$

145

For Exercises 21–28 write the equation for the unknown dimension. Then solve the equation.

| U.S. System | Metric System |

21. Find length *A* on metal plate.

22. Find length *B*.

25–26. Use the diagram below to solve Exercises 21 and 22.

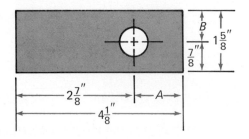
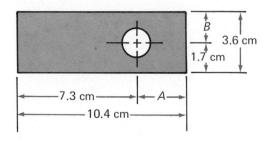

23. Find dimension *X* for spacing the knobs on the drawer.

24. Find dimension *Y*.

27–28. Use the diagram below to solve Exercises 23 and 24.

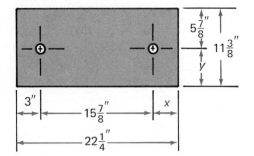
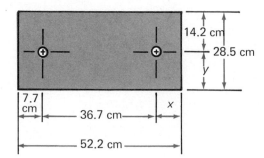

TRICKS OF THE TRADE

To multiply any number by 5, multiply half the number by 10.

$$5 \times 54 = \tfrac{54}{2} \times 10 = 27 \times 10 = 270$$

Odd numbers work the same way.

$$5 \times 23 = \tfrac{23}{2} \times 10 = 11.5 \times 10 = 115$$

An easier way to multiply odd numbers by 5 is to halve the number that is 1 less than the given number. Then affix a final digit 5 to your answer.

$$5 \times 135 \rightarrow 2)\overline{134}^{\;67} \rightarrow 675$$

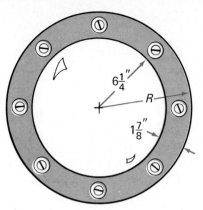

Figure 5-7

5-5 Solving equations by addition

Figure 5-7 shows the seal plate of a ship's porthole. The distance from the center of the glass to the inner seal is $6\frac{1}{4}''$. The seal plate itself is $1\frac{7}{8}''$ wide. What is the distance, R, from the center of the glass to the outer seal? What is the overall diameter of the seal plate?

We can write the following equation based on the information in Figure 5-7:

$$R - 1\frac{7}{8} = 6\frac{1}{4}$$

To find the value of R that solves this equation, we can use the following rule.

> Adding the same number to both sides of an equation does not change the equality of the equation.

Thus,

$$
\begin{aligned}
R - 1\tfrac{7}{8} &= 6\tfrac{1}{4} \\
+ 1\tfrac{7}{8} &= + 1\tfrac{7}{8} \quad \text{(Adding } 1\tfrac{7}{8}) \\
\hline
R &= 8\tfrac{1}{8}
\end{aligned}
$$

Therefore, the distance from the center of the glass to the outer seal is $8\frac{1}{8}''$. Since the diameter of a circle is twice the radius, the overall diameter of the seal plate is $2 \times 8\frac{1}{8}''$, or $16\frac{1}{4}''$.

Here is another example of an equation that is solved by using addition. Study it carefully.

EXAMPLE Solve $x - 14.3 = 17.9$.

SOLUTION
$$x - 14.3 = 17.9$$
$$\underline{x - 14.3 + 14.3} = \underline{17.9 + 14.3} \quad \text{(Adding 14.3)}$$
$$x + 0 = 32.2$$
$$x = \mathbf{32.2}$$

Do you see how adding 14.3 to each side keeps the equation "balanced"?

EXERCISES Use the addition rule to solve the equations.

A
1. $x - 6 = 20$
2. $y - 4 = 7$
3. $a - 8 = 19$
4. $b - 6 = 15$
5. $c - 11 = 15$

6. $x - 8 = 15$
7. $y - 5 = 23$
8. $z - 11 = 18$
9. $a - 21 = 32$
10. $b - 16 = 19$

B
11. $y - \frac{2}{3} = \frac{1}{3}$
12. $d - 3\frac{1}{2} = 6\frac{3}{4}$
13. $x - 9.3 = 21.7$
14. $f - 6.33 = 27.96$
15. $z - 3.5 = 7.9$

16. $z - \frac{1}{4} = 31$
17. $h - 3\frac{1}{4} = 9\frac{7}{8}$
18. $y - 2.18 = 1.78$
19. $d - .065 = 8.183$
20. $x - 1.784 = 14.693$

For Exercises 21–28 write the equation for the unknown dimension. Then solve the equation.

U.S. System

21. What is the size of a rod if .023″ must be ground off in order to have the proper thickness of 1.375″?

22. Find the original width of a piece of aluminum if, after cutting off a $\frac{3}{32}$″ strip, it is $\frac{17}{32}$″ wide.

23. A walnut panel needed for a stereo cabinet must be $22\frac{1}{2}$″. The piece is made by cutting off $1\frac{3}{4}$″ from a longer piece of stock. What is the length of the stock before cutting?

24. After milling off .19″, the thickness of a steel plate is 1.67″. What was the thickness before the milling?

Metric System

25. Find the outside diameter of a piece of plastic tubing which has an inside diameter of 4.31 cm and a thickness of .51 cm.

26. In order to have the proper length of 22.62 cm, a machinist mills a connecting rod down by .11 cm. What is its length before milling?

27. Find the outside diameter of a pipe having an inside diameter of 23.4 mm and a thickness of 4.6 mm.

28. After 1.3 cm is planed off the top, a block of wood is 6.28 cm thick. How thick was the block of wood before planing?

CREATIVE CRAFTSMAN

Construct a wooden puzzle which
   a. is in the form of a geometric shape;
   b. consists of smaller interlocking pieces; and
   c. is challenging to take apart and put together.

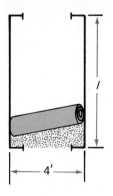

Figure 5-8

5-6 Solving equations by division

The hallway in Figure 5-8 contains 28 sq ft of floor space. An asphalt floor is to be laid in the hallway. If the flooring comes in rolls 4′ wide, how long a piece is needed for the job?

The area of a rectangle is equal to the length times the width. Thus, the area of the hall is $4 \times l$, or simply $4l$. We can show the equation as

$$4l = 28.$$

To solve an equation like this, we use the following rule.

> Dividing both sides of an equation by the same number (except zero) does not change the equality of the equation.

Using this division rule, we solve the equation in this way:

$$4l = 28$$

$$\frac{4l}{4} = \frac{28}{4} \quad \text{(Dividing by 4)}$$

$$l = 7$$

The length of flooring needed is 7′.

Do you see how the division rule allows us to find the unknown quantity? Here are other examples that use the division rule.

EXAMPLE 1   Solve $9m = 38$.

SOLUTION $9m = 38$

$$\frac{9m}{9} = \frac{38}{9} \quad \text{(Dividing by 9)}$$

$$m = \frac{38}{9}$$

$$m = 4\frac{2}{9}$$

EXAMPLE 2   Solve $.7x = .35$.

SOLUTION $.7x = .35$

$$\frac{.7x}{.7} = \frac{.35}{.7} \quad \text{(Dividing by .7)}$$

$$x = .5$$

In Examples 1 and 2 we have the product and one factor. Whenever we must find the other factor, we use the division rule.

EXERCISES   Use the division rule to solve the equation.

A   1. $6a = 24$ 6. $25w = 125$

2. $12d = 60$ 7. $14d = 42$

3. $8x = 32$ 8. $4y = 39$

4. $9y = 63$ 9. $9c = 71$

5. $4t = 44$ 10. $6n = 23$

B   11. $.6y = .54$ 15. $12y = .048$

12. $.2a = 3.8$ 16. $.07r = 5.6$

13. $.4p = 36$ 17. $6b = .18$

14. $7m = 4.9$ 18. $1.3k = .065$

For Exercises 19-26 write the equation for the unknown quantity. Then solve the equation.

U.S. System

19. The area of an appliance store showroom is 9600 square feet. If the width is 80 feet, find the length of the showroom.

20. A temporary spacer made of 3 washers on a bolt measures $1\frac{7}{32}''$ in length. How thick is each washer?

21. A standard sheet of printing paper has an area of 374 sq in. The paper measures 17'' wide. What is the length of the sheet?

Metric System

23. A rectangular airplane wing panel is 7200 sq cm in area. The width of the panel is 60 cm. What is the length?

24. Four table legs can be turned from a piece of pine 422 cm long. How long is each leg?

25. A dining room table has 3 extra leaves. The leaves extend the length of the table 43.5 cm. What is the width of each leaf?

22. To find the circumference (distance around) of a circle, we use the equation $C = \pi d$. Find the diameter d of a circular swimming pool if $C = 63.55'$. Use 3.14 for π.

26. Solve Exercise 22, using 20.5 m for C.

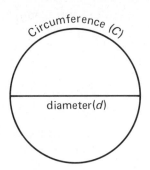

5-7 Solving equations by multiplication

The drill press in Figure 5-9 uses pulleys and pulley belts to transmit power. To vary the speed of rotation, the belt can be changed from one pulley to another.

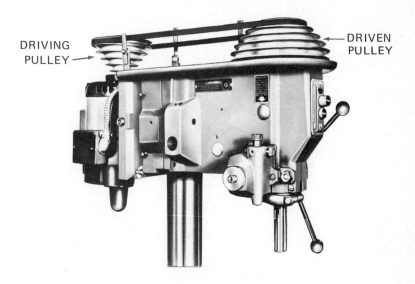

DRIVING PULLEY →

← DRIVEN PULLEY

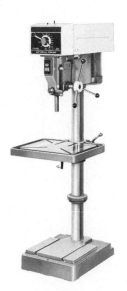

Figure 5-9

Figure 5-10 Step pulleys on a drill press provide different speeds.

The relationship between the diameters of the pulleys and the speeds of the pulleys is given as follows:

$$\frac{\text{speed of driven pulley}(s)}{\text{speed of driving pulley}(S)} = \frac{\text{dia. of driving pulley}(D)}{\text{dia. of driven pulley}(d)}$$

EXAMPLE 1   A driving pulley with a diameter of 15″ and a speed of 600 rpm is connected to a driven pulley which has a diameter of 5″. What is the speed of the driven pulley?

SOLUTION   By substituting the known values in the formula, we get

$$\frac{s}{600} = \frac{15}{5}.$$

To solve an equation like this, we can use the following rule.

> Multiplying both sides of an equation by the same number (except zero) does not change the equality of the equation.

We solve the equation in the following way:

$$\frac{s}{600} = \frac{15}{5}$$

$$\frac{s}{600} \times 600 = \frac{15}{5} \times 600 \quad \text{(Multiplying by 600)}$$

$$\frac{s}{\cancel{600}_{1}} \times \cancel{600}^{1} = \frac{\cancel{15}^{3}}{\cancel{5}_{1}} \times 600$$

$$s = 1800$$

The speed of the driven pulley is 1800 rpm.

EXAMPLE 2   Solve $\dfrac{x}{3.2} = .8$.

SOLUTION $\dfrac{x}{3.2} = .8$.

$$\frac{x}{3.2} \times 3.2 = .8 \times 3.2 \quad \text{(Multiplying by 3.2)}$$

$$x = 2.56$$

152

EXERCISES Use the multiplication rule to solve the equations.

A 1. $\dfrac{x}{5} = 6$ 5. $\dfrac{c}{17} = 9$ 9. $\dfrac{w}{7} = \dfrac{2}{3}$

2. $\dfrac{y}{7} = 3$ 6. $\dfrac{x}{12} = 8$ 10. $\dfrac{y}{7} = \dfrac{7}{8}$

3. $\dfrac{z}{3} = 12$ 7. $\dfrac{d}{5} = 14$ 11. $\dfrac{z}{3} = \dfrac{5}{8}$

4. $\dfrac{a}{15} = 11$ 8. $\dfrac{x}{3} = 18$ 12. $\dfrac{x}{2} = \dfrac{3}{16}$

13. $\dfrac{x}{1.3} = 2.6$ 15. $\dfrac{d}{1.9} = 14$ 17. $\dfrac{x}{4.3} = 0.5$

14. $\dfrac{h}{7} = 1.2$ 16. $\dfrac{y}{5} = .83$ 18. $\dfrac{h}{1.9} = \dfrac{6}{2.3}$

For Exercises 19–24 write the equation for the unknown quantity. Then solve the equation.

U.S. System

Metric System

B 19. The relationship between dimensions d and F of the hex-nut is given by the equation $d = \dfrac{F}{.866}$. If $d = .34''$, find F.

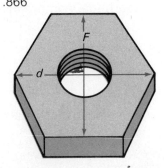

22. The relationship between F and d is the same for a metric hex-nut as for a U.S. hex-nut. This relationship is given by the formula $d = \dfrac{F}{.866}$. Find the dimension F for each of the following size metric hex-nuts:
a. $d = 5.53$ mm
b. $d = 1.2$ cm
c. $d = 1.7$ cm

20. A 6″ driving pulley is connected to a 2″ driven pulley by a V-belt. If the driving pulley turns at 450 rpm, what is the speed of the driven pulley?

21. The resistance of 250′ of electrical wire is 8.9 ohms. Find the resistance of 600′ of the wire. Use the following equation:

$$\dfrac{600}{250} = \dfrac{r}{8.9}.$$

23. A table saw blade is attached to a 9.2 cm pulley. The motor has a 12.4 cm pulley. If the motor pulley turns at 1850 rpm, what is the speed of the saw blade in rpm?

24. The resistance of 30 cm of copper wire is 1.3 ohms. What is the resistance of 160 cm of the wire? Use the following equation:

$$\dfrac{30}{160} = \dfrac{1.3}{r}.$$

5-8 Solving equations by several methods

In your work you will often need to solve equations, using several of the methods you have just studied. The flow chart in Figure 5-11 will help you organize your method of solving such equations.

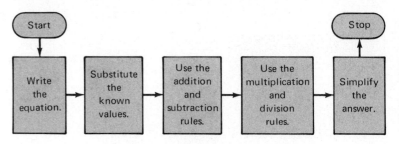

Figure 5-11

EXAMPLE 1 To get an idea of the size of a swimming pool that he wants to build, Mr. Phelps takes some rough measurements. He forms a rectangular loop on the ground with his 100' garden hose. After adjusting the length and width, he finds the best width for the pool is 18'. What will be the length?

SOLUTION The perimeter of a rectangle is given by the equation:

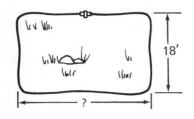

$2l + 2w = P$, where l and w are the length and width.

Since $P = 100$, and $w = 18$, we can substitute these measures in the equation. Thus,

$$2l + 2\,(18) = 100$$
$$\text{or } 2l + 36 = 100$$

To solve this equation we use the subtraction rule first, then the division rule.

$$2l + \underbrace{36 - 36}_{} = \underbrace{100 - 36}_{} \quad \text{(Subtracting 36)}$$
$$2l + 0 = 64$$

or
$$2l = 64$$

Then
$$\underbrace{\frac{2l}{2}}_{} = \underbrace{\frac{64}{2}}_{} \quad \text{(Dividing by 2)}$$
$$l = 32$$

Therefore, the pool will be 32' long.

154

EXAMPLE 2   After a 3 cm by 5 cm part has been stamped from a piece of sheet metal the scrap material, shown by shading, is thrown away. The scrap piece is 8 cm wide and contains 65 sq cm of sheet metal. What is the length of the scrap piece?

SOLUTION   The area of the scrap piece is equal to the difference in the areas of the large and small rectangles.

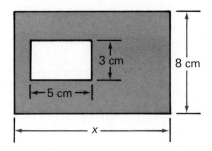

Area of the large rectangle = 8x
Area of the small rectangle = 5 × 3, or 15.

Thus, $8x - 15 = 65$.

To solve the equation, we use the addition rule first, then the division rule.

$$8x - 15 = 65$$
$$8x \underline{- 15 + 15} = \underline{65 + 15} \quad \text{(Adding 15)}$$
$$8x + 0 = 80$$

or $8x = 80$

Then $\dfrac{8x}{8} = \dfrac{80}{8}$ (Dividing by 8)

$$x = 10$$

Therefore, the length of the scrap is 10 cm.

Notice in these examples that we use the rules for solving equations in the order shown in the flow chart in Figure 5-11.

EXERCISES   Solve the equations.

A   1. $2x + 13 = 35$ 7. $3t + 7 = 25$

2. $8x + 41 = 105$ 8. $9y + 8 = 17$

3. $5x - 32 = 53$ 9. $4p - 13 = 27$

4. $9a - 48 = 6$ 10. $8y - 3 = 61$

5. $\dfrac{x}{2} + 1 = 9$ 11. $\dfrac{a}{5} - 3 = 2$

6. $\dfrac{y}{3} + 5 = 29$ 12. $\dfrac{b}{8} - 5 = 1$

155

B 13. $.3y \div 1.8 = 6.5$

14. $1.2z + 4.3 = 115.7$

15. $7y - \frac{4}{3} = \frac{5}{6}$

16. $7t - \frac{5}{8} = \frac{11}{16}$

17. $1.4x + 3 = 7$

18. $.5x - 4 = 1.3$

19. $3a + \frac{3}{4} = \frac{7}{8}$

20. $5y + \frac{1}{6} = \frac{2}{3}$

For exercises 21–28 write the equation for the unknown quantity. Then solve the equation.

U.S. System

21. The perimeter of the triangle below is 26″. The sides marked *s* are equal in length. Find *s*.

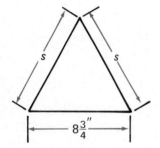

Metric System

25. The lengths of the sides of the triangle are given below. The perimeter of the triangle is 46.6 mm. Find the lengths of sides *AB* and *BC*.

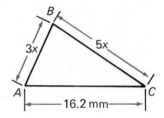

22. A square shaft is milled from a round bar, as shown in the diagram. Find the depth of the cut, *h*.

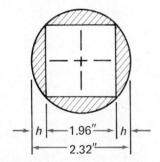

26. Solve Exercise 22, using the dimensions on the figure below.

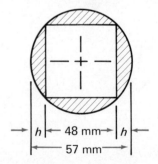

23. Find length x on the light switch plate.

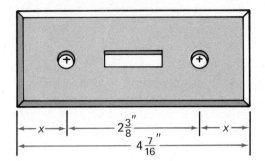

24. Find dimensions x and y on the die pattern.

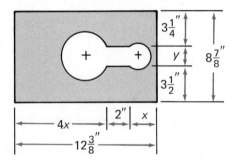

27. Solve Exercise 23, using the dimensions on the figure below.

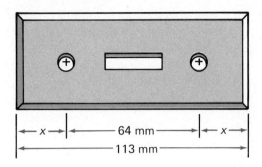

28. Solve Exercise 24, using the dimensions on the figure below.

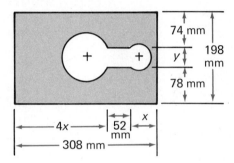

SELF-ANALYSIS TEST 15

Solve the equations.

1. $x + 3.5 = 7.5$

2. $y - 1.34 = 6.65$

3. $16x = 96$

4. $\dfrac{y}{7} = 14$ 98

5. $3x - 8 = 13$

6. $3x + 4x - 2x + 4 = 11$

7. A glazier must install a rubber seal around the frame of a 4′ × 9′3″ display window. How long a piece of sealing does he need in order to have a "continuous" seal?

157

Electronic Computer Operator

The use of computers in industry is increasing. Computers can do simple tasks rapidly and complex tasks very efficiently. Each year additional uses are made of computers and their related hardware. Perhaps the computer industry has a place for you.

Job Description

What do computer operators do?

1. They prepare the data so that it is ready to be put into the computer. This is called providing the "input."
2. They operate the computer console. This means they are responsible for getting the "input" into the computer so the computer can do its work.
3. They operate auxiliary equipment which records the results of the work done by the computer.
4. They operate switches and observe lights which signal the proper operation of all equipment.
5. They often have to locate and correct difficulties when they occur.

Qualifications

Employers usually prefer high school graduates. Some further specialized training is desirable.
Previous work experience is helpful.

Training

In many cases the operators of electronic computers were previously operators of tabulating or bookkeeping machines. Many businesses provide on-the-job instruction for those people who can demonstrate ability in logical thinking. Training sessions are often conducted by the employer or by the computer manufacturer. These sessions may last a few weeks to several months, depending on the nature of the job and the size of the computer. Most senior computer operators are taught how to trace the causes of mechanical failure.

Working Conditions

8 hour shifts each day, with late evening or night shifts
  common.
Rooms where most computer equipment is housed are
  climate-controlled.
Noise level from some computers can be annoying.

Opportunities for Advancement

As computer operators gain experience and training they may
be assigned to operate more complex equipment. Eventually
the operator may be asked to perform supervisory tasks.
Operators may acquire sufficient understanding to move on to
jobs as computer programmers.

Working with formulas

5-9 Writing formulas from rules

Many of the common relationships and processes used in industry can be stated as rules. For example, the appliance industry depends heavily on this rule:

> The power in watts used by an electrical appliance is equal to the product of the voltage and the number of amperes.

Usually an equation representing the rule will be used in performing calculations and measurements. The equation, or formula, for the rule above can be expressed this way:

$$P = V \times A,$$

where P = the power in watts,
V = the voltage in volts,

and A = the current in amperes.

We can use the following general procedure for writing formulas from rules.

---

1. Read the rule, carefully noting the words that represent quantities.
2. Select a letter to stand for the unknown value of each quantity.
3. Determine which operations are used to relate the quantities.
4. Write the letters, together with the operation signs, to make the formula agree with the rule.

EXAMPLE 1   Write a formula for this rule: The number of square centimeters is equal to 10,000 times the number of square meters.

SOLUTION   *Step 1.* The important expressions are "the number of square centimeters" and "the number of square meters."
Step 2. Let c = the number of square centimeters.
Let m = the number of square meters.
Step 3. The quantities are related by multiplication.
Step 4. The formula is $c = 10,000\ m$.

EXAMPLE 2   The number of screw threads per inch is equal to 1 divided by the pitch of the screw.

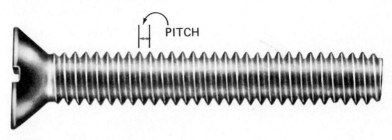

PITCH

SOLUTION   *Step 1.* The important expressions are "the number of screw threads per inch" and "the pitch of the screw."

Step 2. Let t = the number of screw threads per inch.
Let p = the pitch of the screw.

Step 3. The quantities are related by division.

Step 4. The formula is $t = 1 \div p$, or $t = \dfrac{1}{p}$.

EXERCISES   Write a formula for each rule.

A   1. The number of inches is equal to 12 times the number of feet.

2. The number of meters is equal to .01 times the number of centimeters.

3. The number of kilograms is equal to .454 times the number of pounds.

4. The net cost is equal to the marked price less the discount.

5. The area of a sheet of plywood is equal to the length times the width.

6. The number of dollars equals the number of cents divided by 100.

7. The diagonal of a square is equal to 1.414 times the side of the square.

8. To find the circumference of a circle, multiply the diameter by 3.1416.

9. The distance traveled by an automobile equals the number of hours it travels multiplied by the speed.

10. The number of tons is equal to the number of pounds divided by 2000.

Plywood sheets being manufactured.

5-10 Solving with formulas

Every field of industry uses formulas in its daily operation. You should begin now to develop skill in solving problems with formulas. The flow chart in Figure 5-12 gives a method which you can use to solve problems involving industrial formulas.

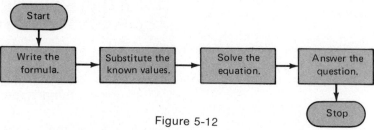

Figure 5-12

EXAMPLE 1 The number of standard bricks needed to build a wall is about 21 times the volume of the wall. How many bricks will it take to build a wall 6″ wide, 8′ high, 14′ long?

SOLUTION We can write the formula for building the wall as follows:

$$n = 21V$$

where n = the number of bricks

and V = the volume of the wall in feet.

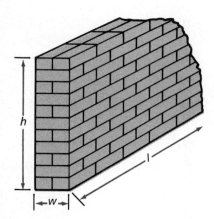

Since the wall is a rectangular solid, its volume in cubic feet can be found by multiplying the length by the width by the height. Thus we can write the formula as:

$$n = 21lwh$$

where n = the number of bricks required

l = the length of the wall in feet

w = the width of the wall in feet

and h = the height of the wall in feet

By substituting the known values in the formula, we get

$$n = 21lwh$$

$$n = 21 \times 14 \times \frac{1}{2} \times 8$$

Thus, $n = 1176$.

Therefore, about 1176 bricks are needed.

In Example 1 we solve the equation easily once we substitute the known quantities in the formula. In the following example we will need to use the multiplication and addition rules to solve the equation.

EXAMPLE 2 The depth h of a gear tooth is found by dividing the difference between the major diameter, D, and the minor diameter, d, by 2. Find the major diameter if the minor diameter is 5.25 cm and the depth of the gear tooth is .25 cm.

SOLUTION We write the formula for the relationship described above as

$$h = \frac{D - d}{2}.$$

Substituting the known values, and solving the equation is done as follows:

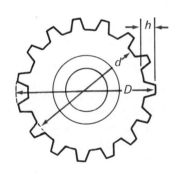

$$h = \frac{D - d}{2}$$

$$.25 = \frac{D - 5.25}{2}$$

$$.25 \times 2 = \frac{D - 5.25}{2} \times 2 \quad \text{(Multiplying by 2)}$$

$$.25 \times 2 = \frac{(D - 5.25) \times \overset{1}{\cancel{2}}}{\underset{1}{\cancel{2}}}$$

$$.50 = D - 5.25$$

$$.50 + 5.25 = D - 5.25 + 5.25 \quad \text{(Adding 5.25)}$$

$$5.75 = D + 0$$

or $\qquad D = 5.75$

Thus, the major diameter is 5.75 cm.

Do you see how the method in the flow chart (Figure 5-12) helps us plan our solutions?

163

Substitute the values into the formula.

Solve the resulting equation.

A 1. $C = 3.14d$
     a. Find C, if $d = .6$.
     b. Find d, if $C = 10.048$.

3. $d = 1.41s$
     a. Find d, if $s = 8.2$.
     b. Find s, if $d = 12.831$.

2. $F = .866D$
     a. Find F, if $D = 1.5$.
     b. Find D, if $F = 1.1258$.

4. $P = 4s$
     a. Find P, if $s = 3\frac{5}{8}$.
     b. Find s, if $P = 58\frac{3}{4}$.

5. $P = 2l + 2w$
     a. Find P, if $l = 16$ and $w = 12$.
     b. Find l, if $P = 48$ and $w = 9\frac{1}{2}$.
     c. Find w, if $P = 36.5$ and $l = 12.75$.

6. $A = \frac{1}{2}bh$
     a. Find A, if $b = 7$ and $h = 18$.
     b. Find b, if $A = 24\frac{3}{8}$ and $h = 7\frac{1}{2}$.
     c. Find h, if $A = 8.14$ and $b = 4.4$

U.S. System

B 7. Using the formula from Example 1, find the number of bricks needed to build a wall 20′ long, 8′ high, and 4″ thick.

8. How many bricks are needed for a wall 30′ long, 4′ high, and 6″ thick?

9. How many bricks are in a wall 48′4″ long, 8′ high, and 8″ thick?

10. The diagonal d of a square is related to the side s of the square by the formula $d = 1.414s$. Find the length of the diagonal of a square table whose side is 32″.

11. Find the length of the diagonal crossbeam of a square shed whose side is 9′ long.

Metric System

12. The minor diameter of a gear is 8.2 cm and the depth of the gear tooth is .35 cm. Using the formula from Example 2, find the major diameter of the gear.

13. The minor diameter of a clock gear is 15.6 cm and the depth of the gear tooth is .83 cm. Find the major diameter.

14. The minor diameter of a watch gear is 7.3 mm and the major diameter is 7.8 mm. What is the depth of the gear tooth?

15. The formula for finding the circumference C of a circle is $C = 3.1416d$, where d is the diameter of the circle. Find the circumference of a circular fish pond having a diameter of 14 m.

16. Find the diameter of a round bird bath having a circumference of 61.7 cm.

SELF-ANALYSIS TEST 16   *Start*

Write a formula for each expression.

1. The density is found by dividing the weight by the volume. $\frac{w}{v}$

2. The perimeter of a square is equal to 4 times the length of a side. $4 \times L$

Substitute the values into the formulas, and solve the equations.

3. $c = 5n$ $1, 0.048$ $5, 8.8$

    a. Find n, if $c = 120$.

    b. Find c, if $n = 8$.

4. $h = \dfrac{P}{2}$ 2.5

    a. Find h, if $P = 3.6$.

    b. Find P, if $h = \frac{7}{16}$.

5. If $y = \dfrac{x + z - w}{2}$ and $y = 1.6$, $z = 1.4$, $w = 1.0$, find x.

SPOTLIGHT ON INDUSTRY

Manufacturers are using a new process for covering surfaces: powder coating. Paint, the old solution, creates harmful fumes in the air while it is being applied. Now that industries are coming under stiffer controls for clean air, they need an alternative to paint. Powder coating a surface is done by spraying finely powdered resin which has been given an electrical charge. The surface to be coated is electrically grounded, making the resin powder stick to it. The coating is then baked in an oven to completely fuse it. Manufacturers of autos and appliances are finding powder coatings superior to paint in many ways. They cover irregular surfaces more uniformly than paint. They also produce a surface more resistant to rust. Another advantage is that surfaces do not have to be primed before they are powder coated.

EXERCISES

1. a. The door of a dishwasher is 65 cm on one side. What is the outside surface area to be painted?

    b. A certain powder coating costs $.13 per sq meter to apply. How much does it cost to paint the door of the dishwasher?

TAKING INVENTORY

1. An **equation** is a statement which indicates that two number expressions are equal. (p. 137)

2. An **exponent** is a symbol which indicates how many times a number is used as a factor. (p. 140)

3. To simplify an expression involving several operations:
   a. Do the operations inside the parentheses.
   b. Do the multiplications and divisions from left to right.
   c. Do the additions and subtractions from left to right. (p. 141)

4. The same number can be subtracted from or added to both sides of an equation without changing the equality of the equation. (pp. 144, 147)

5. Both sides of an equation may be divided by or multiplied by the same number (except zero) without changing the equality of the equation. (pp. 149, 152)

6. A **formula** is an equation which uses symbols to represent a relationship between numbers. (p. 160)

MEASURING YOUR SKILLS

Simplify the expressions. (5-1)

1. $7a + 9a + 4a$

2. $6b - 2b$

Calculate. (5-2)

3. 3^4

4. $\left(\frac{1}{2}\right)^2$

5. $(1.7)^3$ 4,913

Simplify the expression. (5-3)

6. $17 + 5 \times (6 - 2)$

7. $(27 - 3) + (5 - 1)$ 24 + 4 = 28

Solve the equations. (5-4–5-8)

8. $x + 8 = 23$

9. $t + 15 = 17$

10. $9y = \frac{3}{5}$

11. $\frac{y}{8} = \frac{3}{16}$

12. $a - 8 = 13$

13. $b - 1.5 = 4.3$

14. $5x = 3.5$

15. $\dfrac{m}{9} = 6$

16. $6y - 8 = 28$

17. $\dfrac{a}{3} + .04 = .85$

Write a formula for the statements. (5-9)

18. The amount of work done is equal to the product of the force and the distance.

19. The area of a triangle is equal to half the product of the base and the height.

Use the formulas to find the unknown values.

U.S. System

20. The volume of a rectangular container: $V = l \times w \times h$. Use $V = 36$ cu in., $l = 6$ in., $w = 2$ in. to find the value of h.

21. Find the depth of the screw thread, using the formula $H = \dfrac{P}{2} + .01$.

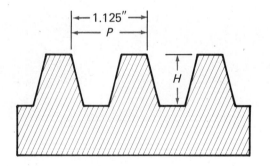

Metric System

22. The volume of a cylindrical container: $V = 3.14r^2h$. Use $r = 3.6$ cm, $h = 7.2$ cm to find the value of V.

23. Find the speed of the driven pulley, using the formula $\dfrac{s}{S} = \dfrac{D}{d}$.

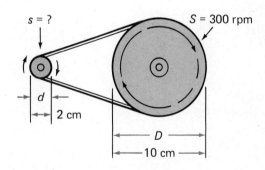

The food industry uses the latest processing and packaging methods to provide ready supplies of convenience foods.

CHAPTER 6 · *Length, Area, Volume*

After completing this chapter, you should be able to:

1. *Find the perimeters of rectangles and the circumferences of circles.*
2. *Find the area of parallelograms, triangles, trapezoids, and circles.*
3. *Find the surface area of cylinders, cones, and spheres.*
4. *Find the volume of rectangular solids, cylinders, cones, pyramids, and spheres.*

Linear measure

6-1 Perimeter of a rectangle or square

The perimeter of any figure is the distance around the figure. You can find the perimeter of any shape by adding the lengths of the sides.

Figure 6-1 shows a rectangle having a length of 4 cm and a width of 3 cm. Because we have two pairs of sides having the same measure we can take the sum of double the length and double the width. So the formula for the perimeter of a rectangle having a length, l, and a width, w, is

$$P = 2l + 2w.$$

For a square having a side, s, we can find the perimeter by this formula:

$$P = 4s$$

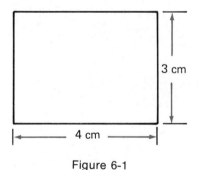

Figure 6-1

3 cm

4 cm

EXAMPLE 1 Find the perimeter of the triangle shown.

SOLUTION 25 + 28 + 22 = 75

The perimeter is 75 mm.

EXAMPLE 2 Find the perimeter of a rectangle having a length of 7 ft and a width of 54 in.

SOLUTION We must convert all the dimensions to the same unit.

$$54 \text{ in.} = \tfrac{54}{12} \text{ ft} = 4\tfrac{1}{2} \text{ ft}$$

$$\begin{aligned} P &= 2l + 2w \\ &= (2 \times 7) + (2 \times 4\tfrac{1}{2}) \\ &= 14 + 9 \\ &= 23 \text{ ft} \end{aligned}$$

EXERCISES

U.S. System

A 1. Find the perimeter of a triangle with sides 3″, 6″, and 5″.

2. Find the perimeter of the figure below.

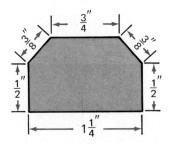

3. Find the perimeter of a rectangle with a length of 5 ft and a width of 39 in.

4. Find the perimeter of a square having sides of 54 in.

5. Find the perimeter of a rectangle having a length of 4 ft 6 in. and a width of 27 in.

Metric System

8. Find the perimeter of a triangle with sides 12 mm, 18 mm, and 21 mm.

9. Find the perimeter of the figure below.

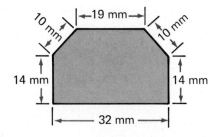

10. Find the perimeter of a rectangle with a length of 230 mm and a width of 560 mm.

11. Find the perimeter of a square having sides of 95 mm.

12. Find the perimeter of a rectangle having a length of 562 mm and a width of 385 mm.

B 6. A room has the shape and dimensions shown below. How much floor molding would be needed for the room?

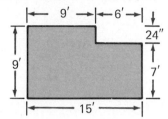

7. The figure below shows the shape of a parking lot. How much fencing is needed to enclose it?

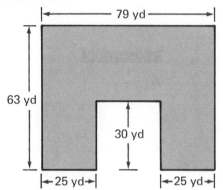

13. A room has the shape and dimensions shown below. How much floor molding would be needed for the room?

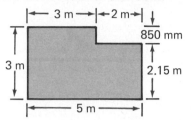

14. The figure below shows the shape of a parking lot. How much fencing is needed to enclose it?

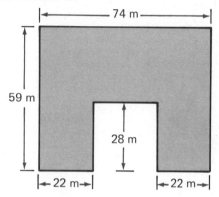

6-2 Circumference

Many parts of machines and tools are circular. Wheels, rings, and pulleys are examples of some of the many circular objects commonly used in industry and the trades. It is important to know the relationships among the measurements of a circle.

Figure 6-2 represents a circular table. Suppose we want to know how much metal edging is needed to put around the table. We are finding the **circumference** of the circle, or the distance around it. We know the **diameter** is 340 mm. So we can use the formula:

$$C = \pi d$$

where

C represents the circumference

d represents the diameter

π is approximately 3.14

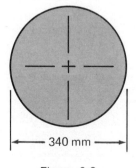

Figure 6-2

171

We can find the amount of edging needed for the circular table in Figure 6-2 as follows

$$C = \pi d$$
$$= 3.14 \times 340$$
$$C = 1067.60 \text{ mm}$$

We should buy 1.068 m of edging.

EXAMPLE 1 Find the circumference of a circle having a diameter of 11 inches.

SOLUTION $C = \pi d$
$$= 3.14 \times 11$$
$$C = 34.54 \text{ in.}$$

The circumference can only be as precise as the diameter. So to the nearest inch, $C = 35$ in.

EXERCISES

U.S. System

A Find the circumference of a circle having the given diameter.

1. $d = 5$ in.

2. $d = 17$ ft

3. $d = 36$ yd

4. $d = 4\frac{3}{8}$ in.

5. $d = 7.22$ in.

B 6. How much edging would it take for the table represented below.

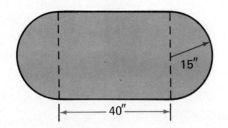

Metric System

Find the circumference of a circle having the given diameter.

10. $d = 5$ cm

11. $d = 1.3$ m

12. $d = 42$ mm

13. $d = 44.3$ m

14. $d = 5.42$ m

15. How much metal edging would it take for the table represented below.

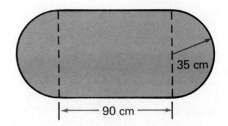

7. Find the circumference of pulley A in Figure 6-3.

8. Find the circumference of pulley B in Figure 6-3.

9. The length of belt needed for the pulleys in Figure 6-3 is found by the formula:

$$L = \tfrac{1}{2}C_A + \tfrac{1}{2}C_B + 2l$$

where C_A = circumference of pulley A
C_B = circumference of pulley B
l = distance between the centers of the pulleys
L = length of the belt

Find L for the pulleys in Figure 6-3.

16. Find the circumference of pulley A in Figure 6-4.

17. Find the circumference of pulley B in Figure 6-4.

18. The length of belt needed for the pulleys in Figure 6-4 is found by the formula:

$$L = \tfrac{1}{2}C_A + \tfrac{1}{2}C_B + 2l$$

where C_A = circumference of pulley A
C_B = circumference of pulley B
l = distance between the centers of the pulleys
L = length of the belt

Find L for the pulleys in Figure 6-4.

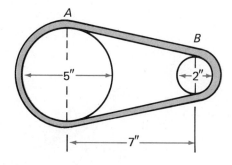

Figure 6-3

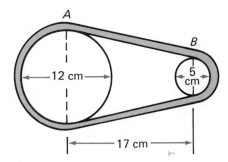

Figure 6-4

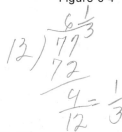

SELF-ANALYSIS TEST 17

U.S. System

1. Find the perimeter of a rectangle having a length of $4\tfrac{1}{2}$ in. and a width of $3\tfrac{1}{2}$ in.

2. Find the perimeter of a square having sides of 44 in.

3. Find the circumference of a circle having a diameter of 12 in.

Metric System

4. Find the perimeter of a rectangle having a length of 38 mm and a width of 19 mm.

5. Find the perimeter of a square having sides of 1.4 m.

6. Find the circumference of a circle whose diameter is 35 mm.

TOOLING UP FOR PRODUCTION

A Universal Domed Structure

The picture below shows an unusual cake-dish cover based on the same design as a domed building containing no interior supports. It is constructed from fifteen equilateral triangles. The base is a regular pentagon. This highly versatile structure can be built to any size. For example, this domed structure can be modified to make a futuristic lamp shade, a portable green house, a bird cage, or even a water- and bug-proof gazebo.

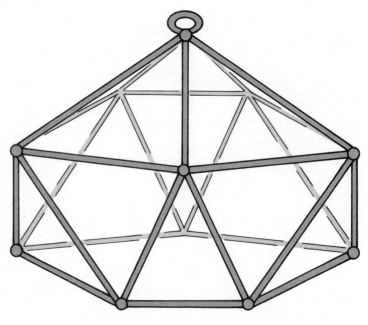

Figure 1

Tools

Hack saw
Fine-toothed hand saw or power saw
Brazing torch

Protractor
Straightedge

Materials

Quantity	Description	Cost
9	18″ brass rods, $\frac{1}{8}$″ diameter (Coat hanger wire may also be used.)	
$\frac{1}{2}$	$\frac{1}{16}$″ vinyl sheet, 21″ × 51″	
1	epoxy resin and hardener kit	
2 ft	silver solder and flux	
1	20″ piece of 2″ × 2″ scrap lumber	
4	3″ nails	

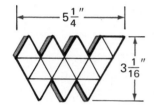

Figure 2

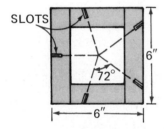

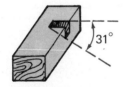

Figure 3

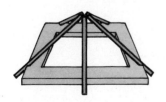

Figure 4

Production Plan

1. Make a pattern out of stiff paper, as shown in Figure 2. Cut the pattern out and fold it to form a model of the domed structure. Use this as a guide to the following construction.
2. Build a jig out of scrap lumber to hold the brass rods for brazing, as shown in Figure 3. To make the slots, drill holes at the given angles, then saw down to the holes.
3. Cut the brass rods into 6″ lengths.
4. Put five 6″ brass rods in the brazing jig so that their ends butt together, as shown in Figure 4. Braze the joint. Do this twice to form two five-pointed "stars."
5. Put the two "stars" in the jig together with three 6″ rods, using your model as a guide for placement. Braze this joint.
6. Continue in this manner until 25 rods are assembled to form the dome. The last five joints will have only four rods being joined.
7. Bend the remaining rod and braze it to the dome as a handle, as shown in Figure 1.
8. Carefully measure the inside dimensions of one triangle in the dome. Cut a piece of plastic to fit inside the brass and epoxy it in place.
9. Continue until all 15 triangles have been installed.

Modifying the Design

1. Suppose you planned to build a screen-enclosed shelter with a wooden frame. If the wooden members (the sides of the triangles) are 6′ long, how many square feet of screen do you need?
2. Can you design a five-sided brazing jig to hold the rods for brazing?

Square measure

6-3 Area of parallelograms

A parallelogram is any four-sided, closed figure with opposite pairs of sides parallel. Can you see that the rectangle and square shown in Figure 6-5 are parallelograms?

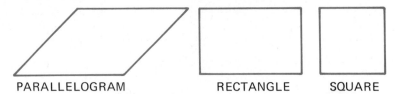

PARALLELOGRAM   RECTANGLE   SQUARE

Figure 6-5

A rectangle is a parallelogram with four right angles. A square is a rectangle having four sides the same length.

The area, or space inside, the rectangle in Figure 6-6 is 12 units, each a square. We always use square units to measure area.

Figure 6-6

To find the area of the parallelogram shown in Figure 6-7, imagine that you cut off the triangular region *DAF* and paste it over the triangular region *CBE*. Can you see that the area of parallelogram *ABCD* is 5 × 3, or 15 square units? The distance *AF* is called the height of the parallelogram, and is perpendicular to the base, *AB*.

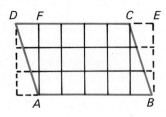

Figure 6-7

So to find the area of any parallelogram we can use the formula,

$$A = bh$$

for a rectangle, the area formula is usually written,

$$A = lw$$

and for the area of a square, we have the formula:

$$A = s \times s$$
$$A = s^2$$

176

EXAMPLE Find the area of a rectangle having a length of 14.3 cm and a width of 6.1 cm.

SOLUTION a. 14.3

b. 6.1

(70.4

c. 14.3 × 6.1 = 87.23

d. 87.23 square centimeters

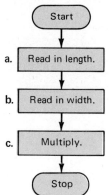

Start

a. Read in length.

b. Read in width.

c. Multiply.

Stop

EXERCISES

U.S. System

A Copy and complete the table. Find the area of a rectangle with length and width given.

	length	width	Area
1.	18 ft	8 ft	3/?2
2.	27 yd	16 yd	?
3.	6 ft	42 in.	?
4.	$3\frac{1}{8}$ in.	$2\frac{7}{8}$ in.	?

Find the area of a square with the sides given.

5. $s = 16$ ft   6. $s = \frac{3}{4}$ in.

Copy and complete the table. Find the area of a parallelogram with base and height given.

	base	height	Area
7.	9 ft	3 ft	?
8.	$5\frac{1}{2}$ in.	4 in.	?
9.	14.2 ft	6.7 ft	253.4

B 10. A rectangular driveway measures 51 yd by 4 yd. How much would it cost to blacktop the driveway at $7.28 per square yard?

Metric System

Copy and complete the table. Find the area of a rectangle with length and width given.

	length	width	Area
11.	16 m 216	9 m	?
12.	36 m	24 m	?
13.	5 cm	1.4 cm	?
14.	3.4 m	6.72 m	?

Find the area of a square with the sides given.

15. $s = 15$ cm   16. $s = 12.3$ m

Copy and complete the table. Find the area of a parallelogram with base and height given.

	base	height	Area
17.	14 cm	9 cm	?
18.	16.3 cm	5.6 cm	?
19.	12.3 m	4.12 m	?

20. A rectangular driveway measures 54 m by 4 m. How much would it cost to blacktop the driveway at $7.28 per square meter?

177

6-4 Area of triangles and trapezoids

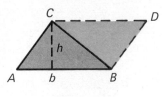

Figure 6-8

The area of a **triangle** is related to the area of a parallelogram. Figure 6-8 shows triangle *ABC* having a **base (*b*)** and a **height (*h*)** perpendicular to the base. Does the gray region appear to be the same size and shape as the red region? Together, the red and gray region make up parallelogram *ABCD*. So the area of triangle *ABC* is $\frac{1}{2}$ of the area of *ABCD*.

So we have the formula for the area of a triangle:

$$A = \tfrac{1}{2}bh$$

EXAMPLE 1 Find the area of a triangle having a base of 14 cm and a height of 8 cm.

SOLUTION
a. 14

b. $\frac{1}{2} \times 14 = 7$

c. 8

d. $8 \times 7 = 56$

e. 56 sq cm

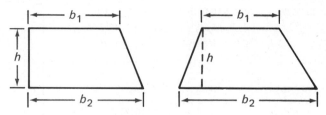

A **trapezoid** is a four-sided figure having exactly one pair of parallel sides. Two different trapezoids are shown in Figure 6-9. All trapezoids have two different length bases. We refer to them as b_1 and b_2.

Figure 6-9

The area of a trapezoid can be found by using the formula:

$$A = \tfrac{1}{2}h(b_1 + b_2)$$

EXAMPLE 2 Find the area of a trapezoid having bases of 14 cm and 18 cm and a height of 6 cm.

SOLUTION   **a.** 6

b. $\frac{1}{2} \times 6 = 3$

c. 14

d. 18

e. 14 + 18 = 32

f. 32 × 3 = 96

g. 96 sq cm

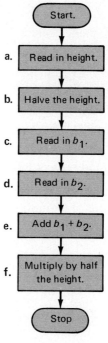

EXERCISES

U.S. System

Find the area of a triangle having the height and base given.

1. $b = 14$ in., $h = 10$ in.

2. $b = 7\frac{1}{2}$ in., $h = 5$ in.

3. $b = 120$ ft, $h = 80$ ft

4. $b = \frac{5}{8}$ in., $h = \frac{3}{4}$ in.

Copy and complete the table. Find the area of a trapezoid with the bases and height given.

	b_1	b_2	h	A
5.	12 in.	16 in.	10 in.	?
6.	5 in.	3 in.	$7\frac{1}{2}$ in.	?
7.	120 ft	110 ft	80 ft	?
8.	$\frac{3}{4}$ in.	1 in.	$\frac{5}{8}$ in.	?

Metric System

Find the area of a triangle having the height and base given.

11. $b = 14$ cm, $h = 10$ cm

12. $b = 165$ mm, $h = 85$ mm

13. $b = 1.2$ m, $h = .5$ m

14. $b = 110$ cm, $h = 50$ cm

Copy and complete the table. Find the area of a trapezoid with the bases and height given.

	b_1	b_2	h	A
15.	16 cm	12 cm	5 cm	?
16.	180 mm	240 mm	80 mm	?
17.	1.2 m	.5 m	.25 m	?
18.	2.32 cm	2.82 cm	1.6 cm	?

179

B **9.** A trapezoidal table top has bases of 30 in. and 60 in. The height is $25\frac{1}{2}$ in.

  a. How many square inches of vinyl are needed to cover the table top?

  b. If the vinyl is cut from a rectangular piece which is 30 in. by 60 in., how much vinyl is wasted?

C **10.** A metal plate is made using the dimensions in the figure below.

  a. Find the area of the trapezoid.

  b. Find the area of the rectangle which is cut out of the trapezoid.

  c. Find the area of the plate.

19. A trapezoidal table top has bases of 75 cm and 150 cm. The height is 67.5 cm.

  a. How many square centimeters of vinyl are needed to cover the table top?

  b. If the vinyl is cut from a rectangular piece which is 75 cm by 150 cm, how much vinyl is wasted?

20. A metal plate is made using the dimensions in the figure below.

  a. Find the area of the trapezoid.

  b. Find the area of the rectangle which is cut out of the trapezoid.

  c. Find the area of the plate.

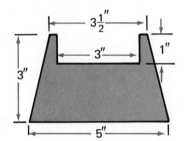

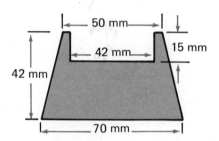

RESEARCH PROJECT

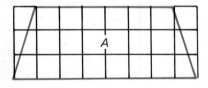

Use grid paper to draw a trapezoid A having bases of 8 units and 6 units and a height of 3 units as shown. Draw another identical trapezoid B on grid paper. Cut out B and place it upside down next to A so that you have a parallelogram. What is the area of the parallelogram you have formed? How does the area of each trapezoid compare to the area of the parallelogram?

The formula for the area of a trapezoid may be written:

$$A = \frac{h \times (b_1 + b_2)}{2}$$

Do the results of your project help you see where this formula comes from?

6-5 Areas of special regions

Sometimes we use more than one formula to find the area of a region.

For example to find the area of the sheet metal plate shown in Figure 6-10, we find the area of the large rectangle and then subtract from it the area of the square.

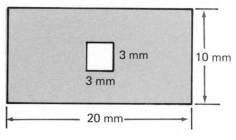

Figure 6-10

Area of rectangle = 20 × 10 = 200
Area of square = 3 × 3 = 9
Area of plate = Area of rectangle − Area of square
= 200 − 9
= 191 sq mm

Sometimes we add to find the area of a region. Study the example below.

EXAMPLE 1   Find the area of the L-shaped patio shown at the right.

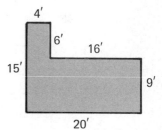

SOLUTION   We can divide the region into 2 rectangles, and then combine the two areas.

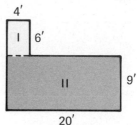

Area of I = 4 × 6
= 24 sq ft

Area of II = 9 × 20
= 180 sq ft

Total area = 24 + 180
= 204 sq ft

EXAMPLE 2   Find the area of the cross section of the I-beam shown at the right.

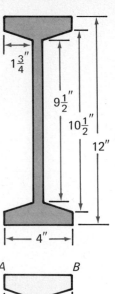

SOLUTION   We can draw a rectangle that encloses the region. Then we can find the area of the 2 trapezoids and subtract them.

Area of $ABCD = 4 \times 12$
$$= 48$$

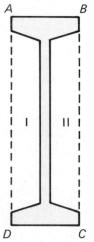

Area of I $= \frac{1}{2}h(b_1 + b_2)$
$$= \frac{1}{2} \times 1\frac{3}{4}(9\frac{1}{2} + 10\frac{1}{2})$$
$$= \frac{1}{2} \times \frac{7}{4} \times \frac{20}{1}$$
$$= \frac{7 \times 5}{2}$$
$$= 17\frac{1}{2} \text{ sq in.}$$

Area of II $= 17\frac{1}{2}$ sq in.

Area of beam $= 48 - (17\frac{1}{2} + 17\frac{1}{2})$
$$= 48 - 35$$
$$= 13 \text{ sq in.}$$

EXERCISES

U.S. System

A 1. Find the area of the L-shaped patio shown in Figure 6-11.

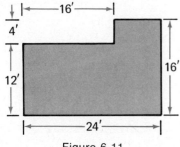

Figure 6-11

Metric System

6. Find the area of the L-shaped patio shown in Figure 6-12.

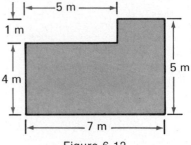

Figure 6-12

2. Find the area of the cross section of the concrete wall and footing shown below.

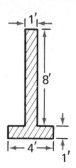

3. Find the area of the side of the building shown in the figure below.

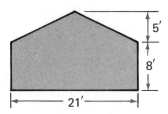

4. Find the area of the template shown in the figure below.

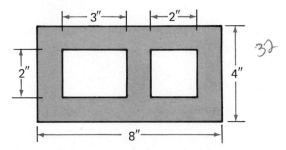

B 5. Find the area of the cross section of the concrete highway support shown in the figure below.

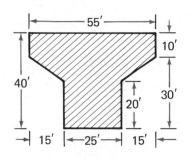

7. Find the area of the cross section of the concrete wall and footing shown below.

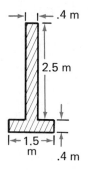

8. Find the area of the side of the building shown in the figure below.

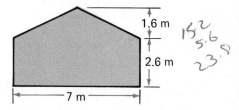

9. Find the area of the template shown in the figure below.

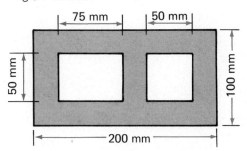

10. Find the area of the cross section of the concrete highway support shown in the figure below.

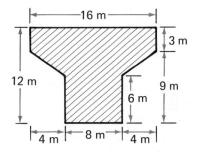

183

6-6 Areas of circles

Recall from section 6-2 that to find the circumference of a circle, we needed to use the number π, which is approximately equal to 3.14.

To find the area of a circle we also need to use this famous Greek number. The formula for the area of a circle is:

$$A = \pi \times r \times r \text{ or } A = \pi r^2$$

Remember that r^2 means to multiply the radius times itself, not times 2.

EXAMPLE 1   Find the area of the circle shown.

SOLUTION   The radius is 6 cm.

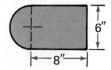

$A = \pi r^2$

$A = 3.14 \times 6 \times 6$
    $= 3.14 \times 36$

$A = 113$ (approx.)

The area is about 113 sq cm.

EXAMPLE 2   Find the area of the region shown.

SOLUTION   The region is composed of a rectangle and a semicircle (half of a circle). First we find the area of the rectangle.

$A = lw$

$A = 8 \times 6 = 48$ sq in.

Now we find the area of the semicircle. To do this we find half the area of a circle whose radius is 3″. (Note that 6″ shown in the diagram is the diameter, not the radius.)

$A = \pi r^2$
    $= 3.14 \times 3 \times 3$

$A = 28.26$ sq in.

Now to find the area of the semicircle, divide 28.26 by 2.
$28.26 \div 2 = 14.13$ sq in.

Now we add the area of the rectangle to the semicircle.
$14.13 + 48 = 62.13$
The area of the region is about 62 sq in.

EXERCISES

U.S. System	Metric System

A Find the area of a circle having the radius given.

Find the area of a circle having the radius given.

1. 5 in.

2. 8 ft

3. 15 yd

4. 7.3 in.

5. $4\frac{1}{2}$ in.

6. .25 in.

10. 6 mm

11. 100 mm

12. 1.3 m

13. 3.7 cm

14. 35 mm

15. 1.02 m

B 7. Find the area of the top of a circular tank having a diameter of 12 ft.

16. Find the area of a camera lens having a diameter of 50 mm.

8. Find the area of the metal blank shown below.

17. Find the area of the metal blank shown below.

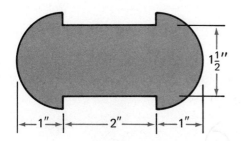

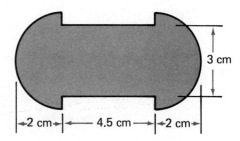

C 9. A cross section of a pipe is shown below. Find the area as follows:
a. Find the area of the outer circle.
b. Find the area of the inner circle and subtract it.

18. A cross section of a pipe is shown below. Find the area as follows:
a. Find the area of the outer circle.
b. Find the area of the inner circle and subtract it.

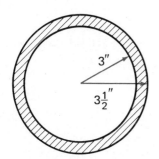

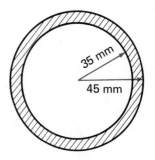

6-7 Areas of cylinders, spheres, and cones

Suppose we need to know the area of metal used to make the pipes shown in Figure 6-13. Each pipe has the shape of an open-ended cylinder.

Figure 6-13

When we find the area of the metal used for the pipes we are finding the lateral area of a cylinder.

The formula for the lateral area, (L), of a cylinder is

$$L = 2\pi rh$$

So if a pipe is 6 feet long and has a radius of 6 inches we can find the area of metal used as follows:

$$L = 2\pi rh$$
$$= 2 \times 3.14 \times \tfrac{1}{2} \times 6 \text{ (changing 6'' to } \tfrac{1}{2}')$$
$$L = 18.84 \text{ sq ft}$$

Sometimes we may wish to find the total surface area of a cylinder. To the lateral area, we must add the area of the two bases, which are circular. So the formula for the total surface area, (S) of a cylinder is the following:

$$S = \text{Lateral area} + 2 \times (\text{area of one base})$$
$$S = 2\pi rh + 2\pi r^2$$

EXAMPLE 1 Find the total surface area of a cylindrical can having a radius of 3 cm and a height of 8 cm.

SOLUTION $S = 2\pi rh + 2\pi r^2$
$$= (2 \times 3.14 \times 3 \times 8) + (2 \times 3.14 \times 3 \times 3)$$
$$= 150.72 + 56.52$$
$$S = 207.24 \text{ sq cm}$$

The figure at left shows a labeled cylinder with height h, radius r, LATERAL AREA, and BASE. CYLINDER

186

To find the area of the spherical fuel tanks shown in Figure 6-14 we use the formula for the **surface area of a sphere**:

$$S = 4\pi r^2$$

EXAMPLE 2 Find the area of the spherical fuel tank if it has a radius of 10 meters.

SOLUTION $S = 4\pi r^2$
$= 4 \times 3.14 \times 10 \times 10$
$S = 1256$ square meters

Figure 6-14

Sometimes we want to calculate the surface area of a **cone**. For example the funnel at the bottom of the exhaust collector shown in Figure 6-15 has the shape of a cone.

The **lateral area, (L),** of a cone can be found by using the formula: $L = \pi rs$

where r = the radius of the base
s = the slant height.

To find the **total surface area, (S),** of a cone we add the area of the base to the lateral area.

$$S = \pi r^2 + \pi rs$$

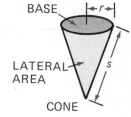

Figure 6-15

EXAMPLE 3 Find the surface area of a cone having a radius of 5 cm and a slant height of 8 cm.

SOLUTION $S = \pi r^2 + \pi rs$
$= (3.14 \times 5 \times 5) + (3.14 \times 5 \times 8)$
$= 78.50 + 125.60$
$S = 204.10$ sq cm

CREATIVE CRAFTSMAN

Design and build an all-wood device that
  a. consists of at least 3 different geometric shapes;
  b. is exciting to watch; and
  c. makes noise by the travel of a coin.

EXERCISES

U.S. System

A Find the total surface area of a cylinder with the radius and height given.

1. $r = 5$ in., $h = 10$ in.

2. $r = 8$ in., $h = 12$ in.

3. $r = 1\frac{1}{2}$ in., $h = 3$ in.

4. $r = 3.4$ in., $h = 1.1$ in.

Find the surface area of a sphere with the radius given.

5. $r = 4$ in.   6. $r = 6$ ft

Find the surface area of a cone with the radius and slant height given.

7. $r = 2$ in., $s = 5$ in.

8. $r = 10$ ft, $s = 12$ ft

9. $r = 80$ yd, $s = 150$ yd

B 10. How many square inches of sheet metal are needed to make the can shown?

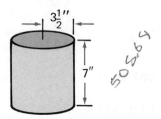

11. How many square inches of metal are needed to make a cone-shaped funnel like the one shown?

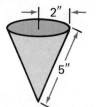

C 12. A spherical gas tank has a diameter of 20 ft. How many gallons of paint would it take to paint the tank if one gallon covers 200 sq ft?

Metric System

Find the total surface area of a cylinder with the radius and height given.

13. $r = 6$ cm, $h = 10$ cm

14. $r = 10$ mm, $h = 25$ mm

15. $r = 1.1$ m, $h = .5$ m

16. $r = 40$ mm, $h = 80$ mm

Find the surface area of a sphere with the radius given.

17. $r = 5$ cm   18. $r = 40$ mm

Find the surface area of a cone with the radius and slant height given.

19. $r = 50$ mm, $s = 80$ mm

20. $r = 9$ m, $s = 14$ m

21. $r = 3.5$ m, $s = 6$ m

22. How many square millimeters of sheet metal are needed to make the can shown?

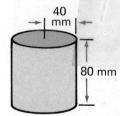

23. How many square millimeters of metal are needed to make a cone-shaped funnel like the one shown.

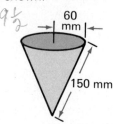

24. A spherical gas tank has a diameter of 6 m. How many cans of paint would it take to paint the tank if one can covers 18 sq m?

188

SELF-ANALYSIS TEST 18

U.S. System

1. Find the area of a parallelogram with a base of 9 in. and a height of $5\frac{1}{2}$ in. $42\frac{1}{2}$ "

2. Find the area of a trapezoid having bases of 12 in. and 18 in. and a height of 4 in.

3. Find the area of the region shown.

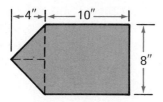

4. Find the area of a circle having a radius of 12 ft.

5. Find the surface area of the cylinder shown.

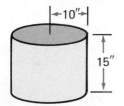

Metric System

6. Find the area of a rectangle with a length of 90 mm and a width of 25 mm.

7. Find the area of a triangle having a base of 40.2 cm and a height of 35.4 cm.

8. Find the area of the region shaded.

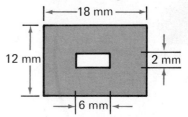

9. Find the area of a circle having a radius of 120 mm.

10. Find the surface area of the cone shown.

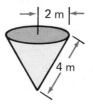

SPOTLIGHT ON INDUSTRY

A new process called extrusion has been discovered to produce very long metal parts. Hot metal is forced into a die like squeezing toothpaste from a tube. Steel, aluminum, and other metals are being formed by this process. Automobile bumpers, seats for sports stadiums, and frames for doors and windows are all being made by extrusion. Many parts which used to require assembling can now be made in one piece by extrusion.

EXERCISES

1. The volume of metal in a solid extruded bar is the product of the cross-section and the length of the bar. How many cubic meters are in 1.7 meters of a bar with a cross section of
   a. 5 sq cm?   b. 36 sq cm?   c. 98 sq cm?

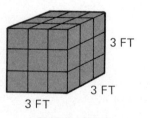

Figure 6-16

Cubic measure

6-8 Volumes of rectangular solids

The industrial containers shown in Figure 6-16 each have the shape of a rectangular solid. Each box is composed of 6 rectangles, called the faces of the solid.

To find the **volume,** or amount of space inside a rectangular solid, we use **cubic measure.** Whereas in measuring area, we used square units, in measuring volume we use cubic units. For example, to find the volume of the solid shown in Figure 6-17, we count the number of red cubes that will fit in the solid.

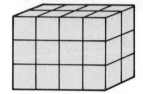

Figure 6-17

You can see that there are 4 × 2, or 8 units in one layer. There are 3 layers, so there are 4 × 2 × 3 cubic units in all. The volume is 24 cubic units.

To find the volume of any rectangular solid whose length, width and height we know, we can use the formula:

$$V = lwh$$

EXAMPLE How many cubic yards of dirt must be excavated to form a basement 35 ft × 20 ft × 8 ft?

SOLUTION
$V = lwh$
$\qquad = 35 \times 20 \times 8$
$V = 5600 \text{ cu ft}$

But we need our answer in cubic yards.
To find how many cubic feet are in one cubic yard, look at Figure 6-18. You can see that there are 3 × 3 × 3, or 27 cubic feet in one cubic yard.
So we can divide 5600 by 27 to find the number of cubic yards.

$5600 \div 27 = 207.4$ (approx.)

About 207 cubic yards of dirt must be removed.

3 FT

3 FT

3 FT

1 CUBIC YARD

Figure 6-18

EXERCISES

U.S. System

A Find the volume of a rectangular solid with the dimensions given.

1. $l = 8$ in., $w = 6$ in., $h = 5$ in.

2. $l = 15$ ft, $w = 9$ ft, $h = 20$ ft

3. $l = 9\frac{1}{2}''$, $w = 4\frac{1}{2}''$, $h = 3''$

4. $l = 5\frac{3}{4}''$, $w = 1\frac{3}{8}''$, $h = \frac{5}{8}''$

B 5. A swimming pool is to be excavated. Its dimensions are 40 ft × 20 ft × 8 ft. How many cubic yards of dirt must be removed?

6. How many cubic yards of concrete are needed to construct a driveway 50 ft long, 10 ft wide, and 8 in. deep?

7. A rectangular trough measures 30 ft × 3 ft × 2 ft. How many gallons of water will it hold if 1 cubic foot = $7\frac{1}{2}$ gallons?

8. What volume of concrete is needed to build a roadway 45 ft wide, 1 ft thick and 10 miles long?

9. One cubic inch of cast aluminum weighs .093 lb. How much would a bar 1 inch thick, 2 inches wide, and 3 feet long weigh?

C 10. An 8-foot deep basement is to be excavated for the L-shaped building shown below. How many cubic yards of dirt must be removed?

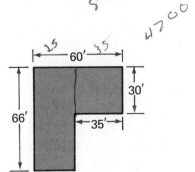

Metric System

Find the volume of a rectangular solid with the dimensions given.

11. $l = 5$ cm, $w = 9$ cm, $h = 4$ cm

12. $l = 20$ mm, $w = 35$ mm, $h = 50$ mm

13. $l = 3.5$ m, $w = 2.8$ m, $h = 5$ m

14. $l = 2.6$ m, $w = 3.55$ m, $h = 4$ m

15. A swimming pool is to be excavated. Its dimensions are 12 m × 6.2 m × 3 m. How many cubic meters of dirt must be removed?

16. How many cubic meters of concrete are needed to construct a driveway 17 m long, 3.1 m wide and 200 mm deep?

17. A rectangular trough measures 9 m × .75 m × .6 m. How many liters of water will it hold if 1 cubic meter = 1000 liters?

18. What volume of concrete is needed to build a roadway 13.5 m wide, .3 m thick, and 8000 m long?

19. 1000 cu mm of cast aluminum weigh 2.58 grams. How much would a bar of cast aluminum 25 mm thick, 50 mm wide, and 900 mm long weigh?

20. A basement 2.4 meters deep is to be excavated for the L-shaped building shown below. How many cubic meters of dirt must be removed?

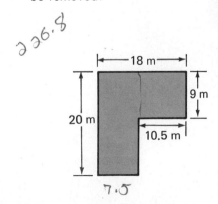

6-9 Volumes of cylinders

Many everyday objects have the shape of a cylinder. Pipes and cans are the most common examples. Figure 6-19 shows how the cylinder for a lightweight steel beverage can is manufactured.

Figure 6-19

We find the volume of a cylinder much like we find volumes of rectangular solids. In a rectangular solid we multiplied the area of the base, in this case, a rectangle, by the height of the solid.

$$V = \text{Area of base} \times h$$
$$V = lwh$$

In a cylinder, the base is a circle. Recall that the formula for the area of a circle is πr^2. So the formula for the volume of a cylinder is parallel to the formula for the volume of a rectangular solid

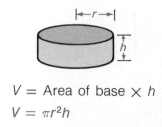

$$V = \text{Area of base} \times h$$
$$V = \pi r^2 h$$

EXAMPLE   Find the volume of a cylinder having a radius of 1.5 cm and
a height of 9 cm.

SOLUTION $V = \pi r^2 h$
$= 3.14 \times 1.5 \times 1.5 \times 9$
$V = 63.5850$

The volume is about 63.6 cu cm.

EXERCISES

U.S. System

A Find the volume of a cylinder having the radius
and height given.

1. $r = 10$ in., $h = 8$ in.

2. $r = 4$ in., $h = 18$ in.

3. $r = 2\frac{1}{2}$ in., $h = 5$ in.

4. $r = 180$ yd, $h = 120$ yd

5. $r = \frac{3}{8}$ in., $h = \frac{3}{4}$ in.

B 6. A cylinder tank has a diameter of 30 ft and
a height of 40 ft. How many gallons would
it hold if one cubic foot will hold about 7.5
gallons?

7. The half-round steel rod shown has a diameter of $\frac{1}{2}$ in. and a length of 14 in. Find the
volume of the rod.

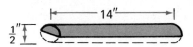

Metric System

Find the volume of a cylinder having the radius
and height given.

8. $r = 10$ mm, $h = 20$ mm

9. $r = 9$ cm, $h = 15$ cm

10. $r = 2.8$ cm, $h = 3.5$ cm

11. $r = 3.5$ m, $h = 5.7$ m

12. $r = .85$ m, $h = 1.23$ m

13. A cylindrical tank has a diameter of 9 m and
a height of 12 m. How many liters would
it hold if one cubic meter will hold 1000
liters?

14. The half-round steel rod shown has a diameter of 3 cm and a length of 25 cm. Find
the volume of the rod.

6-10 Volumes of cones, pyramids, and spheres

A funnel is one of the most common examples of a design
based on a cone.

FUNNEL

CONE

Figure 6-20 shows a cone and a cylinder having the same base and height. How do you think the volume of the cone compares to the volume of the cylinder?

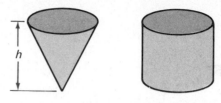

Figure 6-20

The volume of the cone is exactly one-third the volume of the cylinder. So the formula for the volume of a cone is:

$$V = \tfrac{1}{3}\pi r^2 h$$

EXAMPLE 1   Find the volume of a cone having a radius of 3 in. and a height of 5 in.

SOLUTION $V = \tfrac{1}{3}\pi r^2 h$
$\qquad = \tfrac{1}{3} \times 3.14 \times 3 \times 3 \times 5$
$V = 47.10$

The volume is about 47 cu in.

Compare the size of the **rectangular pyramid** in Figure 6-21 with the rectangular solid having the same base and height. You might guess that the volume of these two solid figures would compare in the same way as the volume of a cone and a cylinder having the same base and height.

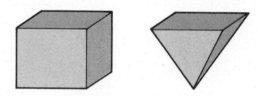

Figure 6-21

Indeed, the formula for the volume of a rectangular pyramid is:

$$V = \tfrac{1}{3}lwh$$

194

EXAMPLE 2 Find the volume of the pyramid shown.

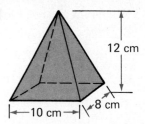

12 cm

10 cm

8 cm

SOLUTION $V = \frac{1}{3} lwh$

$= \frac{1}{3} \times 10 \times 8 \times 12$

$V = 320$ cu cm

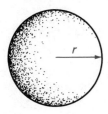

r

An interesting thing about spheres is that they have the greatest volume for the amount of their surface area. It is for this reason that spherical tanks are commonly used to store gas and water.

The volume of a sphere can be found by using the formula:

$$V = \frac{4}{3} \pi r^3$$

EXAMPLE 3 Find the volume of a sphere having a radius 3 cm.

SOLUTION $V = \frac{4}{3} \pi r^3$

$= \frac{4}{3} \times 3.14 \times 3 \times 3 \times 3$

$V = 113.04$

The volume is about 113 cu cm.

EXERCISES

U.S. System

A Find the volume of a cone having the radius and height given.

1. $r = 10$ in., $h = 6$ in.

2. $r = 18$ ft, $h = 12$ ft

3. $r = 1\frac{1}{2}$ in., $h = 5$ in.

4. $r = 50$ ft, $h = 20$ ft

Metric System

Find the volume of a cone having the radius and height given.

15. $r = 100$ mm, $h = 90$ mm

16. $r = 210$ mm, $h = 350$ mm

17. $r = 3.3$ m, $h = 7$ m

18. $r = .6$ m, $h = 1.2$ m

Find the volume of a rectangular pyramid having the length, width, and height given.

5. $l = 11$ in., $w = 9$ in., $h = 5$ in.

6. $l = 4$ ft, $w = 3$ ft, $h = 5$ ft

7. $l = 15$ in., $w = 18$ in., $h = 10$ in.

8. $l = 2\frac{1}{2}$ in., $w = 1\frac{1}{4}$ in., $h = 9$ in.

Find the volume of a sphere having the radius given.

9. $r = 10$ in.

10. $r = 6$ ft

11. $r = 300$ yd

B 12. A spherical water tank has a radius of 24 ft. How many gallons of water will it hold if 1 cubic foot holds about 7.5 gallons?

13. A cone-shaped container has a radius of 14 in. and a height of 10 in. How many gallons will it hold? (231 cu in. = 1 gallon)

C 14. A concrete base for a light pole is constructed in the form of a square pyramid with the top section cut off, as shown below. Find the volume of the light pole base.

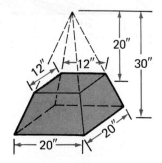

Find the volume of a rectangular pyramid having the length, width, and height given.

19. $l = 10$ mm, $w = 9$ mm, $h = 11$ mm

20. $l = 32$ cm, $w = 15$ cm, $h = 12$ cm

21. $l = 30$ mm, $w = 50$ mm, $h = 85$ mm

22. $l = 3.6$ m, $w = 2.1$ m, $h = .5$ m

Find the volume of a sphere having the radius given.

23. $r = 100$ mm

24. $r = 90$ m

25. $r = 3.3$ m

26. A spherical water tank has a radius of 7.2 m. How many liters of water will it hold if 1 cubic meter holds 1000 liters?

27. A cone-shaped container has a radius of 35 cm and a height of 25 cm. How many liters will it hold? (1000 cu cm = 1 liter)

28. A concrete base for a light pole is constructed in the form of a square pyramid with the top section cut off, as shown below. Find the volume of the light pole base.

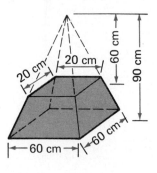

RESEARCH PROJECT

Construct a cone and a cylinder having the same radius and height. Use sand or water to compare the volume of the cone to the volume of the cylinder.

SELF-ANALYSIS TEST 19

U.S. System

1. Find the volume of a rectangular solid having a length of 10 in., a width of 5 in., and a height of 6 in.

2. Find the volume of a cylinder having a radius of 10 ft and a height of 20 ft.

3. Find the volume of a cone having a radius of 9 in. and a height of 20 in.

4. Find the volume of a rectangular pyramid having a length of 12 in., a width of 4 in., and a height of 15 in.

5. Find the volume of a sphere having a radius of 30 in.

6. Find the volume of the concrete in the hollow cinder block shown below.

Metric System

7. Find the volume of a rectangular solid having a length of 8 cm, a width of 10 cm, and a height of 4 cm.

8. Find the volume of a cylinder having a radius of 100 mm and a height of 250 mm.

9. Find the volume of a cone having a radius of 30 mm and a height of 65 mm.

10. Find the volume of a rectangular pyramid having a length of 150 mm, a width of 90 mm, and a height of 200 mm.

11. Find the volume of a sphere having a radius of 90 mm.

12. Find the volume of the concrete in the hollow cinder block below.

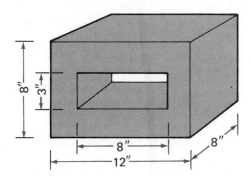

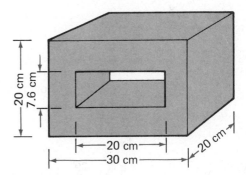

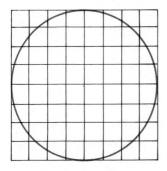

RESEARCH PROJECT

Using graph or grid paper and a compass, draw a circle having a radius of 4 units as shown at the left. Estimate the number of squares inside the circle. To do this, count the number of whole squares inside the circle. Then add to it an estimate of the fractional part of the squares partially included inside the circle.

Now use a value of 4 for the radius in the formula $A = \pi r^2$. How close did your estimate come to the actual area in square units given by the formula?

Food Processing Technician

Many of the foods we eat are processed by industrial firms. Some of these companies package, can, or freeze food after processing. Others take raw materials to make a finished product, such as a loaf of bread or a candy bar. These firms need technicians to help with research, development, and supervisory work. Technicians help make sure that the food produced is tasty and safe. Perhaps you are interested in a career in this important area.

Job Description

What do food processing technicians do?
1. They help food scientists make better food products and create new ones. They also help to improve the production processes involved.
2. They use instruments to make tests on raw materials and finished products.
3. They supervise the overall processing of food products.
4. They help identify sanitary problems, recommend solutions, and direct cleaning crews.
5. They may sometimes inspect food sources for quality and cleanliness.

Qualifications

High school graduates who have taken courses in biology, chemistry, and mathematics are preferred.
Technical training beyond high school is encouraged.

Training

Food technicians can get on-the-job training or take courses part-time at a technical school. A food technician usually begins as a trainee under an experienced food scientist.

Working Conditions

A 40-hour week.
Work is done in very clean plants or labs.
Some travel to food sources may be necessary.
Generally, work is done as part of a team.

Opportunities for Advancement

Technicians with ability can advance to supervisory positions. Some are able to become production managers, depending on their training, ability, and experience. Others become salespersons or purchasing agents.

TAKING INVENTORY

P = Perimeter, C = Circumference, A = Area,
L = Lateral area, S = Surface area, V = Volume

$P = 4s$ (p. 169)

$A = s^2$ (p. 176)

$P = 2l + 2w$ (p. 169)

$A = lw$ (p. 176)

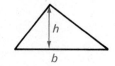

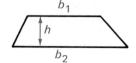

$A = \frac{1}{2}bh$ (p. 178)

$A = \frac{1}{2}h(b_1 + b_2)$ (p. 178)

$C = \pi d$ (p. 171)

$A = \pi r^2$ (p. 184)

$S = 4\pi r^2$ (p. 187)

$V = \frac{4}{3}\pi r^3$ (p. 195)

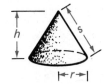

$L = 2\pi rh$ (p. 186)

$S = 2\pi rh + 2\pi r^2$ (p. 186)

$V = \pi r^2 h$ (p. 192)

$L = \pi rs$ (p. 187)

$S = \pi r^2 + \pi rs$ (p. 187)

$V = \frac{1}{3}\pi r^2 h$ (p. 194)

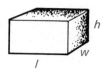

$V = lwh$ (p. 190)

$V = \frac{1}{3}lwh$ (p. 194)

MEASURING YOUR SKILLS

U.S. System

1. Find the perimeter of a rectangle having a length of 8 in. and a width of 5 in. (6-1)

2. Find the circumference of a circle having a diameter of 5 in. (6-2)

3. Find the area of a parallelogram having a base of 18 in. and a height of 5 in. (6-3)

4. Find the area of a triangle having a base of $3\frac{1}{2}$ in. and a height of 2 in. (6-4)

5. Find the area of the region shown below. (6-5)

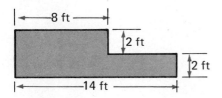

6. Find the area of a circle having a radius of 4 ft. (6-6)

7. Find the total surface area of a cylinder having a radius of 6 in. and a height of 9 in. (6-7)

8. Find the volume of a rectangular solid having a length of 9 in., a width of 10 in., and a height of 3 in. (6-8)

9. Find the volume of a cylinder having a radius of 8 ft and a height of 12 ft. (6-9)

10. Find the volume of a cone having a radius of 9 in. and a height of 20 in. (6-10)

Metric System

11. Find the perimeter of a rectangle having a length of 12 cm and a width of 16 cm. (6-1)

12. Find the circumference of a circle having a diameter of 8 cm. (6-2)

13. Find the area of a parallelogram having a base of 25 mm and a height of 18 mm. (6-3)

14. Find the area of a trapezoid having bases of 14 cm and 18 cm and a height of 9 cm. (6-4)

15. Find the area of the region shown below. (6-5)

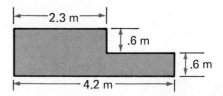

16. Find the area of a circle having a radius of 5 m. (6-6)

17. Find the surface area of a sphere having a radius of 30 mm. (6-7)

18. Find the volume of a rectangular solid having a length of 15 mm, a width of 20 mm, and a height of 8 mm. (6-8)

19. Find the volume of a cylinder having a radius of 25 mm and a height of 40 mm. (6-9)

20. Find the volume of a sphere having a radius of 10 mm. (6-10)

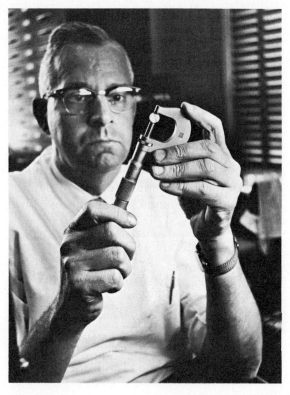

A variety of measuring instruments suggests the need for precision in industrial measurements.

7 *Systems of Measurement*

After completing this chapter, you should be able to:

1. *Convert measures from one unit to another in the United States system.*
2. *Convert measures from one unit to another in the metric system.*
3. *Convert measures in the United States system to measures in the metric system, and vice versa.*
4. *Convert from the Celsius system to Fahrenheit, and vice versa.*
5. *Solve problems involving the metric and United States systems.*

Figure 7-1

Length, area, volume

7-1 Linear measures

Labels or signs like those in Figure 7-1 will no doubt be commonplace before very long. It is therefore important for you to learn to think in the metric system. Since you may be "on the job" before the changeover is complete, you will need to feel at home with whichever system, United States or metric, is used.

The metric system has become world wide, because it is so easy to use. It is based on the decimal system. To convert from one unit to another, you simply multiply by 10 or 100 or 1000 or their reciprocals, .1, or .01, or .001, and so on.

There are three basic units in the metric system, the meter, the gram, and the liter.

A *meter* is about $3\frac{1}{2}''$ longer than a yard.

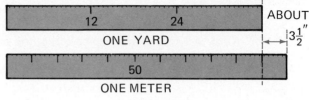

Figure 7-2

The *gram* is a small weight, equal to about .035 oz. You will see measures in grams on tire-balancing weights.

The *liter* is a little more than a quart. You would buy gas for your car by the liter.

Figure 7-3

Units larger or smaller than these basic units are named by using prefixes. For example, "kilo" is used with "gram" to form "kilogram," "centi" with "meter" to form "centimeter," and so on. The most common prefixes, with their meaning, are the following:

milli: one-thousandth (.001)
centi: one-hundredth (.01)
deci: one-tenth (.1)
kilo: one thousand times (1000)

The following table shows the relationships between the commonly used linear metric units. Some of these relationships should be familiar to you by now.

Metric Linear Units

10 *milli*meters (mm) = 1 *centi*meter (cm)	or 1 mm = .1 cm
10 *centi*meters = 1 *deci*meter (dm)	or 1 cm = .1 dm
10 *deci*meters = 1 meter (m)	or 1 dm = .1 m
1000 meters = 1 *kilo*meter (km)	or 1 m = .001 km

Figure 7-4

Earlier you studied the relative size of the centimeter and millimeter compared to the inch. Recall that it takes 2.54 cm to make an inch (see Figure 7-5).

Figure 7-5

A **meter** is about 39.37 inches, or a little more than a yard.

A **kilometer** is about $\frac{5}{8}$ of a mile.

Because metric measurements are used widely in industry, you should become familiar with the different units. Study the following examples.

EXAMPLE 1   3.5 m = ___?___ cm

SOLUTION   Since 100 cm = 1 m, the *conversion factor* for changing meters to centimeters is *100*.

3.5 m = (100 × 3.5) cm
    = 350 cm

EXAMPLE 2   11.3 km = ___?___ m

SOLUTION   Since 1000 m = 1 km, the conversion factor for changing kilometers to meters is 1000.

11.3 km = (1000 × 11.3) m
    = 11,300 m

EXAMPLE 3 A rectangular piece of plywood is 120 cm wide and 240 cm long. What are the dimensions in meters?

SOLUTION Since 100 cm = 1 m, the conversion factor is .01; that is, we divide by 100 or multiply by .01.

$$\text{Width: } 120 \text{ cm} = (120 \times .01) \text{ m} = 1.2 \text{ m}$$
$$\text{Length: } 240 \text{ cm} = (240 \times .01) \text{ m} = 2.4 \text{ m}$$
$$\text{Dimensions: } 1.2 \text{ m by } 2.4 \text{ m}$$

In Example 3, why is the conversion factor .01 instead of 100 as in Example 1? The reason is that you are changing from a smaller unit to a larger one. Example 1 is just the opposite—you are changing from a larger unit to a smaller one.

EXERCISES A

1. Read the ruler at the points indicated.

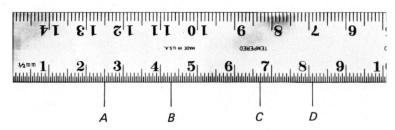

Estimate the lengths of the following segments to the nearest centimeter. Check your estimates with your ruler.

2. _____

3. _____

4. _____

Complete.

5. 152 cm = __?__ m   9. 3 km = __?__ cm

6. 14 m = __?__ cm   10. 6.7 m = __?__ mm

7. 14 m = __?__ mm   11. 1784 m = __?__ km

8. 3 km = __?__ m   12. 14.3 m = __?__ cm

Copy and complete the table.

	mm	cm	dm	m
B 13.	?	1	?	?
14.	?	?	1	?
15.	1	?	?	?
16.	?	?	?	1

C 17. A micron = .000001 meters. How many microns are there in 12.5 mm? (*Micro* means $\frac{1}{1,000,000}$ part of.)

18. A TV station broadcasts at a frequency of 50 megacycles. (*Mega* means 1,000,000 times.) State the frequency in kilo-cycles.

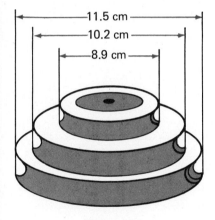

Figure 7-6

7-2 Linear conversions

For the 3-step pulley in Figure 7-6, the diameters are 11.5 cm, 10.2 cm, and 8.9 cm. To replace the assembly with a pulley with measurements in the United States system, what approximate measurements would you use?

This problem is typical of the kind of problem that a changeover to the metric system will bring. To solve this problem, we need a conversion table. This table shows the United States system equivalents of the common metric linear units. To convert measures, multiply by the appropriate conversion factor.

Approximately Equivalent Linear Units

1 in. = 25.4 mm (exact)	1 mm = .0394 in.
1 in. = 2.54 cm (exact)	1 cm = .3937 in.
1 ft = 3.05 dm = .305 m	1 dm = .328 ft
1 yd = .9144 m	1 m = 1.0936 yd
1 mi = 1.61 km	1 km = .621 mi

Figure 7-7

In your work with the United States and metric systems, remember this important point.

In changing measurements from one system to another, your answers are approximate whenever the equivalents are approximate.

EXAMPLE 1 12 in. = ___?___ cm
           1 in. = 2.54 cm

SOLUTION The conversion factor is 2.54. An estimate for the answer
          is "somewhere between 24 and 36," since $2 \times 12 = 24$
          and $3 \times 12 = 36$.

          12 in. = (12×2.54) cm
                 = 30.48 cm

          Is the answer reasonable?

EXAMPLE 2 For the pulley assembly in Figure 7-6, convert the diameters
           to inches. Tell whether a 3-step pulley with diameters of
           $3\frac{1}{2}$ in., 4 in., and $4\frac{1}{2}$ in. is a reasonable replacement.

SOLUTION 1 cm = .3937 in. The conversion factor is .3937.

          11.5 cm = $(11.5 \times .3937)$ in.
                  = 4.52755 in., or 4.5 in.
          10.2 cm = $(10.2 \times .3937)$ in.
                  = 4.01574 in., or 4.0 in.
          8.9 cm = $(8.9 \times .3937)$ in.
                 = 3.50393 in., or 3.5 in.

          Is the replacement part a reasonable one to use?

EXAMPLE 3 A road sign lists the speed limit as 50 miles per hour. If
           you are driving a European car which shows speed in kilo-
           meters per hour, what is the speed limit?

SOLUTION 1 mi = 1.61 km. The conversion factor is 1.61.

          50 miles = (50×1.61) km
                   = 80.5 km, or 81 km

          The speed limit is 81 km per hour.

EXERCISES Decide which is the greater length.
        A   1. 4 cm or 1 in.

              2. 1 ft or 1 m

              3. $\frac{1}{2}$ in. or 1 cm

              4. $\frac{1}{2}$ km or 1 mi

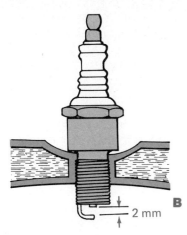

Figure 7-8

Figure 7-9

Arrange the following lengths from the longest to the shortest.

5. 1 ft, $\frac{1}{2}$ m, $\frac{1}{2}$ yd

6. 55 cm, 1 ft, $\frac{1}{2}$ m

Complete the conversions, rounding to the nearest tenth.

7. 3.8 mi = ___?___ km

11. 100 yd = ___?___ m

8. 15 km = ___?___ mi

12. 1760 yd = ___?___ m

9. 4 in. = ___?___ cm

13. 1 mi = ___?___ m

10. 25 mm = ___?___ in.

14. 76.7 cm = ___?___ ft

B

15. A set of metric wrenches has the following sizes: 6 mm, 8 mm, 10 mm, 12 mm, and 14 mm. Change these measurements to the United States system. Give your answer to the nearest thousandth of an inch.

16. The gap of the spark plug in Figure 7-8 is 2 mm. What is the gap in inches?

C

17. A micrometer measures the diameter of the wrist watch in Figure 7-9 to be 3 cm. What is the diameter of the watch in millimeters? in inches?

18. A builder must use glass at least $\frac{3}{16}$″ thick for a construction job. To the nearest millimeter, how thick must the glass be?

7-3 Area measurement

Any area which is equivalent to the area of a square one inch on a side is a square inch. Each diagram below is 1 sq in. in area.

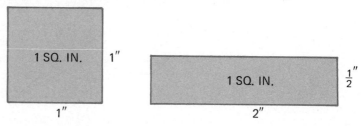

Can you check that each diagram below has an area of 1 sq cm?

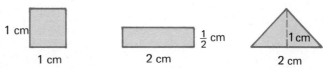

To convert an area measurement to a different unit of measure, multiply by the appropriate conversion factor. The following tables show the common conversion units for area in both systems.

United States Area Measure

144 sq in. = 1 sq ft	1 sq in. = $\frac{1}{144}$ sq ft
9 sq ft = 1 sq yd	1 sq ft = $\frac{1}{9}$ sq yd

Figure 7-10

Metric Area Measure

100 sq mm = 1 sq cm	1 sq mm = .01 sq cm
100 sq cm = 1 sq dm	1 sq cm = .01 sq dm
100 sq dm = 1 sq m	1 sq dm = .01 sq m

Figure 7-11

Start

Select the conversion factor.

Multiply by the conversion factor.

Stop

Figure 7-12

The flow chart in Figure 7-12 tells how to change a measure from one unit to another.

EXAMPLE 1   54 sq ft = ___?___ sq yd

SOLUTION

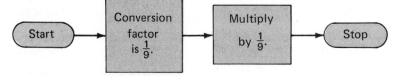

Start → Conversion factor is $\frac{1}{9}$. → Multiply by $\frac{1}{9}$. → Stop

$$54 \text{ sq ft} = (54 \times \tfrac{1}{9}) \text{ sq yd}$$
$$= 6 \text{ sq yd}$$

EXAMPLE 2   56,400 sq cm = ___?___ sq m

SOLUTION

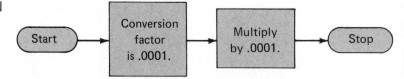

Start → Conversion factor is .0001. → Multiply by .0001. → Stop

1 sq cm = .01 sq dm
1 sq dm = .01 sq m
Therefore, 1 sq cm = (.01 × .01) sq m
$$= .0001 \text{ sq m}$$

56,400 sq cm = (56,400 × .0001) sq m
$$= 5.64 \text{ sq m}$$

EXAMPLE 3 A house contains approximately 1040 sq ft of living space. What is the area in square yards? in square meters?

SOLUTION *Step 1.* 1040 sq ft = (1040 × $\frac{1}{9}$) sq yd
$$= 116 \text{ sq yd (approx.)}$$

Step 2. From Figure 7-7,
$$1 \text{ ft} = .305 \text{ m}$$
$$1 \text{ sq ft} = (.305)^2 \text{ sq m}$$
$$= (.305 \times .305) \text{ sq mi}$$
$$= .09 \text{ sq m (approx.)}$$

1040 sq ft = (1040 × .09) sq m
$$= 93.6 \text{ sq m}$$

EXERCISES What factor do we use to make the following conversions?

A 1. Square inches to square feet

2. Square yards to square inches

3. Square millimeters to square centimeters

4. Square meters to square centimeters

5. Square feet to square yards

Complete the following statements.

6. 152 sq ft = ___?___ sq yd   9. 3.6 sq m = ___?___ sq dm

7. 3.5 sq cm = ___?___ sq mm   10. 300 sq in. = ___?___ sq ft

8. $9\frac{1}{2}$ sq yd = ___?___ sq ft   11. $15\frac{1}{2}$ sq ft = ___?___ sq in.

B 12. A parking lot measures 2520 sq ft in area. How much would it cost to blacktop the driveway at a cost of $5.60 per sq yd?

13. A storage shed contains approximately 108 sq ft. How much would it cost to carpet the room at $9.75 per sq yd?

14. The press room at a lithograph company has a length of 60 ft and a width of 40 ft. What is the area in square yards?

15. How much would it cost to install a suspended ceiling in a room measuring 9 ft by 27 ft? The ceiling tiles are 12″ square and cost $.27 each?

16. The blueprint of a house includes a 4 m by 5 m patio. What would be the cost of laying a flagstone patio, if the flagstone costs $6.95 per sq m?

7-4 Volume measurement

Any volume equivalent to the volume of a cube having an edge one inch in length is called a **cubic inch.**

Similarly, any volume equivalent to the volume of a cube having an edge one centimeter long is a **cubic centimeter.**

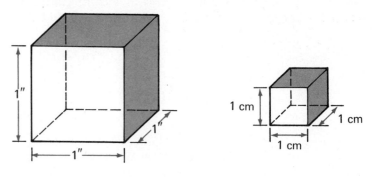

Figure 7-13

The figures above show the relative size of the basic United States unit of volume (the cubic inch) and the basic metric unit of volume (the cubic centimeter).

Some of the common conversion factors for volume units are given in the tables below.

United States Volume Measure

1728 cu in. = 1 cu ft	1 cu in. = $\frac{1}{1728}$ cu ft
27 cu ft = 1 cu yd	1 cu ft = $\frac{1}{27}$ cu yd

Figure 7-14

Metric Volume Measure

1000 cu mm = 1 cu cm	1 cu mm = .001 cu cm
1000 cu cm = 1 cu dm	1 cu cm = .001 cu dm
1000 cu dm = 1 cu m	1 cu dm = .001 cu m

Figure 7-15

Note: Another abbreviation for 1 cu cm is 1 cc (read "one c-c"). Still another is 1 cm^3. You should be familiar with all three.

To convert a particular volume measure to a different unit of measurement, multiply by the appropriate conversion factor.

EXAMPLE 1 $3\frac{1}{2}$ cu yd = ___?___ cu ft

SOLUTION   The conversion factor is 27.

$$3\frac{1}{2} \text{ cu yd} = (3\frac{1}{2} \times 27) \text{ cu ft}$$
$$= 94\frac{1}{2} \text{ cu ft}$$

EXAMPLE 2   35,200 cu mm = ___?___ cu cm

SOLUTION   The conversion factor is .001.

$$35,200 \text{ cu mm} = (35,200 \times .001) \text{ cu cm}$$
$$= 35.2 \text{ cu cm}$$

EXAMPLE 3   12,960 cu in. = ___?___ cu ft

SOLUTION   The conversion factor is $\frac{1}{1728}$.

$$12,960 \text{ cu in.} = (\frac{1}{1728} \times 12,960) \text{ cu ft}$$
$$= 7.5 \text{ cu ft}$$

EXAMPLE 4   A small-parts bin measures 6 cm by 5 cm by 3 cm. What is the volume **a.** in cubic centimeters? **b.** in cubic inches?

SOLUTION   **a.** The formula is $V = l \times w \times h$.

$$V = (6 \times 5 \times 3) \text{ cu cm}$$
$$= 90 \text{ cu cm}$$

b. From the table in Figure 7-7, 1 cm = .39 in.

$$1 \text{ cu cm} = (.39)^3 \text{ cu in.}$$
$$= (.39 \times .39 \times .39) \text{ cu in.}$$
$$= .06 \text{ cu in. (approx.)}$$
$$V = 90 \text{ cu cm} = (90 \times .06) \text{ cu in.}$$
$$= 5.4 \text{ cu in.}$$

EXERCISES   What is the conversion factor for each of the following:

A   1. cubic feet to cubic inches

2. cubic yards to cubic inches

3. cubic millimeters to cubic centimeters

4. cubic meters to cubic centimeters

5. cubic feet to cubic meters

Complete.

6. $2\frac{1}{4}$ cu ft = __?__ cu in.   9. $9\frac{1}{4}$ cu yd = __?__ cu ft

7. 2.1 cu cm = __?__ cu mm   10. 90 cu ft = __?__ cu yd

8. 3.7 cu m = __?__ cu dm   11. $17\frac{1}{3}$ cu yd = __?__ cu ft

B 12. A railway roadbed requires 110,000 cu yd of gravel. The trucks used on the project can haul 229.5 cu ft per load. How many truckloads of gravel will it take to complete the project?

13. The platform of a rapid transit station requires 1440 cu ft of concrete. How much will the concrete cost at $9.55 per cubic yard?

14. A concrete batching plant produces $3\frac{1}{2}$ cu yd of concrete at a time. How many loads of concrete does it take to fill a truck with a capacity of 189 cu ft?

15. How many cubic yards of concrete are needed to lay a 1' deep foundation for a garage measuring 25 ft by 30 ft?

16. If a tank has a volume of 40 cu yd, how many gallons will it hold? (1 cu ft = 7.5 gal, approximately)

17. In building a swimming pool, a contractor excavates an area measuring 18' by 36' to an average depth of 4'. If the excavated soil is used as land fill, how many cubic yards does the excavation yield?

C 18. Skylab, an experimental space station, contains a cylindrical workshop 48 ft long and 21.6 ft in diameter. Express its measurements in meters (to the nearest tenth).

19. In Exercise 18, what is the space available in the workshop to the nearest cubic meter?

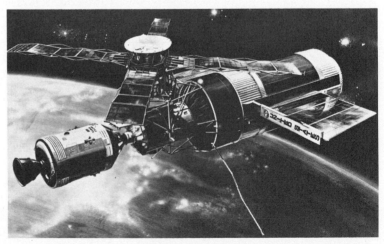

Project Skylab.

SELF-ANALYSIS TEST 20

Complete the statements.

1. 2.5 m = ___?___ cm

2. 20 in. = ___?___ cm

3. 10 sq m = ___?___ sq cm

4. 10 sq m = ___?___ sq yd

5. 5184 cu in. ___?___ cu ft

6. 1 cu m = ___m___ cu mm

7. The stroke of an automobile engine is 7.5 cm. The bore is 9.75 cm. What are these dimensions in inches?

8. A manufacturing plant plans to increase its floor space by 3000 sq ft. About how much is this in sq m?

9. A backyard storage shed contains 540 cu ft of storage space. Give this space in cubic yards.

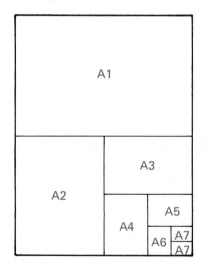

Figure 7-16

SPOTLIGHT ON INDUSTRY

Most countries in the world use the metric system. Like many industries, the graphic arts industry is adopting metric standards to compete with foreign markets. To standardize paper sizes while converting to metric standards, the International Standards Organization (ISO) has planned new paper sizes. Metric units are used, and each size in a series is half the size of the one which comes before it. Figure 7-16 shows how seven different sizes of paper can be cut from one sheet. The large sheet in the A series has an area of one square meter, so A1 is $\frac{1}{2}$ sq m, A2 is $\frac{1}{4}$ sq m, and so on. Changing paper sizes means printing equipment and packaging materials must also be changed. With education and planning these changes can be made with a minimum of problems.

EXERCISES

1. What is the area, in square meters, of A3? A4? A5? A6? A7?

2. What is the area, in square centimeters, of A2? A3? A4?

X-ray Technician

Recent advances in medical care and research have increased the need for trained X-ray technicians. Medical X-rays have become an increasingly important tool in the medical field. The growing practice of X-raying large groups of people as part of disease prevention and control programs will continue to provide job openings. Have you ever considered a career in this field?

Job Description

What do X-ray technicians do?
1. They operate X-ray equipment to take pictures of internal parts of the patient's body. X-rays are usually taken in a special room, though mobile X-ray units are used at a patient's bedside or in surgery.
2. They assist doctors in treating certain diseases by giving prescribed doses of radiation to the patient.
3. They operate equipment for tracing and measuring radioactive materials in the patient's body.

Qualifications

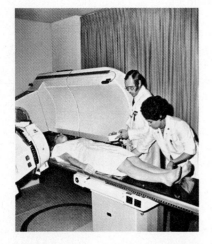

Training schools usually accept only high school graduates. A few training schools require some study beyond high school. High school courses in mathematics, physics, chemistry, biology, and typing are recommended. Good health and endurance are desirable.

Training

Training programs are conducted by hospitals and medical schools. A program usually requires two years to complete, though some programs are longer. Some junior colleges offer a program combining classroom instruction with work experience in hospitals. An X-ray trainee's courses cover the human body, photography, X-ray safety, and equipment care.

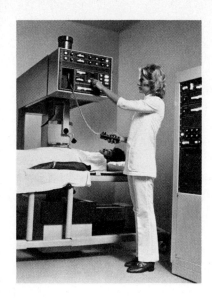

Working Conditions

A 40-hour week is common, but some X-ray technicians may
 be "on call" for night or emergency duty.
Safety rules are followed to protect against overexposure to
 X-rays.

Opportunities for Advancement

Registration with the American Registry of Radiologic
Technologists is an asset in obtaining a highly skilled position.
Completion of an approved program and passing an
examination are required. By completing further training, the
technician can be certified in radiation therapy or nuclear
medicine. Some technicians in large departments can advance
to chief X-ray technician and qualify as instructors in X-ray
techniques.

1 POUND

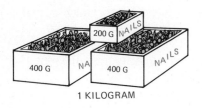

1 KILOGRAM

Figure 7-17

Weight, capacity, temperature

7-5 Weight measurement

The weight of an object is the *amount of force* that gravity exerts on the object. This force varies from place to place. The mass of an object is the *amount of material* of which the object is composed.

For our purpose, we will use the terms interchangeably, since the objects we are studying are affected by the earth's gravity.

The basic unit of weight measurement in the United States system is the pound (lb). The basic unit of weight measurement in the metric system is the gram (g). It takes approximately 454 grams to make a pound. The relative size of these units is shown in Figure 7-17.

The tables below show the relationships among the units of weight.

United States Weight Measure

16 oz = 1 lb	1 oz = $\frac{1}{16}$ lb
2000 lb = 1 ton	1 lb = $\frac{1}{2000}$ ton = .0005 ton

Figure 7-18

Metric Weight Measure

1000 milligrams (mg) = 1 g	1 mg = .001 g
1000 g = 1 kilogram (kg)	1 g = .001 kg
1000 kg = 1 metric ton (mt)	1 kg = .001 mt

Figure 7-19

Approximately Equivalent Units of Weight

1 oz = 28.350 g	1 g = .035 oz
1 lb = .454 kg	1 kg = 2.20 lb
1 ton = .907 mt	1 mt = 1.103 ton

Figure 7-20

As with the other units of measure, you will find that many industrial problems require changing from one unit of weight to another.

EXAMPLE 1 $2\frac{1}{4}$ tons = ___?___ lb

SOLUTION $2\frac{1}{4}$ tons = $(2\frac{1}{4} \times 2000)$ lb
                      = 4500 lb

EXAMPLE 2   4500 g = ___?___ kg

SOLUTION   4500 g = $(4500 \times .001)$ kg
                    = 4.5 kg

EXAMPLE 3   .25 kg = ___?___ oz

SOLUTION   We first change kilograms to grams.
           The conversion factor is 1000.

           .25 kg = $(1000 \times .25)$ g
                   = 250 g

           We now can change grams to ounces.
           The conversion factor is .035.

           250 g = $(.035 \times 250)$ oz
                  = 8.75 oz

           Therefore, .25 kg = 8.75 oz

EXAMPLE 4   If $\frac{1}{2}$ kilogram of nails cost $.45, what is the cost per pound
            of the nails?

SOLUTION   The nails cost $.90 per kg (2 × $.45).

           Since 1 kg = 2.2 lb, we can say that 2.2 lb of nails cost
           $.90.

           Thus, 1 lb of nails cost $\frac{\$.90}{2.2}$ = $.41 (approx.).

EXERCISES   What conversion factor is used to change

A   1. pounds to tons?   4. kilograms to pounds?

        2. metric tons to kilograms?   5. pounds to metric tons?

        3. kilograms to grams?

Complete the weight conversions.

6. $24\frac{1}{4}$ lb = ___?___ oz

7. 2.75 tons = ___?___ lb

8. 22,500 lb = ___?___ tons

9. 2700 kg = ___?___ mt

10. 1.72 kg = ___?___ g

11. 454 g = ___?___ mg

12. .151 mt = ___?___ kg

13. 5 lb = ___?___ kg

14. 5.25 oz = ___?___ g

15. 227 g = ___?___ lb

16. 3.6 mt = ___?___ tons

17. 2.7 kg = ___?___ lb

18. .75 kg = ___?___ oz

B 19. A certain steel alloy weighs .28 lb per cubic inch. If the pipe contains 1200 cu in. of this metal, what is its weight in pounds? in kilograms?

Fueling a nuclear reactor.

20. A rectangular strip of metal is 500 cm long, 200 cm wide, and .5 cm thick. If the metal weighs .0077 kg per cu cm, find the weight of the metal strip in kg. What is the weight in pounds?

21. A commercial vehicle scale has a maximum capacity of 25,000 lb. What is its capacity in metric tons?

22. Test specifications for a certain metal container require it to withstand a force of 400 lb on the lid. If each container weighs 35 kg when full, how many may be safely stacked?

23. A radioactive material used in nuclear power plants costs $350 per gram. What would 1 oz of this material cost?

24. A tank has a volume of 1,000 cu cm. How many kilograms of water can it hold? (1 cc weighs 1 g.)

220

Figure 7-21

7-6 Capacity measurement

Gasoline in the United States is purchased by the gallon. In most countries the price is quoted in liters. The liter (l) is the basic unit of capacity in the metric system.

A race car like the one in Figure 7-21 might be listed as having a 7-liter engine. A liter is equivalent to 1000 cu cm, so a seven-liter engine has a volume of 7000 cu cm.

To change this figure to cubic inches, we multiply by .06, the approximate number of cubic inches in a cubic centimeter. Can you see how to obtain this factor from the table in Figure 7-7?

$$7000 \text{ cu cm} = (7000 \times .06) \text{ cu in.}$$
$$= 420 \text{ cu in.}$$

So a 7-liter engine would be comparable to a 420 cu in. engine.

The tables that follow show the relationships among the common units of capacity.

United States Capacity Measure

16 oz = 1 pt	1 oz = $\frac{1}{16}$ pt
2 pt = 1 qt	1 pt = $\frac{1}{2}$ qt
4 qt = 1 gal	1 qt = $\frac{1}{4}$ gal

Figure 7-22

Metric Capacity Measure

1000 ml = 1 l	1 ml = .001 l
1000 l = 1 kiloliter (kl)	1 l = .001 kl

Figure 7-23

Approximately Equivalent Capacity Units

1 oz = 29.57 ml	1 ml = .034 oz
1 qt = .946 l	1 l = 1.057 qt
1 gal = 3.785 l	1 l = .264 gal

Figure 7-24

EXAMPLE 1   2.25 l = _____?_____ ml

SOLUTION   2.25 l = (1000 × 2.25) ml
            = 2250 ml

EXAMPLE 2   7.5 gal = ___?___ l

SOLUTION   7.5 gal = (3.785 × 7.5) l
                   = 28.3875 l, or 28.4 l

EXAMPLE 3   If gasoline is listed at 42.9¢ per gallon, what is the cost per liter?

SOLUTION   1 l = .264 gal
           .264 × $.429 = $.113256, or 11.3¢ per liter

EXERCISES   Perform the conversions.

A   1. 72 oz = ___?___ qt   7. 25.33 ml = ___?___ l

2. 50 pt = ___?___ gal   8. 500 ml = ___?___ oz

3. 74.5 gal = ___?___ qt   9. 22.5 gal = ___?___ l

4. 1500 kl = ___?___ l   10. 1 pt = ___?___ ml

5. 10.5 l = ___?___ ml   11. 28.7 l = ___?___ gal

6. 1752 l = ___?___ kl   12. 2,500 ml = ___?___ qt

B   13. A spherical tank has a radius of 6 m. How many liters of water will it hold? (Use π = 3.14.) (1 liter = 1000 cu cm)

14. A cylindrical can has a volume of 525 cu cm. How many liters will it hold? (Use π = 3.14.) (1 ml = 1 cu cm)

15. If an automobile has a 450 cu in. engine, what is the capacity in liters?

16. Two milliliters of perfume concentrate are used in one liter of a liquid dishwashing detergent to give it a pleasant scent. If the detergent is packaged in liter containers, how much perfume concentrate must be used to scent 500 bottles of detergent?

17. One liter of a concentrated fertilizer is diluted with water to make 9 gal of fertilizer spray. How many milliliters of concentrate are in 1 gal of the diluted solution?

Spherical storage tank.

CREATIVE CRAFTSMAN

Design and build a set of chess pieces
   a. that consist of combinations of geometric shapes; and
   b. that indicate the moves which the pieces can make by the very shapes of the pieces themselves.

7-7 Temperature formulas

It is 20° indoors and 20° outdoors. How can this be?

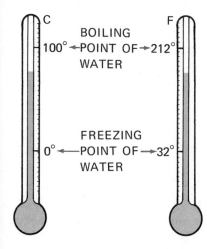

Mr. Strong has a Fahrenheit thermometer in his shop but the one outside the building has two scales, one in Fahrenheit and one in Celsius.

On the Fahrenheit thermometer the freezing point is 32°. The boiling point of water is 212°. On the Celsius thermometer 0° is the freezing point and 100° is the point at which water boils (see Figure 7-26).

Here are two formulas you can use to change the reading on one scale to the other.

$$C = \tfrac{5}{9}(F - 32) \qquad F = \tfrac{9}{5}C + 32$$

EXAMPLE 1 $20°C = \underline{\quad ? \quad} F$

SOLUTION $F = \tfrac{9}{5}C + 32$
$\qquad = \tfrac{9}{5} \times 20 + 32$
$\qquad = 36 + 32 = 68. \quad 68°F$

EXAMPLE 2 $28°F = \underline{\quad ? \quad} °C$

SOLUTION $C = \tfrac{5}{9}(28 - 32)$

If the second number in the parentheses is larger than the first, subtract the first from the second and use the minus sign, as $28 - 32 = -4$. What does the minus sign mean on a thermometer?

Therefore,

$$C = \tfrac{5}{9}(28 - 32) = \tfrac{5}{9}(-4) = -\tfrac{20}{9} = -2\tfrac{2}{9}$$

$-2\tfrac{2}{9}°C$ means $2\tfrac{2}{9}°$ below zero on the Celsius scale.

223

EXERCISES Convert to Fahrenheit or Celsius readings as indicated.

A
1. $32°C = $ __?__ $°F$
2. $62°F = $ __?__ $°C$
3. $160°F = $ __?__ $°C$
4. $100°C = $ __?__ $°F$

5. $200°F = $ __?__ $°C$
6. $16°F = $ __?__ $°C$
7. $45°C = $ __?__ $°F$
8. $95°C = $ __?__ $°F$

B
9. The temperature fell from $80°C$ to $60°C$ in 1 hour. How much did the temperature drop in degrees on the Fahrenheit scale?

10. A soldering iron tip reaches a temperature of $830°F$. What is this temperature in Celsius degrees?

C
11. Mercury freezes at $-39°C$. What is that temperature in Fahrenheit?

12. Wrought iron melts at $1500°C$. Express this in Fahrenheit degrees.

SELF-ANALYSIS TEST 21

1. $1.3 \text{ kg} = $ __?__ g
2. $8 \text{ oz} = $ __?__ g
3. $.5 \text{ kg} = $ __?__ lb
4. $24 \text{ qt} = $ __?__ gal
5. $3.2 \text{ l} = $ __?__ ml
6. $3 \text{ gal} = $ __?__ l

7. On the tailgate of a moving van was painted "MAX LOAD 5000 KG." What is the maximum load in pounds? in tons?

8. At 42¢ per gallon, what is the cost of gasoline per liter?

9. On the Celsius scale a reading is $30°$. Convert to Fahrenheit.

TRICKS OF THE TRADE

To multiply by 25, multiply $\frac{1}{4}$ of the number by 100.

$25 \times 68 = \frac{68}{4} \times 100 = 1700$

$25 \times 97 = 21.25 \times 100 = 2125$

TAKING INVENTORY

1. The metric system and the United States system of measurement can be used for expressing measurements of length, area, volume, weight, and capacity. (p. 203)
2. The metric system is based on the decimal system; the conversion factors within the system are based on tens. (p. 203)
3. The basic units of the United States system are:
   a. the **yard** for length (p. 204)
   b. the **gallon** for capacity (p. 221)
   c. the **pound** for weight. (p. 218)
4. The basic units of the metric system are:
   a. the **meter** for length (p. 205)
   b. the **liter** for capacity (p. 221)
   c. the **gram** for weight (p. 218)
5. The Celsius thermometer is scaled so that 0° corresponds to the freezing point of water and 100° its boiling point. These points on the Fahrenheit scale are 32° and 212°, respectively. (p. 223)

MEASURING YOUR SKILLS

1. 4.3 m = ___?___ cm = ___?___ mm (7-1)

2. .42 km = ___?___ m = ___?___ cm (7-1)

3. 1 ft = ___?___ cm (7-2)

4. $4\frac{1}{2}$ mi = ___?___ km (7-2)

5. 45 sq ft = ___?___ sq yd (7-3)

6. 1500 sq m = ___?___ sq km (7-3)

7. 10 sq m = ___?___ sq yd (7-3)

8. If a rectangular patio floor is 24 ft long, 14 ft wide and 4 in. thick, how many cubic meters of concrete will it take to construct the floor? (7-4)

9. 1.3 kg = ___?___ g (7-5)

10. 1.3 mg = ___?___ g (7-5)

11. 3.5 lb = ___?___ kg (7-5)

12. 1460 ml = ___?___ l (7-6)

13. 13.5 l = ___?___ gal (7-6)

14. 21.5 gal = ___?___ l (7-6)

15. If film developer costs $1.35 per gallon, what is the cost per liter? (7-6)

16. 85°C = ___?___ F (7-7)

17. 85°F = ___?___ C (7-7)

RESEARCH WITH A COMPUTER

In Chapter 7 you learned how to make conversions between the United States system and the metric system of measurement. If an electronic computer is available, you can use the following BASIC program to convert from inches to centimeters.

```
10  PRINT "LENGTH IN INCHES IS";
20  INPUT L
30  PRINT "LENGTH IS";2.54*L;" CM"
40  END
```

Why does the program multiply L by 2.54?

EXERCISES

1. RUN the program, using the following measurements.

a. 7″	d. 148″	g. 71″
b. 3″	e. 12″	h. 3.95″
c. 2.87″	f. 35″	i. 75.83″

2. A mechanic measures the bore of cylinder as 3.875″. What is this dimension in centimeters?

3. The diameter of a pump rotor is 2.1875″. What is the size of a replacement part in metric dimensions?

The next program converts pounds to kilograms.

```
10  PRINT "WEIGHT IN POUNDS IS";
20  INPUT W
30  PRINT "WEIGHT IS"; .454*W;" KG"
40  END
```

How is this program like the previous one?

EXERCISES

4. RUN the program, using the following weights.

a. 5 lb	d. 37 lb	g. 51.25 lb
b. 2.2 lb	e. 18 lb	h. 154 lb
c. 73.5 lb	f. 139 lb	i. 7.77 lb

5. Using the programs given thus far as models, write a program that will convert

   a. miles to kilometers

   b. yards to meters

   c. ounces to grams

   The next program converts quarts to liters. It then uses the fact that

1 liter = 1000 ml = 1000 cc

to give the capacity in cu cm, or cc.

```
10  PRINT "CAPACITY IN QUARTS IS";
20  INPUT C
30  LET M=.946*C
40  PRINT "CAPACITY IS";M;" LITERS"
50  PRINT "CAPACITY IS";1000*M;" CU CM"
60  END
```

EXERCISES

6. RUN the program with the following measurements.

a. 1 qt	d. 17 qt	g. 1.78 qt
b. 4 qt	e. 21.5 qt	h. 55.87 qt
c. .25 qt	f. .134 qt	i. 11.2 qt

7. An industrial lubricant sells for $.37 per liter. At this rate, what is the cost of 75 quarts of the lubricant?

8. Use these programs to solve some of the exercises in Chapter 7. Compare the results. What are some advantages and disadvantages of using the computer to find equivalent measurements in the U.S. and metric systems?

Surveyors and architects use a knowledge of geometry in planning residential and commercial construction.

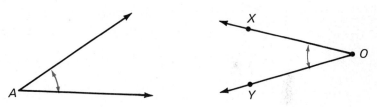

CHAPTER 8 *Geometry*

After completing this chapter, you should be able to:

1. *Use a protractor, a compass, and a straight edge to perform geometric constructions.*
2. *Apply geometric constructions to solve problems.*
3. *Use similar triangles and congruent triangles to solve measurement problems.*
4. *Use the rule of Pythagoras to solve problems involving right triangles.*

Angles

8-1 Measuring angles

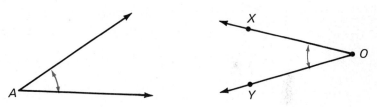

From earlier courses you will recall that angles, as $\angle A$ and $\angle XOY$, can be measured in degrees. In most work in the industry and trades you will often find a need for angles. Bolts and screws, for example, differ in the angle between the threads.

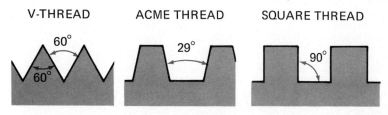

Cross sections of screws.

To measure an angle, you can use a protractor, as illustrated in Figure 8-1. There are two scales. Use whichever is the more convenient.

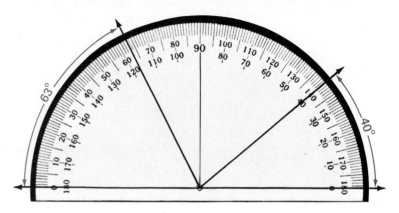

Figure 8-1

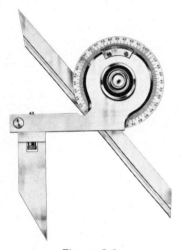

Figure 8-2

As you can easily see, you can use a protractor either to measure a given angle or to draw one of a certain measure. A bevel protractor, shown in Figure 8-2, is used to measure the angle of beveled edges like those in picture frames.

Two special angles are shown here. $\angle ABC$ is a **right** angle, and $\angle XOY$ is a **straight** angle.

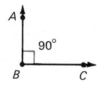

Right angle. 90°

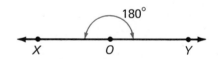

The sides of a straight angle (180°) form a straight line.

EXERCISES A 1. In Figure 8-3 on the next page, read the measures of:

    a. $\angle BAC$

    b. $\angle BAD$

    c. $\angle EAC$

    d. $\angle DAE$

    e. $\angle CAD$

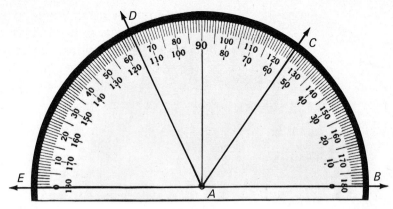

Figure 8-3

2. Using a protractor, draw angles having the following measures:

    a. 45°   **b.** 75°   **c.** 90°   **d.** 125°   **e.** 78°   **f.** 112°

B 3. Draw a triangle having a right angle, and make the two sides of the triangle forming the right angle 4 inches long. Find the measures of the two remaining angles.

  4. Draw triangle *ABC* having the following dimensions:

    side *AB* is 10 cm long;

    ∠*ABC* is a right angle;

    ∠*BAC* is a 30° angle.

    a. What is the measure of ∠*BCA*?

    b. How long is side *BC*?

    c. How long is side *AC*?

C 5. Draw a parallelogram having two sides 7 cm long, two sides 4.5 cm long, and two angles of 50°.

8-2 Central angles

    The parts, or **arcs,** of a circle have the same measure as corresponding central angles. The number of degrees around a point is 360° (2 straight angles); the number of degrees in a circle is 360°. In the watch shown at the left, equal divisions on the circle were found by drawing 12 equal angles at the center, or 12 equal **central angles.** How do you find the size of each angle? (360° ÷ 12) 360° ÷ 12 = 30°, so each central angle is 30°.

231

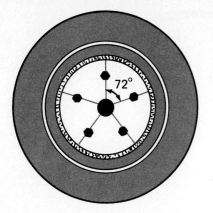

A car designer needs to know where to position the 5 lugs which hold the wheel to the car. Once he locates the center of the wheel, he can use central angles to locate the position of the lugs. The central angle for each lug would be 360° ÷ 5, or 72°.

EXERCISES

U.S. System

Using a protractor to measure the central angles, locate equally-spaced points around the circle described.

1. 4 points on a circle with a 5-inch diameter.

2. 5 points on a circle with a 4.5-inch diameter.

Metric System

Using a protractor to measure the central angles, locate equally-spaced points around the circle described.

3. A circle with a 15-centimeter diameter and 4 points.

4. A circle with a 10.3-centimeter diameter and 10 points.

8-3 Angle relationships

Angles *BAC* and *CAD* are adjacent angles. They have the same vertex, *A* and a side, *AC* in common.

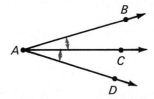

In Figure 8-4 angles *XOZ* and *ZOY* are adjacent angles. They are also complementary angles because their sum is 90°.

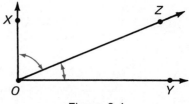

Figure 8-4

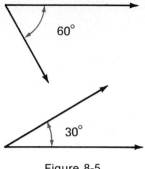

Figure 8-5

Complementary angles do not have to be adjacent angles. The angles in Figure 8-5 are complementary also.

If the sum of the measures of two angles is 180°, the angles are called **supplementary angles**. The figure below shows pairs of supplementary angles. Note that supplementary angles do not have to be adjacent angles.

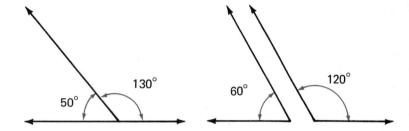

Another very special sum gives us 180° also. This is the sum of the angles of a triangle. Measure $\angle A$, $\angle B$, and $\angle C$ and find their sum.

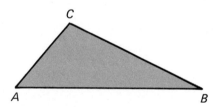

The sum of the angles of a triangle is 180°.

EXAMPLE 1   Suppose we want to splice two boards to form a tight joint. If $\angle ABC = 45°$, what must $\angle DEX$ measure?

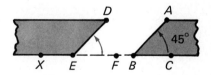

SOLUTION   Points X, E, and C must lie in a straight line. That is, $\angle ABC$ and $\angle DEX$ *must* be supplementary.

Thus $\angle DEX = 180° - \angle ABC$
$$= 180° - 45°$$
$$= 135°$$

EXAMPLE 2 For a right-angled mitre joint shown, assuming ∠1 = ∠2, what are the sizes of ∠1 and ∠2?

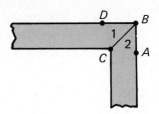

SOLUTION ∠1 and ∠2 are complementary. So the sum of their measures is 90°. Since ∠1 = ∠2, each must be half of 90°.
$$90 \div 2 = 45$$

∠1 and ∠2 each measure 45°.

EXAMPLE 3 In the diagram below, ∠ACD is a straight angle. Find the measure of ∠1 and the measure of ∠2.

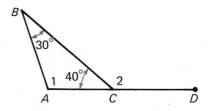

SOLUTION The sum of the angles in the triangle is 180°.

a. ∠1 + 30° + 40° = 180°
∠1 + 70° = 180°
∠1 = 180° − 70°
∠1 = 110°

b. ∠2 and ∠BCA are supplementary angles.

∠2 + 40° = 180°
∠2 = 180° − 40°
∠2 = 140°

EXERCISES A 1. Two angles of a triangle measure 35° and 55°. What is the measure of the third angle?

2. Draw a pair of adjacent supplementary angles, one of which has a measure of 72°. What is the measure of the other angle?

3. Two angles are complementary. One of them has a measure of 45°. What is the measure of the other angle?

B 4. If ∠*ABC* in Figure 8-6 measures 75°, how large is angle *DEF*? (Assume that there is one board under the T-square.)

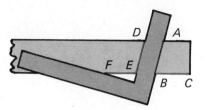

Figure 8-6

5. For the dovetail joint shown in Figure 8-7 if ∠1 = 82°, how large is ∠2?

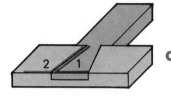

Figure 8-7

C 6. The L-square can be used to size the lumber for a rafter. If the plate angle in Figure 8-8 is 40°, what is the ridge angle?

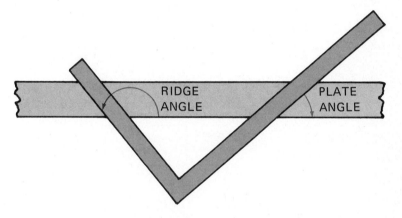

Figure 8-8

SELF-ANALYSIS TEST 22

1. Use a protractor to draw an angle which measures 78°.

2. Give the measure of each central angle of a circle which is divided into 10 equal parts.

3. Two angles of a triangle measure 32° and 53°. What is the measure of the third angle?

4. Give the measure of ∠2 in the figure below.

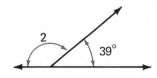

TOOLING UP FOR PRODUCTION

A Holder for Wood Lathe Tools

Here is a holder to keep your tools organized and handy while you are working the wood lathe. One of these holders, mounted within easy reach, will make your work space neat and efficient.

Tools

Screwdriver	Straightedge
Saw	Pencil
Compass	Drill and bits

Materials

Quantity	Description	Cost
2	12″ × 12″ pieces of $\frac{3}{4}$″ plywood	
1	70″ piece of ballister stock ($1\frac{3}{8}$″ × $1\frac{3}{8}$″ actual size)	
8	$1\frac{1}{2}$″ No. 6 wood screws	

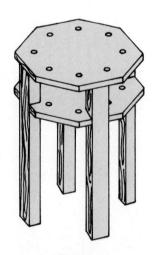

Figure 1

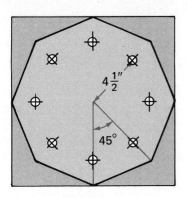

Figure 2

Production Plan

1. Draw regular 8-sided polygons (octagons) on the two squares of plywood, as shown in Figure 2.

2. Saw out the octagons.

3. Locate the centers of the 8 holes for holding the lathe tools, as in Figure 2.

4. Drill the holes in both octagons. The diameters of the holes will vary, depending on the sizes of the tools to be placed in the holder. Most lathe tools will seat handily in a $\frac{3}{4}''$ hole.

5. Cut notches to receive the legs in one of the octagons, as shown in Figure 3. The notches are to be centered on the sides.

6. Cut the 70'' ballister stock into four equal lengths.

7. Assemble the holder, as shown in Figure 1, using the wood screws. The tops of the two octagons are to be located $4\frac{1}{2}''$ apart.

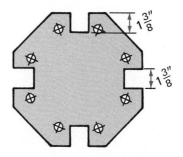

Figure 3

Modifying the Design

1. How many sides would the polygons have if the central angles in the circle have 20°? How many sides if the central angles are 45°?

2. How many degrees should the central angles measure if the holder is designed for 12 tools? for 15 tools?

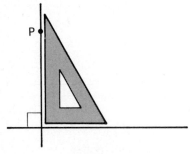

Figure 8-9

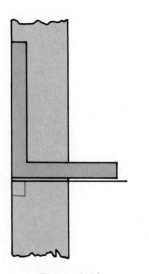

Figure 8-10

Constructions involving perpendiculars

8-4 Perpendicular lines

Lines which meet at right angles are called perpendicular lines, or simply perpendiculars. Perhaps you are familiar with the draftsman's triangle shown in Figure 8-9 or the carpenter's square, shown in Figure 8-10. Both are useful for drawing or testing perpendiculars.

Sometimes, however, you will need or prefer to use just the compass and straightedge. On your own paper, copy the constructions shown step by step below.

Constructing a Perpendicular at a Point *on* a Line

You are given line *l* and point *A*.
Draw *DA* perpendicular to *BC* through *A*.

Step 1

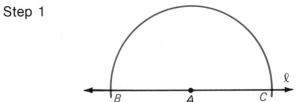

Step 2

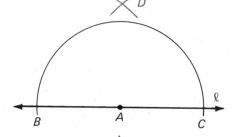

Step 3

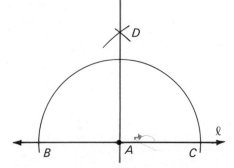

Constructing a Perpendicular From a Point to a Line

You are given line *l* and point *P*.
Draw *PS* perpendicular to *l* from *P*.

Step 1

Step 2

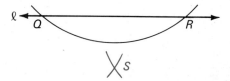

Step 3

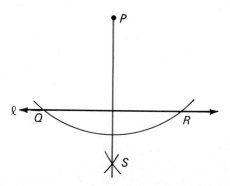

Constructing the Perpendicular Bisector of a Line Segment

You are given line segment *AB*.
Bisect *AB* (cut in half) with a perpendicular, *CD*.

Step 1

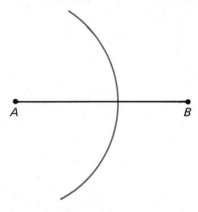

Step 2

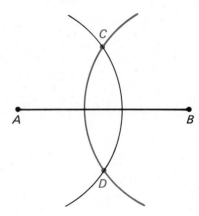

Step 3

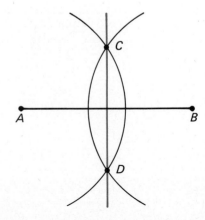

EXERCISES

A 1. Draw a line and locate a point on it. Draw a perpendicular to the line through the point.

2. Draw a line 3 inches long. Construct a perpendicular at each of its endpoints.

3. Draw a line segment 5 inches long. Construct its perpendicular bisector. Divide it into 4 equal parts with 2 more perpendicular bisectors.

B 4. Construct a square having sides 3 inches long.

5. Draw a circle having a 2-inch radius. Divide the circular region into 4 equal parts.

6. Draw a circle having a radius of 3 inches. Divide the circular region into 8 equal parts.

C 7. Draw a circle with a 2-inch diameter. Construct 2 perpendicular diameters. Connect the endpoints of the diameters in order around the circle. What figure have you made?

8. Draw a line and locate a point above it. Draw a perpendicular to the line through the point.

9. Draw a line 10 cm long. Construct a perpendicular at each of its endpoints.

10. Draw a line segment 13 cm long. Construct its perpendicular bisector. Divide it into 4 equal parts with 2 more perpendicular bisectors.

11. Construct a rectangle having a length of 9 cm and a width of 4.5 cm.

12. Draw a circle having a 9-centimeter radius. Divide the circular region into 4 equal parts.

13. Draw a circle having a radius of 8 centimeters. Divide the circular region into 3 equal parts.

14. Draw a circle with a 5-centimeter radius. Construct 2 perpendicular diameters. Connect the endpoints of the diameters in order around the circle. What figure have you made?

SPOTLIGHT ON INDUSTRY

Much effort has been put into producing printed products more quickly and efficiently. The computer and graphic arts industries have produced equipment to help simplify and shorten the process. Typewriters are now being designed to allow the operator to compose, edit, proofread, and correct copy all in one step. Attached to the typewriter, a Visual Display Terminal (VDT) shows the copy as it is being prepared. Then the copy is fed into an Optical Character Reader (OCR). The OCR "reads" the copy and punches a tape in code. The tape may then be stored in a computer and later printed out by a phototypesetter.

8-5 Circles

In Figure 8-11 lines *CA* and *CB* are tangents to circle *O*. Tangents are lines which touch a circle at just one point.

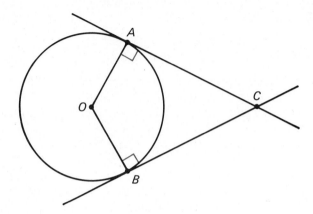

Figure 8-11

Notice that radius *OA* and radius *OB* are perpendicular to the tangents at *A* and *B*. Knowing this means that we can construct a tangent at any given point on a circle. On your own paper, copy the constructions shown step by step below.

Constructing a Tangent to a Given Point on a Circle

You are given circle *O* and point *A* on the circle.
Draw a tangent *l* through point *A*.

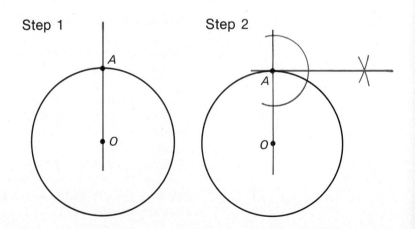

In Figure 8-12, *AB* and *CD* are chords of circle *O*. A chord is any line segment which has its endpoints on the circle.

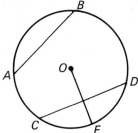

Figure 8-12

OF is the perpendicular bisector of chord *CD*. The perpendicular bisector of any chord always passes through the center of a circle. We can use this fact to find the center of any circle.

Locating the Center of a Circle

You are given a circle.
Draw any 2 chords.
Construct the perpendicular bisector of each to locate the center, *O*.

Step 1

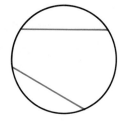

Step 2   **Step 3**

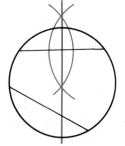   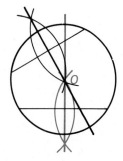

A 1. Draw a large circle *O* and radius *OX*. Construct the tangent at *X*.

2. Trace a circular object such as a can. Locate the center of the circle you have drawn.

B 3. Draw a circle *O* with a diameter *AB*. Construct tangents at *A* and *B*. Construct the perpendicular bisector of *AB*. At each of its endpoints, construct a tangent. What figure have you made?

4. Draw a triangle and construct the perpendicular bisectors of all three sides. What do you notice about the three lines you have constructed? Construct a circle passing through the corners of the triangle.

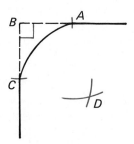

Figure 8-13

C 5. Figure 8-13 suggests a method for "rounding off" the corner of a drawing. "Round off" the corners of a sheet of paper, using this method.

SELF-ANALYSIS TEST 23

1. Draw a line and locate a point below it. Construct a perpendicular from the point to the line.

2. Draw a line segment. Construct its perpendicular bisector.

3. Draw a circle *O* with a radius *OA*. Construct a tangent to circle *O* at point *A*.

4. Trace a circular object. Locate the center of the circle you have traced.

Basic angle constructions

8-6 Angles

In section 8-4 you learned how to bisect, or cut in half, a line segment. We can also use just a compass and straightedge to **bisect an angle**. By doing this, we will form two smaller angles, each half the measure of the original angle.

Bisecting an Angle

You are given ∠A.
Construct bisector AD so that ∠BAD = ∠CAD.

Step 1

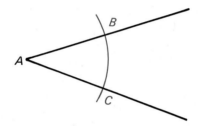

Step 2

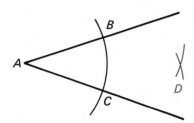

Step 3

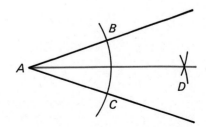

A draftsman was asked to extend this drawing of a cross section of an Acme screw so as to include another thread cross section. This meant constructing at point *C* an angle equal to ∠*ABC*, and at points *D* and *E* angles equal to ∠*BAF*.

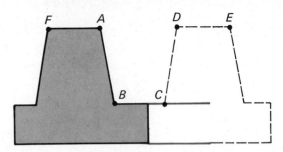

Practice the following construction until you can reproduce an angle quite precisely. A sharp lead will be essential.

Constructing an Angle Equal to a Given Angle

You are given ∠*B* and line *l*.
Construct an angle at *P* on *l* equal to ∠*B*.

Step 1

Make *PQ* = *BC*

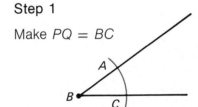

Step 2

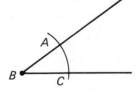
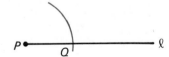

Step 3

Make *QR* = *CA*

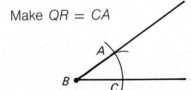
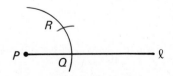

Step 4

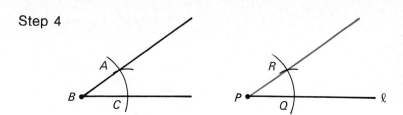

EXERCISES A

1. Draw an angle less than 90°. Construct its bisector.

2. Draw an angle which measures more than 90°. Construct its bisector.

3. Construct a triangle which has two equal angles.

4. Draw a triangle. Using a ruler to copy the length of one side only, construct another triangle identical to the one you drew.

B 5. Draw a triangle. Bisect each of its three angles. What do you notice about the angle bisectors? Draw a circle inside the triangle to which all three sides are tangent.

6. Construct an angle which measures 45°, using only a compass and a straightedge.

7. Figure 8-14 shows a cross section of a V-thread. Trace the drawing and extend it to include 2 more threads.

Figure 8-14

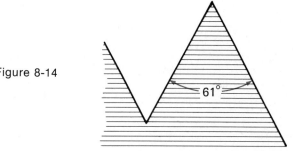

TRICKS OF THE TRADE

To join two pieces of stock at a 90° angle, cut the stock at 45° angles. The pieces fit as shown.

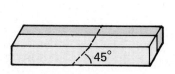

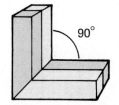

8-7 Parallel lines

Parallel lines are lines on a flat surface which do not meet. The opposite edges of a table illustrate parallel lines.

A triangle or a bevel may be used to draw parallel lines as shown in Figures 8-15 and 8-16. However, it is a good idea to learn how to use the compass for this purpose. Two methods are shown below.

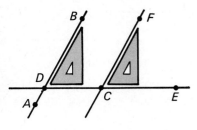

Figure 8-15

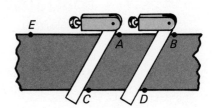

Figure 8-16

Constructing a Line Parallel to a Given Line through a Given Point

You are given line *l* and point *P*.
Draw a line *m* through *P* parallel to *l*.

Step 1

Step 2

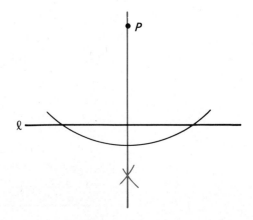

Step 3

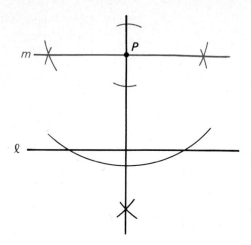

EXERCISES   A   1. Draw a horizontal line and place a point above the line. Construct a line through the point which is parallel to the original line.

2. Draw a vertical line and place a point to the right of the line. Construct a line through the point parallel to the original line.

3. Draw an angle greater than 90°. Label it ∠BAC.

Copy ∠BAC at point B as shown. Measure ∠DBA and ∠BAC and compare their sizes.

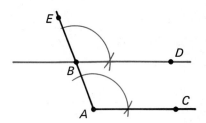

4. Draw an angle less than 90°. Label it ∠PQR.

Copy angle PQR on the opposite side of P as shown. Measure ∠PQR and ∠SPQ to check your construction.

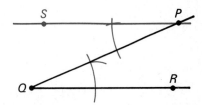

B 5. Copy Figure 8-17 and construct parallels to line *AE* through each of points *B*, *C*, and *D*.

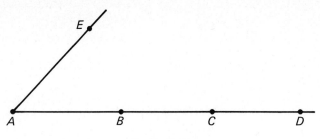

Figure 8-17

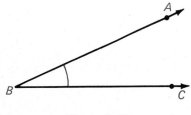

Figure 8-18

SELF-ANALYSIS TEST 24

1. Trace the angle shown in Figure 8-18. Draw ∠*CDE* so that ∠*ABC* = ∠*CDE*.

2. Construct the bisector of ∠*ABC* that you have traced.

3. Draw two parallel lines, using only a compass and straightedge.

Triangles

8-8 **Congruent and similar triangles**

We use the word congruent to describe figures having the same shape and the same size. For example, △*ABC* and △*DEF* are congruent.

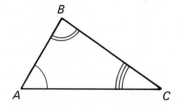
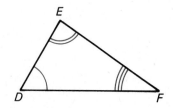

Notice that the corresponding angles are equal as well as the corresponding sides. That is,

$$\angle A = \angle D, \ \angle B = \angle E, \ \angle C = \angle F$$
$$AB = DE, \ BC = EF, \ AC = DF$$

We give a special name to triangles that have the same shape, but not necessarily the same size. They are **similar triangles.**

Similar triangles, such as $\triangle ABC$ and $\triangle XYZ$ below, have these important properties:

1. Corresponding angles are equal.

2. Corresponding sides are in proportion.

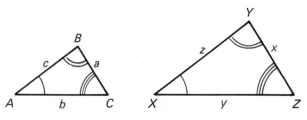

Figure 8-19

That is, $\angle A = \angle X, \angle B = \angle Y, \angle C = \angle Z.$

$$\frac{a}{x} = \frac{b}{y}, \frac{a}{x} = \frac{c}{z}, \frac{b}{y} = \frac{c}{z}$$

EXAMPLE   In Figure 8-19, if $a = 30$ m, $x = 10$ m, and $z = 20$ m, find the length of side c.

SOLUTION   Use the proportion containing the three given measurements.

$$\frac{a}{x} = \frac{c}{z}$$

$$\frac{30}{10} = \frac{c}{20}$$

$$c = 60 \text{ m.}$$

EXERCISES A 1. Draw a triangle XYZ with all angles less than 90°. Construct $\triangle MNQ$ congruent to it. Use three different methods.

2. Draw a triangle ABC with $\angle B$ greater than 90°. Construct $\triangle LMN$ congruent to $\triangle ABC$. Which method did you use?

3. Draw a large triangle ABC. Construct one similar to it with sides half as long. Show all construction marks.

251

4. △MNO is similar to △PQR. What is the measure of ∠O; ∠P; ∠Q; ∠R?

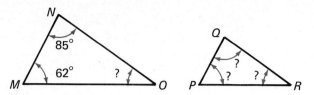

5. △ABC is similar to △XYZ. Use proportions to find the lengths of XZ and YZ.

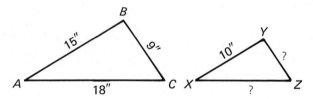

8-9 Right triangles

One of the oldest and most useful formulas in all sorts of work is the one called the Rule of Pythagoras. It can be applied to every right triangle, that is, a triangle with one right angle.

In *every* right triangle, the square of the hypotenuse (side opposite the right angle) equals the sum of the squares of the other two sides.

In Figure 8-20, does

$$5^2 = 3^2 + 4^2?$$
$$5 \times 5 = (3 \times 3) + (4 \times 4)$$
$$25 = 9 + 16$$
$$25 = 25$$

Yes, 5^2 does equal $3^2 + 4^2$.

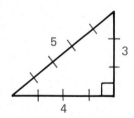

Figure 8-20

We can use the formula

$$c^2 = a^2 + b^2$$

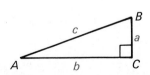

where c is the hypotenuse and a and b the other two sides.

Square Roots of Whole Numbers from 1 to 100

Number	Square Root	Number	Square Root	Number	Square Root	Number	Square Root
1	1.000	26	5.099	51	7.141	76	8.718
2	1.414	27	5.196	52	7.211	77	8.775
3	1.732	28	5.292	53	7.280	78	8.832
4	2.000	29	5.385	54	7.348	79	8.888
5	2.236	30	5.477	55	7.416	80	8.944
6	2.449	31	5.568	56	7.483	81	9.000
7	2.646	32	5.657	57	7.550	82	9.055
8	2.828	33	5.745	58	7.616	83	9.110
9	3.000	34	5.831	59	7.681	84	9.165
10	3.162	35	5.916	60	7.746	85	9.220
11	3.317	36	6.000	61	7.810	86	9.274
12	3.464	37	6.083	62	7.874	87	9.327
13	3.606	38	6.164	63	7.937	88	9.381
14	3.742	39	6.245	64	8.000	89	9.434
15	3.873	40	6.325	65	8.062	90	9.487
16	4.000	41	6.403	66	8.124	91	9.539
17	4.123	42	6.481	67	8.185	92	9.592
18	4.243	43	6.557	68	8.246	93	9.644
19	4.359	44	6.633	69	8.307	94	9.695
20	4.472	45	6.708	70	8.367	95	9.747
21	4.583	46	6.782	71	8.426	96	9.798
22	4.690	47	6.856	72	8.485	97	9.849
23	4.796	48	6.928	73	8.544	98	9.899
24	4.899	49	7.000	74	8.602	99	9.950
25	5.000	50	7.071	75	8.660	100	10.000

EXAMPLE   Find $\sqrt{62}$ to the nearest tenth.

SOLUTION   Locate 62 in the third column headed "Number." Its square root is shown in the next column to the right.

$\sqrt{62}$ = 7.874, or **7.9** to the nearest tenth

EXAMPLE 1 Find the length of PR as shown.

SOLUTION We determine that PQ is the hypotenuse. So we can use the formula:

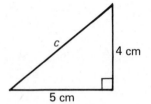

$$c^2 = a^2 + b^2$$
$$13^2 = a^2 + 12^2$$
$$169 = a^2 + 144$$
$$a^2 = 169 - 144$$
$$a^2 = 25$$
$$a = \sqrt{25}$$

Refer to the table of square roots on page 253.

$\sqrt{25} = 5$, so $PR = 5$ in.

EXAMPLE 2 In the right triangle shown, find the length of side c. Use the table of square roots on page 253.

SOLUTION
$$c^2 = a^2 + b^2$$
$$c^2 = 5^2 + 4^2$$
$$= 25 + 16$$
$$c^2 = 41$$
$$c = \sqrt{41}$$
$$c = 6.4 \text{ (approx.)}$$

EXERCISES In the following problems, c represents the length of the hypotenuse of a right triangle. a and b represent the lengths of the other two sides. Find the missing dimensions. Use the table of square roots.

	a	b	c
A 1.	3 cm	5 cm	?
2.	7 m	?	9 m
3.	8 in.	?	10 in.
4.	2 ft	4 ft	?

254

B 5. Find the length of the diagonal of a square having a side whose length is

a. 5 cm

b. 2 in.

c. 3 ft

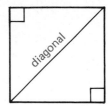

6. Find the lengths of the diagonals of rectangles having the following dimensions:

a. l = 4 in. w = 3 in.

b. l = 6 mm w = 8 mm

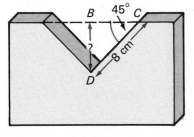

Figure 8-21

7. For the V-block in Figure 8-21, find the depth of the cut (*BD*). Hint: $BD = BC$

8. A square bar 1 inch on a side is to be milled from a circular rod. If we have available rods which are 1 in., $1\frac{1}{4}$ in., and $1\frac{1}{2}$ in. in diameter, which rod should we use? (Refer to Figure 8-22.)

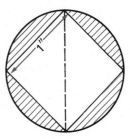

Figure 8-22

CREATIVE CRAFTSMAN

Design and build an object that appears to be

a. a circle when viewed from one direction;

b. a square when viewed from another direction, and

c. a hexagon when viewed from a third direction.

255

SELF-ANALYSIS TEST 25

1. △ABC is similar to △DEF. Find the lengths of DF and EF.

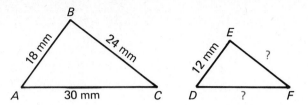

2. Find the length of a in Figure 8-23. You may use the table of square roots.

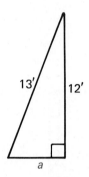

Figure 8-23

TAKING INVENTORY

You have learned to:

1. Measure angles and know the relationship between complementary angles and supplementary angles. (pp. 228–231)

2. Construct perpendicular lines. (pp. 236–238)

3. Construct tangents to a circle and locate the center of a circle. (pp. 240–241)

4. Copy and bisect an angle. (pp. 243–244)

5. Construct parallel lines. (pp. 246–247)

6. Find the missing dimensions of similar triangles. (p. 249)

7. Find a missing dimension for a right triangle when two of the sides are given. (p. 252)

MEASURING YOUR SKILLS

1. Using a protractor, draw an angle whose measure is 33°. (8-1)

2. How large must a central angle be for each spoke on a wheel if there are 6 spokes? (8-2)

3. Two angles of a triangle measure 46° and 38°. What is the measure of the third angle? (8-3)

4. What is the measure of ∠1 in Figure 8-24? *AB* is a straight line. (8-3)

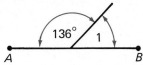

Figure 8-24

5. Draw a line segment 4 inches long. Construct its perpendicular bisector. (8-4)

6. Draw a circle *O* and a radius *OB*. Construct a tangent to circle *O* at point *B*. (8-5)

7. Trace a circular object and locate the center of the circle you drew. (8-5)

8. Draw an angle whose measure is greater than 90° and bisect it. (8-6)

9. Draw a vertical line *l* and locate point *P* to the right of it. Construct a line parallel to *l* through *P*. (8-7)

10. Find the measure of *JK* and *JL* in Figure 8-25. △*ABC* is similar to △*JKL*. (8-8)

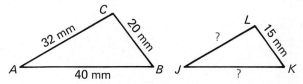

Figure 8-25

11. Find the measure of *a* in Figure 8-26. Use the table of square roots. (8-11)

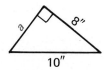

Figure 8-26

Media technicians use sophisticated electronic equipment to convey information through sight and sound.

CHAPTER 9 *Ratio, Proportion, Scale*

After completing this chapter, you should be able to:

1. *Use ratios to compare quantities.*
2. *Find the missing term of a proportion.*
3. *Find lengths and areas of similar objects.*
4. *Read and draw scale drawings.*

Ratios

9-1 Meaning of ratio

In Figure 9-1 gear *A* has 72 teeth. Gear *B* has 32 teeth. The ratio of the number of teeth of gear *A* to the number of teeth of gear *B* is $72:32$, or $\dfrac{72}{32} = \dfrac{9}{4}$.

B

A

Figure 9-1

Figure 9-2

Base coat $1:2:4$ Finish coat $1:2$

Concrete mixtures like those used in Figure 9-2 are also given in terms of ratios. For example, a $1:2:4$ mixture for the base coat consists of 1 part cement, 2 parts sand, and 4 parts crushed rock. A $1:2$ finish coat consists of 1 part cement and 2 parts sand.

As these examples show, a *ratio* is a comparison of numbers by division. Ratios are usually written as a fraction like $\frac{3}{4}$, although sometimes the form 3:4 is used.

Ratios occur widely in industry and the trades. Consider the following examples.

EXAMPLE 1   What is the ratio of the diameter of pulley *A* to the diameter of pulley *B* in Figure 9-3?

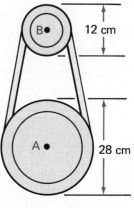

Figure 9-3

SOLUTION $\dfrac{\text{diameter of pulley } A}{\text{diameter of pulley } B} = \dfrac{28 \text{ cm}}{12 \text{ cm}} = \dfrac{7}{3}$

The ratio is 7:3.

Notice that we are comparing two dimensions, 28 cm and 12 cm, which are expressed in the same units of measure. The ratio 7:3, however, is a fraction. It is not expressed in units of measure.

EXAMPLE 2   What is the ratio of 30″ to 7′6″?

SOLUTION   To compare these lengths, we need to express them in the same units.

Change the 7′6″ to inches.

$$7'6'' = (7 \times 12) + 6 \text{ in.} = 84 + 6 = 90''$$

The ratio of 30″ to 90″ is 1:3.

260

EXERCISES

U.S. System   Metric System

A Express the following ratios in their simplest form.

1. 18″ to 24″

2. 3′ to 30′

3. 3″ to 12″

4. 2″ to 3½″ (Hint: Multiply by 2.)

5. 4″ to 18″

6. 2 yd to 1.5 yd

Express the following ratios in their simplest form.

14. 9 cm to 24 cm

15. 3 m to 6 m

16. 15 cm to 100 cm

17. 15 mm to 1 mm

18. 4 cm to 150 cm

19. 3 m to 1.5 m

Measure the line segments below in inches. Write the ratios in their simplest form.

7. a:c   9. d:a   11. c:d

8. e:c   10. a:b   12. e:a

20–25. Measure the line segments below in millimeters. Write the ratios in Exercises 7–12 in their simplest form.

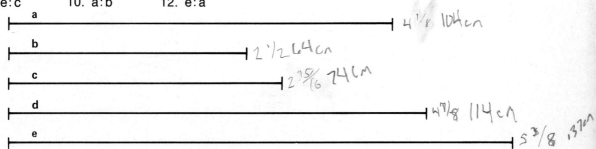

a   4⅛ 104cm

b   2½ 64cm

c   2¹⁵⁄₁₆ 74cm

d   4⁷⁄₈ 114cn

e   5³⁄₈ 137cm

The *pitch,* or steepness, of a roof is the ratio of the rise to the run.

$$pitch = \frac{rise}{run}$$

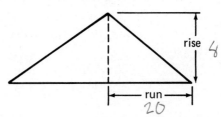

rise 4

run 20

B 13. Find the pitch of a roof with these dimensions:

    a. rise = 8′, run = 20′

    b. rise = 6′, run = 24′

    c. rise = 6′, run = 18′

    d. rise = 5′, run = 22′6″

    e. rise = 4½′, run = 20′3″

26. Using the information at the left, find the pitch of a roof with these dimensions.

    a. rise = 1.5 m, run = 7.5 m

    b. rise = 1.2 m, run = 8.4 m

    c. rise = 1.6 m, run = 6.4 m

    d. rise = 1.75 m, run = 10.5 m

    e. rise = .95 m, run = 3.8 m

9-2 Screw threads

Screw threads are designed to meet a variety of industrial needs. Three common screw threads are shown in Figure 9-4. The ratio of the depth of the thread, D, and the number of threads per inch, N, for each kind of thread is given by the formulas.

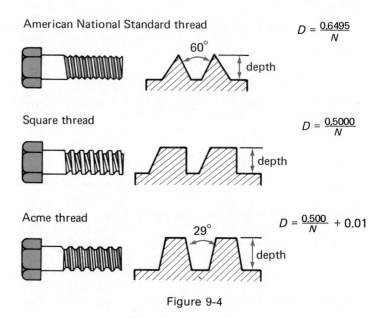

American National Standard thread

$$D = \frac{0.6495}{N}$$

Square thread

$$D = \frac{0.5000}{N}$$

Acme thread

$$D = \frac{0.500}{N} + 0.01$$

Figure 9-4

Screws are machined to fine tolerances. Therefore, a machinist must be familiar with these formulas in order to set the controls on the threading lathe.

EXAMPLE 1   What must be the depth setting on a lathe to machine an American National Standard screw having 12 threads per inch?

SOLUTION $D = \dfrac{.6495}{N} = \dfrac{.6495}{12} = .0541$ (approx.)

The thread depth must be .0541″.

EXAMPLE 2   How many threads per inch does an Acme screw have if its thread depth is .04125″?

SOLUTION

$$D = \frac{.5000}{N} + .01$$

$$.04125 = \frac{.5000}{N} + .01$$

$$.03125 = \frac{.5000}{N} \text{ (Subtracting .01)}$$

$$.03125\,N = .5000 \text{ (Multiplying by } N)$$

$$N = \frac{.5000}{.03125} \text{ (Dividing by .03125)}$$

$$N = 16$$

There are 16 threads per inch.

EXERCISES   Exercises 1 and 2 refer to the American National Standard thread.

A 1. Find the depth of the thread if there are
   a. 13 threads per inch.
   b. 40 threads per inch.

2. Find the number of threads per inch

   a. if the depth is .027″.
   b. if the depth is .059″.
   c. if the depth is .0203″.

B 3. In an Acme screw, the number of threads per inch is 25. Find the depth.

4. In a square thread, the number of threads per inch is 36. Find the depth.

SELF-ANALYSIS TEST 26

Express the following ratios in their simplest form.

1. 9″ to 36″   4. 6 yd to 9 ft

2. 4′ to 12′   5. 5 m to 7 m

3. 3 cm to 27 cm   6. 10′ to 10″

7. Find the depth of an American National Standard thread if there are 15 threads per inch.

8. In a square thread, the number of threads per inch is 10. Find the depth.

Figure 9-5

Proportions

9-3 The meaning of proportion

Sometimes we need to change the size of a drawing. To enlarge or reduce a drawing, we can use a photocopying machine which enlarges or reduces, as in Figure 9-5.

No matter which method we use, we must be sure that we change the height and the width *by the same ratio*. For example, a template for extruding a plastic grille is shown in a $\frac{1}{2}$-size drawing in Figure 9-6.

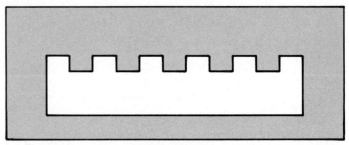

Figure 9-6

In the drawing the length of the block is $3\frac{5}{8}''$. The height is $1\frac{3}{8}''$. The actual dimensions of the block are:

$$w = 2 \times 3\tfrac{5}{8}'' = 7\tfrac{1}{4}''; \; h = 2 \times 1\tfrac{3}{8}'' = 2\tfrac{3}{4}''$$

Would you agree with the following statement?

$$\frac{\text{Width of drawing}}{\text{Width of actual template}} = \frac{\text{Height of drawing}}{\text{Height of actual template}}$$

Or, $\;\;$ Ratio of $\;1$ to 2 $\;\dfrac{3\frac{5}{8}''}{7\frac{1}{4}''} = \dfrac{1\frac{3}{8}''}{2\frac{3}{4}''}\;$ Ratio of 1 to 2

The ratio of $3\frac{5}{8}''$ to $7\frac{1}{4}''$ is the same ratio as $1\frac{3}{8}''$ to $2\frac{3}{4}''$. An equation of two ratios is called a proportion. The terms of a proportion have special names, as shown below.

First term (extreme) $\searrow$ $\;\;$ Third term (mean) $\swarrow$

$$\frac{3\frac{5}{8}}{7\frac{1}{4}} = \frac{1\frac{3}{8}}{2\frac{3}{4}}$$

Second term (mean) $\nearrow$ $\;\;$ Fourth term (extreme) $\nwarrow$

Notice that the product of the means is $7\frac{1}{4} \times 1\frac{3}{8} = 9\frac{31}{32}$. The product of the extremes is $3\frac{5}{8} \times 2\frac{3}{4} = 9\frac{31}{32}$. This fact suggests the following rule.

In a proportion the product of the means is equal to the product of the extremes.

We can solve a proportion with a missing term using the rule of means and extremes.

EXAMPLE 1 Solve $\dfrac{7}{x} = \dfrac{21}{24}$.

SOLUTION
$$\dfrac{7}{x} = \dfrac{21}{24}$$

$21x = 7 \times 24$ (Means, extremes)
$21x = 168$

$\dfrac{21x}{21} = \dfrac{168}{21}$ (Dividing by 21)

$x = 8$

EXAMPLE 2 A pattern for a rectangular end table is printed in a book. The pattern measures 7″ by $10\frac{1}{2}$″. If the width of the finished table is to be $17\frac{1}{2}$″, what will be the finished length?

SOLUTION The proportion for the finished length is

$$\dfrac{7}{17\frac{1}{2}} = \dfrac{10\frac{1}{2}}{l}$$

$7l = 10\frac{1}{2} \times 17\frac{1}{2}$ (Means, extremes)

$l = \dfrac{10\frac{1}{2} \times 17\frac{1}{2}}{7}$ (Dividing by 7)

$l = 26\frac{1}{4}$

The table will be $26\frac{1}{4}$″ long.

EXERCISES Solve the following proportions.

A

1. $\dfrac{x}{2} = \dfrac{3}{4}$

2. $\dfrac{3}{y} = \dfrac{9}{21}$

3. $\dfrac{7}{8} = \dfrac{l}{24}$

4. $\dfrac{3}{8} = \dfrac{12}{p}$

5. $\dfrac{x}{3\frac{1}{5}} = \dfrac{6}{16}$

6. $\dfrac{5}{4\frac{1}{2}} = \dfrac{y}{27}$

7. $\dfrac{\frac{1}{2}}{400} = \dfrac{a}{100}$ 8. $\dfrac{\frac{3}{4}}{150} = \dfrac{2}{s}$

B   9. The watch below is shown twice the actual size. Use proportions to find the dimensions of parts *A*, *B*, and *C*.

10. The plan for a 12′ by 14′ rectangular room is drawn 18″ by 21″. Use a proportion to find the dimensions of a closet shown in the drawing as $4\frac{1}{2}$″ by 9″.

9-4 Inverse proportions

The speeds at which a pair of gears turn is related to the number of teeth in the gears. In figure 9-7 the ratio of the number of teeth in gear *A* to the number of teeth in gear *B* is 12:25 or $\frac{12}{25}$.

Gear *A* will make more revolutions per minute (rpm) than gear *B*. In particular, gear *A* will turn 25 times while gear *B* turns just 12 times. The ratio, $\frac{25}{12}$, is the *reciprocal* of the ratio of the numbers of teeth. It is called the gear ratio.

The following formula describes the relationship:

$$\frac{\text{Speed of gear } A}{\text{Speed of gear } B} = \frac{\text{Number of teeth in gear } B}{\text{Number of teeth in gear } A}$$

A proportion in which the ratios are based on reciprocal relationships is called an **inverse proportion**.

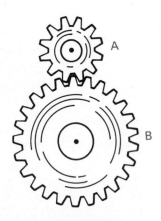

Figure 9-7

EXAMPLE 1   If gear *A* in Figure 9-7 is turning at 300 rpm, what is the speed of gear *B*?

SOLUTION $\dfrac{\text{Speed of } A}{\text{Speed of } B} = \dfrac{\text{Number of teeth in } B}{\text{Number of teeth in } A}$

$$\frac{300}{s} = \frac{25}{12}$$
$$25s = 12 \times 300$$
$$25s = 3600$$
$$s = 144$$

The speed of gear *B* is 144 rpm.

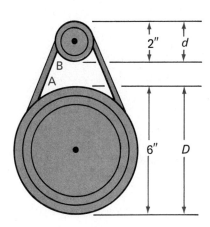

Figure 9-8

Another example of an inverse proportion is illustrated in Figure 9-8. The speed at which a pair of pulleys, connected by a belt, revolve are inversely proportional to the diameters of the pulleys. Thus,

$$\frac{\text{Speed of } A}{\text{Speed of } B} = \frac{\text{Diameter of } B}{\text{Diameter of } A}.$$

EXAMPLE 2   If pulley *A* in Figure 9-8 is rotating at 200 rpm, what is the speed of pulley *B*?

SOLUTION $\dfrac{\text{Speed of } A}{\text{Speed of } B} = \dfrac{\text{Diameter of } B}{\text{Diameter of } A}$

$$\frac{200}{x} = \frac{2}{6}$$
$$2x = 1200$$
$$x = 600$$

The speed of pulley *B* is 600 rpm.

A third example of an inverse proportion is shown in Figure 9-9. In an automobile engine the rocker arm is used to change the upward force of the pushrod to a downward force on the valve. The adjusting nut serves as a fulcrum, or pivot point, for the rocker arm.

The proportion below describes the operations of the valve system:

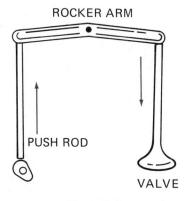

Figure 9-9

$$\frac{\text{Upward force on pushrod}}{\text{Downward force on valve}} = \frac{\text{Pivot-to-valve distance}}{\text{Pivot-to-pushrod distance}}$$

Can you see why this is an inverse proportion?

EXAMPLE 3　Find the downward force on the valve in Figure 9-9. The upward force of the pushrod is 220 lb. The valve stem is .875″ from the pivot point. The pushrod seat is 1.0625″ from the pivot.

SOLUTION　The proportion will be

$$\frac{220}{F} = \frac{.875}{1.0625}$$

$.875F = 220 \times 1.0625$ (Means, extremes)

$$F = \frac{220 \times 1.0625}{.875}$$ (Dividing by .875)

$F = 267.14$ (approx.)

The downward force on the valve is 267.14 lb.

EXERCISES　Copy and complete the table. Use the formula in Example 1.

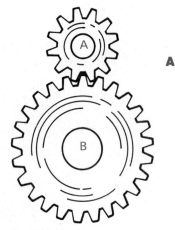

A

		Teeth in gear A	Teeth in gear B	Speed of gear A	Speed of gear B
1.		12	25	400 rpm	?
2.		12	24	?	1170 rpm
3.		?	15	750 rpm	350 rpm
4.		20	?	360 rpm	800 rpm
5.		15	10	320 rpm	?
6.		48	18	?	360 rpm

Copy and complete the table. Use the formula in Example 2.

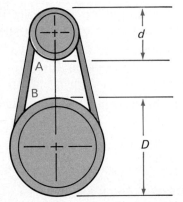

	Diameter of pulley A	Diameter of pulley B	Speed of pulley A	Speed of pulley B
7.	4″	?	300 rpm	400 rpm
8.	$4\frac{1}{4}″$	$8\frac{1}{2}″$	?	350 rpm
9.	15″	10″	350 rpm	?
10.	45 cm	30 cm	350 rpm	?
11.	15.3 cm	45.9 cm	?	240 rpm
12.	?	15.5 cm	600 rpm	750 rpm

B 13. The motor for a table saw runs at 1750 rpm and has a pulley 4″ in diameter. The saw blade is turned by a shaft with a pulley 6″ in diameter. At what speed does the saw blade revolve?

16. The motor used to run a drill press turns at 1950 rpm. It has a pulley 10 cm in diameter. The drill is turned by a shaft with a pulley 15 cm in diameter. At what speed does the drill bit revolve?

14. A 28-tooth gear is set on the shaft of a motor running at 1200 rpm. It meshes with a 64-tooth gear. What is the speed of the second gear?

17. A 42-tooth gear is on the shaft of an electric motor running at 3600 rpm. The gear meshes with a 70-tooth gear. What is the speed of the second gear?

15. A machinist must replace a broken pressure spring on a printing press. The spring is activated by an arm that receives 360 lb of force. The location of the pivot point on the arm is shown below. What must be the strength of the replacement spring in order to "balance" the force of the arm?

18. To replace a defective valve spring, a mechanic measures the upward force of the pushrod. He also measures the distance from the pivot point of the rocker arm to the valve stem and to the pushrod set. What should be the strength of the spring?

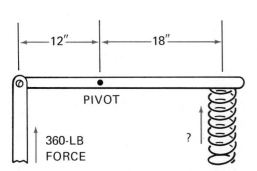

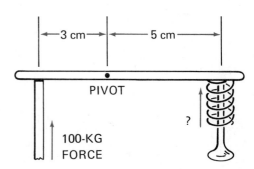

SELF-ANALYSIS TEST 27

Solve the proportions.

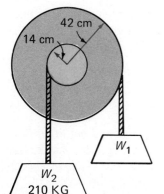

1. $\dfrac{x}{4} = \dfrac{10}{8}$

2. $\dfrac{9}{y} = \dfrac{18}{6}$

3. $\dfrac{7}{4} = \dfrac{a}{28}$

4. $\dfrac{16}{12} = \dfrac{4}{b}$

5. A special windlass like the one shown at the left is used to lift an engine from an automobile. Find the amount of force that is needed to lift an engine weighing 210 kg. Use this formula:

$$\frac{\text{Force on rope}}{\text{Weight of engine}} = \frac{\text{Diameter of small pulley}}{\text{Diameter of large pulley}}$$

Photographic Laboratory Technician

The volume of commercial photography used in industry has grown rapidly in recent years. At the same time, pocket-size cameras and film cartridges have made amateur photography a very popular hobby. Processing the great amounts of professional and amateur photos requires the services of trained photographic laboratory technicians. Have you ever considered a career for yourself in this growing field?

Job Description

What do darkroom technicians do?
1. They develop film by placing it in tanks and trays of chemical solutions. They vary the developing process according to the kind of film used—black and white negative, color negative, and so on.
2. They make photographs by transferring the image from a negative to photographic paper. During this printing process they can do minor touch-up work on the photo.
3. They enlarge or reduce photographs.
4. They may set up lights and cameras, and assist a photographer in his work.

Qualifications

Preference is given to high school graduates who have had courses in mathematics, physics, and chemistry.
Trade courses in photography or hobby experience in developing film are also helpful.

Training

Photographic laboratory technicians usually get informal on-the-job training. In most cases they begin as assistants to experienced technicians. After three or four years of apprentice work, the technician is ready to handle a wide variety of laboratory processes.

Working Conditions

A 40-hour week with possible overtime.

Overtime is common during peak seasons or in meeting
   commercial deadlines.

Most jobs are not usually physically strenuous, though eye
   strain can occur. Care must be exercised around chemicals.

Laboratories are generally clean, quiet and well lighted.

Opportunities for Advancement

Many technicians advance to supervisory positions in the
laboratory. Those whose experience has been in smaller
laboratories may eventually transfer to large, automated
laboratories. Frequently, a technician will continue on and
become a professional photographer.

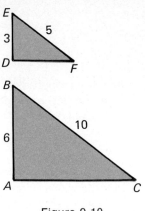

Figure 9-10

Similar figures

9-5 Finding lengths with similar figures

In Chapter 8 you learned about similar triangles like those shown in Figure 9-10. Recall that in similar figures the corresponding sides have equal ratios. By corresponding sides, we mean the sides opposite the equal angles. In triangles *ABC* and *DEF* the corresponding sides are *AB* and *DE*, *AC* and *DF*, *BC* and *EF*. The ratios of the corresponding sides are equal. Thus,

$$\frac{AB}{DE} = \frac{AC}{DF} = \frac{BC}{EF}.$$

EXAMPLE
A graphic arts specialist wants to make a "blow up" of a 8″ by 10″ photo. If the width of the "blow up" is to be 44″, what will be the height?

SOLUTION
The proportion for this enlargement is

$$\frac{\text{Width of original photo}}{\text{Width of enlargement}} = \frac{\text{Height of original photo}}{\text{Height of enlargement}}$$

$$\frac{8}{44} = \frac{10}{h}$$

$$8h = 44 \times 10$$

$$h = \frac{44 \times 10}{8}$$

$$h = 55''$$

EXERCISES
Find the missing lengths of the similar triangles *MNO* and *PQR*.

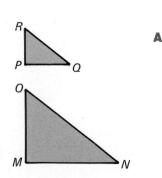

A

		PQ	PR	QR	MN	MO	ON
	1.	4″	6″	7″	8″	?	?
	2.	18″	15″	12″	$4\frac{1}{2}$″	?	?
	3.	6″	$7\frac{1}{2}$″	$5\frac{1}{2}$″	9″	?	?
	4.	?	?	2.5 cm	6 cm	9 cm	10 cm
	5.	?	?	12 cm	8 cm	7 cm	4 cm
	6.	?	?	15 m	7 cm	5 cm	3 cm

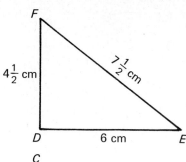

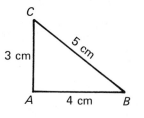

Figure 9-11

9-6 Finding areas with similar figures

Figure 9-11 shows a pair of similar triangles. Would you agree that the ratio between any pair of corresponding sides is 2:3?

Using the formula for area which we studied in Chapter 6, we see that the area of triangle ABC is:

$$(\tfrac{1}{2} \times 4 \times 3) \text{ sq cm} = 6 \text{ sq cm}$$

The area of triangle DEF is:

$$(\tfrac{1}{2} \times 6 \times 4.5) \text{ sq cm} = 13.5 \text{ sq cm}$$

The ratio of the area of triangle ABC to the area of triangle DEF is $\frac{6}{13.5}$, or $\frac{4}{9}$.

Notice that if we take the squares of each pair of corresponding sides, we get the following ratios:

$$AB:DE = 4^2:6^2 = 16:36 = 4:9$$
$$AC:DF = 3^2:(4\tfrac{1}{2})^2 = 9:\tfrac{81}{4} = 4:9$$
$$BC:EF = 5^2:(7\tfrac{1}{2})^2 = 25:\tfrac{225}{4} = 4:9$$

This pattern suggests the following rule.

The ratio of the areas of similar figures is equal to the ratio of the squares of any pair of corresponding sides of the figures.

EXAMPLE 1   What is the ratio between the areas of two circles having diameters of 2″ and 3″?

SOLUTION   Since all circles are similar, the ratio of the areas is equal to the ratio of the squares of the diameters. The ratio is:

$$2^2:3^2 = 4:9$$

Thus, the area of the 2″ circle is $\frac{4}{9}$ of the area of the 3″ circle. Or, the area of the 3″ circle is $2\tfrac{1}{4}$ times the area of the 2″ circle.

EXAMPLE 2   Two pipes, each 3″ in diameter, are joined into a single pipe by a "Y". What must be the diameter of the larger pipe in order to carry off the flow of the two smaller pipes?

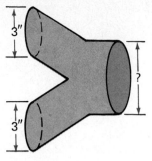

SOLUTION   We need to know the diameter, D, of a pipe whose cross section has twice the area of a pipe 3″ in diameter. Since the areas of circles are in the same ratio as the squares of their diameters, we can write the following proportion:

$$\frac{\text{(Diameter of large pipe)}^2}{\text{(Diameter of small pipe)}^2} = \frac{2}{1}$$

or

$$\frac{d^2}{3^2} = \frac{2}{1}$$

$$d^2 = 18$$

$$d = 4.25 \text{ (approx.)}$$

We need a pipe with a diameter of $4\frac{1}{4}$″ or more.

EXERCISES

U.S. System

A 1. What is the ratio between the areas of a 4″ circle and a 3″ circle?

2. How many times greater than the area of a 1″ circle is the area of
   a. a 3″ circle?
   b. a 4″ circle?
   c. a $5\frac{1}{2}$″ circle?

3. A triangle has an area of 144 sq ft. One of the sides of the triangle is 9′ long. Find the area of a similar triangle having a corresponding side with a length of
   a. 3′.   c. 21′.
   b. $4\frac{1}{2}$′.   d. 14.5′.

Metric System

8. What is the ratio between the areas of a 3 cm circle and a 5 cm circle?

9. How many times greater than the area of a 1 cm circle is the area of
   a. a 4 cm circle?
   b. a 4.5 cm circle?
   c. a 5.5 cm circle?

10. A triangle has an area of 72 sq cm. One of the sides of the triangle is 8 cm long. Find the area of a similar triangle having a corresponding side with a length of
   a. 2 cm.   c. 6.5 cm.
   b. 5 cm.   d. 20 cm.

4. What is the ratio of the areas of two squares when
   a. the ratio of the sides is $\frac{1}{2}$?
   b. the ratio of the sides is $\frac{2}{3}$?
   c. the sides are 4″ and 16″?

B 5. A 4″ water pipe is to be replaced by 2″ pipes. How many smaller pipes are needed to carry the same amount of water?

6. A circular heating duct is 12″ in diameter. How many ducts 8″ in diameter are needed to carry the same volume of air?

7. How many 1″ pipes are needed to carry as much water as one 2″ pipe?

11. What is the ratio of the areas of two squares when
    a. the ratio of the sides is 2 to 4?
    b. the ratio of the sides is 3 to 5?
    c. the sides are 8 cm and 24 cm?

12. A 10 cm water pipe is to be replaced with 4 cm pipes. How many smaller pipes are needed to carry the same amount of water?

13. A circular heating duct is 30 cm in diameter. How many ducts 20 cm in diameter are needed to carry the same volume of air?

14. How many 2.5 cm pipes are required to carry as much water as one 5 cm pipe?

SELF-ANALYSIS TEST 28

U.S. System

1. Triangles *ABC* and *DEF* are similar. Find the lengths of sides *DF* and *EF*.

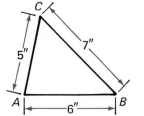

Metric System

3. Answer Exercise 1, using the similar triangles *ABC* and *DEF* below.

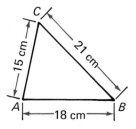 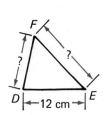

2. Circles *P* and *Q* are similar. Find the ratio of their areas.

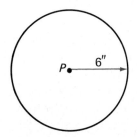 

4. Answer Exercise 2, using the circles below.

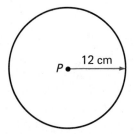

Scales

9-7 The architect's scale

So far in this chapter we have studied ways by which we can find dimensions if we know the size of a similar object. The methods which we studied can be used in many industrial fields, such as graphic arts, manufacturing, and so on.

When a draftsman wants to find certain dimensions, as on a **scale drawing** or a blueprint, he uses a special tool called an **architect's scale**. Figure 9-12 shows an architect's triangular ruler.

Figure 9-12

The architect's rule contains 10 different scales that are frequently used in drafting. These scales, in order of increasing size, are $\frac{3}{32}$, $\frac{3}{16}$, $\frac{1}{8}$, $\frac{1}{4}$, $\frac{3}{8}$, $\frac{1}{2}$, $\frac{3}{4}$, 1, $1\frac{1}{2}$, and 3.

A section of the $\frac{1}{2}$-scale is shown in Figure 9-13.

Figure 9-13

Notice that the $\frac{1}{2}$-scale runs from the right to the left across the ruler. The numbers 10, 9, 8, and 7 refer to the scale which begins at the other end of the ruler. We ignore these numbers when we are using the $\frac{1}{2}$-scale.

EXAMPLE 1   Represent a length of 4', using the ½-scale.

SOLUTION   To do this, we draw a line 4 units long, beginning at the 0-mark and ending at the 4-mark. Thus, in a scale drawing where all the lengths are given in the scale of $\frac{1}{2}'' = 1'$, the length of AB would represent 4'.

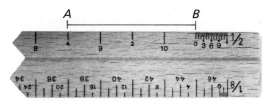

EXAMPLE 2   Represent a length of 5', using the ½-scale.

SOLUTION   To do this we draw a line 5 units long, beginning at the 0-mark and ending at the 8-mark. Note carefully that even though line CD ends at the 8-mark, CD is only 5 units long. We ignore the 8, of course, because it is part of the scale which runs from the left to the right.

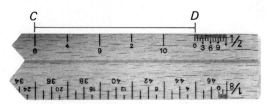

EXAMPLE 3   Represent a length of 5'3'' on the ½-scale.

SOLUTION   As in Example 2, the distance CD represents 5'. How do we represent an additional 3'' on the ½-scale? Notice the small subdivisions at the end of the scales. The numbers 3, 6, 9, and 12 (not shown) represent the lengths $\frac{3}{12}$, $\frac{6}{12}$, $\frac{9}{12}$, and $\frac{12}{12}$ of the scale unit. Since 3'' is $\frac{3}{12}$ of a foot, the distance from D to E represents 3''. Thus, we show a length of 5'3'' on the ½-scale by line CE, as in the figure below.

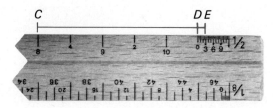

EXERCISES **A** 1. Using the $\frac{1}{2}$-scale on an architect's rule, represent the following lengths:

    a. 18'   c. 5'   e. 7'6"

    b. 10'   d. 3'   f. 9'9"

2. Using the $\frac{1}{8}$-scale, represent the following lengths:

    a. 12'   c. 9'   e. 6'5"

    b. 18'   d. 13'   f. 2'11"

3. Using the $\frac{3}{8}$-scale, represent the following lengths:

    a. 20'   c. 13'   e. 9'6"

    b. 12'   d. 17'   f. 19'2"

B 4. Assuming that Figure 9-14 was drawn using the 1-scale (1" = 1'), redraw it:

    a. Using the $\frac{3}{4}$-scale.   c. Using the $\frac{1}{2}$-scale.

    b. Using the $\frac{1}{8}$-scale.

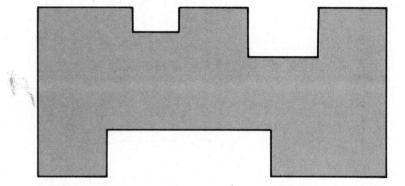

Figure 9-14

5. Using the architect's scale, make an oversize drawing of the lock plate shown below using the $1\frac{1}{2}$-scale.

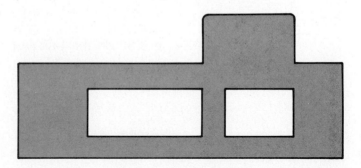

9-8 Scale drawings

Because it is not practical to make full-size drawings or models of objects, scale drawings and scale models are used widely in industry.

The actual objects may be too large, as in the case of the buildings represented by the scale model in Figure 9-15.

Figure 9-15

In other cases, a drawing must be larger than the object in order to show the important details, as with the cross section of an American National Standard screw thread in Figure 9-16.

Scale drawings usually have the scale indicated on the drawing. Which scale is used depends on the space available to make the drawing and the amount of detail on the drawing.

Figure 9-16

The following rule can be helpful in preparing scale drawings.

> To find the measurements to be used in a scale drawing, multiply the dimensions of the actual object by the scale ratio.

EXAMPLE 1   What lengths of lines should be used to represent dimensions A and B of the V-block in a scale of $1'' = 6''$?

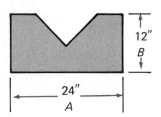

SOLUTION   The scale ratio is $\frac{1''}{6''}$, or $\frac{1}{6}$. Therefore, each dimension in the drawing must be multiplied by $\frac{1}{6}$. Thus

$$\text{Scale length of } A = \tfrac{1}{6} \times 24 = 4$$
$$\text{Scale length of } B = \tfrac{1}{6} \times 12 = 2$$

Therefore, on the scale drawing of the V-block A will be drawn $4''$ long. B will be drawn $2''$ long.

279

EXAMPLE 2   The floor plan shown below must be drawn in a scale of $\frac{3}{4}'' = 1'$. What length of lines will be used to represent the length and width of the floor plan?

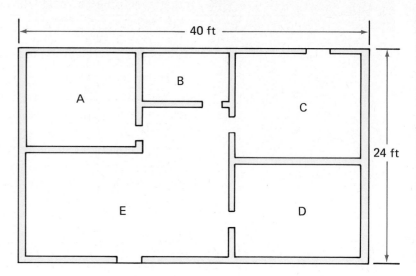

SOLUTION   The scale ratio is $\dfrac{\frac{3}{4}''}{1'}$, or $\dfrac{\frac{3}{4}''}{12''} = \frac{1}{16}$. Therefore, each dimen-

sion shown in the floor plan must be multiplied by $\frac{1}{16}$.

Scale length of plan $= \frac{1}{16} \times 40' = 2\frac{1}{2}'$, or $30''$

Scale width of plan $= \frac{1}{16} \times 24' = 1\frac{1}{2}'$ or $18''$

Occasionally plans are given in a scale version only, so that they can be adapted to fit a variety of size requirements. In such case the following rule can help us.

> To find the dimensions of the actual objects from a scale drawing, multiply each length on the drawing by the *reciprocal* of the scale ratio.

EXAMPLE 3   A plan for an automated assembly line is drawn in a scale of $\frac{1}{4}'' = 1'$. The overall length of the assembly line on the drawing is $12\frac{1}{4}''$. How long should the actual assembly line be?

SOLUTION   The scale ratio is $\dfrac{\frac{1}{4}''}{1'}$ or $\dfrac{\frac{1}{4}''}{12''} = \frac{1}{48}$. The reciprocal of $\frac{1}{48}$ is 48. Thus,

$$48 \times 12\frac{1}{4}'' = 48 \times \frac{49}{4} = 588'', \text{ or } 49'$$

EXERCISES Complete the following table.

		Scale	Scale ratio	Dimension being represented	Length of line on drawing
A	1.	$1'' = 6''$	$\frac{1}{6}$	$24''$	?
	2.	$1'' = 3''$	$\frac{1}{3}$	$48''$	?
	3.	$\frac{1}{2}'' = 6''$	?	$90''$	?
	4.	$\frac{1}{4}'' = 6''$	?	?	$3''$
	5.	$\frac{1}{8}'' = 6''$	?	?	$4\frac{1}{8}''$
	6.	$\frac{1}{8}'' = 1'$	$\frac{1}{96}$	$36'$	?
	7.	$\frac{1}{4}'' = 1'$	$\frac{1}{48}$	$48\frac{1}{2}'$	?
	8.	$\frac{1}{16}'' = 1'$	?	$240'$	?
	9.	$\frac{3}{16}'' = 1'$	?	?	$14\frac{3}{4}''$
	10.	$\frac{3}{16}'' = 1'$	?	?	$22\frac{3}{8}''$

B 11. Measure the length of lines A, B, and C. Using the scale given for each line, find the length being represented by lines A, B, and C.

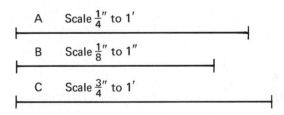

A   Scale $\frac{1}{4}''$ to $1'$

B   Scale $\frac{1}{8}''$ to $1''$

C   Scale $\frac{3}{4}''$ to $1'$

12. Find the actual dimensions of rooms B, C, D and E in the floor plan in Example 2. The scale of the plan is $\frac{3}{32}'' = 1'$.

13. The chair leg below must be drawn in a scale of $1\frac{1}{2}'' = 1'$. How long should each of the dimensions be drawn on the scale drawing?

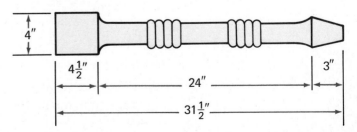

SELF-ANALYSIS TEST 29

1. Using an architect's rule, draw the following:

   a. a line representing 6', on the $\frac{1}{2}$-scale.

   b. a line representing 7'6", on the $\frac{1}{4}$-scale.

   c. a line representing 9'4", on the $\frac{3}{8}$-scale.

2. How long a line would you draw to represent a line

   a. 10' long, using a scale of $\frac{1}{4}'' = 1'$?

   b. 5' long, using a scale of $\frac{3}{8}'' = 1'$?

3. Find the actual length of a dimension that is represented by a line

   a. 3'' long, in drawing having a scale of $\frac{1}{4}'' = 1'$.

   b. $7\frac{3}{16}''$ long, in a drawing having a scale of $\frac{3}{16}'' = 1'$.

RESEARCH PROJECT

Plans and blueprints of homes and buildings may be found in your local library. Study a few of these plans. In which scale are most of them drawn? Check the accuracy of the lengths of important lines on the blueprints, using an architect's rule.

TAKING INVENTORY

1. A **ratio** is a comparison of numbers by division. (p. 258)

2. A **proportion** is a statement of two equal ratios. (p. 262)

3. In a proportion the product of the means is equal to the product of the extremes. (p. 262)

4. Corresponding sides of similar figures are proportional. (p. 270)

5. The ratio of the areas of similar figures is equal to the ratio of the squares of the corresponding sides in the figures. (p. 271)

6. The **scale** of a drawing is the ratio of a length on the drawing to the corresponding length on the actual object. (p. 277)

MEASURING YOUR SKILLS

Express as a ratio in simplest form. (9-1)

1. 2′ to 3″

2. 2.5 cm to 1.2 m

3. Find the depth of an American National Standard thread if there are 18 threads per inch. (9-2)

Solve the following proportions. (9-3)

4. $\dfrac{9}{x} = \dfrac{12}{16}$

6. $\dfrac{3}{8} = \dfrac{7}{x}$

5. $\dfrac{3}{x} = \dfrac{9}{1}$

7. $\dfrac{5}{8} = \dfrac{x}{20}$

8. Two gears have a gear ratio of 2:5. The smaller gear has 16 teeth. How many teeth does the larger gear have? (9-4)

9. For the gears in Exercise 8, the larger gear revolves at a speed of 1800 rpm. What is the speed of the smaller gear? (9-4)

10. The sides of triangle ABC are 3″, 4″, and 5″ long. The shortest side of similar triangle DEF is $2\frac{1}{2}$″ long. What are the lengths of the other sides of DEF? (9-5)

11. The corresponding sides of a pair of similar triangles are 30 cm and 60 cm. The area of the smaller triangle is 160 sq cm. What is the area of the larger triangle? (9-6)

area = 160 sq cm

30 cm

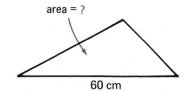
area = ?

60 cm

12. Using an architect's rule, draw the following:
    a. a line representing 9′8″, on the $\frac{3}{4}$-scale. (9-7)

    b. a line representing 6′2″, on the $\frac{1}{8}$-scale. (9-7)

13. A drawing is made in a scale of $\frac{3}{8}$″ = 1′. A line on the drawing is $7\frac{3}{8}$″ long. Find the actual dimension that is being represented by the line. (9-8)

14. In a scale of $\frac{3}{16}$″ = 1′, how long a line must be drawn to represent a distance of $4′2\frac{5}{8}$″? (9-8)

RESEARCH WITH A COMPUTER

In Sections 9-7 and 9-8 you studied scales, and how to make scale drawings. If an electronic computer that uses BASIC is available, you can RUN the following program. It will tell you how long to draw a line according to the indicated scale.

```
10  PRINT "SCALE IS";
20  INPUT A,B
30  LET S=A/B
40  PRINT "ACTUAL LENGTH IN FEET IS";
50  INPUT L
60  IF L=-1 THEN 90
70  PRINT "LINE SHOULD BE DRAWN";L*S;" IN."
80  GO TO 40
90  END
```

Note: When you INPUT the scale for line 20, type the numerator, then a comma, then the denominator. Further, most architectural drawings involve a number of lines that must be drawn to scale. This program will continue to run until you have converted all the lines in the drawing to their scale length. To END the program, simply type in −1 when it asks, "ACTUAL LENGTH IN FEET IS?"

EXERCISES

1. RUN the program to find the length that must be used to represent the following dimensions on a drawing in a scale of $\frac{1}{8}''$ to 1′.

   a. 4′ c. 21′ e. 8.5′
   b. 7′ d. 27.5′ f. 3.25′

2. Using the lengths in Exercise 1, RUN the program for a scale drawing with a scale of $\frac{3}{4}''$ to 1′. Compare the results.

3. Using the lengths in Exercise 1, RUN the program for a scale drawing having a scale of $\frac{3}{32}''$ to 1′. Compare the results with Exercise 1 and with Exercise 2.

Sometimes a scale drawing may contain objects that are too small to be shown accurately in one scale. In such cases, the draftsman may show an enlarged, or "detailed" view of the object, using a different scale. The following program will indicate the correct length to draw a line on a detailed scale drawing, when you know the length of the line in the original scale drawing.

284

```
10  PRINT "FIRST SCALE IS";
20  INPUT A,B
30  PRINT "NEW SCALE IS";
40  INPUT C,D
50  LET S=(C/D)/(A/B)
60  PRINT "LENGTH ON THE FIRST DRAWING IS";
70  INPUT L
80  IF L=-1 THEN 110
90  PRINT "LINE SHOULD BE"; S*L;" IN.
    ON NEW DRAWING"
100  GO TO 60
110  END
```

As in the previous program, INPUT the scales by typing numerator, comma, denominator. Also type −1 when you want to END the program.

EXERCISES

4. The blueprint below must be drawn in a scale of $\frac{1}{2}''$ to 1'. Use the first program to find the length that each line should be drawn. Then use the second program to give a detailed view of the kitchen floor plan in a scale of $\frac{7}{8}''$ to 1'. Before you begin, change dimensions given in feet and inches to feet only. (10'6'' to 10.5')

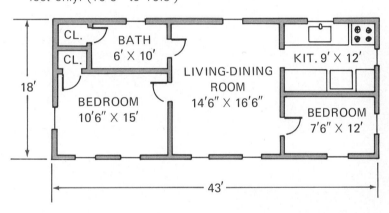

MEASURING YOUR PROGRESS

Simplify the expressions. (5-1–5-3)

1. $3x + 4x$ 3. 7^2 5. $6 + (3 \times 9) - 8$

2. $12y - 4y$ 4. 4^3 6. $8 \div 4 + 1 - 3$

Solve the equations. (5-4–5-8)

7. $x + 4.3 = 7.1$ 9. $6s = 4.56$

8. $y - \frac{3}{8} = 1\frac{3}{16}$ 10. $\frac{4}{9}x = 2\frac{1}{4}$

Substitute the values into the formulas. Then solve the equations. (5-9–5-10)

11. $d = \dfrac{W}{V}$,

     where $W = 18$
     and $V = 64$

12. $P = 2l + 2w$,

     where $l = 3.6$
     and $w = 5.9$

13. Find the perimeter of a square storage area which is 300' on each side. (6-1–6-2)

14. Find the area of the hole made by an expansion-bit drill having a radius of 1.5″. (6-3–6-7)

15. Find the surface area of a spherical water tank having a radius of 12.5 m. (6-7)

16. Find the volume of a cylindrical tank having a radius of 9' and a height of 25'. (6-8–6-10)

17. Find the volume of a pyramid having a base with an area of 27 sq cm and a height of 7 cm. (6-10)

Complete the statements. (7-1–7-4)

18. 2.6 m = __?__ cm   20. 5 sq ft = __?__ sq m

19. 10 in. = __?__ cm   21. 900 cu cm = __?__ cu in.

22. A truck scale has a capacity of 40,000 lb. What is this capacity in kilograms? (7-5–7-7)

23. The kindling temperature of paper is 451°F. What is this temperature in Celsius degrees?

24. If two angles of a triangle measure 67° and 38° respectively, how large is the third angle? (8-1–8-3)

25. Use a protractor to draw a 150° angle. Use a compass and straightedge to divide it into 2 equal angles. (8-6)

26. A right triangle has a side 14.5 cm long and a hypotenuse 16.5 cm long. Find the length of the other side. (8-9)

Express as a ratio in simplest form. (9-1–9-2)

27. 12.5 oz to 16 oz

28. 9 mm to 3 cm

Solve the proportions. (9-3–9-4)

29. $\dfrac{x}{3.2} = \dfrac{4.6}{9.2}$ 　　　　　　30. $\dfrac{4}{8} = \dfrac{x}{16}$

31. A pair of gears has a 1:3 gear ratio. If the smaller gear turns at 1200 rpm, what is the speed of the larger gear? (9-4)

32. The sides of a triangle are 3.6 cm, 7.2 cm and 10.8 cm long. The shortest side of a similar triangle is 5.4 cm long. What are the lengths of the other sides of the second triangle? (9-5–9-6)

33. A blue print of a factory is to be drawn in a scale of $\frac{3}{4}'' = 1'$. How long a line should be used to represent a 28' hallway? (9-7–9-8)

TRICKS OF THE TRADE

To join stock at an odd angle, cut the stock at an angle that is exactly half of the angle that you want. For example, to join the pieces at a 110° angle, cut the stock at a 55° angle. The pieces must be rotated to fit together.

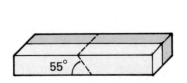
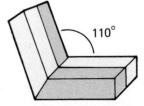

The limited supply of natural resources makes the efficient use of power and energy a growing concern.

CHAPTER 10

Power and Energy

After completing this chapter, you should be able to:

1. Describe power and how it is measured.
2. Describe some of the factors that affect horsepower, such as engine displacement and compression ratios.
3. Describe how power is transmitted by gears and pulleys.
4. Describe how we measure the power of hydraulic, pneumatic, and electrical systems.

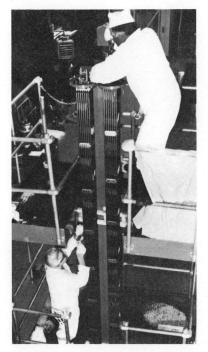

Maintenance of a power plant.

Power

10-1 Power and energy

What is it that drives our machines, heats our buildings, and runs our autos and appliances? Energy, in all its forms, is what sustains our lives and makes it possible for us to produce. Energy really means the ability to do work. There are many sources of energy, such as electrical, mechanical, chemical, atomic, and solar energy.

We measure energy by measuring how much work it can do. Here we do not mean the everyday meaning of work, but a specific meaning. Doing work means applying a force through a distance. So work is the product of *force* times *distance*.

$$\text{Work} = \text{force} \times \text{distance}$$

$$W = f \times d$$

A common U.S. unit of work is the foot-pound. You do one foot-pound of work when you move one pound a distance of one foot.

EXAMPLE 1   Find the work done in lifting a 3 lb weight a distance of 2 ft.

SOLUTION $W = f \times d$

$= 3 \times 2$

$W = 6$ ft-lb

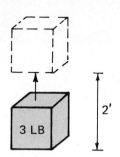

The work done is 6 foot-pounds.

Sometimes the terms "power" and "work" are confused. Power means the rate of doing work. So power is measured in work per unit time.

$$\text{Power} = \frac{\text{work}}{\text{time}} \text{ or } P = \frac{f \times d}{t}$$

Sometimes power is measured in foot-pounds per second or foot-pounds per minute.

EXAMPLE 2   Find the power needed to lift 100 lb of steel 12 ft in 3 sec.

SOLUTION $P = \dfrac{f \times d}{t}$

$= \dfrac{100 \times 12}{3}$

$P = 400$ ft-lb per sec

A standard U.S. unit of power is the horsepower. This unit was introduced by James Watt, who developed the steam engine. He wanted to compare the amount of work his engines could do with the work his horses could do. He found that an average horse could lift 550 pounds a distance of one foot in one second. This rate of doing work, 550 foot-pounds per second, he called one horsepower (hp).

1 hp = 550 ft-lb/sec

In one *minute*, Watt's average horse could do 60 times the amount of work done in one second.

$550 \times 60 = 33,000$
1 hp = 33,000 ft-lb/min

Since 1 horsepower = 550 ft-lb/sec, we divide a power in ft-lb per sec by 550 to find the horsepower.

$$hp = \frac{\text{ft-lb per sec}}{550} \text{ or } \frac{\text{ft} \times \text{lb}}{\text{sec} \times 550}$$

If the power is given in ft-lb per minute, we divide by 33,000 to find horsepower.

$$hp = \frac{\text{ft-lb per min}}{33,000} \text{ or } \frac{\text{ft} \times \text{lb}}{\text{min} \times 33,000}$$

EXAMPLE 3   What horsepower is needed to raise 330 lb of steel 20 ft in 4 sec.?

SOLUTION $hp = \dfrac{\text{ft} \times \text{lb}}{\text{sec} \times 550}$

$= \dfrac{330 \times 20}{4 \times 550}$

$= \dfrac{6600}{2200}$

$hp = 3$

EXERCISES A   1. How much work is done when a force of 60 lb moves an object 15 ft?

2. Find the work done in lifting a 200 lb object a distance of 35 feet.

3. A force of 30 lb moves an object 8 ft in 2 sec. How much power is used?

4. Find the horsepower needed to lift a 5500 lb object 20 ft in 5 sec.

B   5. A gasoline engine lifts 84 lb a distance of 60 ft in 12 sec. How much power was used?

6. What horsepower is needed to raise a 2100 lb object 50 ft in 3 min? Give the answer to the nearest hp.

7. It takes a 50 pound force to pull a 200 lb crate 3 feet up a platform. How much work is done?

C   8. An object was moved by a 5 lb force. How far was it moved, if the work done was 350 ft-lb?

9. It takes a 5 hp engine one minute to raise a 1650 lb car to the top of a junk pile. How high is the pile?

10-2 Measuring horsepower

How can the horsepower of an engine or electric motor be measured? Any device which measures the power output of a machine is called a dynamometer. One way a dynamometer can measure the horsepower output of an engine is by measuring the force required to brake the engine. This method measures **brake horsepower (bhp)**, the most widely used measure of engine horsepower. One device used to measure horsepower output is a prony brake. Figure 10-1 shows a diagram of a prony brake.

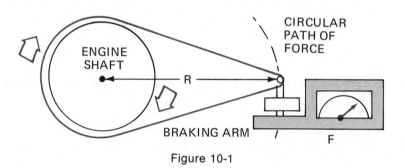

Figure 10-1

This method of finding brake horsepower uses the force needed to brake a running engine to a specific number of revolutions per minute (rpm). The engine crankshaft moves in a circular path. So the distance the crankshaft moves in one minute is the circumference ($2\pi R$) times the number of revolutions per minute (N).

$$\text{Distance} = 2\pi R \times N$$

$$\text{bhp} = \frac{(2\pi RN)}{33,000} \times F$$

Since $\dfrac{2\pi}{33,000} = \dfrac{1}{5252}$, the formula can be written more simply as:

$$\text{bhp} = \frac{RNF}{5252} \text{ where}$$

R = length of the arm in feet
N = rpm of engine
F = force in pounds

EXAMPLE 1   If the arm is 3 ft long, the force needed to brake is 100 lb, and the engine speed is 1000 rpm, find the brake horsepower.

SOLUTION $bhp = \dfrac{RNF}{5252}$

$bhp = \dfrac{3 \times 1000 \times 100}{5252}$

$bhp = 57.12$

The brake horsepower is about 57.

Another measure of horsepower is based on the power input through the pistons to the engine. This measurement of power is called indicated horsepower (ihp). It is based on the average pressure to each square inch of piston, the number of power strokes per minute, and the length of each stroke. The formula for indicated horsepower is:

$$ihp = \dfrac{PLAN}{33,000} \text{ where}$$

$P =$ average pressure in pounds per square inch
$L =$ length of the stroke in ft
$A =$ area of piston in sq in.
$N =$ number of power strokes per min

EXAMPLE 2   Find the indicated horsepower of an engine with a bore of 6″, a stroke of $2\frac{3}{4}$″, average pressure of 125 lb per sq in. and 6000 power strokes per minute. ($\pi = 3.14$)

SOLUTION   First we must change to the proper dimensions:
The stroke of $2\frac{3}{4}$″ must be changed to feet. To convert inches to feet, we divide by 12.

$2\frac{3}{4} \div 12 = \frac{11}{4} \times \frac{1}{12}$
$\qquad\qquad = \frac{11}{48} = .229$

The stroke is about .23 feet.

The area of the piston is found by using the formula for the area of a circle. Since the bore is 6″, the radius of the piston is 3″.

293

$A = \pi r^2$

$\quad = 3.14 \times (3)^2$

$\quad = 3.14 \times 9$

$\quad = 28.26$

The area of the piston is about 28.3 sq in.

So $\quad P = 125 \qquad A = 28.3$

$\qquad L = .23 \qquad N = 6000$

$ihp = \dfrac{PLAN}{33,000}$

$\quad = \dfrac{125 \times .23 \times 28.3 \times 6000}{33,000}$

$\quad = \dfrac{4881.75}{33}$

$ihp = 148$ (approx.)

The indicated horsepower is about 148.

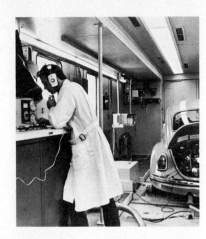

Periodic checkups insure maximum horsepower.

EXERCISES Find the answer to the nearest horsepower.

A 1. What is the brake horsepower of a gasoline engine if the arm is 3′ long, the force is 300 lb, and $N = 3000$ rpm?

2. Find the brake horsepower of an engine that registers 135 lb at the end of a prony brake arm $2\frac{1}{2}$ ft long. The engine is running at 4600 rpm.

3. Find the indicated horsepower for an engine which has an average pressure of 100 lb per sq in., a stroke of .5 ft, pistons each having an area of 20 sq in., and makes 3000 strokes per min.

4. Find the ihp of an engine having an average pressure of 125 lb per sq in., a stroke of .75′, a piston with an area of 22.5 sq in., and 3500 strokes per minute.

B 5. Find the brake horsepower of an engine where the load on the scale is 125 lb at the end of a 2′ 6″ arm when the engine is running at 5500 rpm.

6. Find the indicated horsepower of an engine whose piston has an area of 33.2 sq in., a stroke of 8″, an average pressure of 120 lb per sq in., and makes 4000 strokes per minute.

C 7. Find the indicated horsepower of an engine with a bore of 6″, a stroke of $7\frac{1}{2}$″, an average pressure of 130 lb per sq in., and 3000 power strokes per minute. ($\pi = 3.14$)

SELF-ANALYSIS TEST 30

1. Find the work done in lifting a 300-pound object 20 feet in the air.

2. How much work is done when a 5000-pound automobile is lifted 30 feet by a crane?

3. How much power is used when a 150-lb object is lifted 18 ft in 4 sec?

4. 1100 pounds of scrap metal is lifted to the top of an 18-foot-high pile. How much horsepower is used if a crane does the work in 4 seconds?

5. What is the brake horsepower of an engine if the length of the arm is 10 feet, the force is 130 pounds, and the engine speed is 3000 rpm?

6. Find the indicated horsepower of an engine having an average pressure of 115 pounds per square inch, a stroke of .5 feet, a piston with an area of 25 square inches, and 3000 strokes per minute.

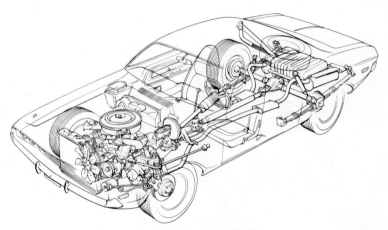

Power train of an automobile.

CREATIVE CRAFTSMAN

Design a device that will turn three shafts at different speeds and in different directions. The device is to be powered by a small electric motor. Use as few parts as possible.

Diesel Mechanic

Many industries are locating their plants in outlying districts, near major highways. This trend has caused sizable increases in transportation of freight by trucks. As the number of trucks on the highways increases the need for skilled diesel mechanics is expected to increase rapidly. You may be interested in pursuing a career in this expanding field.

Job Description

What do diesel truck mechanics do?
1. They repair heavy trucks used for mining, construction, and travel between cities.
2. They do preventive maintenance to assure safe operation of trucks. Regular spot checks help prevent wear and damage to parts, and reduce costly breakdowns.
3. They may specialize in a particular kind of repair. For example, large shops employ mechanics just for transmission repair or engine rebuilding.

Qualifications

Preference is given to high school graduates.
Courses in machine shop and automobile repair are especially useful. Background courses in mathematics and science can give a better understanding of how trucks operate.
Good physical condition is necessary to move heavy equipment.
Good hand coordination is needed in working with tools near exhaust pipes and radiator fans.

Training

Diesel mechanics learn their skills in different ways. Some learn by first working on gasoline-powered engines. They may be an apprentice to an experienced mechanic for several years. Firms that use diesel-powered equipment frequently train their mechanics in courses ranging from 6 to 18 months. Frequently, a beginning mechanic will take extra courses in repair and maintenance at a nearby vocational or trade school. The manufacturers of diesel engines often sponsor training programs for their apprentice mechanics. A combination of classroom training and practical experience is given over a four-year period.

Working Conditions

Most diesel truck mechanics work 40 to 48 hours a week.
Since service around the clock is provided by many firms,
some mechanics work evening and night shifts, usually at a
higher rate of pay.
Emergencies may require mechanics to be on call at any time.
Repair shops vary in the amount of working space, lighting,
heat, and fresh air.
Common hazards include cuts and bruises.
There is danger of injury when repairing heavy parts supported
on jacks and hoists.

Opportunities for Advancement

Experienced mechanics who have supervisory ability may
advance to shop foremen or service managers. Some become
truck salespersons. Others open their own diesel service stations
or independent repair shops.

10-3 Engine displacement

Why are some engines more powerful than others? One factor that affects the horsepower rating of an engine is its displacement. The displacement of one cylinder is the amount of space through which the piston travels in one stroke. Figure 10-2 shows the relationship of the bore and the stroke to the displacement.

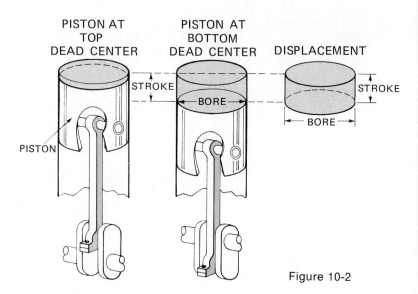

Figure 10-2

Do you see that the displacement of a cylinder is actually a cylinder of space? Recall the formula for the volume of a cylinder:

$$V = \pi r^2 h$$

Since $h =$ the stroke of the engine and $r = \left(\dfrac{\text{bore}}{2}\right)$, we can rewrite the formula for the displacement of a cylinder as

$$D = \pi \times \left(\frac{\text{bore}}{2}\right)^2 \times \text{stroke}$$

$$= \pi \times \frac{(\text{bore})^2}{4} \times \text{stroke}$$

$$= \frac{1}{4} \times \pi \times (\text{bore})^2 \times \text{stroke}$$

Can you find the pistons and the cylinders?

The total displacement of an engine is the sum of the displacement of all the cylinders. We may use the following formula to find the total displacement of an engine.

$$D = \tfrac{1}{4} \times \pi \times (\text{bore})^2 \times \text{stroke} \times \text{no. of cylinders}$$

EXAMPLE 1   Mr. Porter's V-8 engine has a $3\tfrac{3}{4}''$ bore and a $3\tfrac{1}{4}''$ stroke. What is its displacement? $(\pi = \tfrac{22}{7})$

SOLUTION $D = \tfrac{1}{4} \times \tfrac{22}{7} \times (\tfrac{15}{4})^2 \times \tfrac{13}{4} \times 8$

$\qquad = \tfrac{1}{4} \times \tfrac{22}{7} \times \tfrac{225}{16} \times \tfrac{13}{4} \times 8$

$\qquad = \tfrac{32175}{112} = 287$ cu in. (approx.)

Frequently, decimals are used to state engine dimensions, especially dimensions given in metric units. In such cases, we can use a simpler form of the displacement formula.

$$D = \tfrac{1}{4} \times \pi \times (\text{bore})^2 \times \text{stroke} \times \text{no. of cylinders}$$
$$= .25 \times 3.1416 \times (\text{bore})^2 \times \text{stroke} \times \text{no. of cylinders}$$
$$D = .7854 \times (\text{bore})^2 \times \text{stroke} \times \text{no. of cylinders}$$

EXAMPLE 2   Find the displacement of a 4-cylinder engine with a 9.0 cm bore and a 6.7 cm stroke.

SOLUTION $D = .7854 \times (9.0)^2 \times 6.7 \times 4$

$\qquad = .7854 \times 81 \times 6.7 \times 4$

$\qquad = 1705$ cu cm (approx.)

Displacement figures involving metric units are often stated in liters as well as cubic centimeters. Recall that 1 liter = 1000 cubic centimeters. Therefore, the displacement of the engine in Example 2 can be stated as

$$D = 1705 \text{ cu cm or } D = 1.705 \text{ l}$$

Sometimes we can use a flow chart to help us solve a problem. Study the flow chart for finding engine displacement in Example 3 on the next page.

EXAMPLE 3   What is the displacement of a
V-8 engine having a 3.5″ bore
and 3.25″ stroke?

SOLUTION   a. 3.5
               ↓
            b. 3.5 × 3.5 = 12.25

            c. .7854
               ↓
            d. .7854 × 12.25 = 9.62115

            e. 3.25
               ↓
            f. 3.25 × 9.62115 = 31.2687375

            g. 8
               ↓
            h. 8 × 31.2687375 = 250.1499

            i. 250.1499 = 250 (approx.)

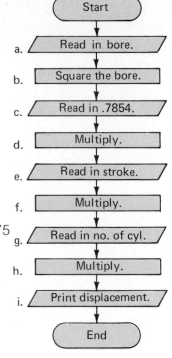

a. Read in bore.
b. Square the bore.
c. Read in .7854.
d. Multiply.
e. Read in stroke.
f. Multiply.
g. Read in no. of cyl.
h. Multiply.
i. Print displacement.

EXERCISES

U.S. System

Find the displacement of the following engines
in cubic inches.

A 1. A V-8, with a 3″ bore and a 3″ stroke.

2. A 6, with a $3\frac{1}{2}″$ bore and a 3″ stroke.

3. A 6, with a 4″ bore and a $3\frac{3}{8}″$ stroke.

B 4. A 6-cylinder pick-up truck engine has a
displacement of 265 cubic inches. If the
bore is $3\frac{3}{4}″$, what is the stroke?

5. Mrs. Brown's 6-cylinder engine has a bore
of 3.5″ and a displacement of 255 cubic
inches. What is the stroke?

C 6. An economy 6-cylinder engine has a displacement of 196 cubic inches. If the stroke
is 2.75″, what is the bore?

Metric System

Find the displacement of the following engines
a) in cubic centimeters and b) in liters.

7. A V-8, with a 9.0 cm bore and a 7.0 cm
stroke.

8. A V-8, with a 8.3 cm bore and a 8.0 cm
stroke.

9. A 6, with a 8.75 cm bore and a 7.7 cm
stroke.

10. A standard 6-cylinder engine has a displacement of 3780 cu cm. If the bore is
9.8 cm, what is the stroke?

11. An optional V-8 engine has a displacement
of 4770 cu cm. If the bore is 9.75 cm, what
is the stroke?

12. Find the bore of a 4-cylinder engine, if the
displacement is 1340 cu cm and the stroke
is 7.25 cm.

Cutaway view of a 4-cylinder engine. Can you estimate the compression ratio?

10-4 Compression ratios

Mr. Peters and Mr. Salvador each have a 270 cu in. V-8 engine in their cars. Mr. Peters buys regular gas for his car but Mr. Salvador must buy premium, higher octane gas for his car. The difference is that Mr. Peter's car has a higher compression ratio. Compression ratios are closely related to engine displacement.

Recall that engine displacement is the difference between the amount of space when the piston is at the top of its stroke and the amount of space when it is at the bottom of its stroke.

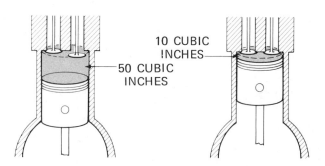

Figure 10-3

Figure 10-3 shows a cylinder having a maximum of 50 cu in. at the bottom of the piston's stroke and a minimum of 10 cu in. at the top of the piston's stroke. The ratio of the maximum space in the cylinder to the minimum space in the cylinder is called the **compression ratio** of an engine. So the compression ratio of the engine in Figure 10-3 is

$$\frac{50}{10} \text{ or } \frac{5}{1}.$$

A ratio of $\frac{5}{1}$ is usually written as 5 to 1 or 5:1. Compression ratios are always written so the second number in the ratio is 1. Many car engines today have compression ratios of $8\frac{1}{2}$:1 to $9\frac{1}{2}$:1.

Note the relationship between the compression ratio and the displacement of the cylinder in Figure 10-3. The displacement in the cylinder is the difference between the two numbers used to find the compression ratio.

$$50 \text{ cu in.} - 10 \text{ cu in.} = 40 \text{ cu in.}$$

So the displacement of the cylinder is 40 cu in.

This computerized test can check compression ratio.

EXAMPLE 1   What is the compression ratio if there are 42 cu in. of space when the piston is at the bottom of its stroke and only 7 cu in. when the piston is at the top of its stroke?

SOLUTION $\frac{42}{7} = \frac{6}{1}$

The compression ratio is 6:1.

EXAMPLE 2   Mr. Jones' car engine has a compression ratio of 9 to 1. If there are 38 cu cm when the piston is at the top of its stroke, what is the cylinder's displacement?

SOLUTION   First we must find the number of cubic centimeters when the piston is at the bottom of its stroke

$$\text{compression ratio} = \frac{\text{maximum space}}{\text{minimum space}}$$

$$\frac{9}{1} = \frac{\text{maximum space}}{38}$$

$$\text{maximum space} = 9 \times 38$$
$$= 342 \text{ cu cm}$$

$$\text{displacement} = \text{maximum space} - \text{minimum space}$$
$$= 342 - 38$$
$$= 304$$

The displacement of the cylinder is 304 cu cm.

Careful testing of auto emissions can help reduce air pollution.

EXERCISES

U.S. System

A 1. A cylinder contains 40 cubic inches of space when the piston is at bottom dead center and 5 cubic inches when the piston is at top dead center. What is the compression ratio?

2. The compression ratio of an engine is 9:1. When the piston is at the top of its stroke there are 6 cu in. of space in the cylinder. How much space is there when the piston is at the bottom of its stroke?

3. A cylinder has a maximum amount of 45 cu in. of space when the piston is at the bottom of its stroke. The compression ratio is 8:1. How much space is there when the piston is at the top of its stroke?

4. An engine has a compression ratio of $8\frac{1}{2}$ to 1. There are 4 cu in. of space in the cylinder when the piston is at the top of its stroke. How much space is there when the piston is at the bottom of its stroke?

B 5. There are 50 cubic inches of space in the cylinder when the piston is at bottom dead center and the displacement of the cylinder is 40 cu in. How many cubic inches of space are there when the piston is at top dead center?

6. Mrs. Matthews' car engine has a compression ratio of 8:1. If one of its cylinders has 4 cu in. of space when the piston is at the top of its stroke, what is the cylinder's displacement?

C 7. Mr. Peron has a 6-cylinder car with a compression ratio of 9:1. In each cylinder, there are 36 cu in. of space when the piston is at the bottom of its stroke. What is the engine's displacement?

Metric System

8. A cylinder has 220 cu cm of space when the piston is at the bottom of its stroke and 22 cu cm of space when the piston is at the top of its stroke. What is the compression ratio?

9. The compression ratio is 8 to 1 and there are 328 cubic centimeters of space in the cylinder when the piston is at the bottom of its stroke. How much space is there when the piston is at the top of its stroke?

10. There are 35 cu cm of space in a cylinder when the piston is at the top of its stroke. The compression ratio is 9 to 1. How much space is there in the cylinder when the piston is at the bottom of its stroke?

11. There are 42 cu cm of space in a cylinder when the piston is at the top of its stroke. There are 399 cu cm of space when the piston is at the bottom of its stroke. What is the compression ratio?

12. Mrs. Perella's car engine has a displacement of 280 cu cm in each cylinder. There are 40 cu cm of space in each cylinder when the piston is at the top of its stroke. How much space is there in each cylinder when the piston is at the bottom of its stroke?

13. A car engine has a compression ratio of 9:1. Each of its cylinders has a maximum of 450 cu cm of space when the piston is at the bottom of its stroke. What is the displacement in each of its cylinders?

14. Mr. Tamura's car has a displacement of 2025 cu cm in 6 cylinders. There are 37.5 cu cm of space in each cylinder when the piston is at the top of its stroke. What is the engine's compression ratio?

SELF-ANALYSIS TEST 31

U.S. System

1. What is the engine displacement of a V-8 engine if the bore is 4″ and the stroke is $3\frac{1}{2}$″?

2. A cylinder contains 40 cu in. when the piston is at the bottom of its stroke and 4 cu in. at the top of its stroke. What is the compression ratio?

3. The compression ratio of an engine is $8\frac{1}{2}$ to 1. There are 5 cubic inches in the cylinder when the piston is at the top of its stroke. How much space is there when the piston is at the bottom of its stroke?

Metric System

4. Find the displacement of a 6 cylinder engine if the bore is 6 cm and the stroke is 5 cm.

5. There are 420 cu cm of space in the cylinder when the piston is at the bottom of its stroke. When it is at the top of its stroke there are 60 cu cm of space in the cylinder. What is the compression ratio?

6. The compression ratio of an engine is $9\frac{1}{2}$ to 1. At the top of the piston's stroke there are 45 cu cm of space in the cylinder. How much space does the cylinder contain at the bottom of the stroke?

SPOTLIGHT ON INDUSTRY

As our natural resources of fuel are being used up, scientists are turning to the sun for a source of energy. Solar power has already been used in satellites which use the sun as their continuing power source. Their photo power cells convert solar energy directly into electrical energy. It has been suggested that a great number of these cells be put in a desert to supply electrical power. Another idea is to have satellites with photo power cells beam electrical power back to the earth. Solar power can also be converted to electrical power by heating water. The steam produced could drive turbines in existing power plants. These ideas have not yet been applied on a large scale. However, scientists estimate that solar power could provide up to 20% of the world's electrical power needs.

Gears and pulleys

10-5 Gears

Machines must be able to transfer their energy output to the proper moving parts. One method for transferring power is to use gears. For example, the speed reducer shown in Figure 10-4 enables a craftsman to either double or halve the speed of a power drill. The gear diagram shows the bevel gears inside this device.

Gears can be used to change the speed, force, and direction of motion. In Figure 10-5, two spur gears are shown.

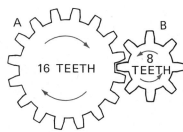

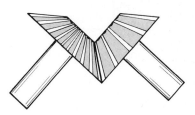

Figure 10-4

Figure 10-5

In this case, the gears produce a change in both direction and speed of the motion produced. You can see that when gear A moves clockwise, gear B moves counterclockwise. Notice that gear A has twice as many teeth as gear B. So whenever gear A makes one turn, gear B makes two turns. This means that gear B is turning twice as fast as gear A. We say that the **gear ratio** of A to B is 1 to 2. The gear ratio of B to A is 2:1. The gear ratio of two gears is the ratio of their speeds. Notice how the gear ratio is related to the number of teeth in each gear.

$$\text{gear ratio of A to B} = \frac{\text{speed of A}}{\text{speed of B}} = \frac{\text{teeth in B}}{\text{teeth in A}}$$

So you see that the gear ratio is always the *reciprocal* of the ratio of the number of teeth.

EXAMPLE 1   If gear C has 60 teeth and gear D has 20 teeth, what is the gear ratio of C to D?

SOLUTION   The teeth ratio of C to D is $\frac{60}{20}$.
The gear ratio is the reciprocal of $\frac{60}{20}$, so it is $\frac{20}{60}$ or $\frac{1}{3}$.
The gear ratio of C to D is $1:3$.

Power is transmitted from the engine to the wheels of an auto by a series of gears. There are many common gear ratios which describe how the engine speed is changed to the rear axle speed. The transmission in the automobile is a gear train, or series of connected gears, that changes the speed of the engine to the speed of the drive shaft. Figure 10-6 shows a cut-away view of a fully synchronized 3-speed manual transmission.

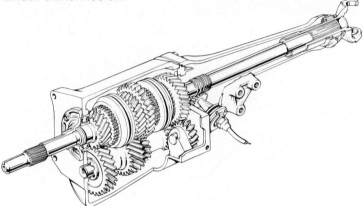

Figure 10-6

The transmission ratio is the ratio of the engine speed to the drive shaft speed.

$$\text{transmission ratio} = \frac{\text{engine speed}}{\text{drive shaft speed}}$$

A transmission ratio of 4 to 1 means the rpm (revolutions per minute) of the engine is 4 times the rpm of the drive shaft.

EXAMPLE 2   If the engine is running at 2000 rpm and the transmission ratio is 5 to 1, what is the speed of the drive shaft?

SOLUTION $\text{transmission ratio} = \dfrac{\text{engine speed}}{\text{drive shaft speed}(s)}$

$$\frac{5}{1} = \frac{2000}{s}$$

$$5 \times s = 2000 \times 1$$

$$s = \frac{2000}{5}$$

$$s = 400 \text{ rpm}$$

The rear axle ratio describes how the speed of the drive shaft is changed by gears to the speed of the rear axle.

$$\text{rear axle ratio} = \frac{\text{drive shaft speed}}{\text{rear axle speed}}$$

The two gears involved in the rear axle are shown in Figure 10-7.

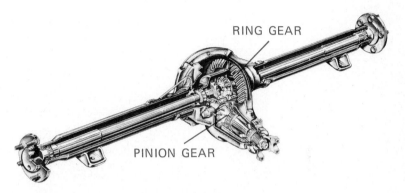

RING GEAR

PINION GEAR

Figure 10-7

Connected to the drive shaft is the pinion gear, which drives the ring gear. The ring gear is connected to the rear axle. Recall that the gear speed ratio is the reciprocal of the ratio of the number of teeth. So another way to find the rear axle ratio is from the number of teeth in the ring gear and in the pinion gear.

$$\text{rear axle ratio} = \frac{\text{teeth in ring gear}}{\text{teeth in pinion gear}}$$

EXAMPLE 3   If the pinion gear has 20 teeth and the ring gear has 60 teeth, what is the rear axle ratio?

SOLUTION $\text{rear axle ratio} = \dfrac{\text{teeth in ring gear}}{\text{teeth in pinion gear}}$

$$= \frac{60}{20}$$

$$= \frac{3}{1}$$

The rear axle ratio is 3:1.

To determine the gear ratio of the engine speed to the rear axle speed, we can multiply the transmission ratio by the rear axle ratio.

EXAMPLE 4   If the transmission ratio is 4 to 1 and the rear axle ratio is 5 to 1, what is the gear ratio from the engine to the rear axle?

SOLUTION $\frac{4}{1} \times \frac{5}{1} = \frac{20}{1}$

The gear ratio from the engine to the rear axle is 20 to 1.

EXERCISES A   1. If gear A has 20 teeth and gear B has 60 teeth, what is the gear ratio of A to B?

2. If gear A has 30 teeth and gear B has 70 teeth, what is the gear ratio of A to B? What is the gear ratio of B to A?

3. The engine speed is 2400 rpm while the drive shaft speed is 800 rpm. What is the transmission ratio?

4. The rear wheels are turning at 240 rpm while the drive shaft is turning at 1200 rpm. What is the rear axle ratio?

B   5. If the gear ratio of A to B is 3 to 1 and gear A has 9 teeth, how many teeth does gear B have?

6. The transmission ratio is 3 to 1. The engine speed is 1500 rpm. Find the drive shaft speed.

7. The rear axle ratio is 4 to 1. The rear axle is turning at 600 rpm. What is the speed of the drive shaft?

8. If the rear axle ratio is 4.2 to 1 and the pinion gear has 15 teeth, find the number of teeth in the ring gear.

9. Find the engine-to-rear-axle ratio if the engine speed is 4800 rpm, the drive shaft speed is 1200 rpm, and the rear axle speed is 400 rpm.

C   10. The engine is running at 2960 rpm. The transmission ratio is 2 to 1 and the rear axle ratio is 4 to 1. What is the speed of the rear wheels?

RESEARCH PROJECT

Measure the circumference of the rear wheels of a car. Find out from a mechanic or a dealer the rear axle ratio and the transmission ratio of this car. Calculate how fast the engine must run in order to move the car at 60 miles per hour.

Figure 10-8

10-6 Pulleys

Pulleys are another device used to transfer power from one place to another. A common use for pulleys is in lifting heavy objects. Figure 10-8 shows a pulley device commonly used in service stations to lift cars. Pulleys transfer power much like gears do. Figure 10-9 shows two pulleys connected by a belt.

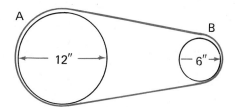

Figure 10-9

Pulley A has a diameter twice that of pulley B. Therefore the belt has to travel twice as far around pulley A as around pulley B. When pulley A makes one turn, pulley B makes two turns. Pulley speed ratios are like gear ratios. Recall that a gear ratio is the reciprocal of the ratio of the number of teeth. In the same way, a pulley speed ratio is the reciprocal of the ratio of the diameters of the pulley,

$$\frac{\text{speed of pulley A}}{\text{speed of pulley B}} = \frac{\text{diameter of B}}{\text{diameter of A}}$$

EXAMPLE   Pulley C is 35″ in diameter and pulley D is 7″ in diameter. What is the ratio of the speed of C to the speed of D?

SOLUTION $\dfrac{\text{speed of C}}{\text{speed of D}} = \dfrac{\text{diameter of D}}{\text{diameter of C}}$

$$= \frac{7}{35}$$

$$= \frac{1}{5}$$

The ratio of the speeds of C to D is $1:5$.

EXERCISES A   1. The diameter of one pulley is 13″ and the diameter of a second pulley is 4″. Find the ratio of the speed of the first pulley to the speed of the second pulley.

2. Pulley A has a 15″ diameter and pulley B has a 3″ diameter. Find the ratio of the speed of B to the speed of A.

3. Pulley C has a 7″ radius and pulley D has a 2″ radius. Find the ratio of the speeds of C to D.

B 4. Pulley R has a diameter of 12″ and pulley S has a radius of 3″. If pulley R is turning at 500 rpm, how fast is pulley S turning?

5. One pulley turns at 100 rpm and a connected pulley turns at 25 rpm. If the diameter of the first pulley is 2″, what is the diameter of the second pulley?

C 6. Find the rpm of the alternator pulley in Figure 10-10 if the crankshaft turns at 1200 rpm.

7. Find the rpm of the fan pulley in Figure 10-10 if the crankshaft turns at 1200 rpm.

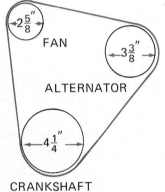

FAN

ALTERNATOR

CRANKSHAFT

Figure 10-10

SELF-ANALYSIS TEST 32

1. If gear A has 25 teeth and gear B has 50 teeth, what is the gear ratio of A to B?

2. Find the number of teeth in the smaller of two gears if the gear ratio is 9 to 4 and the larger gear has 36 teeth.

3. An engine turns at 3600 rpm while the drive shaft turns at 1200 rpm. What is the transmission ratio?

4. What is the rear axle ratio if the speed of the drive shaft is 1500 rpm and the speed of the rear wheels is 500 rpm?

5. Pulley A has a diameter of 8″ and pulley B has a diameter of 2″. What is the ratio of the speeds of A to B?

6. One pulley's speed is 5 times that of a second pulley's speed. The smaller pulley has a diameter of 10 in. What is the diameter of the larger pulley?

RESEARCH PROJECT

Obtain several advertising brochures from your local automobile dealer. Use the specifications for bore and stroke given in the brochure to check the indicated displacement. How do your figures compare with those in the brochure? Can you explain any differences?

The Rotary Combustion Engine

For years automotive engineers have tried to develop a power source that is less expensive, lighter in weight, more efficient, and gives off cleaner exhaust than the conventional piston engine. Of the many designs that have been proposed and developed, one engine appears to satisfy these requirements. It is known as the Wankel engine, in honor of the German engineer who invented it, Felix Wankel. It is also referred to as the rotary combustion engine, or simply, the rotary engine.

Operation

The diagram on page B compares the operation of the familiar reciprocating engine and the rotary engine. Notice that in the reciprocating engine, the piston makes 4 strokes — two up and two down — in order to complete a full cycle of intake, compression, ignition, expansion, and exhaust. There is only one power stroke in each cycle of 4 strokes. In the reciprocating engine these strokes are converted to circular motion by means of a crankshaft.

The operation of the rotary engine also includes intake, compression, ignition, expansion, and exhaust phases. However, a triangular rotor with slightly curved sides rotates within a housing that is shaped like an oval pinched in the middle. For each complete revolution of the rotor there are three power "strokes." In the rotary engine the rotor rides directly on the main shaft, and turns it in the same direction. Because the movement is at all times circular, the rotary engine tends to be freer of vibration than the reciprocating engine.

From the outside the rotary engine looks like the familiar reciprocating engine. Visual 1 shows some of these common external components: (1) air intake and filter, (2) carburetor, (3) twin distributors, (4) ignition coils, (5) vacuum-operated spark advance, (6) alternator, (7) spark plugs, (8) cooling fan, (9) auxiliary drive pulley, (10) oil pan.

The interior of the rotary engine (Visual 2) shows the simplicity of its design. It takes just two rotors, side by side, to make an automobile engine. The rotors rotate in two oval-shaped engine housings which are slightly narrowed at midsection. This shape is traced out by each apex of the rotor during its cycle. The front portion of one chamber is shown by dotted lines.

As with piston engines, the engine block contains hollow passages. This permits a coolant to pass through the block to carry away internal heat.

Notice that the rotary engine is ignited by two spark plugs. The dual ignition systems cause the fuel mixture to burn smoothly and efficiently.

On the right is the timing gear (11) around which the rotor "walks" during its rotations.

Continued on page D.

A

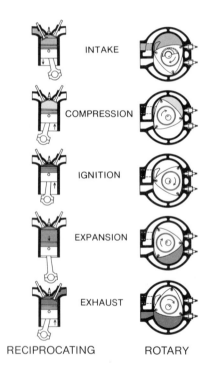

INTAKE

COMPRESSION

IGNITION

EXPANSION

EXHAUST

RECIPROCATING   ROTARY

Comparing the Reciprocating and Rotary
Engines

B

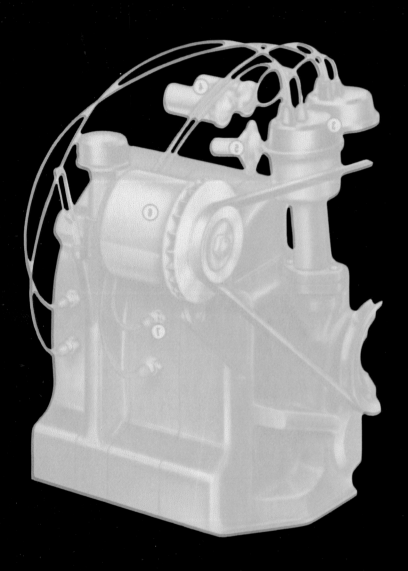

Visual 1 External Components of the Rotary Engine

(1) air intake and filter
(2) carburetor
(3) twin distributors
(4) ignition coils
(5) vacuum-operated spark advance
(6) alternator
(7) spark plugs
(8) cooling fan
(9) auxiliary drive pulley
(10) oil pan

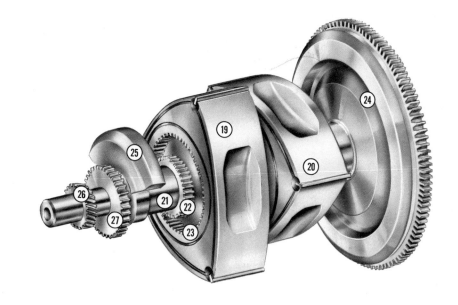

 INTAKE
MIXTURE

COMPRESSED
MIXTURE

COMBUSTION
GASES

EXPANDING
GASES

EXHAUST
GASES

COOLING
MEDIUM

LUBRICATING AND
COOLING OIL

Power Train Assembly

(19) and (20) rotors
(21) main shaft
(22) housing gear

(23) rotor gear
(24) flywheel
(25) balance weight
(26) distributor drive gear
(27) oil pump drive gear

c

Visual 3 gives a clear view of the triangular rotors in their housings. Where two of the faces of the rotors come together, there is a sliding apex seal. On the side of the rotor there are also side seals. These create the separate moving chambers as the rotor turns within the housing.

The incoming fuel-air mixture (blue) enters through the ports in the upper portion of the chambers. As the rotor turns, the mixture is compressed in the narrow midsection of the chamber (yellow). It is ignited by the twin spark plugs (red). The expanding gases (orange) force the rotor to turn clockwise, thereby transferring the power to the main shaft. When the rotation of the rotor uncovers the exhaust port, the spent gases are swept away (pink), completing the cycle. Notice that the entire process from intake to exhaust happens three times for each complete rotation of the rotor.

The arrows in Visual 4 show the path of the fuel mixture through the intake (14) and exhaust (15) manifolds. This engine has been equipped with a thermal reactor (16). Inside the reactor the unburned substances in the exhaust gases are mixed with a fresh supply of air from the auxiliary air pump (17), and are burned again. When the exhaust passes out of the high-temperature reactor, the polluting elements have been removed and the exhaust is virtually "clean."

Because the rotary engine has a number of seals that are in constant contact with the interior surfaces of the housing, adequate lubrication is essential. An oil metering device (18) is used to make certain that adequate oil is sent to these areas.

The power train of the rotary engine is shown on page C. The triangular rotors (19) and (20) and the main shaft (21) are the three principal moving parts. The proper working relationship between the rotors and the main shaft is maintained by the fixed housing gear (22) and by the internal "walking" gear of the rotor (23). The flywheel (24), which is part of the main shaft, provides the connection to the clutch, transmission, and the other components of the power train. The flywheel and the balance weight (25) smooth out the turning of the shaft, and dampen engine vibration. The distributor drive gear (26) and the oil pump drive gear (27) are also found on the main shaft.

Advantages

Automotive engineers are excited about the advantages of the rotary engine over the piston engine. A few of these advantages are:

1. The rotary engine weighs about 40% less than a piston engine of the same power.
2. The rotary engine is more compact, affording more space for passengers and storage.
3. The rotary engine contains fewer parts, simplifying maintenance.
4. The rotary engine makes more effective use of its fuel and gives off relatively clean exhaust.

These facts have caused many to consider the rotary engine to be the engine of tomorrow *today*.

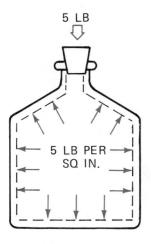

Figure 10-11

Fluid and electrical power

10-7 Hydraulic power

Fluid power systems use the fluids of liquids and gases to control and carry power. Fluid power is based on pressure applied to a confined liquid or gas. When a liquid, usually oil, transmits the power, we call it hydraulic power. When the power is transmitted through air or gas, it is called pneumatic power.

Fluid power is one of the fast growing types of power systems. It can produce a great force in a small space, and it is very flexible. It can carry power wherever tubes or pipes can be placed. Fluid power is used in many industrial machines, including the sewerage pumps shown in Figure 10-11.

Fluid power works because of this principle: pressure on a confined fluid acts equally in all directions. Pressure is the measure of fluid force. To see how pressure is measured, look at Figure 10-12. The stopper on the bottle has an area of 1 square inch. A force of 5 pounds is pushing down on it. This pressure acts equally on all the air in the bottle. So every square inch of bottle has a force of 5 pounds pushing it out. We call this a pressure of 5 pounds per square inch, or 5 psi.

The hydraulic lift shown in Figure 10-13 is used in service stations to make it easier for mechanics to work on cars.

5 LB

5 LB PER
SQ IN.

Figure 10-12

Figure 10-13

To understand how a hydraulic device works, look at Figure 10-14. An outside force of 50 pounds is pushing on the left piston. The piston has an area of 5 square inches. Each square inch receives its equal share of the 50 pound force.

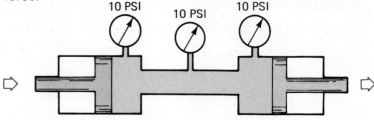

INPUT FORCE = 50 LB   AREA OF PISTON = 5 SQ. IN.
AREA OF PISTON = 5 SQ. IN.   OUTPUT FORCE = 50 LB

Figure 10-14

To find the pressure on the liquid, remember that pressure can be measured in pounds per square inch (psi).

$$\text{Pressure} = \frac{\text{Force}}{\text{Area}}$$

$$= \frac{50 \text{ pounds}}{5 \text{ square inches}}$$

$$= 10 \text{ psi}$$

This pressure of 10 psi acts on all the liquid in the cylinder. So the piston on the right is getting its share, too. The force with which it is pushed depends on its area. Each of its 5 square inches gets 10 pounds of force. So the entire piston receives 50 pounds of force.

EXAMPLE 1   The piston in Figure 10-15 receives a force of 96 lb. The area of the piston is 8 sq in. What is the pressure?

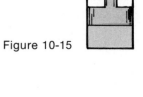

96 LB

Figure 10-15

SOLUTION $\text{Pressure} = \dfrac{\text{Force}}{\text{Area}}$

$$= \frac{96}{8}$$

$$= 12 \text{ psi}$$

Sometimes we want more output force than input force. To do this, we can make the area of the output piston larger. Figure 10-16 shows what happens.

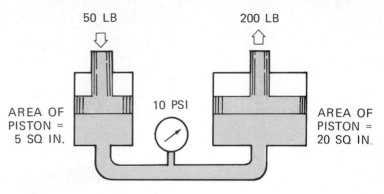

Figure 10-16

When a 50-lb force acts on 5 sq in. we have a pressure of 10 psi. The larger piston has an area of 20 sq in. So it receives a force of 10 pounds for each square inch.

$$\text{Force} = \text{Pressure} \times \text{Area}$$
$$= 10 \times 20$$
$$= 200 \text{ pounds}$$

Thus the output piston receives a force of 200 pounds. However, the output piston can do no more *work* than the input piston. Remember that work is the product of force times distance. For the two cylinders to do equal work, the output piston moves $\frac{1}{4}$ the distance of the input piston. This is because it has 4 times the force of the input piston. So to have more output force in a hydraulic system we always sacrifice distance.

EXAMPLE 2   In a hydraulic system the input piston has an area of 8 sq in. The output piston has an area of 24 sq in. If the force on the input piston is 25 pounds, what is the force on the output piston.

SOLUTION $$\text{Pressure} = \frac{\text{pounds}}{\text{square inches}}$$
$$= \frac{25}{8}$$
$$= 3.125 \text{ psi}$$

Now find the force on the output piston.

$$\text{Force} = \text{Pressure} \times \text{Area}$$
$$= 3.125 \times 24$$
$$= 75 \text{ pounds}$$

EXERCISES **A** 1. A force of 20 pounds acts on 2 sq in. What is the pressure?

2. The liquid in a cylinder has a pressure of 15 psi. The force on the input piston is 45 pounds. What is the area of the piston?

3. A piston with an area of 10 sq in. produces a pressure of 45 psi. How much outside force is it receiving?

4. The pressure in a hydraulic system is 20 psi. The output piston has an area of 4 sq in. What is the output force?

5. The smaller piston in a hydraulic system has an area of 5 sq in. It receives a force of 190 pounds. What is the pressure in the system?

B 6. The input piston in a hydraulic system has an area of 8 sq in. The area of the output piston is 25 sq in. If the input force is 40 pounds, what is the output force?

7. The small piston in a hydraulic system has an area of 6 sq in. It receives a force of 30 pounds. The large piston puts out a force of 120 pounds. Find the area of the large piston.

8. In a hydraulic system an input force of 50 pounds produces an output of 125 pounds. The pressure in the cylinder is 25 psi. Find the area of both the input piston and the output piston.

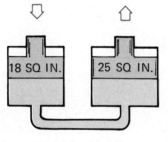

Figure 10-17

C 9. Find the output force in Figure 10-17. How far up does the output piston move when the input piston moves down 10″?

10-8 Pneumatic power

Hydraulic power is based on the principle that liquids under pressure do not compress. This means that when we apply a force to a liquid, the pressure goes up, but the volume stays the same. However, if you put pressure on a gas, it compresses to a smaller volume with more pressure. Look at Figure 10-18 to see how this works.

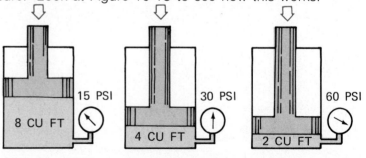

Figure 10-18

When 4 cubic feet of air is compressed to half its original volume, the pressure is doubled. When the air space is one-fourth its original space (2 cubic feet), the pressure is multiplied four times. Notice that the product of volume and pressure remains the same.

$$8 \times 15 = 4 \times 30 = 2 \times 60.$$
$$120 = 120 = 120$$

We can use this fact to find the pressure of a gas after it has been compressed.

Old Pressure $\times$ Old Volume = New Pressure $\times$ New Volume

$$P_1 \times V_1 = P_2 \times V_2$$

EXAMPLE 1   The piston in Figure 10-19 compresses 10 cu ft of gas to 2 cu ft. What is the new pressure?

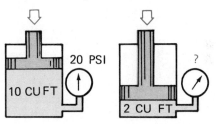

Figure 10-19

SOLUTION

$$P_1 V_1 = P_2 V_2$$
$$20 \times 10 = P_2 \times 2$$
$$200 = P_2 \times 2$$
$$100 = P_2$$

The new pressure is 100 psi.

Figure 10-20

Because air does not maintain the same volume under pressure, a pneumatic power system cannot work like a hydraulic system. Pneumatic systems require a constant volume of compressed air. This is done with an air compressor. The air compressor takes in air at the normal pressure of 15 psi and raises its pressure to meet the demands of the system. It stays at a constant volume under the same pressure. So its fluid force can be used to produce motion in the output piston. For example, the pneumatic jackhammer shown in Figure 10-20 uses this principle of pneumatic power.

A simplified pneumatic system is shown in Figure 10-21. Notice that the air compressor supplies a large volume of pressurized air to the air storage tank, to be used by the output piston.

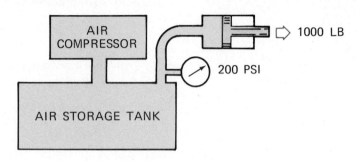

Figure 10-21

EXAMPLE 2   What is the area of the piston in Figure 10-21?

SOLUTION   Force = Pressure × Area
1000 = 200 × Area
$\frac{1000}{200}$ = Area
Area = 5 sq in.

EXERCISES A   1. A piston compresses 20 cu ft of air at 15 psi to 5 cu ft. What is the new pressure?

2. Air at 20 psi is compressed so its new pressure is 35 psi. If the original volume was $3\frac{1}{2}$ cu in., what is the new volume?

3. How much air pressure results when 10 cu ft of air at 15 psi is compressed to 1 cu ft?

4. Air at 15 psi is compressed so its volume is 4 cu in. and its pressure is 60 psi. What was the original volume?

5. An air compressor supplies a constant pressure of 150 psi to a piston. If the area of the piston is 5 sq in., what is the resulting force on the piston?

B   6. How much air pressure is needed to lift a 300 lb object if the area of the piston is 4 sq in.?

7. If 2 cu ft of air at 15 psi is compressed to 40 cu in., what is the new pressure?

8. A volume of air at 15 psi is compressed to 3 cu ft, with a resulting pressure of 100 psi. What was the original volume?

10-9 Electrical power

We use electricity every day for light, heat, appliances, as well as for radio, television and other communication. Industries depend on electricity to run tools and machines, provide heat for processes such as steelmaking, and many other purposes. The source of electrical power is sometimes water power from dams. This water power is changed to electrical power by the huge generators shown in Figure 10-22. Electricity for smaller systems, like a car's ignition system, is available from the chemical energy produced by and stored in batteries, like the one in Figure 10-23.

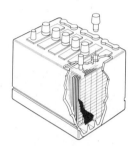

Figure 10-23

The energy of electricity is controlled and transmitted by conductors, usually metal wires. The flow of electricity, or electrical current, is measured in three ways.

1. The *rate of flow* of a current is measured in amperes. This can be compared to the rate of water flowing through a pipe, as shown in Figure 10-24.

2. The *pressure* under which the current flows is the measure of its voltage. Figure 10-25 compares the voltage of a current to pressure in a water pipe.

Figure 10-22

Figure 10-25

CURRENT FLOW

VOLTS

BATTERY
(VOLTAGE SOURCE)

PSI

PUMP
(PRESSURE SOURCE)

WATER FLOW

AMPERES
(ELECTRONS PER SECOND)

CURRENT FLOW

Figure 10-24

RATE
(GALLONS PER SECOND)

WATER FLOW

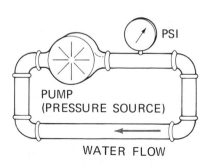

3. The *resistance* that the wire offers to the current's flow is measured in **ohms**. The resistance of the wire depends on the type of metal used and the length and diameter of the wire.

Volts, amperes, and ohms are all related. It takes one volt to force one ampere of current through a resistance of one ohm. This can be shown by the following formula.

$$\text{Volts} = \text{Amperes} \times \text{Ohms}$$

EXAMPLE 1   How large a current will 120 volts send through a resistance of 2 ohms?

SOLUTION

This steam turbine plant can produce 380,000 kilowatts.

Volts = Amps × Ohms

120 = Amps × 2

Amps = $\frac{120}{2}$

= 60 amps

How do we measure the rate of work done by an electrical system? The unit of power used for electricity is the **watt**. One watt of power is used when one volt produces a current of one ampere.

$$\text{Watts} = \text{Volts} \times \text{Amperes}$$

A watt is a small unit of power compared to one horsepower, used earlier in this chapter. It takes 746 watts to make one horsepower.

$$1 \text{ hp} = 746 \text{ watts}$$

Since the watt is such a small unit, a larger unit, the kilowatt (1000 watts) is sometimes used.

EXAMPLE 2   What is the wattage of a circuit using 10 amperes when the resistance is 12 ohms?

SOLUTION   To find the wattage we must know the voltage.

Volts = Amperes × Ohms
= 10 × 12
= 120 volts

Watts = Volts × Amperes
= 120 × 10
= 1200 watts

EXERCISES A

1. How many volts are needed to send a current of 2 amperes through a resistance of 60 ohms?

2. It takes 110 volts to send a current of 5 amperes through an electric toaster. Find the resistance of the toaster.

3. How many amperes will 120 volts send through a resistance of 3 ohms?

4. How many watts of power are used by an electric range that draws 5 amperes of current on a 240-volt line?

5. In a 12-volt auto electrical system, it takes 8 amperes to light the headlights. How much power is used?

6. A 12-volt battery has an output of 75 amperes. How much power is available from this battery?

7. An industrial machine uses 50 amperes of current on a 240-volt line. How many kilowatts does it use?

B 8. What is the wattage produced by 12 amperes when the resistance is 15 ohms?

9. The resistance of an iron is 11 ohms when the iron is using 110 volts. How many watts are being used?

10. Find the resistance of a 60 watt light bulb on a 120 volt line.

C 11. A one-horsepower electric motor is connected to a 120-volt line. How many amperes of current does it require?

12. A three-horsepower motor is connected to a 220-volt line. How much resistance does this motor have?

SELF-ANALYSIS TEST 33

1. A hydraulic system has an output piston with an area of 9 sq in. If the pressure in the system is 25 psi, what is the output force?

2. An input piston in a hydraulic system receives a force of 32 pounds. If its area is 4 sq in., what is the pressure in the system?

3. A 20-cu ft volume of air is compressed to 5 cu ft. If its original pressure is 15 psi, what is the pressure after compression?

4. How much resistance does an electric mixer offer if it is rated at 5 amperes with 110 volts?

5. How many watts are used by a 3-ampere electric dishwasher when it is connected to a 240-volt line?

RESEARCH WITH A COMPUTER

In Section 10-3 you learned how to find the displacement of an engine by using a flow chart and the following formula:

$$D = .7854 \times (\text{bore})^2 \times \text{stroke} \times \text{no. of cylinders}$$

If you have access to an electronic computer that uses the BASIC "language," you can use the program below to find engine displacement in cubic inches or cubic centimeters.

```
10 PRINT "BORE =";
20 INPUT B
30 PRINT "STROKE =";
40 INPUT S
50 PRINT "NUMBER OF CYLINDERS =";
60 INPUT N
70 LET D = .7854 * B↑2 * S * N
80 PRINT "DISPLACEMENT ="; D
90 END
```

Do you recognize the displacement formula in line 70? How is "(bore)^2" shown in the program?

EXERCISES

1. RUN the program with $B = 3.5$, $S = 3.25$, and $N = 8$. Compare the result with Example 3 on page 300.

2. RUN the program with $B = 9.0$, $S = 6.7$, and $N = 4$. Compare the result with Example 2 on page 299.

3. Change line 70 in the program above to

    ```
    70 LET D = INT( .7854 * B↑2 * S * N +.5)
    ```

4. Repeat Exercises 1 and 2. What do you notice?

RUN the program above using the bore and stroke measurements given in an automobile brochure. Compare the result with the displacement stated in the brochure.

Automobile makers frequently state engine specifications in both U.S. and metric units. The next program uses the measurements of bore and stroke, in inches, to find the displacement, in cubic inches. It also prints out the metric equivalents of the bore and stroke, in centimeters, and the displacement, in both cubic centimeters and liters.

```
10 PRINT "BORE (IN.) =";
20 INPUT B
30 PRINT "STROKE (IN.) =";
40 INPUT S
50 PRINT "NUMBER OF CYLINDERS =";
60 INPUT N
70 LET D=INT(.7854*B↑2*S*N+.5)
80 LET M=(INT(10*D*16.39+.5))/10
90 LET B=(INT(100*B*2.54+.5))/100
100 LET S=(INT(100*S*2.54+.5))/100
110 LET L=(INT(10*M/1000+.5))/10
120 PRINT "DISPLACEMENT (CU IN.) =";D
130 PRINT
140 PRINT "BORE (CM) =";B
150 PRINT "STROKE (CM) =";S
160 PRINT "DISPLACEMENT (CU CM) =";M
170 PRINT "DISPLACEMENT (L) =";L
180 END
```

EXERCISES

5. RUN the program with $B = 3.36$, $S = 2.72$, and $N = 4$.
   a. Compare the number of centimeters for the bore with the number of inches. Is the number of centimeters about $2\frac{1}{2}$ times the number of inches? Are these two measurements equivalent?

   b. Compare the number of centimeters for the stroke with the number of inches. Is the number of centimeters about $2\frac{1}{2}$ times the number of inches? Are these two measurements equivalent?

   c. Compare the liter displacement with the cubic-centimeter displacement. Is the number of liters about $\frac{1}{1000}$ the number of cubic centimeters? To which place is the number of liters rounded?

6. RUN the program with $B = 3.54$, $S = 2.60$, and $N = 4$.
   a. Is the displacement of this engine greater or less than the engine in Exercise 5? By how many cubic inches? By how many cubic centimeters?

   b. Is the bore of this engine greater or less than the bore of the engine in Exercise 5? By how many inches? By how many centimeters?

   c. Is the stroke greater or less than the stroke of the engine in Exercise 5? By how many inches? By how many centimeters?

TAKING INVENTORY

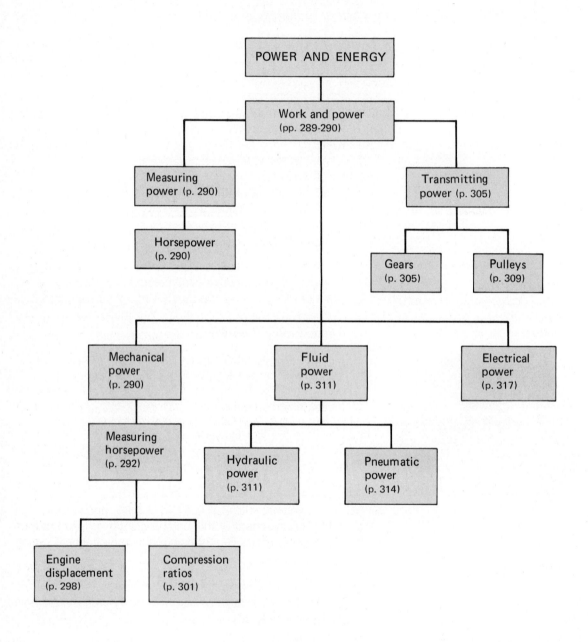

MEASURING YOUR SKILLS

1. Find the amount of work done in lifting 500 lb 3 ft. (10-1)

2. Find the horsepower needed to raise a 2750-lb car 3 ft in 5 sec. (10-1)

3. What is the brake horsepower of an engine that registers 200 lb on the end of an arm 2 ft long when the engine speed is 2800 rpm? Find the answer to the nearest horsepower. (10-2)

4. Find, to the nearest horsepower, the ihp of an engine whose pistons have an area of 15 sq in., a stroke of 5 ft, an average pressure of 80 lb per sq in., and 2000 piston strokes per minute. (10-2)

U.S. System

5. Find the displacement of a V-8 engine with a 4″ bore and a $3\frac{1}{2}$″ stroke. $(\pi = \frac{22}{7})$ (10-3)

6. There are 3 cu in. of space in a cylinder when the piston is at the top of its stroke. If the compression ratio is 9:1, how much space is there when the piston is at the bottom of its stroke? (10-4)

Metric System

7. What is the displacement of a 6-cylinder engine whose bore is 9 cm and whose stroke is 9 cm? (10-3)

8. A cylinder contains 200 cu cm of space when the piston is at the bottom of its stroke. There are 25 cu cm of space when it is at the top of its stroke. What is the compression ratio? (10-4)

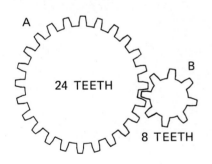

24 TEETH

8 TEETH

Figure 10-26

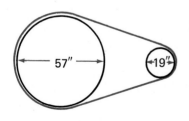

57″   19″

Figure 10-27

9. What is the gear ratio of A to B in Figure 10-26? (10-5)

10. The engine speed of a car is 3600 rpm while the drive shaft speed is 1200 rpm. What is the transmission ratio? (10-5)

11. The rear axle ratio is 5:1. If the drive shaft is turning at 2500 rpm, at what speed is the rear axle turning? (10-5)

12. What is the ratio of the speed of pulley A to pulley B in Figure 10-27? (10-6)

13. The liquid in a cylinder has a pressure of 20 psi. The output piston has an area of 8 sq in. What is the output force? (10-7)

14. 30 cu ft of air is compressed to 6 cu ft. The air pressure was 15 psi before compression? What is the pressure after compression? (10-8)

15. A 5-ampere electric drill requires 110 volts. What is its resistance? (10-9)

16. How much electrical power is used for a 6-ampere electric lawn mower connected to a 240-volt line? (10-9)

To keep up with the demand for commercial and residential buildings skilled construction workers use hand tools and heavy equipment.

CHAPTER **11** *Construction*

After completing this chapter you should be able to:

1. *Read blueprints and working drawings.*
2. *Estimate costs of projects.*
3. *Determine quantities of materials needed for various construction projects.*

From drawing to foundations

11-1 Plans and estimating costs

Before you start building anything, you need a plan. It might be a simple sketch or a detailed blueprint. Figure 11-1 shows a working drawing for adding a patio to a house.

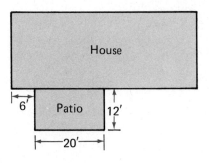

Figure 11-1

To build a complete house, more detailed drawings are necessary. A floor plan for a two-bedroom house is shown in Figure 11-2.

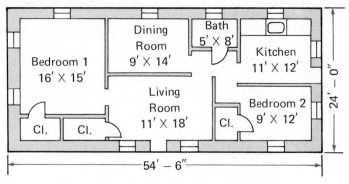

Figure 11-2

EXAMPLE 1   How many square feet of floor space is in the house shown in Figure 11-2?

SOLUTION $54'6'' = 54\frac{1}{2}$ ft
$54.5 \times 24 = 1308$ sq ft

The architect's blueprints help him make an estimate of the cost of construction. Then the contractor uses the architect's blueprints to make his own estimate. The estimated cost of a building is usually given in dollars per square foot.

EXAMPLE 2   An architect estimates that a house can be built for $15 per square foot. The house has 1800 square feet of floor space. What is the estimated cost?

SOLUTION $15 \times 1800 = 27000$

The estimated cost is $27,000.

EXERCISES   Use the floor plan in Figure 11-2 for Exercises 1–10.
Find the number of square feet in each of the following rooms.

A   1. living room   4. bedroom 1

2. kitchen   5. bedroom 2

3. bathroom

6. The estimated cost of the house in Figure 11-2 is $16 per square foot. What is the estimated cost of construction?

B 7. How many square yards of carpet are needed to carpet the two bedrooms?

8. If the price of carpeting is $12.50 per square yard, what is the cost of carpeting the living room?

9. One square foot of floor tiling for the kitchen costs $1.20. How much would it cost to tile the kitchen floor? (The 3′ × 12′ countertop should be subtracted.)

C 10. A contractor wishes to carpet all the rooms shown except the kitchen and bathroom. If the carpet costs $8.95 per square yard, what would be the cost of the carpet?

11-2 Excavations

Figure 11-3

Before any building can be started, excavation is usually necessary. The photograph in Figure 11-3 shows excavation being done prior to construction. Excavation for foundations, footings, or basements is usually computed in cubic yards.

The cost of excavating depends on the type of material which must be dug up. Another cost factor is the distance the material must be hauled for disposal.

EXAMPLE   An underground parking lot requires excavation 200 feet long, 150 feet wide, and 33 feet deep. The cost will be $6.00 per cubic yard. What will the excavation cost?

SOLUTION   200 ft = $\frac{200}{3}$ yd; 150 ft = 50 yd; 33 ft = 11 yd

$\frac{200}{3} \times 50 \times 11 = \frac{200}{3} \times \frac{50}{1} \times \frac{11}{1}$

$= \frac{110000}{3}$

$= 36,667$ (approx.)

There are 36,667 cubic yards to be excavated.

$36,667 \times 6 = 220,002$

The cost will be $220,002.

EXERCISES **A**   1. A warehouse basement requires an excavation 10′ deep, 78′ wide, and 96′ long. How many cubic yards of earth must be removed for this basement?

2. How many hours will it take a contractor to dig the basement in Exercise 1 if he can remove 60 cubic yards per hour?

3. A trucker can haul 10 cubic yards of earth per trip from an excavation to a landfill. He makes 2 trips per hour. How many cubic yards can he haul in an 8-hour day?

4. An excavation of 750 cubic yards is to be done by an earth-mover who will charge $3.00 per cubic yard. What will it cost to get the job done?

B 5. If the basement of the house in Figure 11-2 requires an excavation 9 feet deep, how many cubic yards of earth need to be removed?

6. The cost of excavating a 9-foot-deep basement in Figure 11-2 is $7.00 per cubic yard. What is the cost of excavating?

C 7. A basement requires an excavation 9 feet deep, 54 feet long, and 30 feet wide. An earth mover can dig this basement at a rate of 50 cubic yards per hour. If he charges $150.00 per hour, what is the cost of the excavation?

11-3 Footings

Before a building can be planned, the architect must know the bearing capacity of the soil. The number of pounds per square foot that the soil will support is the bearing capacity of the soil. The total weight of a building divided by the bearing capacity of the soil determines the area of footing on which the building should rest.

$$\text{Area of footing} = \frac{\text{weight}}{\text{bearing capacity}}$$

Figure 11-4 illustrates part of a foundation and the footing on which it rests.

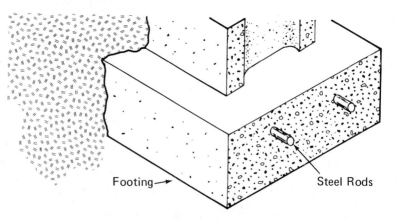

Footing→   Steel Rods

Figure 11-4

EXAMPLE 1 The bearing capacity of a soil is 2500 pounds per square foot. If the footing is required to sustain a load of 60,000 pounds, what should be the area of the footing?

SOLUTION Area of footing $= \dfrac{\text{weight}}{\text{bearing capacity}}$

$$= \dfrac{60,000}{2500}$$

$$= 24$$

24 sq ft of footing is needed.

The materials used for footings vary with the type of building constructed. Reinforced concrete is a popular material in use for footings. The reinforcement consists of metal rods placed in the concrete, as shown in Figure 11-4.

Reinforcing rod is usually sold by the foot and is available in different diameters. The cost of various widths of reinforcing rods is shown in Figure 11-5.

Number	Diameter	Price per ft
#3	$\frac{3}{8}''$	6.6¢
#4	$\frac{1}{2}''$	9.3¢
#5	$\frac{5}{8}''$	13.5¢
#6	$\frac{3}{4}''$	22.2¢

Figure 11-5

EXAMPLE 2 The footing for the house in Figure 11-2 has #3 reinforcing rods in it. Find the number of feet required if 2 parallel rods are required. What is the cost of these rods?

SOLUTION First we must find the perimeter.

$54\frac{1}{2} + 54\frac{1}{2} + 24 + 24 = 157$ ft

Since 2 rods are required we get

$2 \times 157 = 314$ ft

Thus we need 314 feet of reinforcing rod.

The cost of #3 rod is $.066 per foot

$$314 \times .066 = 20.724$$

The cost is $20.72.

EXERCISES A

1. If the bearing capacity of the soil is 2100 pounds per square foot and the area of the footing is 30 square feet, what is the maximum weight this footing will support?

2. A building will weigh 150,000 pounds. If the bearing capacity of the soil is 2000 lb per sq ft, what area of footing is required?

3. A structure weighing 50,000 pounds is to be built on soil which has a bearing capacity of 1800 lb per sq ft. What is the area of footing needed?

4. How many cubic yards of concrete are needed for a footing 18″ wide, 9″ deep and 120 feet long?

5. Use Figure 11-5 to find the cost of 75 feet of ½″ reinforcing rod.

B

6. A concrete footing 24 inches wide, 9 inches thick, 240 feet long, and reinforced with #4 rod is to be constructed. Three sets of reinforcing rods are placed lengthwise in the footing. Determine the cost of the reinforcing rods.

C

7. The concrete for the footing in Exercise 6 weighs 935 pounds per cubic yard. What is the weight of the concrete used?

11-4 Foundations

The type of foundation used for a building depends on its structure and location. In areas with a high risk of flooding or earthquakes, houses may be built on a concrete slab foundation. Otherwise they are usually constructed with basements. Foundations under houses having basements are commonly built with poured concrete or concrete blocks. Figure 11-6 shows a top view of the foundation wall of a house and a cross-section of the foundation and its footing.

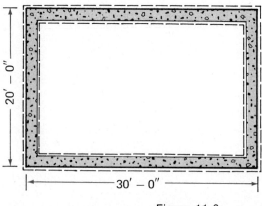

Slab foundation

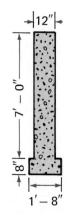

Figure 11-6

EXAMPLE 1   How many cubic yards of concrete are needed for the foundation shown in Figure 11-6?

SOLUTION   Two walls are 30′ × 7′ × 1′

$$30 \times 7 \times 1 = 210 \text{ cu ft}$$
$$210 \times 2 = 420 \text{ cu ft}$$

Two walls are 20′ × 7′ × 1′

$$20 \times 7 \times 1 = 140 \text{ cu ft}$$
$$2 \times 140 = 280 \text{ cu ft}$$
$$420 + 280 = 700 \text{ cu ft}$$

There are 27 cu ft in 1 cu yd.

$$700 \div 27 = 25.9 \text{ (approx.)}$$

26 cubic yards of concrete are needed.

Sometimes concrete blocks rather than poured concrete are used for foundations. Concrete blocks like those shown in Figure 11-7 are held together by mortar. Figure 11-8 shows that one **course** of blocks is the block itself, together with its mortar joint.

Figure 11-7

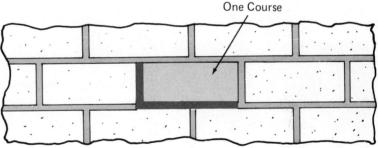

One Course

Figure 11-8

One course of concrete blocks measures 8″ high and 16″ long.

EXAMPLE 2   How many concrete blocks are needed to build a foundation wall 8 feet high and 40 feet long?

SOLUTION   First we find the area of the wall.

$$8 \times 40 = 320 \text{ sq ft}$$

Since one course of blocks is 16″ × 8″, or 128 sq in. we need to convert 320 sq ft to sq in.   (cont. on next page)

There are 144 sq in. in 1 sq ft.

$320 \times 144 = 46{,}080$

So there are 46,080 sq in. of wall. To find the number of blocks needed, divide by the area of one course.

$46{,}080 \div 128 = 360$

360 blocks are needed.

Concrete blocks can sometimes be broken. So contractors frequently add on a percentage for breakage when ordering.

EXAMPLE 3   If 10% is allowed for breakage in Example 2, how many concrete blocks should be ordered?

SOLUTION

$$10\% \text{ of } 360 = .10 \times 360$$
$$= 36$$

We need 36 more blocks.

$360 + 36 = 396$ blocks

EXERCISES A

1. A concrete slab foundation 6″ thick, 20 feet wide, and 25 feet long is to be poured. How many cubic yards of concrete must be ordered?

2. A poured concrete foundation wall is 10″ thick, 8 ft high and 40 ft long. How many cubic yards of concrete are required?

3. How many concrete blocks are needed to build a wall 10 ft high and 25 ft long?

4. A contractor determines that he needs 450 concrete blocks for a foundation. If he allows 8% for breakage, how many blocks should he order?

5. A warehouse requires a concrete foundation wall 9″ thick, and 3 ft high. The building measures 38 ft by 82 ft. How many cubic yards of concrete are needed for the foundation?

6. It costs Mr. Rivera $.45 each for concrete blocks. He wishes to build an 8-foot-high foundation for a 25′ × 45′ house. If he allows 5% for breakage, how much will the concrete blocks for the foundation cost?

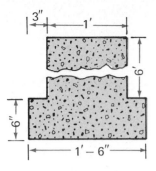

Figure 11-9

B 7. Ready mixed concrete will be delivered to the construction site for $21.00 per cubic yard. What will concrete cost for the foundation and footing for a 60′ × 100′ building. The cross section of the foundation and footing is shown in Figure 11-9.

SELF-ANALYSIS TEST 34

1. A 25′ × 40′ house is planned to cost $15 per square foot. What is the estimated cost of construction?

2. The foundations of a large building require an excavation 45 feet deep, 150 feet long, and 150 feet wide. How many cubic yards of earth must be removed?

3. A building is planned to weigh 856,000 pounds. The bearing capacity of the soil on which it will be built is 300 lb per sq ft. How large a footing is needed?

4. How many cubic yards of concrete are needed to build a one-foot-thick by one-foot-deep foundation wall for a 30′ × 50′ building?

SPOTLIGHT ON INDUSTRY

The demand for low-cost, flexible housing is being met by modular construction. Houses are put together from factory-assembled and finished modules. Each section of the house is made up of two rectangular modules side by side. All the plumbing, wiring, and duct work is done at the factory. The modules are shipped to the house site on trucks. Once assembled on the foundation, they are ready for use. Since all the units are rectangles, a variety of room arrangements can be planned. The buyer can choose a suitable floor plan. Some advantages of modular housing are the low cost and the flexibility of room arrangements.

EXERCISES 1. A house can be built on site for $35,000. A similar modular house would cost $22,000. How much could be saved by buying the modular house?

2. Carpet for three bedrooms of a modular house costs $8 per square yard. Each bedroom measures 12 ft x 18 ft. How much would it cost to carpet the three bedrooms?

Framing and exterior

11-5 Framing

The framework of most houses built today is made of wood. Figure 11-10 shows the framework of a house.

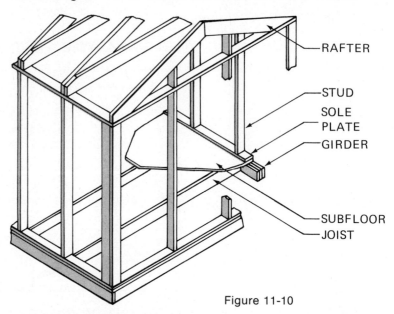

Figure 11-10

The contractor orders wood for the frame in board feet, the standard measuring unit for lumber. One board foot is a piece of lumber one foot long, one foot wide and one inch thick. Sometimes a larger unit, M, is used for 1000 board feet. Boards come in varying widths of 2″, 3″, 4″, 5″, 6″, 8″, 10″, and 12″. The thickness may vary, too, but standard units are 1″, $1\frac{1}{4}$″, $1\frac{1}{2}$″, 2″, 3″, 4″, 6″, 8″, and so forth. In calculating board feet, lumber less than 1″ thick is counted as 1″ thick. One board foot may be any piece with the same volume as $1' \times 1' \times 1''$. Figure 11-11 shows 3 pieces of lumber which measure 1 board foot.

Figure 11-11

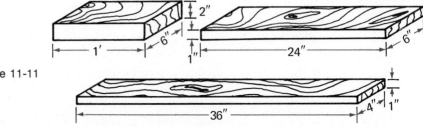

To find the number of board feet in a piece of lumber we can use the formula

$$bd\ ft = lwt$$

where l = length in feet
w = width in feet
t = thickness in inches

EXAMPLE 1   Find the number of board feet in a 2 by 4 that is 6 feet long.

SOLUTION $Bd\ ft = lwt$

$$= 6 \times \tfrac{4}{12} \times 2$$

$$= 4\ bd\ ft$$

EXAMPLE 2   Find the cost of 8 timbers 6″ × 10″ × 20′ at $200 per M.

SOLUTION $bd\ ft = lwt$

$$= 20 \times \frac{10}{12} \times 6$$

$$= 100\ bd\ ft$$

$$8 \times 100 = 800\ bd\ ft$$

$$cost = \frac{bd\ ft \times price\ per\ M}{1000}$$

$$= \frac{800 \times 200}{1000}$$

$$= 160$$

The cost is $160.

There are many places in construction where pieces are spaced the same distance apart. For example, floor joists, wall studs, and roof rafters are usually placed 16″ apart. We indicate this as 16″ o.c. (on center).

EXAMPLE 3   How many 16″ o.c. floor joists are needed for an 8-foot-long room?

SOLUTION   We must divide the length by 16″.

$$8 \times 12 = 96″\ long$$

$$96 \div 16 = 6$$

(cont. on next page)

Figure 11-12 illustrates the joists.

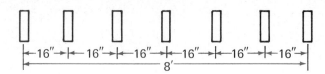

Figure 11-12

6 + 1, or 7 joists are needed, because we must add one for a starter.

EXERCISES   Find the number of board feet.

A   1. 6 boards, each 2″ × 8″ × 12′

2. Twenty 2 × 6's, each 14 ft long

3. 15 pieces, $\frac{3}{4}$″ × 10″ × 8′, and 5 pieces, $\frac{3}{4}$″ × 10″ × 2′

4. How many wall studs are needed for a 20-foot wall if the studs are 16″ o.c.?

5. How many roof rafters are needed for a 42-foot-long roof if the rafters are 16″ o.c.?

B   6. The cost of a certain kind of lumber is $190 per M. Find the cost of 150 pieces, each 2″ × 8″ × 12′, at this price.

7. A 12-foot wall needs 2 × 4 studs placed 16″ o.c. If the height of the wall is 8 feet, find the number of board feet of studs to be ordered.

C   8. Good quality 2 × 6's used for rafters sell for $238 per M. Find the cost of rafters for the roof shown in Figure 11-13 if they are placed 16″ o.c.

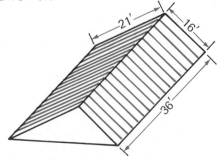

Figure 11-13

11-6 Roofing

After the completion of the frame, the house is ready for roofing. Many different kinds of roofs are available. Some varieties are shown in Figure 11-14.

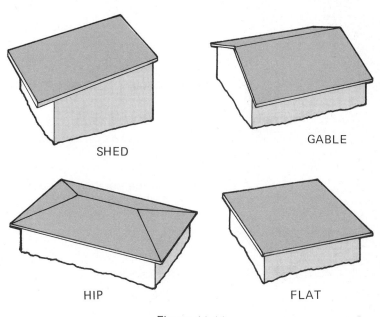

SHED

GABLE

HIP

FLAT

Figure 11-14

The materials chosen for roofing vary with the appearance desired, the climate, and the cost of materials and labor.

Shingles are commonly used for most gable or shed roofs. One of the most popular kind of shingle used is the asphalt strip shingle. Asphalt shingles are measured in squares. One square of shingles will cover 100 square feet of roof. For example, if a roof has an area of 900 square feet, 9 squares of shingles will be needed to cover it.

Generally, a layer of roofing felt is laid down before the shingles are attached. Roofing felt comes in rolls 3 feet wide and 144 feet long. So, one roll will cover 3 × 144, or 432 square feet.

Another material needed for the roofing process is nails, for attaching the shingles. About 2 pounds of nails should be allowed for one square of shingles.

EXAMPLE The gable roof pictured in Figure 11-15 is 30 feet long and has rafters $16\frac{1}{2}$ feet long. How many squares of shingles are needed to cover it?

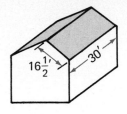

Figure 11-15

SOLUTION   Half of roof = $16\frac{1}{2} \times 30$

$\qquad\qquad\qquad$ = 495 sq ft

Area of roof = 2 × 495 = 990 sq ft

1 square of roofing covers 100 sq ft.

990 ÷ 100 = 9.9

10 squares of roofing are needed.

EXERCISES   Find the number of squares needed for the following roofs.

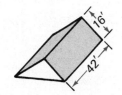

Figure 11-16

A 1. A gable roof 42 feet long with 16-foot rafters. (See Figure 11-16.)

2. A gable roof 27 feet long with 12-foot rafters

3. A shed roof 20 feet long with 14-foot rafters (See Figure 11-17.)

4. A shed roof 30 feet long with 15-foot rafters

B 5. Find the cost of the shingles for a gable roof 35 feet long with 15-foot rafters if shingles cost $7.50 per square.

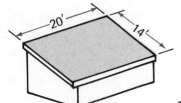

Figure 11-17

6. Find the cost of the roofing nails needed for the roof in Exercise 5 if nails cost $0.20 per pound.

7. How many rolls of roofing felt are needed for a shed roof which is 24 feet long and has rafters 16 feet long?

C 8. What is the cost of roofing materials for a 1680-square-foot roof? Assume that shingles cost $7.90 per square, roofing felt costs $2.75 per roll, and nails are $.25 per pound.

9. Find the cost of roofing the building in Figure 11-18 if shingles cost $7.88 per square, roofing felt, $2.80 per roll, and nails, $.19 per lb.

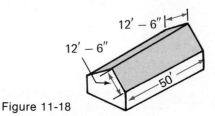

Figure 11-18

11-7 Windows and doors

The size, type, and number of windows and doors is planned along with the rest of the house. Various kinds of windows are available, as shown in Figure 11-19.

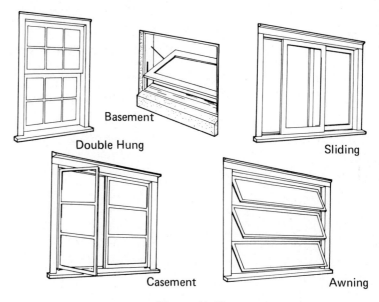

Figure 11-19

When the windows are planned, FHA (Federal Housing Administration) requirements must be followed. FHA requires that the window area of a house be at least 10% of the floor space.

EXAMPLE What should be the minimum window area for a house whose floor area is 1800 sq ft?

SOLUTION 10% of 1800 = .10 × 1800
= 180 sq ft

The cost of windows can vary with the type of glass used. To provide better insulation, some windows are made with two pieces of glass having an air space between them. These welded glass windows are naturally more expensive, as they have twice as much glass.

The price of doors also varies with the type of wood or metal used.

1. What is the price of 7 double-hung windows with 28″ × 20″ welded glass, if the price of each is $70.84?

2. A double hung 28″ × 20″ window with regular glass costs $14.70. What will 5 of these windows cost?

3. Welded glass windows cost $70.84 each and regular glass windows the same size cost $46.86 each. How much more will welded glass windows cost, if 8 windows are ordered?

4. A contractor needs 9 room and closet doors. What will he pay, if each door costs $12.90?

B 5. How many windows with an area of 9 square feet are needed to meet FHA requirements for a 25′ × 40′ house?

6. A builder needs 9 double-hung 28″ × 20″ windows, 2 basement windows, 1 bay window, 9 plywood doors, and 2 mahogany doors. Find his cost if the prices are as follows:

28″ × 20″ double-hung window	$53.90
basement window	$35.40
bay window	$85.75
plywood door	$13.85
mahogany door	$59.40

11-8 Siding

To be finished on the outside a house needs siding or other material to cover the exterior walls. Siding is sometimes made of wood. More recently, aluminum, steel, and vinyl siding have become popular. These pre-finished sidings require little or no maintenance and are easy to apply. The man at the left is installing siding for a house under construction.

To calculate the amount of siding needed for a house it is necessary to subtract the space for windows and doors. A common rule-of-thumb is to subtract 5 square feet for each window and 10 square feet for each door. So we must calculate the total number of square feet for the walls of the house and then use the rule-of-thumb to subtract the window and door area.

EXAMPLE The house shown in Figure 11-20 on the next page has 2 doors and 8 windows. Use the rule-of-thumb to find the area to be sided.

SOLUTION   Perimeter = (2 × 30) + (2 × 48)
                    = 156 ft

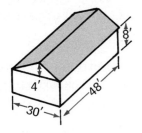

Figure 11-20

The area without the two triangular roof sections is the perimeter × height.

156 × 8 = 1248 sq ft

Triangular area = $\frac{1}{2}$ × 30 × 4
                    = 60 sq ft

2 triangular areas = 2 × 60 = 120 sq ft

1248 + 120 = 1368 sq ft

Now we subtract 5 sq ft for each window and 10 sq ft for each door.

(8 × 5) + (2 × 10) = 60

1368 − 60 = 1308

The area to be sided is 1308 sq ft

EXERCISES A

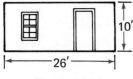

Figure 11-21

1. A wall 30 feet long and 8 feet high is to be sided. The wall contains 2 windows and one door. Estimate the total area that is to be sided.

2. Estimate the number of square feet that are to be sided in the wall pictured in Figure 11-21.

3. A wall 15 feet high and 25 feet long contains 4 windows and a door. Estimate the area of the wall to be sided.

B 4. A flat roof house has exterior walls 10 ft high. The dimensions of the house are 40′ × 25′. There are 8 windows and 2 doors. Estimate the area to be sided.

5. Estimate the total area that is to be sided on the end of the house shown in Figure 11-22.

6. The house sketched in Figure 11-23 has 10 windows and 3 doors. Estimate the area to be sided.

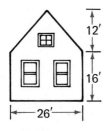

Figure 11-22

Figure 11-23

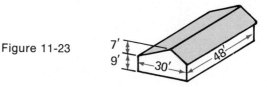

341

11-9 Brickwork

Another method of finishing the exterior of a house is with brickwork. Brick facing is commonly put on all or part of the exterior of a house.

The standard size of a brick is $2\frac{1}{4}'' \times 3\frac{3}{4}'' \times 8''$. Other sizes are available and many different textures and colors are available in face brick. Where the brick will be seen, face brick is used, and it is considerably more expensive than common brick.

Mortar is used to bond the brick together. Some varieties of bonding are available, but the most common is the running bond. The thickness of the mortar joints may vary from $\frac{1}{4}''$ to $\frac{1}{2}''$. If thicker mortar joints are used, there are less bricks per square foot. Figure 11-24 shows how the number of bricks laid in running bond varies with the thickness of the mortar.

Running Bond

Thickness of mortar joint	$\frac{1}{4}''$	$\frac{3}{8}''$	$\frac{1}{2}''$
Number of bricks per 100 sq ft	698	655	616

Figure 11-24

This information can be used to determine how many bricks should be ordered. As with concrete block, a percentage is usually allowed for breakage. Bricks are usually sold in flats, with 300 bricks per flat.

EXAMPLE A 25' $\times$ 10' wall of a house is to have bricks laid in running bond with $\frac{1}{4}''$ mortar joints. If the bricks sell for $40.00 per flat, how much will the bricks cost?

SOLUTION The area to be bricked is 25 $\times$ 10, or 250 sq ft.
The number of bricks is 698 per 100 sq ft.

$$\frac{250 \times 698}{100}$$

$2.5 \times 698 = 1745.0$

1745 bricks are needed.

To find the number of flats, divide by 300.

$1745 \div 300 = 5.8$

6 flats are needed

$6 \times \$40 = \$240$

The cost of the bricks is $240.

EXERCISES A 1. How many standard bricks laid in running bond are needed for a 200-square-foot wall if the mortar joints are $\frac{3}{8}''$ wide?

2. The cost of a flat of a face brick is $45.00. The front of a house, which measures $45' \times 12'$, is to be faced with bricks laid in running bond with $\frac{1}{4}''$ mortar joints. How much will the bricks cost?

B 3. A contractor needs to face an entire house with bricks laid in running bond having $\frac{1}{4}''$ joints. The dimensions of the house are $30' \times 45'$ with 10' high walls all around. Allowing 3% of breakage, how many bricks should he order?

C 4. A house is to be faced with running bond brick 2 layers deep. The mortar joints will be $\frac{3}{8}''$ thick. The house has 12' high walls with outer dimensions $25' \times 40'$. The cost of a flat of bricks is $55.00. How much will the bricks cost if 4% is added for breakage?

SELF-ANALYSIS TEST 35

1. Find the number of board feet in a piece of lumber $2'' \times 10'' \times 16'$.

2. How many floor joists are needed for a 12-ft long room if the joists are placed 16" o.c.?

3. Find the cost of asphalt shingles for a gable roof 20 feet long with 16-foot rafters, if the cost per square of shingles is $8.00.

4. Find the cost of 4 windows at $36.50 each and 2 doors at $45.90 each.

5. Find the number of square feet of siding to be ordered for a $20' \times 8'$ wall having 4 windows.

6. Bricks are laid so that there are 675 bricks in 100 sq ft. How many bricks should be ordered to face a $25' \times 12'$ wall of a house?

Waste Water Treatment Plant Operator

Clean water is necessary for life. The expansion of industry and the boom in home construction are making greater demands on our water supply. The proper treatment of waste water is one way to ensure that the quality of our water remains high. Treatment plant operators must see that waste water is pollution-free. Perhaps you are interested in following a career in this vital area.

Job Description

What do treatment plant operators do?
1. They supervise the operation of equipment that removes domestic and industrial wastes from sewage water, or makes these wastes harmless.
2. They test and correct levels of chemicals that remove harmful germs from the water.
3. They operate valves and pumps to keep the water moving through the treatment process. This prevents sludge from building up in the sedimentation tanks.
4. They read meters and record important data on a log sheet.
5. They make minor repairs in the equipment. Under emergency conditions, they may be required to make major repairs.

Qualifications

Most larger plants prefer high school graduates.
Applicants should have some experience with machines.
Background in mathematics, chemistry, mechanics, and earth science is helpful.
Good physical condition is required for climbing ladders.

Training

Most states offer courses for the training of treatment plant operators. Among the subjects studied in these courses are basic chemistry and methods of measuring water flow. Usually a treatment plant operator will combine classroom instruction

with training in the plant. Apprentice operators learn by helping in regular duties like meter reading, taking samples, and adjusting pumps.

Working Conditions

Work is usually done in several daily shifts.
Overtime is sometimes needed during emergencies.
Work hazards include exposure to unpleasant odors, noise, and
  dangerous chemicals.
Work is done indoors and outdoors, in all weather conditions.

Opportunities for Advancement

Operators with ability and experience may become supervisors or chief operators. Some operators may become technicians for state or local water pollution control groups. Some operators may choose to work as consulting engineers for private industries. Chances for advancement are improved by passing state tests for treatment plant operations. Further study beyond high school can help in getting a supervisory job in a larger plant.

Finishing the job

11-10 **Electrical wiring**

While carpenters are busy shingling and siding a building, the electricians and plumbers are busy installing their systems.

Recall from Chapter 10 that we measure electrical power in watts or kilowatts. Remember also that

$$\text{watts} = \text{volts} \times \text{amperes}.$$

The voltage entering a house is about 120 volts or 240 volts. So the factor that determines how many watts are available is amperage. The amperage is restricted at the service entrance, the part of the electrical system linked to the outside power source. The service entrance is connected by a meter to the distribution panel. Fuses or circuit breakers are contained in the distribution panel to protect electrical equipment. Out of the distribution panel, branch circuits carry current to various locations in the house. There is a fuse or circuit breaker to control the amount of current for each circuit.

EXAMPLE   A 20-ampere circuit breaker is placed on a 110-volt circuit. How many watts of power can be used on this circuit.

SOLUTION   Watts = Volts × Amperes
$$= 110 \times 20$$
$$= 2200$$

2200 watts or 2.2 kilowatts can be used.

EXERCISES A

1. A 15-ampere fuse is placed in a 120-volt circuit. How many watts of power are available through this circuit?

2. A 30-ampere circuit breaker is located in a 220-volt circuit. How many kilowatts of power are available through this circuit?

3. An electric motor requires 1.7 amperes on a 115-volt circuit. How many watts of power does it use?

4. An electrical code requires an outlet every 8 feet or less. How many outlets are necessary for a room that is 14 feet wide and 20 feet long?

11-11 Plumbing

A plumbing system uses pipes of various sizes and materials. Before the foundation is completed, a line from the water main and a water meter are positioned. The drain pipe leading to the sewer is also put in place early in the construction process.

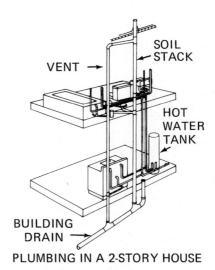

PLUMBING IN A 2-STORY HOUSE

The pipes of a plumbing system used to be made of cast iron or galvanized iron. Copper pipes were an improvement, but now plastic pipes are used extensively. Plastic pipes are less expensive, less easily corroded, and easy to use.

EXAMPLE   The price of $\frac{1}{2}''$ copper pipe is $.50 per foot and the price of $\frac{1}{2}''$ plastic pipe is $.26 per foot. A plumbing job requires 340 feet of $\frac{1}{2}''$ pipe. How much less will the pipe cost if plastic is used instead of metal?

SOLUTION   Cost of copper pipe: 340 × .50 = 170.00

Cost of plastic pipe: 340 × .26 = 88.40

170.00 − 88.40 = $81.60 less

EXERCISES A   1. The price of 4'' cast iron soil pipe is $1.57 per foot and plastic soil pipe of the same diameter costs $0.44 per foot. What is the difference in price per foot?

347

2. If $\frac{1}{2}''$ plastic pipe costs \$0.25 per foot, find the cost of 180 feet of this pipe.

3. If a plumber works for 37 hours in one week and is paid \$6.75 per hour, how much does he earn?

B 4. If 4'' plastic soil pipe costs \$43.90 per hundred feet, find the cost of 2000 feet of this pipe.

5. A repair project required 40 feet of $\frac{1}{2}''$ plastic pipe at \$0.26 per foot, 12 feet of 6'' soil pipe at \$1.10 per foot, and 5 hours of labor at \$5.25 per hour. What did the repair project cost?

11-12 Interior finishing

In seasonal climates, insulation is one of the first steps in interior finishing. The insulation must be placed between the wall frame and the interior wall finish. A variety of materials can be used to finish the interior walls. Gypsum lath, metal lath, or plaster board (sheet rock) is commonly used as wall board. This can then be plastered, painted, wallpapered or panelled.

To determine the amount of wall covering needed, we can use a simple rule-of-thumb: Four times the floor space will give the approximate wall and ceiling area to be covered.

EXAMPLE 1   How much plaster board should be ordered to cover the interior walls and ceilings for a 23' × 46' house?

SOLUTION   23 × 46 = 1058 sq ft of floor

1058 × 4 = 4232 sq ft

4232 sq ft of plaster board should be ordered.

Wallpaper is very popular as a wall covering. It is usually sold in 18''-wide rolls either 24 feet or 48 feet long.

EXAMPLE 2   How many 24-foot rolls of wallpaper 18'' wide should be ordered for a 8' × 10' room with an 8-foot ceiling?

SOLUTION   The area of the 4 walls is:

(8 × 8) + (8 × 8) + (8 × 10) + (8 × 10)

64 + 64 + 80 + 80 = 288 sq ft

Area of one roll of paper:

$1\frac{1}{2}' \times 24' = 36$ sq ft

$288 \div 36 = 8$

8 rolls of paper should be ordered.

Painting is another popular wall and ceiling covering. The area that a volume of paint will cover varies with the type of paint used and whether a primer coat has been applied first.

EXAMPLE 3   One gallon of paint will cover 460 sq ft. How many gallons and quarts should be ordered for a 15' × 20' room with an 8-foot ceiling?

SOLUTION   The area of the 4 walls is:

$(15 \times 8) + (15 \times 8) + (20 \times 8) + (20 \times 8)$
$120 + 120 + 160 + 160 = 560$ sq ft
$560 \div 460 = 1.2$ (approx.)

1 gallon and 1 quart should be ordered.

Various types of floor covering are in use today. Hardwood, tile, linoleum, and carpet are available in a variety of colors, sizes, patterns, and textures. Hardwood is sold by the board foot but the others are sold by the square yard, or by the piece.

EXAMPLE 4   A room 12' × 15' is to be carpeted with carpet costing $13.00 per square yard. What will the carpet cost?

SOLUTION   Changing the feet to yards gives

$\frac{12}{3} \times \frac{15}{3} = 4 \times 5$
$\qquad\quad = 20$ sq yd
$20 \times 13.00 = 260.00$

The carpet will cost $260.00.

EXERCISES A   1. If the floor area of a house is 1800 sq ft, estimate the number of square feet of gypsum lath needed for the interior of this house.

2. About how many square feet of wallboard are needed for a 30' × 45' house?

3. How many rolls of wallpaper 18″ wide and 24′ long are needed to paper a wall 8 ft high and 27 ft long?

4. A 15′ × 25′ living room with an 8-foot ceiling is to be papered with 18″ wide wallpaper. If the rolls are 24 feet long, how many rolls should be ordered?

5. One gallon of paint will cover 500 sq ft. How many gallons are needed for 2700 sq ft?

6. How many square yards of carpeting are needed for a 15′ × 18′ room?

B 7. If one piece of gypsum lath is 16″ wide and 48″ long, estimate the number of pieces of lath needed for a house with 2500 square feet of floor space.

8. If indoor-outdoor carpet costs $6.00 per square yard, find the cost of carpeting a patio that is 12 ft × 18 ft.

9. A 12′ × 15′ master bedroom is to be wallpapered with 18″ × 24′ rolls costing $5.65 per roll. If the bedroom ceiling is 8′ high, what will be the cost of the wallpaper?

C 10. A 20′ × 24′ living room has an 8-foot ceiling. Wall-to-wall carpeting is ordered at $9.00 per sq yd. $5.75-per-roll wallpaper is also picked out. The rolls of wallpaper are 18″ wide and 24′ long. What is the cost of carpet and wallpaper for the room?

TRICKS OF THE TRADE

To divide a board into strips of the same width without calculating, use this method.

    a. Lay a rule at an angle across the width of the board so that the distance on the rule is easily divisible by the number of strips you want. Mark these points.

    b. Repeat the procedure at another part of the board.

    c. Join the marks and extend the lines to the ends of the board.

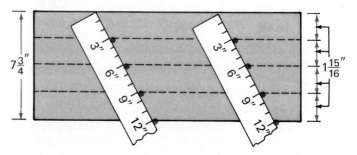

11-13 Landscaping

One of the last steps in completing the construction of a house or commercial building is the landscaping. **Landscaping** means grading the earth and planting trees, shrubs, and grass.

Grading or sloping the earth may require more excavation or fill to raise the level of the ground. The fill is usually covered with topsoil, which can support grass and shrubs. Both fill and topsoil are sold by the cubic yard. Sometimes sod is applied, as a shortcut to planting grass seed. Sod is sold by the square yard.

Landscaping for a commercial building.

EXAMPLE 1   A lot 100 ft wide and 165 ft long is to be covered with topsoil to a depth of 4″. Topsoil will be delivered to the site for $4.00 per cubic yard. What will the topsoil cost?

SOLUTION   Changing the feet and inches to yards, we multiply to get the volume.

$$V = \frac{100}{3} \times \frac{165}{3} \times \frac{4}{36}$$
$$= \frac{100}{3} \times \frac{55}{1} \times \frac{1}{9}$$
$$= \frac{5500}{27}$$
$$= 203.7 \text{ (approx.)}$$

204 cubic yards are needed.

$204 \times 4.00 = 816.00$

The topsoil will cost $816.00.

EXAMPLE 2 The lot in Example 1 is to be sodded. The sod costs $.75 per square yard. How much will the sod cost?

SOLUTION We convert to yards to find the area.

$$A = \frac{100}{3} \times \frac{165}{3}$$
$$= \frac{100}{3} \times \frac{55}{1}$$
$$= \frac{5500}{3}$$
$$= 1833.3 \text{ (approx.)}$$

1834 sq yd of sod is needed.

$1834 \times \$.75 = \$1375.50$

The sod will cost $1375.50.

EXERCISES A 1. Fill can be bought for $3.50 per cubic yard. If 35 cubic yards are needed for one job and 45 cubic yards for another job, how much will the fill cost for both jobs?

2. If topsoil, delivered to the site, costs $4.50 per cubic yard, what will 21 cubic yards cost?

3. A 60' × 75' plot needs 4" of topsoil. How many cubic yards of topsoil should be ordered?

4. Sod is being ordered for a 40' × 60' yard. How many square yards should be ordered?

5. What is the cost of 375 sq yd of sod at $.65 per square yard?

B 6. What is the total cost of the following list of trees and shrubs?

   1 mountain ash tree at $14.00
   5 junipers at $12.00 each
   6 rose bushes at $2.75 each
   3 seedless ash trees at $5.00 each

7. Six inches of topsoil are needed for a 60' × 90' lot. At $4.50 per cubic yard, what will the topsoil cost?

8. A contractor needs to lay sod for a 50' × 60' lot. If the sod costs $.75 per square yard, how much will the contractor pay for the sod?

C 9. Topsoil can be delivered to a lot for $4.75 per cubic yard. How much will it cost to lay topsoil for a 45' × 75' lot to a depth of 3"?

10. Figure 11-25 is a sketch of a house and lot. Find the cost of sodding this lawn if sod costs $0.60 per square yard.

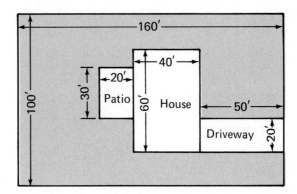

Figure 11-25

SELF-ANALYSIS TEST 36

1. A 20-ampere fuse is placed in a 120-volt circuit. How many watts of power can be used on this circuit?

2. One-inch plastic piping costs $.32 per foot. Copper piping of the same size costs $.42 per foot. If 85 feet of piping are needed, how much can be saved by using the plastic piping?

3. How many gallons of paint should be ordered to paint two 10' × 12' bedrooms if one gallon covers 400 sq ft? The ceilings in the bedrooms are 8 ft.

4. How many square yards of carpeting should be ordered for a 18' × 24' living room?

5. Find the cost of sod for a 20' × 45' yard at $.55 per square yard.

6. How many cubic yards of topsoil should be ordered for a 50' × 75' lot if the desired depth is 4"?

CREATIVE CRAFTSMAN

Make working drawings for an A-frame house which includes at least one hexagon-shaped room.

TAKING INVENTORY

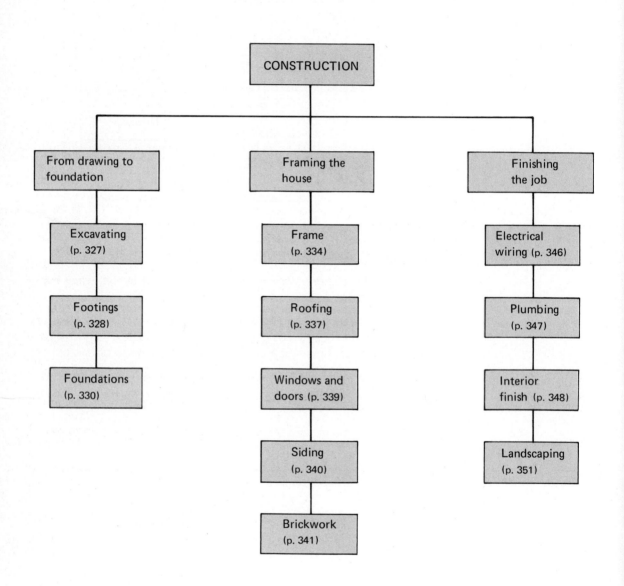

MEASURING YOUR SKILLS

Refer to the floor plan in Figure 11-26 for Exercises 1-8.

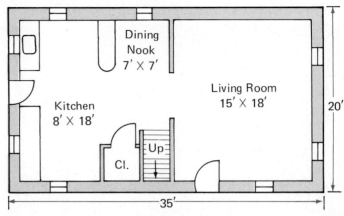

Figure 11-26

1. The contractor estimates that he can build the house for $16 per square foot. What is the estimated cost of construction of the floor shown in Figure 11-26? (11-1)

2. The excavation for the basement of the house is to be 8 feet deep. How many cubic yards of dirt must be removed? (11-2)

3. The bearing capacity of the soil is 1600 lb per sq ft. If the house is to weigh 27,000 lb, what area of footing should the house have? (11-3)

4. Twenty 2 × 4 wall studs, each 8' long, are ordered for the living room. How many board feet is this? (11-5)

5. How many squares of shingles should be ordered for a gable roof on the house if the rafters are 12 ft long? (11-6)

6. What is the cost of 8 double hung windows if the price of each is $60.55? (11-7)

7. How much siding is needed for the 35' × 20' wall having three windows? (11-8)

8. Bricks are laid in bonding that gives 660 bricks per 100 sq ft. How many bricks should be ordered for a one-layer-deep facing of a 35' × 10' wall? (11-9)

9. A 30-ampere fuse is placed in a 120-volt circuit. How many watts of power does this circuit provide? (11-10)

10. Find the cost of 38 ft of plastic piping at $.23 per foot. (11-11)

11. What is the cost of $9-a-square-yard carpeting for a 15' × 18' room? (11-12)

Newly developed techniques and machinery account for the increasing list of manufactured items.

CHAPTER 12 *Manufacturing*

After completing this chapter, you should be able to:

1. *Find the amounts of materials needed to produce various items.*
2. *Work problems relating to forming, joining, and separating materials.*
3. *Work problems relating to packaging and marketing.*

Forming and conditioning

Figure 12-1

12-1 Casting

A manufacturer must produce a product that people need or will use. The first step in making a new product is testing to see if people will buy it. Then the manufacturer must find the best way to make the product with the greatest profit. Figure 12-1 shows a product being tested in a laboratory before it is put on the market.

Many different processes are involved in making products. One step is to take a material and make it into a desired shape. One method of shaping involves casting. This means pouring molten or fluid materials into a mold. The mold forms the material, so that when it hardens, it will be the desired shape. Many kinds of metals, plastics, rubber, glass, and concrete are cast in molds. Bottles and tires are two examples of products made by casting.

357

EXAMPLE   A new washing machine is planned to have a water pump made of cast aluminum. Each pump requires 2 pounds of aluminum. How many tons of aluminum are needed to make 175,000 washing machines?

SOLUTION   2 × 175,000 = 350,000

There are 2000 lb in 1 ton.

350,000 ÷ 2000 = 175

175 tons of aluminum are needed.

EXERCISES   A

1. A certain type of casting requires 2.54 pounds of cast iron.
   a. How much cast iron is needed to make 175 castings?
   b. How many castings can be made from 1270 pounds of molten iron?

2. One mold can be used to produce 5 castings per hour. How many castings can be produced by 2 molds in 3 hours?

3. After being cast in the mold, the casting cools at a rate of 15 degrees every 2 minutes. How many minutes are needed for the casting to cool 75 degrees?

B 4. A machine can produce cast soft drink bottles at a rate of 6 bottles per minute. How many bottles can be made by one machine in an 8-hour shift?

5. If molten iron is to be used for making castings, about 10% of it is lost during the casting process and is re-cycled for future use. How much iron is recycled if one ton of molten iron is used?

6. A machine will produce model cars at a rate of one car every 12 seconds. Each car requires 1.5 ounces of plastic. How much plastic is needed when the machine runs for 3 hours?

7. After casting a block for an engine, 3% of the material is removed by drilling, tapping, grinding, and other processes that are necessary to produce a finished block. If the finished block weighs 175 pounds, what was its original weight?

8. It costs a soft drink company 1.5 cents to produce one new bottle. The company uses 3 million bottles per year. 80% of the bottles it uses have been recycled and the rest are new. What is the cost of producing new bottles each year?

Hot metal casting.

12-2 Compressing and stretching

Another way of forming parts is by compressing or stretching. Sometimes this is done by large presses which shape the material.

Forging is press work usually done with a heated metal which can be shaped as desired more easily. Figure 12-2 shows molten metal used in the forging process.

Figure 12-2

EXAMPLE It takes a pressure of 7 tons per square inch to press a design into a piece of metal. How much force will be needed to press a piece with a surface of 5 square inches?

SOLUTION We multiply the pressure per sq in. by the area.

$7 \times 5 = 35$

35 tons of force are needed.

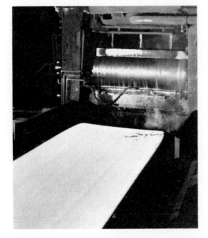

Figure 12-3

Press work can also involve any stamping device which shapes the material. Parts for appliances and aluminum siding are commonly made by a stamping process.

When a material is needed in sheets, a *rolling* process is used to stretch the material. Rolling reduces the thickness of the material and increases the length or width. Some materials, like aluminum foil, are rolled at room temperature. In other cases, the piece of material is heated to make the rolling easier. This process is called hot-rolling and is shown in Figure 12-3.

EXERCISES A 1. A pressure of 4 tons per square inch is needed to forge a metal part. How much force is required to forge a part having an area of $9\frac{1}{2}$ square inches?

2. A forging machine can produce 35 tons of force. An object to be forged is 17.5 square inches. How many pounds of pressure is this piece getting on each square inch?

U.S. System

3. A piece of aluminum 2 in. × 4 in. × 6 in. is rolled to a thickness of .01 in. It stays 4 in. wide. How long is it? (Hint: Volume is constant.)

4. Each time an iron bar passes through the roller of a rolling machine its thickness is decreased by $\frac{3}{8}''$. How many times must a bar 4″ thick be rolled to produce a bar $2\frac{1}{8}''$ thick?

B 5. A press stamps metal parts. Each part contains .25 pounds of metal. How many tons of metal are needed to produce 1 million parts?

Metric System

6. A piece of aluminum 10 mm × 25 mm × 100 mm is rolled to a thickness of .1 mm. If it stays 25 mm wide, how long is it?

7. Each time a metal bar is passed through a rolling machine its thickness is decreased by 2 mm. How many times must a bar 15 mm thick be rolled to produce a bar 5 mm thick?

8. A press stamps metal parts. Each part contains 25 grams of metal. How many kilograms of metal are needed to produce 1 million parts?

12-3 Conditioning

Changing the properties of a material is sometimes needed. **Thermal conditioning** means changing a material by heat treatments. The exposure to extreme heat can add hardness and strength to some materials.

Materials can also be hardened by **chemical conditioning**. For example, the plastic part of a washing machine, shown in Figure 12-4, has probably been hardened by chemical treatments.

The properties of a material can also be changed by **physical conditioning**, such as magnetism. For example, in upholstery shops, tack hammers like the one shown in Figure 12-5 have their heads magnetized to make it easier to apply tacks.

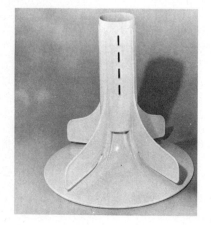

Figure 12-4

EXERCISES A 1. A 2″ round iron bar is heated and then cooled with water. The rate of cooling is 550° per second. How many degrees will it cool in 3 seconds?

Figure 12-5

2. The center of the iron rod in Exercise 1 above will cool at the rate of 46° per second. How long will it take the center to cool 230°?

3. If the same 2″ round bar is cooled with oil instead of water, the rate of cooling at the surface is 81° per second. How long will it take for the surface to cool 405°?

4. How long will it take for the surface of the bar in Exercise 3 above to cool 1620°?

SELF-ANALYSIS TEST 37

1. A certain part of a car is cast using 1.75 pounds of steel. How much steel is needed for 500 parts?

2. A forging machine can produce a pressure of 3500 pounds per square inch. How much force is received by a piece of metal with an area of 15 square inches?

3. An iron rod is heated at the rate of 50° per second. If the starting temperature is 55°, how long will it take to reach 2555°?

SPOTLIGHT ON INDUSTRY

Glass is one of the large elements of solid wastes. Since it does not burn or break down, scientists are working to find solutions to the problem of waste glass. One solution is to mix it with chemicals to make a foam. This material can be molded to fit any shape. It can be used for insulation and other construction purposes. This glass foam is fireproof and cannot be damaged by water or acid. Scientists have come up with another way to solve the waste glass problem. When mixed with tar, it can be used for paving roads. It has been nicknamed glassphalt.

EXERCISES

1. A glass jar contains 7 cu in. of glass. How many jars are needed to make 1400 cu in. of crushed glass?
2. A bottle contains 125 cu cm of glass. How many of these bottles are needed to make 100 cubic meters of crushed glass?

Separating materials

Bench grinder.

12-4 Shearing and chip removal

In addition to forming and conditioning, materials can be altered by **separation**. Here separating means to remove excess material. This can be done by shearing, by chip removal, or with chemicals, heat, and electricity.

Cutting paper with scissors is an example of **shearing**. Large industrial presses can produce enough pressure to shear metals, plastics, paper, fabrics, and other materials. Figure 12-6 shows steel being sheared.

Figure 12-6

Separating materials by removing small bits and pieces is called **chip removal**. This is done by saws, drills, grinding wheels, milling cutters, and lathes, like the one shown in Figure 12-7.

Chip removal is usually done by a circular sawing motion. The cutting speed of any tool used for chip removal is important. The distance that the cutting edge of the tool moves in one revolution is the circumference of the tool. So the **cutting speed**, in feet per minute (fpm), is the circumference times the number of revolutions per minute (rpm).

$$S = \text{circumference in feet} \times \text{rpm}$$
$$S = \pi \times \text{diameter in feet} \times \text{rpm}$$

Figure 12-7

However, the diameter of drills and grinding wheels is usually given in inches. So we can write the formula like this:

$$S = \frac{3.1416 \times \text{diameter in inches} \times \text{rpm}}{12}$$

Since $\frac{3.1416}{12} = .2618$ the formula can be simplified as

$$S = .2618 \times d \text{ in inches} \times \text{rpm}$$

EXAMPLE A grinding wheel with a 9-inch diameter turns at 1850 rpm. What is its cutting speed?

SOLUTION $S = .2618 \times d \times \text{rpm}$

$$= .2618 \times 9 \times 1850$$

$$= 4358.97$$

The cutting speed is about 4359 ft per min.

EXERCISES What is the cutting speed in each of the following?

A 1. A circular saw blade, 12 inches in diameter, rotating at 3450 rpm.

2. A grinding wheel, 6 inches in diameter, rotating at 1750 rpm.

3. A surface planer with blades $4\frac{1}{2}$ inches in diameter, rotating at 3600 rpm.

4. A router with a $\frac{3}{8}$-inch diameter cutting bit, rotating at 25,000 rpm.

5. A $\frac{5}{8}$-inch drill bit rotating at 400 rpm.

6. A grinding wheel with an 8-inch diameter, rotating at 2500 rpm.

B 7. The recommended cutting speed for brass is 120 fpm. If a piece of stock 3 inches in diameter is being turned in a lathe, what should be the rpm of the lathe?

8. A high speed steel drill bit has a cutting speed of 70 fpm. If the drill bit has a diameter of $\frac{3}{8}$ inch, what is the rpm of the bit?

9. A piece of wood with a diameter of $\frac{1}{3}$ ft is being turned in a wood lathe at 550 rpm. What is the cutting speed?

Hand router.

12-5 Separating by heat, chemicals, and electricity

Styrofoam can be cut by using a thin hot wire, and metals can be cut with the aid of a cutting torch. Separating with the aid of heat is called thermal erosion.

When acids are used to "eat away" material to create a certain pattern, design, or texture, the material is being etched. Etching is an example of chemical separating.

We can cause some materials to separate by passing electric currents through them. This is electrochemical separating.

If we can cause a material to break along a certain line we are using induced-fracture separating. Gem and glass cutters use this form of separating.

EXERCISES A

Printed circuit board.

1. A gas cutting torch is capable of cutting a certain type of steel at a rate of 18 inches per minute. How many inches of this steel can be cut in one hour?

2. It takes 40 seconds to etch a printed circuit for a television set. A company wishes to produce 10,000 sets. How much time must be allowed for the etching of the circuits?

3. Electrochemical machining removes 2 milligrams of material per second from a fragile material. How many milligrams will be removed in 3 periods, each 10 seconds in length?

B

4. A glass-cutting device cuts pieces of glass for 8″ × 11″ picture frames. How many pieces will be cut from a sheet of glass that measures 48″ × 60″?

5. A laser beam is capable of cutting the pieces for 150 suits in 15 minutes. Older techniques could cut only 5 suits in 20 minutes. How many times faster is the method of cutting with a laser beam?

6. A gas cutting torch will burn for 4 hours on one tank of gas. If the torch is capable of cutting 6 pieces per minute, how many pieces can be cut with one tank of gas?

SELF-ANALYSIS TEST 38

1. Find the cutting speed of a grinding wheel 6″ in diameter at 5500 rpm.

2. A cutting torch can cut metal at the rate of $\frac{1}{2}$″ per second. How long will it take the machine to cut 20 ft of metal?

Combining materials

12-6 Mixing and coating

When some items are manufactured it is necessary to combine materials or to coat them with some other material. One way of combining materials is with a **mixing process**. This means stirring ingredients together until they are spread evenly throughout the mixture. The mixing process is used in making the doughnuts being prepared by the machine shown in Figure 12-8.

Figure 12-8

In order to make the plastic part of the washing machine that is shown in Figure 12-4, various chemical elements were mixed to form the fluid plastic which later hardened as a result of a chemical reaction.

Materials can also be made more durable and attractive by **coating**. Various kinds of paints are available and can now be applied easily. Figure 12-9 shows an automated auto painter.

Porcelain and ceramic coatings are used on large appliances, bathroom fixtures, and even rocket nose cones.

Protective coatings made of metals such as zinc, nickel, and chromium prevent rust and corrosion.

Sometimes metal coatings are applied by **electroplating**. In this process a direct current of electricity is used. The current causes particles of metal in a solution to be deposited on another metal.

Figure 12-9

1. A building with 1500 sq ft of wall area is to be painted. A gallon of paint will cover about 400 sq ft. How much paint is needed to paint the building?

2. Paint sells for $6.00 per gallon or $2.00 when bought by the quart. Find the cost of paint for the building in Exercise 1.

3. If a painter paints at a rate of 200 sq ft per hour, how many hours will he need to paint 1500 sq ft?

4. A current of 20 amperes per square foot is needed to nickel-plate a surface. How many amperes of current are needed to plate a surface of 3.5 square feet?

5. A current of 20 amperes per square foot will nickel-plate a surface to a thickness of .001″ per hour. How much time is needed to nickel-plate a surface to a thickness of .015″ with a 20-ampere current?

B 6. A painter applies a primer coat at the rate of 150 sq ft per hour and is paid $5.50 per hour. How much will it cost to have the painter paint 1200 sq ft?

7. With a voltage of 115 volts, a current of 20 amperes per square foot will give a nickel-plating .001″ thick. How many watts of power are needed to nickel-plate an area of 1 sq ft to a thickness .001″?

12-7 Bonding

A popular method of joining solid parts is by bonding. We call it adhesive bonding when the two solid parts are held together with an adhesive such as glue, paste or cement. When the parts are heated to the point that they flow together and then cool to make a rigid bond, we call it fusion bonding.

Many types of adhesive materials are available for adhesive bonding. Those used in woodworking form a long-lasting rigid bond and are applied when needed. Others can be applied at a factory and are ready to use when needed, like the glue on envelopes.

Solder, which is a combination of tin and lead, is used as an adhesive for certain types of metals. Solder melts at a relatively low temperature. A plumber uses solder for joining copper pipes.

Welding is an example of fusion bonding. Arc welding uses electricity to fuse the materials. The two people shown in Figure 12-10 are using electric welding equipment to weld an auto body.

Figure 12-10

EXERCISES A

1. One quart of contact cement will cover about 100 square feet of surface. How much cement is needed for a counter top that measures 3 feet by 8 feet? Both the surfaces need to be covered with cement.

2. One gallon of white glue weighs 11 pounds and sells for $5.44. What is the price per pound of this glue?

3. Rosin-core solder for use in printed circuits contains 60% tin and 40% lead. How much tin is contained in a 1-pound spool of this solder?

4. The glue sticks for an electric glue gun cost $2.39 for a box of 60 sticks. What is the cost per stick?

5. If one welding rod will weld a joint 8 inches long, how many rods are needed to weld a joint that is 3 feet 4 inches in length?

6. A package of hard-surface welding rods contains 23 pieces and costs $1.97. What is the price of each piece?

CREATIVE CRAFTSMAN

Design and build an all-metal device that moves and makes sounds when heated by sunlight.

12-8 Mechanical fasteners

How many kinds of fasteners can you find in Figure 12-11?

Figure 12-11

Nails, hooks, snaps, staples, zippers, screws, bolts, and nuts are a few of the mechanical fasteners in use today. Bolts and screws are called **threaded fasteners**. The size, type, and nature of the thread is determined by the use that will be made of the bolts and screws. The bolts and screws used in a fine Swiss watch will differ from those used in a piece of heavy industrial equipment.

The majority of threaded fastening devices in the United States use the American National and Unified Thread Series. Two of the most commonly used series are the National Coarse (NC) and the National Fine (NF). The NC series is used on most machine tools and the NF series is used in automobile work.

Screws and bolts are identified by their **diameter** and the **number of threads per inch.** A $\frac{5}{16}$"-18 NC bolt means a diameter of $\frac{5}{16}$", 18 threads per inch, and National Coarse series.

A 1. A package of 1000 staples for a stapler costs $2.41. What is the cost of 5 packages of staples?

2. How many threads per inch are there on a $\frac{3}{8}''$-16 NC threaded bolt?

3. A package of 100 assorted bolts weighing 5 pounds, 8 ounces sells for $3.39. What is the price per pound?

B 4. What is the maximum diameter of a bolt that will fit in a $\frac{1}{2}''$ diameter hole if $\frac{1}{64}''$ clearance is needed on all sides of the bolt?

5. If one bolt is capable of holding 2 tons, how many bolts are needed for a 60-ton load if we add 20% more bolts for safety?

SELF-ANALYSIS TEST 39

1. An automated auto-painter can paint 54 cars in an hour. How long will it take to paint 1000 cars?

2. A glue gun operator can fasten 250 boxes in an hour. How long will it take 3 persons to glue 2500 boxes?

3. How many threads per inch are there on a $\frac{5}{8}''$-11 NC screw?

Visual inspection of truck bodies on an assembly line.

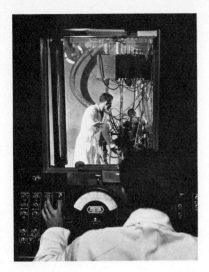

Laboratory testing.

Testing and marketing the product

12-9 Quality control

In order for a manufacturer to sell his product, he must be sure that it is free from major defects. It also should meet the requirements for which it was designed. The testing of a product before, during, and after its development is called quality control.

Inspection is one way of testing the quality of a product. Measuring various parts and even X-raying of internal parts can determine the quality without destroying the product.

Another kind of testing destroys a product. An example of destructive testing is setting off a flash bulb to see if it will flash. Some products are tested to see how long it will take to wear out the product. Sometimes this is done by using the product the way it was designed to be used. For example, a car might be driven 10,000 miles, but in the period of only a week. Other types of wear testing use machines to wear out the product, as shown in Figure 12-12.

Figure 12-12

During the production of some items it may not be practical to test every item. Of course, this is true if destructive testing is involved. If it is impractical to test every item, a representative sample is tested.

EXERCISES A 1. At a bottling company the bottles pass by a visual inspection point at the rate of 5 bottles per second. How many bottles must be inspected each hour?

2. In a visual inspection on an assembly line, 18 defective items were found in an hour. If the items move through the line at the rate of 500 items per minute, what percent were defective?

3. A certain type of tire has $\frac{1}{4}''$ of usable tread. Testing indicates that under normal conditions $\frac{1}{32}''$ of tread is used for each 6000 miles of travel. For how many miles should this tire last?

4. During testing of transistors it was found that 5 out of 600 tested were defective. What percent were defective?

B 5. Standards set by a certain company require that the maximum percent of defective parts is .15%. How many defective parts are allowed for each 10,000 parts?

6. A factory produces 5,000 light bulbs per 8-hour shift. One bulb of each 150 is tested. How many bulbs must be tested during each shift?

7. The thickness tolerance of cold rolled metal .250'' thick and 20'' wide is .0055''. What is the maximum and minimum thickness of this type of metal sheet?

12-10 Packaging

Putting caps on bottles.

After a product has been completed it must be prepared for distribution. Most finished products must be put in some type of container. This is called packaging.

The containers that are used for packaging are designed with a number of purposes in mind. A container should make it easier to handle the product. It should also protect the product, identify it, and look attractive.

The size, shape, and nature of the product will determine the kind of container that is needed. Cans, bottles, jars, bags, crates, boxes, and sacks are some of the types of containers being made today.

The shape of the container, as well as the type of material used, will determine its cost. For example, a cylindrical can with a radius of 2'' and a height of 9'' will contain the same volume as a can with a radius of 3'' and a height of 4''. However, about 132 square inches of material are needed to make the can with a 3''-radius and a 4''-height while about 138 square inches of material are required to make the other can.

EXERCISES

<table>
<tr><td align="center">U.S. System</td><td align="center">Metric System</td></tr>
</table>

A 1. A rectangular box has a length of 8″, a width of 6″, and a height of 5″. How many cubic inches does the box contain?

7. A rectangular box has a length of 10 cm, a width of 8 cm, and a height of 4 cm. How many cubic centimeters does it contain?

2. A rectangular box has a length of 10″, a width of 8″, and a height of 5″. What is the surface area of this box?

8. A rectangular container has a length of 8 cm, a width of 6 cm, and a height of 12 cm. What is the surface area of the box?

3. A container in the shape of a rectangular solid is being designed. It must have an 8″-square base and a volume of 1280 cubic inches. How high is the container?

9. A rectangular box has a 5 cm × 8 cm base. If it is to contain 480 cu cm, how high should it be?

B 4. A container must hold 450 cu in. If it is to be a box find 2 sets of dimensions.

10. A container must hold 360 cu cm. If it is to be a box, find 2 sets of dimensions.

5. The rectangular-shaped bottom of a container has an area of 35 sq in. and a perimeter of 24 inches. Find the dimensions of the bottom.

11. A rectangular box has a volume of 224 cu cm. If the height of the box is 7 cm, find the area of the base.

C 6. A container in the shape of a rectangular solid is to be designed to contain 512 cu in. Try to find the dimensions of the container using the least amount of material.

12. A rectangular container 9 cm × 14 cm × 25 cm costs $.015 per square cm to produce. How much will it cost to produce 100 containers?

12-11 Marketing the product

The marketing of a product involves pricing, advertising, and selling. The price of the product is determined by many factors. The cost of making the product, plus all the expenses of packaging, shipping, storing, advertising, and selling it determine the manufacturer's cost. In determining the selling price, the manufacturer adds an amount for profit. The profit cannot be too large, or the product will not sell. Also, many industries have government regulations about the amount of profit they can show. The following formula relates the selling price to the cost, expenses, and profit.

Selling price = cost + expenses + profit

EXAMPLE What is the selling price of a washing machine if the cost to the dealer is $192.50, the expenses are $66.00 and the profit is $16.50?

SOLUTION Selling price = 192.50 + 66.00 + 16.50
= $275.00

EXERCISES A
1. What is the selling price of an item if the cost to the merchant is $2.98, his expenses are $0.23, and his profit is $0.29?

2. If an item sells for $10.95 and the cost and expenses to the dealer are $8.75, what is his profit?

3. An item sells for $12.98. The dealer knows that 20% of the selling price must be used to pay expenses. How much were the expenses on this item?

4. A company has gross sales of $1.5 million. It spends $120,000 for advertising. What percent of its gross is spent on advertising?

B 5. What is the percent of profits on an item that sells for $49.95 if the expenses are $5.00 and the cost is $39.95?

C 6. A dealer wishes to make a 15% profit on an item whose costs and expenses are $150.00. What should his selling price be? (Hint: The profit is a percentage of the selling price.)

SELF-ANALYSIS TEST 40

1. If .05% of the items tested are defective, how many defective items should you expect to find if 10,000 are tested?

2. How many cubic inches of material can be put into a container 10″ × 12″ × 18″?

3. What is the selling price of an item if the cost to the dealer is $3.98, his expenses are $.40, and his profit is $.25?

CREATIVE CRAFTSMAN

Design and build a device that
    a. produces different colors of light by means of colored filters; and
    b. uses a motor to move the filters.

TOOLING UP FOR PRODUCTION

A Shadow Box

Here is a decorative shadow box which you can make to hang on the wall as a knick-knack holder. The pleasing appearance of this shadow box is the result of the proportional rectangles *ABCD* and *WXYZ,* as shown in Figure 1 on the next page. A shadow box like this can be a useful and attractive display shelf for any room in the house.

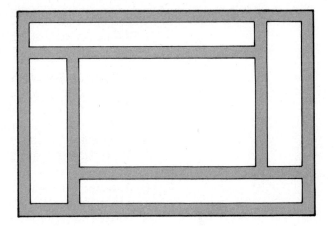

Tools

Screwdriver   Paint brush
Saw   Sandpaper
Drill

Materials

Quantity	Description	Cost
2	5′ lengths of $\frac{1}{2}''$ × 3″ hardwood	
24	$1\frac{1}{2}''$ No. 6 wood screws	
1	can of paint, color optional	
1	can of wood putty	
2	$1\frac{1}{2}''$ × $1\frac{1}{2}''$ × $\frac{1}{2}''$ inside corners	
2	3″ × $\frac{1}{8}''$ split-wing toggle bolts	

Production Plan

1. Cut the $\frac{1}{2}'' \times 3''$ lumber to fit the dimensions in Figure 2.
2. Assemble the shadow box using the wood screws. Plug the screw holes with wood putty.
3. Attach the inside corners to the rear underside of the top shelf.
4. Sand and finish the shadow box. The "shadow box" effect is enhanced by painting it the same color as the wall.
5. Locate, mark, and drill $\frac{3}{8}''$ holes in the wall for mounting. Use the toggle bolts to hang the shadow box on the wall.

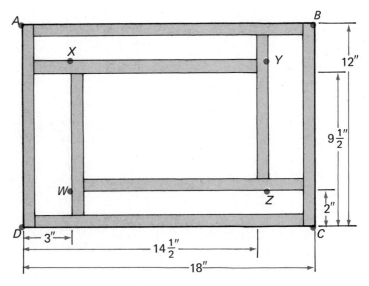

Figure 1

Modifying the Design

1. Suppose the dimensions of the exterior rectangle are to be 20'' by 30'' and the interior rectangle will have a length of 13''. Find the width of the interior rectangle that will make the rectangles proportional.
2. What other shapes could you use to design a shadow box? Can you make a proportional shadow box using hexagons?
3. What other materials could you use to make a shadow box? What might you use to make a box with curved shapes?
4. A "golden rectangle" is one whose sides are in a certain ratio called a "golden section," a ratio of about 1 to 1.6. Find out more about golden rectangles. Can you design a shadow box made only of golden rectangles?

TAKING INVENTORY

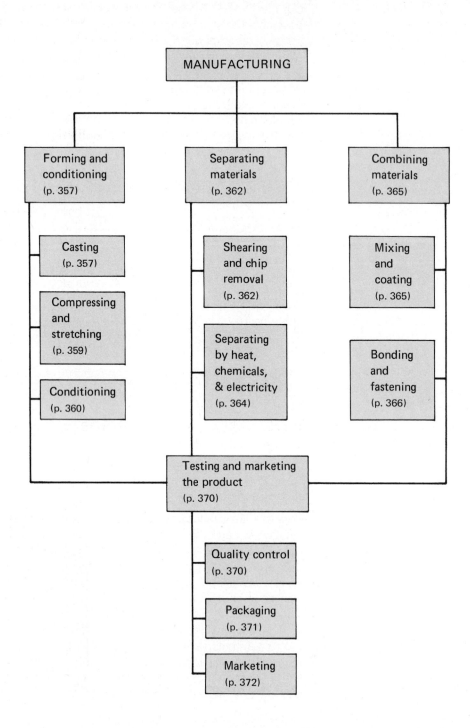

MEASURING YOUR SKILLS

1. The water pump for a new automobile is made from cast iron. If it takes 2.74 pounds of iron for each water pump, how many pounds of iron are needed if 1,275,300 cars are built? (12-1)

2. A forging machine is capable of exerting 80 tons of force. If the object being forged has an area of 27.5 sq in., how many pounds of pressure can be exerted on each sq in.? (12-2)

3. A certain type of iron part is heat-treated so it can support 5000 pounds per square inch. How much weight could be supported by a piece measuring 8″ × 12″? (12-3)

4. What is the cutting speed of a grinding wheel with a 6″ diameter, if the wheel turns at 1650 rpm? (12-4)

5. A glass cutter can cut 500 parts in one hour. A manufactured item contains 8 of these glass parts. How long will it take the glass cutter to make glass parts for 5000 items? (12-5)

6. An automated painter can paint 135 items per minute. How many items can be painted in an 8-hour shift? (12-6)

7. 21 staples are needed to assemble each container. How many staples are needed for 25,000 containers? (12-7)

8. What is the diameter of a $\frac{9}{16}$″-12 NC bolt? (12-8)

9. During testing it was found that 1 out of each 150 items tested was defective. How many defective items should you expect to find if you tested 1200 items? (12-9)

10. A rectangular container measures 5″ × 3″ × $8\frac{1}{2}$″. How many cubic inches of material will it hold? (12-10)

11. What is the selling price of an item if the cost to the merchant is $5.23, his expenses are $.52, and his profit is $.48? (12-11)

Automated glass cutter.

To meet the growing demand for diversified printed matter the graphic arts industry uses the latest in photographic and printing equipment.

CHAPTER **13** *Graphic Arts*

After completing this chapter, you should be able to:

1. *Calculate space with points, picas, ems, and column inches.*
2. *Describe the differences between letterpress, lithography, and gravure printing.*
3. *Calculate materials, cost, and time involved in the steps in printing.*

Measuring type

13-1 **The point system**

The point and the pica are the units used in printing in all English-speaking countries. The point system is used to measure type sizes, to mark copy, and to measure distances in printed matter.

A point measures .01384″ or approximately $\frac{1}{72}$ inch. So there are 72 points to an inch. One pica is approximately $\frac{1}{6}$ inch, or 12 points. So we have these approximate measures:

$$6 \text{ picas} = 1 \text{ inch}$$
$$12 \text{ points} = 1 \text{ pica}$$
$$72 \text{ points} = 1 \text{ inch}$$

The pica ruler, shown in Figure 13-1 shows units of $\frac{1}{2}$ pica, or 6 points. To see how big one point is, look at the width of the red line across page 383. You are looking at a one-point line.

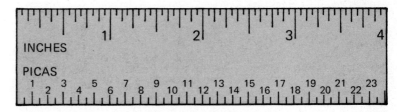

Figure 13-1

Many different sizes and styles of typefaces are available today. Figure 13-2 shows a variety of styles as well as sizes.

This is 24 point Lucia Script

This is 24 point Palatino Italic

This is 24 point Bodoni Book

This is 18 point Imperial Bold

This is 18 point Optima Semibold

THIS IS 14 POINT NEWS GOTHIC BOLD

This is 12 point Baskerville

This is 10 point Futura Bold Condensed

This is 12 point Futura Bold Condensed

Figure 13-2

For most purposes it is important for type to be readable. Typefaces which resemble handwriting or elaborate script are used for a decorative appearance.

It is sometimes necessary to convert measurements given in picas and points to measurements in inches.

EXAMPLE How many inches long is a 39-pica line?

SOLUTION Since there are 6 picas to an inch, we divide 39 by 6:

$$39 \div 6 = 6\frac{1}{2}$$

The line is $6\frac{1}{2}$ inches long.

EXERCISES Change the following measures to inches.

A 1. 18 picas   3. 42 points

2. 23 picas   4. 24 points

5. 36 picas

7. 20 picas

6. 41 picas

8. 48 picas

B   9. Give the size of a card in picas if it is $4\frac{1}{2}''$ wide and $6\frac{1}{2}''$ long.

10. A form has a width of 54 picas and a depth of 78 picas. Find the area, in square inches, of this form.

11. A copy that measures 39 picas wide is centered on a page that is $8\frac{1}{2}''$ wide. How wide are the side margins in picas? in inches?

13-2 The em

In the printing trade, picas and points are used to measure length. A printer measures area in terms of a unit called an em. An **em** is the area occupied by the letter M in a given type size. The printed capital letter M always takes up a perfectly square space. Thus an em is as long as it is wide. As the point size of the type varies, so does the size of an em of that size. Figure 13-3 shows the size of an em in four different sizes of type.

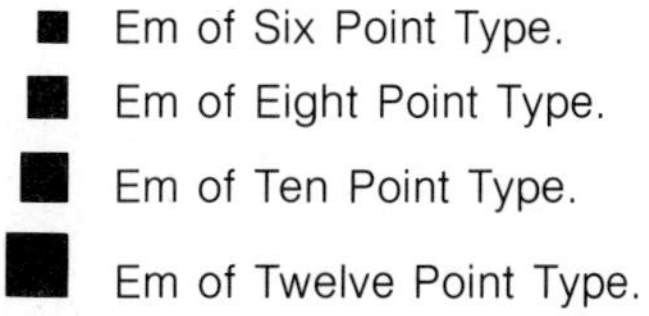

■   Em of Six Point Type.

■   Em of Eight Point Type.

■   Em of Ten Point Type.

■   Em of Twelve Point Type.

Figure 13-3

Because the em is a measure of area, it can be used to determine how much type will fit in a given area.

EXAMPLE   How many ems of 8-point type are there in a page with type set 288 points wide and 504 points deep?

SOLUTION   To find the number of ems in one line, we divide the length in points by 8:

$288 \div 8 = 36$ ems per line

To find the number of lines on the page, divide the depth in points by 8:

504 points $\div$ 8 = 63 lines

63 lines $\times$ 36 ems per line = 2268 ems

1. How many ems of 7-point type are there in a line 217 points long?

2. How many ems of 5-point type are there in a line 24 picas long?

3. How many points of length are used by 27 ems of 4-point?

4. How many picas of length are used by 15 ems of 12-point?

5. How many lines of 6-point type are there in a page 546 points deep?

6. How many lines of 8-point type are there in a page 44 picas deep?

How many ems are there in pages of these sizes set with the given type size?

B 7. A page 291 points wide, 504 points deep, set with 7-point type.

8. A page $4\frac{1}{4}$ inches wide, 7 inches deep, set with 6-point type.

9. A page 24 picas wide, 36 picas deep, set with 8-point type.

10. A page $4\frac{1}{3}$ inches wide, $7\frac{1}{2}$ inches deep, set with 12-point type.

13-3 Column inch

In newspaper publishing a different standard measure is used, the column inch. One column inch is an area one column wide and one inch deep. The American Newspaper Publishers Association has set the standard width of a newspaper column at $11\frac{1}{2}$ picas. Advertising in newspapers is usually priced by the column inch. The price per column inch depends on the newspaper.

EXAMPLE Find the cost of an advertisement 2 columns wide and 3 inches deep at $3.60 per column inch.

SOLUTION First we find the number of column inches.

2 columns × 3 inches = 6 column inches

6 × $3.60 = $21.60

The cost is $21.60

Find the number of column inches in an advertisement that is

1. 1 column wide and 3 inches deep.

2. 2 columns wide and 1 inch deep.

3. 3 columns wide and 2 inches deep.

4. 5 columns wide and 5 inches deep.

5. 8 columns wide and $20\frac{1}{2}$ inches deep.

Find the cost of an advertisement that is:

6. 6 column inches at $2.40 per column inch.

7. 3 columns wide and 2 inches deep at $5.60 per column inch.

8. 8 columns wide and $10\frac{1}{4}$ inches deep at $4.80 per column inch.

9. 4 inches deep and 3 columns wide at $7.50 per column inch.

10. What is the cost of a full-page advertisement if a full page is 8 columns wide and $20\frac{1}{2}$ inches long and the advertising rate is $18.50 per column inch?

11. If a full page is 8 columns wide and $20\frac{1}{2}$ inches deep, find the cost of a half-page advertisement at $9.50 per column inch.

SELF-ANALYSIS TEST 41

1. Find the width in inches of a page that is 42 picas wide.

2. Find the width in inches of a line that measures 31 picas 6 points.

3. How many ems of 9-point type are there in a line 30 picas long?

4. Find the price of a newspaper advertisement that is 3 columns wide and 4 inches long if the rate is $5.55 per column inch.

CREATIVE CRAFTSMAN

Design a symbol (sometimes called a "logo") for an imaginary company. Make two versions of the logo:
   a. using black and white only;
   b. using 2 colors.

Printing processes

13-4 Letterpress

The method by which a printed image is transferred to paper depends on the kind of printing process used. The oldest and most common method of printing, illustrated in Figure 13-4, is the letterpress. In this process, ink is applied to a raised surface and transferred directly to the paper by means of pressure.

Figure 13-4 Attaching a plate to a cylinder letterpress.

There are three kinds of presses used in this process: the platen press, the cylinder press, and the rotary press. All kinds of printed material, including newspapers, pamphlets, catalogues, books, and packaging materials are printed on these presses. The most common type of press used for books is the rotary press. Two-color material, such as this book, and four-color work is usually printed on rotary presses. A continuous roll, or web, of paper is used in web-fed rotary presses.

EXERCISES A

1. If a cylinder press can print 5,000 sheets per hour, what is the cost of printing 3,000 sheets at $25.75 per hour?

2. A folded-sheet pamphlet is printed on a sheet-fed rotary press which runs at 35 sheets per minute. Two passes through the press are necessary to print each pamphlet. How many pamphlets can be printed in one hour?

3. A carton can be printed and cut on a flat-bed cylinder press at the rate of 800 cartons per hour. How long will it take to print and cut 22,000 cartons?

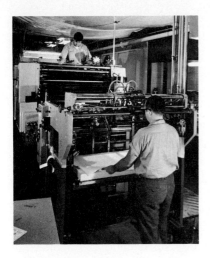

Paper being inserted into a small sheet-fed offset press.

13-5 Lithography

One of the newest and fastest-growing printing processes is lithography, sometimes called offset printing. Lithography is printing from a *flat* surface, rather than a raised surface, as in letterpress. The basic principle behind lithography is that greasy surfaces will attract greasy ink and repel water, and wet surfaces will attract water and repel greasy ink.

Photo-offset lithography is a type of lithographic process that is becoming very popular today. Offset refers to the process which uses three cylinders, instead of the two used in letterpress. Figure 13-5 illustrates the three cylinders used in an offset press.

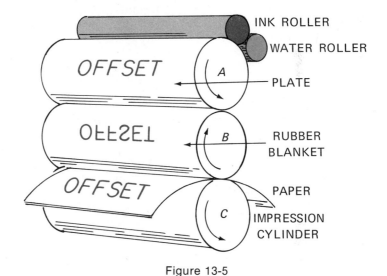

Figure 13-5

The plate is inked and watered in A, and then prints onto the rubber blanket in B. The rubber blanket *offsets* this ink impression to the paper held in the impression cylinder C. The rubber blanket prints a clearer impression on a wide variety of papers and other materials than the metallic plates used in letterpress.

Another way that photo-offset printing differs from letterpress is that anything which can be photographed can be used as original copy. So illustrations and photographs can be used with less preparation, and therefore with less expense.

The image carrier placed on the plate can be made of a variety of materials. Plastic carriers can be made, costing as little as 10 cents for a $8\frac{1}{2}''\times 11''$ page. For long press runs, the plates are made of combinations of copper and aluminum. Such plates can produce up to 500,000 copies.

Small printing jobs are frequently run on offset duplicators. They are ideal for quick printing of office and plant forms, inventory sheets, price lists, bulletins, sales letters, programs, and schedules. Plates for offset duplicators can be prepared easily.

EXERCISES A

1. If it costs $4.50 to make a copper-aluminum plate for printing 8 pages, what will the plates cost for printing 128 pages?

2. A printer will do small printing jobs for 1¢ per page plus 10¢ for the lithographic plate. What is the cost of a job that involves 250 pages?

3. What will it cost to print 250 copies of the program for a high school band concert if the printing office charges 10 cents for the lithographic plate and two cents for each copy printed?

4. If an offset press can print 50,000 pages per hour, how long will it take to print 1,000,000 pages?

5. An offset duplicator can print 300 copies per minute from an aluminum plate. How long will it take to produce 1800 copies?

13-6 Gravure

While letterpress uses a *raised* surface, and offset a *flat* surface, gravure printing uses a sunken or depressed surface for transferring the image. The lines to be printed are cut into the plate, the plate is coated with ink, and then wiped off. The ink remaining in the depressed surface is then deposited on the paper. This makes the ink stand out from the paper or printing surface.

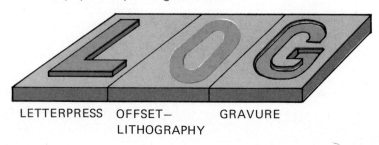

LETTERPRESS   OFFSET—   GRAVURE
               LITHOGRAPHY

Gravure printing is considered to be the finest method of reproducing pictures, but the higher cost of plate-making limits its use to long runs. As with the rotary letterpress, gravure presses are made for both sheets (sheet-fed gravure) and rolls (rotogravure) of paper. Some publications printed on commonly rotogravure presses are Sunday newspaper magazine sections, premium stamp catalogues, and large mail-order catalogues. Some interesting examples of gravure printing are vinyl floor coverings, vinyl upholstery fabrics, and pre-pasted wallpaper.

EXERCISES A

1. A rotogravure press can print 10,000 copies per hour and an offset press can print 50,000 copies per hour. If both presses run for 3 hours, how many more copies will be printed with the offset than with the rotogravure?

2. If a rotogravure press can print 10,000 copies per hour, how long will it take to print 25,000 copies?

3. If a rotogravure plate costs $5.00 and the paper costs $.003 per copy what will the plate and paper cost for 20,000 copies of one page?

4. A printer charges 3 cents per page for the first 5000 copies, 2 cents per page for the next 5000 copies and one cent for each page over 10,000. What will it cost to have 12,000 copies printed?

5. A printer charges $6.00 for making a rotogravure plate, 2 cents per copy for the first 5,000 copies, and one cent per copy for each copy over 5,000. What will it cost for a plate and 12,000 copies?

6. Each rotogravure plate costs $3.50 and each printed page costs 2 cents. What will it cost to make 10,000 copies of a 4-page bulletin? Assume one plate is needed for each page.

Removing a plate from a rotogravure cylinder.

SELF-ANALYSIS TEST 42

1. A sheet-fed rotary press can print 4,000 sheets per hour. How long will it take to print 200,000 copies?

2. If paper costs $.015 per page and one offset plate costs $.12, how much will it cost to print 2000 copies of a 10-page pamphlet? Assume one plate is needed for each page.

3. Plates for printing a vinyl floor covering on a gravure press cost $1.50 and the vinyl costs $.30 per foot. What is the cost of printing 20,000 feet of floor covering?

Duplicating Machine Service Technician

Duplicating machines and copiers are used extensively in business offices in all branches of industry. Their ability to produce copies of printed material has shortened the time for order processing and accounting. To keep these invaluable machines working, the services of a skilled service technician are required. Perhaps this is a career that you would like to follow.

Job Description

What do service technicians do?
1. They maintain and service equipment on a regular basis to insure its proper operation.
2. They adjust, oil, clean, and replace parts including rollers, belts and gears.
3. They check electronic components with meters to determine the need for adjustment or replacement.
4. They make repairs on defective machines. Repairs are made either on location or in central repair shops, if major repairs are needed.

Qualifications

Employers prefer high school graduates who have mechanical aptitudes.
Courses in mathematics, physics, and electricity are particularly helpful in this line of work.
A pleasant appearance and the ability to meet the public are desirable traits.

Training

Service technicians usually begin as trainees. They acquire their skills through on-the-job training and experience in the field. Usually, they will also attend the manufacturer's training courses. The length of these courses varies from 6 months to 2 years. Some state and city vocational schools also offer training in this field.

Working Conditions

Usually works on the site, requiring some travel.
Work schedule corresponds to usual business office hours.
Work is cleaner and lighter than most other mechanical repairs.
Work is relatively free from the danger of accident.

Opportunities for Advancement

Many service technicians work for one particular manufacturer of duplicating and copying equipment. Some advance to become salespersons for these companies, usually increasing their earnings. Others, working either for manufacturers or for independent companies, become foremen or get other supervisory positions. Some open their own repair and service firms. Some who do, and who also have sales ability, may expand their repair and service work into sales of duplicating machines and supplies. Service technicians may also become involved in rebuilding machines and selling them.

Steps in printing

13-7 Preparing copy

There are many steps in making a finished book, magazine, or advertising pamphlet. The first step is always preparing the original copy. Usually it is carefully typewritten, so it is easy to read. The typed copy is sometimes prepared by a technical typist, who may be paid by the page or by the hour.

For some offset lithography presses, the copy is prepared on special typewriters. These machines produce the desired typeface with the proper spacing.

Another part of preparing the copy is planning space for illustrations or photographs which will appear as finished copy.

EXERCISES A

1. If a typist can type 80 words per minute, how long will it take to type a 3200-word manuscript?

2. If it takes 2 hours to type a 6000-word manuscript, what is the average number of words being typed per minute?

3. If a typist can type a page in 5 minutes and is paid 30 cents per page, what is the hourly rate?

4. If a typist can type 45 words per minute, how long will it take to type an average page containing 280 words?

5. If it takes 20 seconds to insert the paper in the typewriter, 5 minutes to type the page, $1\frac{1}{2}$ minutes to proofread the page, and 5 seconds to remove the page, how much time is needed to complete one page?

B

6. A technical manuscript is being typed for 80 cents per page. If there are 200 words per page, what is the cost of typing a 15,000-word manuscript?

7. A typist can average 40 words per minute on a certain 18,000-word manuscript. There will be 90 typed pages when completed. Should the typist take the job for 70 cents per page or $8.00 per hour?

8. A typist is hired at $5.00 per hour to type a manuscript which can be done at a rate of one page every 6 minutes. What is the cost per page of typing this manuscript?

9. A manuscript involves 30 pages of regular typing at 60 cents per page, 10 pages of technical typing at 80 cents per page, and 5 pages of charts and tables at $1.00 per page. What is the cost of typing this manuscript?

Setting copy for advertisements on a linotype machine.

13-8 Composition

The next step in the printing process, after the preparation of the original copy, is the composition. Composition involves determining the amount of copy, calculating the area needed, selecting or producing the proper style and size of type, and setting the type.

There are many different kinds of machines for setting type. The earliest kind of typesetting, dating back to the 15th century, was hand-set. Today most type is set by machines, with increasing computer assistance. Type is cast from hot metal on linotype and monotype machines. In linotype work, a whole line is molded in one piece, called a slug. Monotype uses individual molded letters, usually set by the direction of a punched tape.

A newer method of setting type is photo-composition. The various kinds of photo-composing machines produce type directly onto film. This film will later be used to make the plates used in the various printing processes. The machines used in photo composition include linofilm and monophoto, similar to linotype and monotype.

Computers are being used increasingly to set up the line breaks and word breaks from a punched tape containing the characters of the words in a manuscript.

Composition is usually measured in ems and the rate of setting type is given in ems per hour. Recall from section 13-2 that an em is a square of space in a given type size.

EXAMPLE A linotype operator can set 3500 ems per hour. How many pages of 12-point type can he set in 7 hours if each page measures 42 picas × 50 picas?

SOLUTION Determine the number of ems on one page:

12 points = 1 pica, so the em of 12-point type measures 1 pica × 1 pica.

42 × 50 = 2100

There are 2100 ems on one page.

In 7 hours, he can set 7 × 3500, or 24,500 ems.

$24{,}500 \div 2100 = 11\frac{2}{3}$

He can set $11\frac{2}{3}$ pages in 7 hours.

1. One page of copy contains 1280 ems of type. A monotype operator can set 2000 ems per hour. How long will it take to set 50 pages of copy?

2. The cost of setting type in linofilm is $15.00 per hour. What is the cost of linofilm composition for a 250-page book if the operator can set 2 pages per hour?

3. Determine the number of ems of 9-point type on a page if the page measures 30 picas × 45 picas.

4. A linotype operator can set one page of 12-point type that is 39 picas × 55 picas in one hour. What is this rate, in ems per hour?

B

5. In one hour, a linotype operator can set one page of 10-point type that is 30 picas × 40 picas. How many ems per hour is this?

6. The operator of a computer-assisted linofilm machine can set 5000 ems per hour. How long will it take to set 50 pages of 10-point type if each page measures 27 picas × 36 picas?

13-9 Photoengraving

Once the type has been set, in metal or in film, the next step is making the plates to be used on the printing press. At this point there may be photographs or line drawings to be added. Camera copy is compiled using the printed type, if hot metal has been used, along with the photos or line art to be included. If the type was set in film, then the plates are made directly from the film. Photoengraving is the process of etching the metal plates to be used on the press.

Engraving a line plate, which consists of lines and type characters, but no grey tones, is done by a simple photographic and chemical process. For letterpress, the plates are etched in metal such as zinc or copper. In the lithographic process, the etching is done on aluminum or plastic bases.

To reproduce a photograph, a halftone engraving is made. Making a halftone is similar to making a line engraving. A halftone screen is placed between the camera lens and the film. This screen, or grid, breaks up the blacks and whites in a photograph into tiny dots that are etched into the printing plates. The reproduction of color photographs is similar, except that four separate plates are usually

Developing the film from which the metal plates are etched.

made. The red, blue, yellow, and black plates printed on top of each other will give the combined image of the colors in the original photograph.

Photographs are frequently reduced or enlarged from their original size to fit the space allowed for in the copy. This reduction process may be done in the final plate-making stage, or it may be done earlier if the type is set in film. To determine the reduced size of a photograph, we can use a **proportion**. The ratio of the width and depth of the original photo is equal to the ratio of the width and depth of the reduction or enlargement desired.

$$\frac{\text{original width}}{\text{original depth}} = \frac{\text{final width}}{\text{final depth}}$$

EXAMPLE A 5″ × 7″ photograph must be reduced so that it is $3\frac{1}{2}$″ wide. What is the depth of the reduced picture?

SOLUTION

$$\frac{\text{original width}}{\text{original depth}} = \frac{\text{final width}}{\text{final depth}}$$

$$\frac{5}{7} = \frac{3\frac{1}{2}}{d}$$

$$5 \times d = 7 \times 3.5$$

$$d = \frac{7 \times 3.5}{5}$$

$$d = 7 \times .7$$

$$d = 4.9$$

The depth of the reduced picture is 4.9″.

EXERCISES A

1. The cost of engraving plates for a book is $20 per page, plus $5 for each halftone. If the book has 412 pages and 42 halftones, what is the cost of the plates?

2. The cost of preparing plates for a book is $21,000. If the book has 360 pages, what is the cost per page?

U.S. System

3. A 8″ × 10″ photograph must be reduced so its width is $2\frac{5}{8}$″. What is the resulting depth?

4. A 4″ × 5″ photograph must be reduced to fill a column that is 20 picas wide. What will be the resulting depth?

Metric System

8. A 60 mm × 70 mm photograph must be enlarged so it is 75 mm wide. What is the resulting depth?

9. A 200 mm × 250 mm photograph must be reduced to a width of 85 mm. What will be its depth?

B 5. A 8″ × 10″ photograph is reduced to 4″ × 5″. Find the percent of reduction of the width and depth.

6. A 8″ × 10″ photograph is reduced to 4″ × 5″. The area of the reduced photo is what percent of the area of the original?

C 7. A 4″ × 5″ photograph is reduced to 80% of its original dimensions. What percent of the area of the original is the area of the reduction?

10. A 200 mm × 250 mm photograph is reduced to 50% of its original size. What are the resulting dimensions?

11. A 150 mm × 200 mm photograph is reduced to 75 mm × 100 mm. The area of the reduced photo is what percent of the area of the original?

12. A 240 mm × 320 mm photograph is reduced to 75% of its original dimensions. What percent of the area of the original is the area of the reduction?

13-10 Paper

A variety of papers is available for printing. Paper may be selected for its appearance, for its lasting quality, for the texture of its surface, or for its cost and weight. The four basic classifications of paper and sizes presently in use are given in Figure 13-6.

Classification	Use	Basic Sheet Size
Bond	Standard office use, letterheads, typing, etc.	17″ × 22″
Book	Books	25″ × 38″
Cover	Magazine covers	20″ × 26″
Card	Posters, advertising displays	22½″ × 28½″

Figure 13-6

A **ream** of paper consists of 500 sheets of a basic size. The **substance** of paper is the weight of a ream, or 500 sheets. For example, paper is labeled "20-pound bond" if 500 sheets (one ream) of size 17 × 22 weigh 20 pounds. A heavier paper means each sheet is thicker.

Occasionally paper is ordered in special sizes, that is, sizes other than the basic sizes given in Figure 13-6. The weight of a special size is proportional to its increased area. So to find the weight of a special size, we can use the ratios of the area and weight of the paper.

Paper is also available in continuous rolls, or webs, shown here at one end of a web-fed press.

EXAMPLE Find the 500-sheet weight of 18-pound bond in 20″ × 28″ size.

SOLUTION

$$\frac{\text{weight of special size}}{\text{area of special size}} = \frac{\text{weight of standard size}}{\text{area of standard size}}$$

$$\frac{w}{20 \times 28} = \frac{18}{17 \times 22}$$

$$\frac{w}{560} = \frac{18}{374}$$

$$w \times 374 = 18 \times 560$$

$$w = \frac{18 \times 560}{374}$$

$$= \frac{10080}{374}$$

$$= 27 \text{ pounds (approx.)}$$

500 sheets weigh about 27 pounds.

Although the basic size of bond paper is 17 × 22 inches, bond is often used for letterheads, measuring $8\frac{1}{2}$ × 11 inches. Figure 13-7 indicates how a 17 × 22 inch sheet can be cut to give 4 sheets each $8\frac{1}{2}$ × 11 inches.

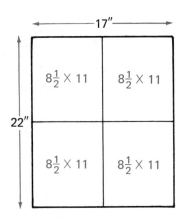

Figure 13-7

EXERCISES A

1. If 500 sheets of 17 × 22 inch bond weigh 20 pounds, how much will 2000 sheets weigh?

2. What is the cost of 2500 sheets of 25″ × 38″ book paper, substance 20, if the paper costs 38¢ per pound?

3. Find the 500-sheet weight of 80-pound book paper in 35 × 46 inch sheets.

4. What is the maximum number of 8 × 9 inch sheets that can be cut from one 25 × 38 inch sheet?

5. If 1000 sheets of 17 × 22 inch bond weigh 56 pounds, what is the substance number of this paper?

B 6. Find the weight of 1500 sheets of substance 120 book paper in a special 38 × 52 inch size.

7. How many $8\frac{1}{2}$ × 11 inch letterheads can be cut from two 500-sheet reams of 17 × 22 inch bond paper?

8. A sheet of 28 × 42 inch book paper is cut into 7 × 9 inch pieces. What is the maximum number of pieces that can be cut from one sheet?

C 9. A printing job requires 3 reams of substance 24 paper at 48 cents per pound and $2\frac{1}{2}$ hours of labor for typesetting and printing at $6.50 per hour. What was the total cost of the job?

Signatures coming off folding machines at the end of a web-fed press.

13-11 Finishing

After the printing is done, there may be other steps necessary to produce the final product. Finishing involves folding, binding, trimming, gluing, or any other activity that is needed to get the product ready for use.

Whenever a printer produces a book, magazine, or other publication, he ordinarily prints several pages on each side of a single sheet of paper. This sheet is then folded and trimmed to form a signature and makes up one section of the publication.

The simplest signature involves two pages. This would be one sheet printed on both sides with no folding. Usually signatures will have 4, 8, 16, 32, or 64 pages. Take a sheet of paper and fold it to see if you can figure out why signatures have 4, 8, 16, 32, or 64 pages.

When printing a 16-page signature it is necessary to arrange the printing of the pages on each side of the sheet so that after folding and trimming, the pages will be in order. The arrangement of type pages is called the imposition. Figure 13-8 shows an imposition for each side of a sheet for a 16-page signature.

A variety of paper-folding machines are available. Some machines can fold a single sheet 5 times to produce a 64-page signature.

Paper for newspapers comes in large rolls and is fed into the presses in a continuous sheet. Rotary folders attached to the delivery end of these presses can fold paper at a rate of 1600 feet per minute. This is equivalent to about 20,000 sheets per hour. By knowing the speed of the folding machine, we can determine how many newspapers can be produced per hour if we know the number of folds required.

EXAMPLE How many 32-page newspapers can be produced per hour if the folding machine can fold 20,000 sheets per hour?

SOLUTION If a sheet of newspaper is cut and folded once to produce a 4-page signature we must divide the number of pages by 4 to get the number of folds per newspaper.

$32 \div 4 = 8$

Thus we have 8 folds per newspaper.

$20,000 \div 8 = 2,500$

Thus our folding machine can produce 2,500 32-page newspapers per hour.

Most of the other finishing activities such as binding, punching, trimming, or stapling are also done by machines. By knowing the rate at which each machine works we can determine the time that is needed to complete a job. Once we know the time that is needed we can calculate the costs involved.

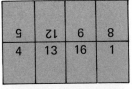

Figure 13-8

RESEARCH PROJECT

Take a sheet of typing paper and label each side as indicated in Figure 13-8. Now fold this sheet as many times as necessary. Now look at the numbers on the pages. Are they in order? If not, try again. Once you have them in order you can trim the edges and you have a 16-page signature.

1. How many times must a single sheet be folded to produce an 8-page signature?

2. If a paper folding machine can fold 20,000 sheets per hour, how long will it take to fold 300 sheets?

3. How many folds are necessary if each sheet of a printing job is folded twice and the job involves 1350 sheets?

4. A machine can trim and bind 5 books per minute. How long will it take to trim and bind 10,000 copies?

B 5. It costs $3.50 per hour to operate the machine in Exercise 4. What is the cost of trimming and binding the job?

6. How many folds are necessary to produce a book that contains ten 32-page signatures?

7. If a machine can make 20,000 folds per hour, how long will it take to do the folding for 5000 copies of the book in Exercise 6?

SELF-ANALYSIS TEST 43

1. If a typist can type 75 words per minute, how long will it take to type 50 pages if each page has about 250 words?

2. A linotype operator can set 2500 ems per hour. How long will it take to set 200 pages of type if each page has 1500 ems?

3. A 5″ × 7″ photo is reduced so its width is 2″. What is the reduced depth?

4. How much will 15,000 sheets of substance 20 book paper weigh?

5. A paper folding machine can make 400 folds per minute. A book requires 5 folds for each of its signatures. How many books can be folded in one hour if each copy contains 4 signatures?

Inspection of waste paper prior to entry into deinking system.

SPOTLIGHT ON INDUSTRY

The paper industry wants to preserve our forests by using recycled pulp. Their research has produced high quality recycled paper. Companies are now making paper having 20% to 100% recycled pulp. Another advantage of recycling paper and paper-based materials is that it lessens the amount of valuable land needed for disposal areas.

EXERCISES

1. It takes 17 trees to make a ton of newsprint. How many trees can be saved by making 85,000 tons of newsprint with 100% recycled paper?
2. A company uses stationery made of 65% recycled paper. If the company uses 586,000 kilograms of paper in one month, how much of the paper has been recycled?

Inspection of deinked and bleached pulp.

RESEARCH WITH A COMPUTER

In Chapter 13 you learned about setting type. The formula for finding the cost of setting type is

$$C = \frac{T}{E} \times H$$

where C = cost of composition,
T = total ems set,
E = ems set per hour,
and H = hourly wage.

Since setting the costs of printing jobs is an important skill to develop, you should try to be as realistic and accurate as you can. If you have access to a computer which uses the BASIC "language," you can use the following program to help you find the cost of composition for a project.

```
10 PRINT "TOTAL EMS SET =";
20 INPUT T
30 PRINT "EMS SET PER HOUR =";
40 INPUT E
50 PRINT "HOURLY WAGE = ";
60 INPUT H
70 LET C = (T/E)* H
80 PRINT "COST OF PROJECT = $"; C
90 END
```

EXERCISES

Do you recognize the formula for setting type in line 70?

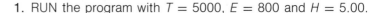

1. RUN the program with $T = 5000$, $E = 800$ and $H = 5.00$.

2. RUN the program in Exercise 1 with $T = 10000$. How do the results compare? What effect does a larger numerator have on the result?

3. RUN the program in Exercise 1 with $E = 3000$. How do the results compare? What effect does a larger denominator have on the result?

4. RUN the program in Exercise 1 with $H = 4.50$. How do the results compare?

5. A total of 22680 ems are needed to set the type for a automotive repair manual. The compositor works at a rate of 800 ems per hour. His wage is $5.90 per hour. Find the cost of setting the type for the manual.

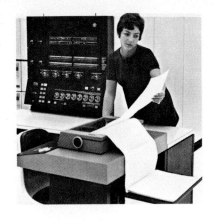

When type is set by machine the cost of running the machine must be figured into the total cost of composition. If it costs D dollars to set 1 em on a photo-composition machine, the cost of running the machine to set T ems is $T*D$. Thus, the total cost of paying the compositor and running the machine, in dollars, is

$$(H*T/E) + (T*D).$$

The following program will compute the cost of setting type for a project.

```
10  PRINT "TOTAL EMS SET =";
20  INPUT T
30  PRINT "EMS SET PER HOUR =";
40  INPUT E
50  PRINT "HOURLY WAGE =";
60  INPUT H
70  PRINT "COST PER EM FOR MACHINE =";
80  INPUT D
90  LET C = (H*T/E) + (T*D)
100 PRINT "COST OF PROJECT = $"; C
110 END
```

Notice the formula for the combined cost of the machine and the compositor in line 90.

EXERCISES

6. RUN the program with $T = 5000$, $E = 800$, $H = 5.00$, and $D = .003$.

7. RUN the program in Exercise 6 with $E = 3000$. What effect does the higher rate of setting ems have on the result?

8. RUN the program in Exercise 6 with $D = .0015$. What effect does the reduced machine cost have on the cost of the project?

9. Which is less expensive:

   a. To hand-set 10000 ems with $E = 800$, $H = 5.50$, and $D = .002$, or

   b. To machine-set 20000 ems with $E = 3000$, $H = 4.00$, and $D = .0015$?

401

TAKING INVENTORY

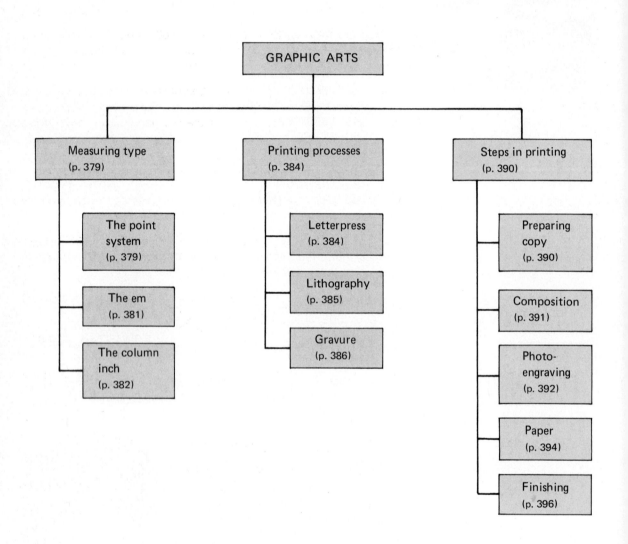

MEASURING YOUR SKILLS

1. A column of type is $4\frac{1}{2}''$. How many picas is this? (13-1)

2. How many ems of 8-point type are there in a line 368 points long? (13-2)

3. Find the cost of an advertisement that is 3 columns wide and 4 inches long if the rate is $12.00 per column inch. (13-3)

4. A sheet-fed rotary press can print 4000 sheets per hour. How long will it take to print 5000 copies of a pamphlet if 3 sheets are used for each pamphlet? (13-4)

5. It costs $3.50 to make a lithographic plate and $.015 per page for paper. What is the cost of plates and paper for 100 copies of a 4-page bulletin if one plate per page is required? (13-5)

6. If a rotogravure press can print 8,000 copies per hour, how long will it take to print 22,000 copies? (13-6)

7. A technical typist can type 4 manuscript pages per hour. At the rate of 50¢ per page, how much should he be paid for typing a 300-page manuscript? (13-7)

8. It costs $14.00 per hour to run the linofilm machine and pay the operator. If 3 pages can be set per hour, what is the cost of composition for a 320-page book? (13-8)

9. A 200 mm × 250 mm photograph is reduced to a width of 120 mm. How deep will it be? (13-9)

10. What is the weight of paper for a book that contains 10 sheets of substance 85 book paper? (13-10)

11. If a paper-folding machine can fold 10,000 sheets per hour, how many books can be folded in an hour if each book requires 8 folds? (13-11)

Paper cutting machine in a book bindery.

MEASURING YOUR PROGRESS

700

1. A force of 50 lb raises an object 14 ft. How much work is done? (10-1)

37,312031

2. Find the displacement of a V-8 engine with a stroke of 4.5 inches and a bore of 3.25 inches. (10-3)

8:1

1:3

3. A cylinder contains 400 cubic centimeters of space when the piston is at the bottom of its stroke and 50 cubic centimeters when it is at the top of its stroke. What is the compression ratio? (10-4)

5400

14.375

4. Gear A has 15 teeth and gear B has 45 teeth. What is the gear ratio of A to B? (10-5)

5. In a hydraulic device a force of 60 pounds is applied to a piston whose area is 1 sq in. What is the force on the larger piston whose area is 90 sq in? (10-7)

6. What is the resistance of an 8-amp air-conditioner using 115 volts? (10-9)

7. How many hours will it take a contractor to dig a basement that measures 9 feet deep, 28 feet wide and 54 feet long if he can remove 60 cubic yards per hour? (11-2)

8. How many cubic yards of concrete are needed for a footing 16 inches wide, 8 inches deep and 120 feet long? (11-3)

9. What is the cost of 10 pounds of roofing nails at $.20 per pound? (11-6)

10. A wall 30 feet long and 8 feet high is to be sided. The wall contains two windows. Estimate the total area that is to be sided. (11-8)

11. A 20-amp fuse is placed in a 115-volt circuit. How many watts of power are available through this circuit? (11-10)

12. If $\frac{1}{2}$-inch plastic pipe costs $0.25 per foot, find the cost of 230 feet of this pipe? (11-11)

13. If a room is 18 ft × 20 ft, find the cost of carpeting at $12.00 per square yard. (11-12)

14. If topsoil, delivered to the site, costs $5.00 per cubic yard, what will 21 cubic yards cost? (11-13)

Chord of a circle A line segment that has its end points on the circle. (p. 243)

Circumference The distance around a circle. (p. 171)

Column inch A standard unit of area measure in newspaper publishing equivalent to an area one column wide by one inch deep. (p. 382)

Compression ratio In the cylinder of an engine the ratio of the maximum space to the minimum space. (p. 301)

Complementary angles Two angles, the sum of whose measures is 90°. (p. 232)

Cone A solid figure with one circular base and a curved region which comes to a point. (p. 187)

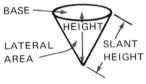

Congruent figures Figures having the same size and shape. (p. 250)

Course (of blocks) A building block together with its mortar joint. (p. 331)

Curved-line graph A presentation of data in which quantities are plotted as a series of dots which are then connected by a smooth curve. (p. 14)

Cutting speed The rate at which a cutting edge moves across a surface, usually expressed in feet per minute (fpm). (p. 362)

Cylinder A solid figure with two circular bases and a curved surface joining them. (p. 186)

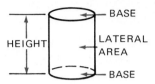

Datum line A fixed line in a technical drawing from which a set of dimensions is referenced. (p. 34)

Decimal A number that uses place value and a decimal point. For example: 45.32 (p. 100)

Deci- A prefix meaning $\frac{1}{10}$. (p. 204)

Degree A unit of measure of angles. The angular measure of a straight line is 180°. (p. 36 and p. 229)

Denominator In $\frac{3}{4}$, 4 is the denominator. (p. 20)

Diameter A line segment connecting two points on a circle, through the center. (p. 171)

Dimension limits Measurements indicating the acceptable range of lengths or sizes. (p. 124)

Dimension lines Lines in a technical drawing showing the specified length of a part of the object. (p. 34)

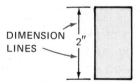

Discount price *See* net price. (p. 122)

Efficiency The ratio of useful energy output to total energy output of a system; especially, the ratio of the energy delivered by a machine to the energy supplied for its operation. (p. 128)

Em A unit of measure of area in the printing trade equal to the square space occupied by the letter M in any given type face. (p. 381)

Energy The ability to do work. (p. 289)

Engine displacement The amount of space through which one piston in the engine travels in one stroke multiplied by the number of pistons in the engine. (p. 298)

Equation A mathematical sentence stating that two expressions are equal. (p. 137)

Equivalent fractions Fractions that have the same value. (p. 23)

Estimate A reasonable guess. (p. 87)

Exponent A small number written above and to the right of another number telling how many times the second number is to be used as a factor. (p. 140)

Expression One or more terms connected by addition or subtraction signs. (p. 137)

Extension lines In a technical drawing, lines extending beyond the edges of an object between which the dimension lines are drawn. (p. 34)

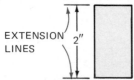

EXTENSION LINES 2″

Extremes In a proportion, the numerator of the first fraction and the denominator of the second fraction. (p. 264)

$$\frac{2}{5} = \frac{4}{10}$$

Face A plane figure that forms one of the sides of a solid figure. (p. 190)

Flat (of bricks) 300 bricks. (p. 342)

Floor plan The view of a horizontal cut through a building, showing the layout of the walls and the room arrangement. (p. 326)

Foot-pound A unit of work equivalent to that done by a one-pound force moving through a distance of one foot. (p. 289)

Formula An equation that states a rule or relationship of physical quantities. (p. 160)

Gear ratio The ratio of the speeds of two gears. It is the reciprocal of the ratio of the number of teeth of each gear. (p. 305)

Gram The basic unit of weight in the metric system. 1 gm = 0.03502 oz (p. 204)

Hidden lines Dashed lines in a technical drawing that indicate a part of the figure that cannot be seen in a particular view. (p. 33)

Horsepower A unit of power equivalent to 550 foot-pounds per second, or 33,000 foot-pounds per minute. (p. 290)

Hydraulic power Power transmitted by a liquid. (p. 311)

Hypotenuse The side of a right triangle opposite the right angle. (p. 252)

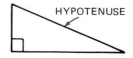

HYPOTENUSE

Indicated horsepower A measure of horsepower based on the power input through the pistons to an engine. (p. 293)

Inverse proportion A proportion in which the ratios are based on reciprocal relationships. (p. 266)

Kilo- A prefix meaning 1000. (p. 204)

Kilowatt-hours (KWH) The basic unit of measure of electrical power consumption. (p. 1)

Leader In a technical drawing, a line, usually curved, used to direct information and symbols to a place in the drawing. (p. 34)

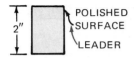

Least common denominator (LCD) The smallest number that can be divided evenly by the denominators of two or more fractions. (p. 48)

Liter The basic unit of volume in the metric system. (1l = 1000 cu cm) (p. 204)

Lowest terms A fraction is in lowest terms when its numerator and denominator cannot be divided evenly by the same number. (p. 25)

Mass The amount of material of which an object is composed. (p. 218)

Means In a proportion, the denominator of the first fraction and the numerator of the second fraction. (p. 264)

$$\frac{2}{3} = \frac{8}{12}$$

Meter The basic unit of length in the metric system. (1 m = 39.37 in.) (p. 204)

Micro- A prefix meaning $\frac{1}{1,000,000}$. (p. 207)

Micrometer An instrument used in making precise measurements. (p. 112)

Milli- A prefix meaning $\frac{1}{1000}$. (p. 204)

Net price Price after deductions, such as dealer discounts, have been made; discount price. (p. 122)

Numerator In $\frac{3}{4}$, 3 is the numerator. (p. 20)

Ohm The basic unit of measure of electrical resistance. (p. 318)

Parallel lines Lines on a flat surface that do not meet no matter how far they are extended. (p. 248)

Parallelogram A four-sided, closed figure with opposite pairs of sides parallel. (p. 176)

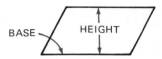

Percent Per hundred. (p. 120)

$$35\% = \frac{35}{100} = .35$$

Perimeter The distance around a figure. (p. 54 and p. 169)

Perpendicular lines Lines that meet at right angles. (p. 238)

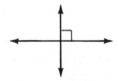

Phantom line A line composed of a long dash and two short dashes that shows the alternate position of a moving part in a technical drawing. (p. 33)

Pica A unit used to measure distances in printed matter equal to about $\frac{1}{6}$ inch. (p. 379)

Pitch The ratio of the rise of a roof to its span. (p. 261)

Pneumatic power Power transmitted through a gas. (p. 311)

Point A unit used to measure the size of printing type equal to .01384 inches or $\frac{1}{12}$ pica. (p. 379)

Pound The basic unit of weight or force in the U.S. system. (p. 218)

Proportion An equation of two ratios. (p. 264)

Power The rate of doing work. (p. 290)

Pressure The force per unit area exerted by a fluid or gas. (p. 311)

Radius A line segment from any point on a circle to its center. (p. 36)

RADIUS

Ratio A comparison of numbers by division. (p. 260)

Ream A standard quantity of paper equal to 500 sheets of a basic size. (p. 394)

Rear axle ratio The ratio of the drive shaft speed to the rear axle speed. (p. 307)

Reciprocals Two numbers whose product is 1. (p. 82) $\frac{5}{4}$ and $\frac{4}{5}$ are reciprocals, since

$$\frac{5}{4} \times \frac{4}{5} = 1$$

Rectangular pyramid A solid figure having a rectangular base and four triangular faces. (p. 194)

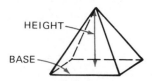

HEIGHT

BASE

Rectangle A parallelogram with four right angles. (p. 176)

Relative error The tolerance of a dimension of a manufactured article compared to the magnitude of the dimension itself. (p. 124)

$$\text{Relative error} = \frac{1}{2} \times \frac{\text{Tolerance}}{\text{Basic size}}$$

Right angle An angle whose measure is 90°. (p. 230)

Rule of Pythagoras "In every right triangle, the square of the hypotenuse equals the sum of the squares of the other two sides." (p. 252)

Scale The ratio of the length of a line in a technical drawing to the corresponding length of the actual object. (p. 279)

Similar figures Figures having the same shape. (p. 251)

Similar terms Terms in the same unknown or terms containing no unknown. (p. 138)

Square A rectangle having four sides the same length. (p. 176)

Square (of shingles) The amount of shingles that will cover an area of 100 square feet. (p. 337)

Straight angle An angle whose measure is 180°. (p. 230)

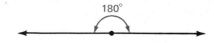

180°

Supplementary angles Two angles, the sum of whose measures is 180°. (p. 233)

Tangent A line that touches a circle at only one point. (p. 242)

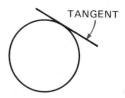

TANGENT

Term A known or unknown quantity in an equation. Terms are connected by addition or subtraction signs. (p. 137)

Tolerance The difference between dimension limits. (p. 124)

Transmission ratio The ratio of the engine speed to the drive shaft speed. (p. 306)

Trapezoid A four-sided figure having exactly one pair of parallel sides, called the *bases*. (p. 178)

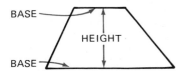

Triangle A three-sided closed figure. (p. 178)

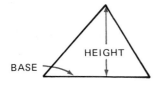

Undirectional dimensioning Dimensioning in a technical drawing in which all dimensions can be read from the bottom of the drawing. (p. 34)

Volt The basic unit of measure of electrical potential. Voltage is analogous to pressure in that it causes electrical current to flow. (p. 317)

Vertex The common end point of the two sides of an angle. (p. 232)

Volume The measure of space inside a solid closed figure. (p. 190)

Watt The basic unit of electrical power. The amount of power produced when one volt produces a one-ampere current. (p. 318)

Weight The amount of force that gravity exerts on an object. (p. 218)

Work The transfer of energy that occurs when a force moves an object through some distance. (p. 289)

Index

Credits

Photo on cover and title page courtesy of Wallace-Murray Corporation.

CHAPTER ONE

X Top Left: A.T. & T.
    Bottom Left: NASA
    Right: A.T. & T.
3 The American Meter Division, Singer Company
5 Simonds Saw and Steel
7 Stewart Warner Corporation
9 Frigidaire Division of General Motors Corporation
11 Frigidaire Division of General Motors Corporation
13 Caterpillar Tractor Company
15 John Deere Company
17 Left: General Electric
    Right: Laser Focus Magazine
18 Top: A.T. & T.
    Bottom: New England Telephone
19 New England Telephone
20 L. S. Starrett Company
21 L. S. Starrett Company (all)
22 L. S. Starrett Company
23 L. S. Starrett Company (all)
27 L. S. Starrett Company
28 L. S. Starrett Company
29 L. S. Starrett Company
30 Top: The Lamson and Sessions Company
    Middle: New Britain Hand Tools
    Bottom: L.S. Starrett Company

31 L. S. Starrett Company
39 Rochester Gas and Electric, Atomic Energy Commission
41 New Britain Hand Tools

CHAPTER TWO

42 Top Left: F.A.O. Photo
    Bottom Left: Ewing Galloway
    Right: H. Armstrong Roberts
43 Reynolds Metal Company
45 The Lamson and Sessions Company
50 Top: National Machinery Company
    Bottom: General Motors Corporation Photo
52 Radio Shack
58 The C-Thru Ruler Company
62 Cadillac Plastic
63 Amoco Chemicals Corporation
64 Top: Owens Corning Fiberglas Corporation
    Bottom: Weyerhaeuser
67 Penn Central Railroad
68 New England Telephone
69 Harry R. Feldman, Inc.
70 Bethlehem Steel Corporation
71 A.T. & T.

423